Pacific Empires

Glyndwr Williams

Pacific Empires

Essays in Honour of Glyndwr Williams

EDITED BY

ALAN FROST

AND

JANE SAMSON

UBC PRESS / VANCOUVER

Published in Canada by UBC Press
6344 Memorial Road
Vancouver, BC V6T 1Z2
www.ubcpress.ubc.ca

Published in Australia by Melbourne University Press.

Designed by Lauren Statham, Alice Graphics
Typeset by Syarikat Seng Teik Sdn. Bhd., Malaysia, in 11/13 point Adobe Garamond
Printed in Australia by Brown Prior Anderson Pty Ltd

Canadian Cataloguing in Publication Data

Main entry under title:
Pacific empires

Includes bibliographical references and index.
ISBN 0-7748-0757-1 (bound) -- ISBN 0-7748-0758-X (pbk.)

1. Pacific Ocean--Discovery and exploration. 2. Pacific Area--
History--18th century. 3. Pacific Area--History--19th century. 4.
Northwest Coast of America--History. 5. Williams, Glyndwr. I.
Frost, Alan, 1943- II. Samson, Jane Dianne, 1962- III. Williams,
Glyndwr.
DU20.P32 1999   910'.9164   C99-910538-8

Preface

In 1995, Professor Michael Osborne, the Vice-Chancellor of La Trobe University, began a major Humanities initiative, when he decided to fund an annual lecture and symposium in North American Studies, both as a recognition of and to enhance further La Trobe's expertise in this area of teaching and research.

The first distinguished visitors were Professor Bernard Bailyn of Harvard University and Professor Christon Archer of the University of Calgary. Subsequently, Professor Bailyn generously agreed that the lecture might be named after him. The University has published his lecture, and those which have followed it, which were given by Dr Barbara Ehrenreich (1996), Professor James Patterson of Brown University (1997), and Professor Norman Yoffee of the University of Michigan (1998).

La Trobe University invited Professor Glyndwr Williams to deliver the fifth Bailyn Lecture in 1999. This seemed an appropriate occasion to undertake a more substantial publication, to coincide with this lecture and the accompanying symposium on native title in Australia, the Pacific Ocean and North America, for, as we explain in our Introduction, Professor Williams's interests have ranged through the reaches of the vast world beyond Europe; and he has had a shaping influence on much of the historiography of European exploration and culture contact which has appeared in English in recent decades.

With the help of Melbourne University Press, this volume is the result.

v

A BRIEF EXPLANATION of some editorial practices in the volume is necessary.

Because imperial measurements appear in the many documents on which the essays are based, these have been retained in the text. Non-standard spellings in quotations from sources have been kept, without being followed by 'sic'.

In order to standardise usage, to avoid unnecessary confusion, and —especially—to avoid any derogatory implications, Greg Dening's usage of Native and Stranger has been followed throughout, with these terms signifying, on the one hand, the people who inhabited a land, and, on the other, the Europeans who travelled and encountered them. The usage also involves the analytic concepts of Self and Other.

A COLLECTION OF essays such as this one appears only after much labour by a number of people. The editors are most grateful to Carol Courtis, Heather Wilkie and Emily Booth, of the Department of History, La Trobe University, for their help with word-processing; and to Sally Nicholls, editor at Melbourne University Press.

Contents

Illustrations

Plates

Glyndwr Williams *frontispiece*

between pages 228 *and* 229

George Ford, soon after his return from the Arctic (Karpeles Manuscript Library)

George Ford in later life (Karpeles Manuscript Library)

Two portraits of Amelia, Lady Douglas (British Columbia Archives and Records Service)

Josette Work as 'Queen Victoria' (British Columbia Archives and Records Service)

Isabella Ross in her widow's weeds (British Columbia Archives and Records Service)

Sophia Lolo (British Columbia Archives and Records Service)

Daughters of Captain W. H. McNeill and Mathilda (British Columbia Archives and Records Service)

Douglas daughters Agnes, Jane and Alice (British Columbia Archives and Records Service)

Studio portrait of Jane Douglas and her sister, Martha (British Columbia Archives and Records Service)

Flora Ross (British Columbia Archives and Records Service)

The four surviving McNeill sisters in 1904 (British Columbia Archives and Records Service)

A page from Martha Harris's album (British Columbia Archives and Records Service)

Maps

Tables

Notes on Contributors

Chris Archer is Professor of History at the University of Calgary. As well as having published numerous articles, he is the author of *The Army in Bourbon Mexico, 1760–1810*, which was awarded the Herbert E. Bolton prize for 1979 and the Pacific Coast Branch, American Historical Association Prize.

William Barr is Professor of Geography at the University of Saskatchewan. His field of expertise is far northern exploration. Among his works are: *The Expeditions of the First International Polar Year, 1882–3* (1985) and (with Glyndwr Williams), *Voyages to Hudson Bay in Search of a Northwest Passage*, 2 vols (1994, 1995).

Andrew Cook is Map Archivist, Oriental and India Office Collections, British Library, London. He has made an extensive study of Alexander Dalrymple, the eighteenth-century hydrographer and cartographer.

Greg Dening is Professor Emeritus, University of Melbourne, and Adjunct Professor, Australian National University. He is the author of *Islands and Beaches* (1980); *The Death of William Gooch* (1988, 1995); *Mr Bligh's Bad Language* (1992); *Performances* (1996); and *Readings/Writings* (1998).

Robin Fisher is Professor of History, University of Northern British Columbia, and Dean of the College of Arts, Social and Health Sciences. He was convenor of the conferences, Captain James Cook and his Times (Vancouver, 1978) and the Vancouver Conference on Exploration and Discovery (Vancouver, 1992). He is the author of *Contact and Conflict* (1977), and of a study of George Vancouver.

Alan Frost is Professor of History at La Trobe University. He is the author of *Convicts and Empire* (1980); *Arthur Phillip, 1738–1814: His Voyaging* (1987); *Botany Bay Mirages* (1994); *The Precarious Life of James Mario Matra* (1995); and *The Voyage of the* Endeavour (1998).

R. J. B. Knight is Deputy Director, National Maritime Museum, Greenwich. He is the editor of the *Guide to Manuscripts in the National Maritime Museum* (1977, 1980), and has written extensively on eighteenth-century British naval administration.

David Mackay is Professor of History and Dean of the Faculty of Arts and Social Sciences, Victoria University of Wellington. He is the author of *A Place of Exile* (1985) and *In the Wake of Cook* (1985).

P. J. Marshall was formerly Rhodes Professor of Imperial History at King's College, London. Among many other works, he is the author of *The Impeachment of Warren Hastings* (1965); *The British Discovery of Hinduism in the Eighteenth Century* (1972); (with Glyndwr Williams) *The Great Map of Mankind* (1982); and *Bengal: The British Bridgehead: Eastern India, 1740–1828* (1987). He has recently edited the second volume of the *Oxford History of the British Empire* (1998).

Andrew Porter is Rhodes Professor of Imperial History at King's College, London. He is the author of several books, including *The Origins of the South African War* (1980) and *European Imperialism 1860–1914* (1994). He has recently edited the third volume of the *Oxford History of the British Empire* (forthcoming 1999).

Jane Samson is Assistant Professor at the University of Alberta. She has been a Killam Post-doctoral Fellow at the University of British Columbia, Caird Junior Research Fellow at the National Maritime Museum, and Senior Research Fellow at the Institute of Commonwealth Studies, London. She is the author of *Imperial Benevolence: Making British Authority on the Pacific Islands* (1998).

Sylvia Van Kirk is Professor of Canadian History and Women's Studies at the University of Toronto. Glyndwr Williams supervised her PhD thesis, which was published as *Many Tender Ties: Women in Fur Trade Society, 1670–1870* (1980). She continues to publish on issues of race and gender in early Western Canada.

Introduction

⁓

J. C. BEAGLEHOLE'S meticulous edition of Cook's journals, with its long introductions and copious annotations, began a new era in the study of the European exploration of the Pacific Ocean in the second half of the eighteenth century, and of the colonisations that commenced towards century's end and continued for more than one hundred years. Others were soon producing kindred editions of fellow explorers (Byron, Carteret) and junior officers, thus swelling the mass of source materials available. In time, added to these sources were sumptuous catalogues of the charts, views and art of the voyages, and of the scientific and ethnographic collections. There were also biographies of the explorers based on modern principles and fresh research in archives. Nor were these developments confined to the English-speaking world. French and then Spanish scholars replicated them where Bougainville, Lapérouse, Entrecasteaux, Baudin and Malaspina were concerned. And with the transformation of information about the Pacific ventures as a model, scholars turned their attention also to other areas of the world explored by Europeans in the eighteenth and nineteenth centuries—to North and South America, Africa and Asia. Now, at the end of the twentieth century, scholars of history, geography, the natural sciences and ethnography have available records of great richness and diversity detailing the encounters of European Strangers with the outer world.

Initially, the scholars of Pacific exploration focused their attention on the geographical results of the voyages, and on their scientific import. Slowly, the recognition grew that science was often deployed in the service of empire, so that increasing attention has been given to the strategic and commercial contexts and implications of the voyages. Progressively, too, scholars have realised that, if read with special interpretative lens, the records may also reveal much of how the Natives encountered the Strangers—as Greg Dening wrote recently,

> Forty-five years ago I made a discovery that changed my life. I found that I could read the accounts of voyagers to the Pacific and Australia—Cook, Banks, Bligh, Bougainville and all the others and their companions—not so much for what they did as what they saw. I wanted to write two-sided history—of the indigenous peoples and of those who intruded upon them. To see the other side of the beach through eyes that were so blinkered, I thought that I needed new reading skills. I thought those reading skills should be anthropological, though I did not know what that meant. But when so much is lost, when so much is distorted, one has to catch at the slightest signs of the ways human beings leave their signatures on life.[1]

FOR ALL HIS professional life, Glyn Williams has been at the forefront of these historiographical developments. His early work concerned British (and European) imperialism; he has edited narratives of exploration; produced atlases of exploration; and written analytical studies, both of where explorers went, and what they saw—or thought they saw. His attention has ranged from North America to the Pacific Ocean to Asia. Along the way, Glyn has deployed historical, geographical, cartographical, artistic, literary and ethnographic perspectives. His has been a most enquiring progress, during which he has consistently disregarded conventional disciplinary boundaries.

Glyn's publication record is so extensive that we have appended a full bibliography of his work at the end of this book. However, some of his contributions deserve particular mention, because of how they prefigure and relate to essays published here. Glyn's leadership role in the Hudson's Bay Record Society and the Hakluyt Society led him to edit a series of journals and correspondence concerning modern exploration in North America and the Pacific. His first two monographs—*The British Search for the Northwest Passage in the Eighteenth Century* (1962) and *The Expansion of*

Europe in the Eighteenth Century (1966)—began to develop themes that would recur throughout his later work, for example the importance of British North America and the Pacific to the eighteenth-century British Empire, and the interaction between the scientific Enlightenment and voyages of discovery.

Both these themes are reflected in the opening essay of this book, Glyn's '"To Make Discoveries of Countries Hitherto Unknown": The Admiralty and Pacific Exploration in the Eighteenth Century', which was the 1995 Caird Medal lecture. As Glyn here points out, while the British were content to have buccaneers and the only-briefly-active South Sea Company exploit possibilities about Spanish America in the first decades of the eighteenth century, the Admiralty took an active role from 1739 onwards, with Anson's expedition to the South Seas, and Middleton's search for the Northwest Passage. Anson then formulated a scheme for deliberate exploration, which, though not finally pursued until 1764, set the pattern for much of what followed in the second half of the century. Glyn stresses the scientific aspect of much of this exploration, while at the same time conceding that it contributed to the imperial rivalry between Britain, France and Spain.

Alan Frost's 'The Spanish Yoke' adds to our understanding of that rivalry. He argues that, in the mid-eighteenth century, the British government began developing a policy aimed at establishing a trans-Pacific trading network of its own. Attacks on Spanish colonies during the Seven Years' War improved Britain's strategic position, and Cook's explorations improved geographical understanding and uncovered several potentially important new products for the China trade. The establishment of the New South Wales colony in 1788 opened up additional possibilities until, in the nineteenth century, creole insurrections and free trade ideology combined to give Britain the opportunity it had long sought to gain access to Latin American markets.

Systematic scientific observation and charting continued to underpin Britain's attempts to dominate maritime trade in the nineteenth century. Significant here was the founding of the Royal Navy's Hydrographic Office in 1795. In 'Alexander Dalrymple and the Hydrographic Office', Andrew Cook shows that, in the first ten-or-so years, Dalrymple oversaw the sorting and incidental publication of accumulated maritime information, for both operational and commercial purposes. From 1808 onwards, however, under Dalrymple's successors, the Office progressively developed the roles of provider of nautical information through systematic publication of charts, and of commissioner of new surveys.

As Jane Samson points out in 'An Empire of Science: The Voyage of HMS *Herald*, 1845–1851', this gathering of scientific data continued to have strategic and commercial significances. There were no published charts of much of the Pacific region until the middle of the nineteenth century. The making of those charts, and their relationship to areas of developing British (and later American) political and commercial interest, is a sadly neglected part of British imperial and Pacific regional history. The *Herald*'s survey was linked to the search for an Atlantic-Pacific canal route, the survey of harbours on Vancouver Island prior to its colonisation in 1849, and the search for a Northwest Passage.

And, as Roger Knight shows in 'John Lort Stokes and the New Zealand Survey, 1848–1851', British hydrographic work was just as entangled with imperial expansion in the South Pacific in the nineteenth century. James Cook had charted the main islands of New Zealand in 1769. British colonisation formally commenced in 1840. This in turn led to the need for a detailed coastal survey, so as to facilitate trade. However, Stokes's work went far beyond this objective, as he searched for coal deposits, catalogued natural resources, and acted as go-between in colonial land negotiations with the Maori. Both Samson's and Knight's essays uncover neglected sources and show not only hydrographic-imperial connections, but the developing web of trans-Pacific British interests.

However, in all this attention to science, strategy and commerce, to the results of both grand oceanic sweeps and detailed coastal surveys, it is easy to overlook human circumstances. It is important to remember that whole ships' companies were involved in the voyages of exploration and survey. William Barr's 'A Warrant Officer in the Arctic: The Journal of George Ford, 1850–1854' introduces us to the unpublished papers of a junior officer on Arctic service during the search for Franklin. Ford's experiences show us how arduous were the conditions endured by those involved in the search, which included the ongoing struggle with scurvy and the social stresses produced during long, icebound winters. His journals also reveal an educated man with his own interests in natural history and ethnology, and an eye for the humorous side of shipboard life.

THE SUBJECT OF culture contact in the Pacific, especially that involving the eighteenth-century British explorers, has given rise to what is now a veritable publishing industry; and over the past thirty years there have been profound shifts in the historiographical focus. J. C. Beaglehole's references to Captain Cook as 'our hero', for example, must now be read against a generation of scholarship drawing on indigenous perspectives. Revisionist imperial history now takes account of those perspectives, and is busily re-examining the historical and cultural contingencies of western colonialism. Glyn Williams has again had a hand in these developments. His '"Far more happier than we Europeans": Reactions to the Australian Aborigines on Cook's voyage' was for him a step towards extended consideration of the realities of Native peoples, and of European representations—and misrepresentations—of them. In some of the essays in *Terra Australis to Australia*, he developed his insights further. Glyn signalled this change—both individual and general—in focus in his summing up of the results of the 1992 'Vancouver Conference on Exploration and Discovery'. Hearkening back to its predecessor, the 'Captain James Cook and his Times' conference in 1978, he noted the transformation that had taken place in approaches to Europe's second age of discovery. Whereas Pacific-island-centred perspectives had been almost absent in 1978, in 1992 they were well represented; in 1978, it had been James Cook who was the dominant historical figure: in 1992, it was the Nootka leader, Maquinna; and whereas in 1978 most of the papers had been straightforwardly historical in their orientation, the 1992 papers were notably interdisciplinary, with writers deploying perspectives of art history, literature and anthropology, as well as of history, to offer fresh insights.

Five essays dealing with aspects of culture contact in both the North and South Pacific constitute Part 2 of this collection.

Greg Dening pioneered the study of the theatre of contact; and in 'The Hegemony of Laughter: Purea's Theatre' he shows how the

Tahitian leader Airoreatua i Ahurai i Farepua and her people used and were used by humour. The Tahitians laughed at their strange and clumsy European visitors; later, in the literature and theatres of Europe, Europeans laughed at 'Queen Purea' and her exotic court. European laughter was powerful, a reflection of imperial hegemony, but Dening reminds us that Tahitian laughter was—and still is— also subversive of that power.

In 'Vancouver's Vision of Native Peoples: The Northwest Coast and Hawai'i', Robin Fisher shows how George Vancouver's experience of Hawai'i and its inhabitants coloured his judgement of the very different peoples of the northwest coast. Fisher points out the tendency for current historiography to generalise about Native–Stranger encounters, so that colonialism becomes the monocausal explanation, or there is deemed to be no possible explanation due to the infinite distance between events and texts. Instead, Fisher reaffirms the importance of studying events in context, and uses the texts of Vancouver's voyage to suggest that a range of aesthetic, political and cultural factors lay behind the captain's response to the different peoples of the Pacific.

Chris Archer's 'Whose Scourge? Smallpox Epidemics on the Northwest Coast' is similarly double-edged. Archer questions the established view that epidemics of smallpox caused widespread mortality among northwest coast Native peoples in the eighteenth century. He argues that the 'Black Legend' of Spanish imperialism, especially as publicised in Britain, pushed stories of epidemics forward in time from the early days of Spanish America—where smallpox had devastated indigenous populations—to the eighteenth century and Spanish activities on the northwest coast. The thrust of Archer's argument is that recent scholarship, much of it driven by the desire to expose the human cost of European imperialism, is simply reinforcing old British arguments about Spanish destructiveness. Careful empirical research suggests instead that it was the nineteenth century that saw the most virulent outbreaks of smallpox on the coast, and by then Spanish (or Russian) influence had been decisively displaced by British and American activity.

In 'The Career of William Ellis: British Missions, the Pacific, and the American Connection', Andrew Porter takes us into the nineteenth century, and reinforces Glyn Williams's contention that

North America and the Pacific continued to be important in British imperial affairs. By examining British-American links in the operations of the London Missionary Society, as highlighted by the activities of missionary William Ellis, Porter shows how Ellis's sojourn with American missionaries in Hawai'i shaped his subsequent career as Foreign Secretary of the Society. Through a network of friendships, correspondence and mutual intellectual interests, Ellis maintained his interest in the Pacific islands and applied this perspective to his management of the Society's activities in Asia and Africa.

Sylvia Van Kirk, too, shows the part larger dynamics—in this case race and gender—played in the context of particular historical circumstances. 'Colonised Lives: The Native Wives and Daughters of Five Founding Families of Victoria' explores the experiences of the part-Native women who, as wives, mothers and daughters, found themselves subjected to the pressures of acculturation during the early colonial years of Vancouver Island. Van Kirk has uncovered rare documentation of these women's lives, along with a selection of photographs which she mines for further information. She concludes that these prominent mixed-race families featured a complicated intersection of race and gender role expectations which added pressure to a society struggling to transform itself from fur trade outpost to colonial settlement.

PART 3 OF this collection comprises two reflective essays. In *The Great Map of Mankind: British Perceptions of the World in the Age of Enlightenment* (1982), Glyn Williams and P. J. Marshall explored British encounters with non-European geographies and peoples. Ten years on, Peter Marshall considers '*The Great Map of Mankind*: The British Encounter with India'. Like his fellow authors here, Marshall is aware of recent developments in theories of colonialism, representation and Otherness; and like them, too, he reaffirms the importance of historical research and argument. Whereas *The Great Map of Mankind* concentrated mainly on the written record of British perceptions, Marshall suggests that were he to undertake the study now, he would pay greater attention to fiction, poetry, music, the visual arts, and a range of other cultural productions. But, he warns, such a study would also need to feature the initiatives of

Indians themselves in shaping the notions of Europeans, and to take account of the fact that 'the British' exhibited a wide range of responses to India. Put bluntly, Marshall believes that simplistic notions of Orientalist or colonialist domination have had their day.

David Mackay makes a similar point concerning the historiography of the European exploration of the Pacific Ocean. In 'Exploring the Pacific, Exploring James Cook', he considers the many faces of Captain Cook, whose iconic significance has shifted from Great Navigator to Great Destroyer depending on who is considering his significance, and when. After a survey of recent Cook literature, including the influence on it of literary theory, Mackay concludes that European and American scholars are often continuing to use the Pacific as a sounding board for the understanding of western experiences. The focus of attention may have shifted from the triumphs of western civilisation to critiques of colonialism; but the scholarship is still profoundly Eurocentric. Only faintly are indigenous Pacific voices—Pacific islander, Maori, Australian Aboriginal, northwest coast First Nations—making their presence felt. Mackay's proposition is that the Pacific is still discovering James Cook, its greatest explorer.

IF GLYN WILLIAMS has consistently exceeded boundaries in his scholarly writings, so has he too in other areas of life. He has worked—and, for varying periods, lived—not only in Britain, but in Canada, the United States, a number of European countries, the West Indies, and Australia and New Zealand. Wherever he has been, he has interested himself in the present life of the country as well as in its past.

Glyndyr Williams has held visiting fellowships, and received numerous invitations to deliver keynote addresses at scholarly gatherings. A number of institutions have recognised his accomplishments by conferring on him Honorary Doctorates.

Yet—and it is from this that Glyn would likely take most satisfaction—it is in the respect and affection felt by so many students and colleagues in the course of his long career at Queen Mary (now Queen Mary and Westfield) College within the University of London that we may perhaps best see his merit. He has enthusiastically taught many undergraduate and postgraduate subjects in British, Imperial, Canadian and Australian history, and always shown himself most approachable and supportive of students.

Nowhere have these qualities—of enthusiasm, approachability and concerned interest—been more manifest than in Glyn's role at the Institute of Historical Research's Imperial History Seminar. As one of its principal organisers, he has always seen that it has had an interdisciplinary, international scope. And, as we might only expect, he has contributed very significantly to its friendly, constructive atmosphere—no small achievement when academic gatherings these days tend to become occasions for the venting of anxious rivalries. Among other features, there has been the habit, which Glyn and the other seminar organisers have developed, of encouraging informal discussion after the seminar at eating and drinking establishments deliberately chosen for their affordability for students.

THE ESSAYS IN this collection have been written by friends and colleagues of Glyn Williams (some of them his former students). All of us could think of no finer tribute, as a gift to him on his retirement, to mark his singular career as a historian, mentor and friend.

Jane Samson
University of Alberta
Canada

Alan Frost
La Trobe University
Melbourne

PART

Explorations, Imperial and Scientific Ventures

'To Make Discoveries of Countries Hitherto Unknown'

The Admiralty and Pacific Exploration in the Eighteenth Century

GLYNDWR WILLIAMS

INTEREST BY THE ADMIRALTY in oceanic discovery was a slow and halting business. Though English vessels had entered the Pacific in the late sixteenth century, the voyages of Cook, Vancouver and their contemporaries two hundred years later formed not so much the climax of a steady process of officially sponsored exploration as an exceptional outburst of activity for which the precedents were few and muffled. The Elizabethan circumnavigations of Drake and Cavendish, in effect plundering expeditions on a grand scale, brought back something in the way of new geographical information, but their primary purpose was treasure rather than knowledge.

Not until the second half of the seventeenth century did another English ship enter the Pacific, and it was a forerunner of sorts since it was a naval vessel. Commanded by John Narborough, the expedition of 1669–71 was a very curious affair. Narborough carried trade goods on board, with orders from the Lord High Admiral, the Duke of York, to head for Chile and Peru 'to make a Discovery both of the Seas and Coasts of that part of the World, and if possible to lay the foundations of a Trade there'.[1] This ill-conceived attempt to combine exploration and trade along the coasts of Spain's Pacific possessions failed miserably. Leaving four of his men in Spanish hands, Narborough retraced his track through the Strait of Magellan, of which he produced a good chart. Otherwise he had done little of note. After his embarrassed return little more was heard about the South Sea in official circles, and interest in England was rather attracted by the exploits in that region of the true successors of Drake and Cavendish—the buccaneers.

It was from their disreputable ranks that the next commander of a naval expedition to the Pacific emerged. This was William Dampier, whose wanderings in Central America, the Pacific and the East Indies were chronicled in his best-selling *New Voyage round the World*, published in 1697. Dampier became a minor celebrity: he dined with Pepys; was consulted by the Council of Trade and Plantations; and corresponded with the First Lord of the Admiralty, the Earl of Orford.[2] From this correspondence emerged the idea of a naval voyage to the Pacific, but there is no evidence that it represented any serious thrust of national policy. The choice of area to be explored seems to have been Dampier's rather than the Admiralty's as he responded to Orford's airy request 'to make a proposal of some voyage wherein I might be serviceable to my Nation'. Dampier's motives were practical and commercial as he proposed a voyage to the unknown shores of Terra Australis on the grounds that it was 'reasonable to conceive that so great a part of the World is not without very valluable commodities'. Having agreed to the venture, the Admiralty seem to have lost interest in it. Dampier was provided with only one vessel instead of the two he had requested, and the *Roebuck* was in a state of disrepair and decay. Whatever his merits as a navigator and writer, Dampier had no experience of command. Quarrelling with his first lieutenant, a regular naval officer who regarded his captain as 'an Old Pyrating Dog', Dampier still managed to nurse the *Roebuck* across the southern reaches of the Atlantic and Indian Oceans as far as New Holland and on to his one major discovery of New Britain. Dampier should now have turned south to explore the unknown east coast of Australia, but the condition of both ship and crew was so poor that he decided to head for home. A year later the bottom fell out of his vessel in mid-Atlantic, and the crew were fortunate to save their lives by scrambling ashore on Ascension Island. When he got back to England, Dampier faced court-martial, was fined all his pay for the voyage, and declared not to be a fit person ever again to command one of the Queen's ships.[3]

For the Navy, if not for privateers, satirists and speculators, the South Sea dropped out of the reckoning as a sphere of activity. Exploration was not yet regarded as a legitimate objective of official attention and funding. When in 1738 the then First Lord of the Admiralty, Sir Charles Wager, was approached with a view to sending naval vessels to Hudson Bay in search of a Northwest Passage his reaction was one of doubt. There was little interest in oceanic discovery, he thought—'a Spirit of that Kind seems to have been asleep for many Years'. Moreover, with tension with Spain increasing, he felt compelled to point out that 'As to Vessels being sent at the Public Expence, tho' it would not be great, yet the Parliament may think, especially at this Time, that we ought not to play with the Money they give us, for other and particular Services'.[4] It needed the intervention of the monarch, George II, before the Admiralty agreed to send two vessels to Hudson Bay in 1741 to search for a route to the Pacific. As with Dampier's voyage, the expedition was commanded not by a regular naval officer but by a seaman granted a commission shortly before the ships sailed. The reasoning was the same. Just as Dampier's knowledge of the South Sea, and particularly of Australian waters, seemed to make him the logical choice in 1699, so Christopher Middleton's experience of northern navigation in the service of the Hudson's Bay Company brought him a command in 1741.

The war with Spain, apprehension of which had moved Wager against 'playing' with government money for discovery purposes, was now used in favour of the Hudson Bay voyage. Arthur Dobbs, promoter of the Middleton expedition, pointed out to Wager that if a passage was discovered, then the following year naval ships could be sent through it into the Pacific to wreak havoc among the unprepared Spaniards: 'Our being capable of attacking them in the South Sea in so easy a Manner would soon humble them, and make them value our Friendship'.[5] Unknown to Dobbs at the time, such a venture was already being planned, and although the route was more orthodox the motives behind George Anson's voyage were similar to those argued by Dobbs. Not in any sense a discovery expedition, at one level Anson's squadron seemed a rerun of the old buccaneering ventures to the South Sea. At another, though, it was a portent of future British interest in the region, with its instructions to open up the Pacific seaboard of Spanish America to British merchants.[6] Middleton was informed that Anson's squadron was expected to be off California by December 1741, and was advised that once through the passage he should meet it there. If he failed to make contact with Anson then he was to find an island 'that may be of use for a future settlement' and winter. If he encountered Japanese or other ships, then he was 'to return, that Ships of Sufficient Force may be sent out next Season to begin a Trade, or make a Settlement without any Apprehension or Disturbance from any powerfull Nation on that Side'.[7]

For the first time there is an anticipation of Admiralty policy in the next reign, when naval vessels ranged the Pacific in search of bases and new markets for British goods. Middleton's voyage marks a tentative step towards this policy, for his instructions make it clear that his expedition was a pathfinder, and that if he found a navigable passage the Admiralty would consider further measures to secure his discovery. Under the protection of 'Ships of Sufficient Force', British merchants would take the shortcut to the western shores of America, and pass on to the rich lands beyond. In the event, Middleton failed to find a passage, and was plunged into an acrimonious pamphlet war on his return. The controversy rumbled on through 1744, but was lost to sight amid the hubbub which followed the return of Anson that summer from a voyage of high drama and compelling public interest. Once more the South Sea became a focus of attention, and newspaper accounts, serial publications, and individual narratives met the demand for information about an expedition whose capture of the Acapulco galleon seemed compensation for the losses of men and ships. After the Mediterranean fleet's failure off Toulon in February the Navy stood in need of a popular triumph, and the seizure of a treasure galleon was the next best thing to a fleet victory.

Some looked beyond the immediate excitement of Anson's return, and pondered the long-term implications of his Pacific experiences. In his monumental collection of voyages and travels John Campbell drew, both from Anson's voyage and earlier ventures, evidence of the opportunities awaiting Britain in the Pacific. The possibility awaited his countrymen, Campbell wrote, of a new commercial empire in the South Pacific ranging from Juan Fernandez in the east to New Holland in the west, and taking in on the way the great southern continent *Terra Australis Incognita*.[8] Another assessment of South Sea opportunities emerged when the long-awaited official account of Anson's voyage was published in 1748. Ostensibly written by Richard Walter, chaplain on the expedition, the literary style of *A Voyage round the World* by George Anson owed much to Benjamin Robins, an experienced pamphleteer; but without doubt the opinions expressed in the book were those of Anson, now reaching a dominant position in naval affairs. In 1745 he was appointed to the Board of Admiralty; he was created a peer in 1747 and promoted to Admiral in 1748; and in 1751 became First Lord of the Admiralty. He exercised close control over the writing of the book, whose Introduction stressed the value of accurate charts, global recordings of magnetic variation, and proper surveys taken from naval vessels. Despite such exhortations, the Royal Navy failed to establish any specialist surveying service, or even a hydrographic office to supervise the publication of charts. In 1766 the setting up of such an office seems to have been discussed by the then First Lord of the Admiralty, the Earl of Egmont, but in the end the matter dropped from view.[9] Other parts of Anson's account analysed the weaknesses in Spain's overseas empire before going on to argue the case for new British bases, both in the South Atlantic and South Pacific.

Developments in 1749, the first year of peace, showed an initial determination to put Anson's recommendations into practice. The Admiralty fitted out an expedition of two sloops which was to survey the Falklands and then pass into the South Sea to Juan Fernández. From there the vessels were 'to make further discoveries' by sailing 3000 miles westward into the Pacific, steering 'a traverse course' between 10°S lat. and 25°S lat.[10] It seems logical and probable that Anson was the inspirer of this project, although the most detailed explanation of the proposed voyage was given by the First Lord of the Admiralty, the Earl of Sandwich. British assurances about the scientific and disinterested nature of the enterprise, and even the cancelling of part of it, failed to mollify the Spaniards. After Anson's destructive sweep through the South Sea they were understandably touchy about further British expeditions to the region, scientific or not. The Spanish concept of the Pacific as *mare*

clausum died hard, and the anxiety of the British government not
to upset the delicate negotiations in progress on the *asiento* and
other issues led it to drop the planned expedition—'for the present',
and without giving up the 'right to send out Ships for the discovery
of unknown & unsettled Parts of the World'.[11] What Britain's
special envoy to Madrid, Benjamin Keene, called 'their whimsical
notions of exclusive rights in those seas' were to be respected, at least
for the time being.[12]

The 'right to send out Ships' was not to be exercised for another
fifteen years, when in 1764 the first discovery expedition of George
III's reign, commanded by Commodore John Byron, sailed for the
Pacific. Perhaps because of the new reign, perhaps because an
account of the expedition appeared in Hawkesworth's *Voyages*,
Byron's voyage traditionally has been linked with the succeeding
Pacific expeditions. In reality it was a throwback to an earlier
period; it was the abortive 1749 expedition writ large. Byron had
been a midshipman on Anson's expedition, on the unlucky *Wager*,
so it was appropriate that he was to command an expedition whose
aims would have been familiar to Anson and to Anson's generation.
Anson had died in 1762—regretting, so the Earl of Shelburne
claimed, that he had not pressed ahead with a settlement on the
Falklands[13]—and Byron received his instructions from Egmont.
There is some evidence that the voyage was planned by the
Admiralty, in direct communication with the King, without other
ministers being kept informed. This may have been a ploy by
Egmont to avoid a repetition of the 1749 episode, when wider
diplomatic considerations had forced the cancellation of the
intended Falklands and South Sea venture.[14]

Certainly Byron's 'Secret Instructions' seem to have been more
secret than most at this time. Their opening lines struck a new note
as they proclaimed that 'nothing can redound more to the honor of
this Nation as a Maritime Power, to the dignity of the Crown of
Great Britain, and to the advancement of the Trade and Navigation
thereof, than to make Discoveries of Countries hitherto unknown
. . .'[15] The body of the instructions, however, contained little fresh.
They represented the bringing together of the plans of earlier generations. 'Trade and Navigation' were to be the chief beneficiaries;
of science there was no mention. Drake and Dampier were the fore-
runners, and the elusive Northwest Passage once more appears.

Egmont's report to the Cabinet as he received news of Byron's arrival at the Falklands confirms the anti-Spanish aims of the expedition. The enterprise was of 'very great Moment & of the most secret nature'. The Falklands, he insisted, were '*the Key to the whole Pacifick Ocean*', for they 'must command the Ports & Trade of Chili[,] Peru, Panama, Acapulco, & in one word all the Spanish Territory upon that Sea. It will render all our Expeditions to those parts most lucrative to ourselves, most fatal to Spain'.[16] It may not be a coincidence that Egmont's papers contain a proposal by a former South Sea Company factor, Henry Hutchinson, who had sailed with Anson, to establish a British settlement on the Pacific coast of South America south of Chile.[17] Only once did Egmont raise wider considerations of oceanic exploration, when he pointed out that the Falklands would serve as a base from which to make 'Discoverys in all that Southern Tract of Ocean both to the East & West of the magellanick Streights'.[18]

But it was these wider considerations which came to the fore in the voyage which immediately followed Byron's, that of Samuel Wallis. For the first time since Dampier the looming shape of *Terra Australis Incognita* appears in official Admiralty instructions: 'whereas there is reason to beleive that Lands, or Islands of great extent, hitherto unvisited by any European Power may be found in the Southern Hemisphere between Cape Horn and New Zeland, in Latitudes convenient for Navigation, and in Climates adapted to the product of Commodities usefull in Commerce'.[19] In this new and portentous directive Byron, usually dismissed as an inadequate explorer, seems to have played an important role. Sailing through the northern fringes of the Tuamotu Archipelago in June 1765 he had been convinced that there was land to the south, and but for unfavourable winds 'I should have fell in with it, & in all Probability made the discovery of the S° Continent'.[20] On his return to England in May 1766 Byron became involved with Egmont's planning of the Wallis expedition, and it appears to have been his 'posative oppinion' on the existence of 'a Continent of Great Extent never yet Explored or seen' which persuaded Egmont to point Wallis towards its discovery.[21]

In the event, the expedition was almost cancelled. On 13 August 1766 Egmont resigned because of opposition in the Cabinet to his hardline policy on the Falklands; but he signed Wallis's instructions before his resignation became effective, and the ships sailed on 21 August. It was perhaps a sign of Egmont's declining influence that the special perquisites arranged for Byron's expedition were not repeated. There was no appointment to commodore for Wallis, and no double pay for the crews. More worrying, the consort vessel was the *Swallow*, a sloop described by its commander Philip Carteret as 'above 30 years old, and one of the worst, if not the very worst of her kind; in his majesty's Navy'. It was ironic that the Lord of the Admiralty who seems to have been most unresponsive to Carteret's requests for extra fittings and supplies was Charles Saunders, who a quarter-century before had sailed around the world with Anson.[22]

Adequately fitted or not (and there were few problems with Wallis's *Dolphin*), the expedition sparked off a rumbling dispute with the Spanish ambassador, the Prince of Masserano, which went well beyond the question of the Falklands. On 25 September the ambassador was challenged by Shelburne, newly appointed Secretary of State for the Southern Department. On being shown on a map the extent of Spanish claims over the Pacific from Cape Horn to the Philippines, Shelburne exclaimed 'that Spain's ideas were vast'. Masserano retorted that England's were still 'greater'.[23]

Meanwhile, the *Dolphin* and *Swallow* were sailing south, but after a hard passage through the Strait of Magellan the ships became separated and made independent voyages. Wallis showed little initiative in his track across the Pacific, but his voyage was marked by his chance discovery of Tahiti, and perhaps much else. As the high peaks of Tahiti came over the horizon, so farther south an even more exciting vista lay open to view, or at least to the view of the master, George Robertson, who described in his journal seeing the tops of a range of mountains 60 miles away which could only be part of the southern continent.[24] To Robertson's disgust, after spending a month at Tahiti, Wallis sailed without exploring to the south. Carteret, by contrast, despite his problems with the *Swallow*, stuck to his instructions and crossed the Pacific farther south than any previous explorer, so making considerable inroads into the supposed southern continent. As he struggled through the last leg of his voyage in the Atlantic he was overhauled by a French ship, Bougainville's *La Boudeuse*. It, too, though Carteret was unaware of this, had been on a Pacific voyage, and one consciously intended to rival those of the British.

Wallis arrived back in May 1768, a year earlier than Carteret, and found another Pacific expedition in preparation. This, to begin with at least, was different, for its immediate objective was clearly and narrowly scientific. It was to answer the request of the Royal Society that the Admiralty should send a ship to the South Pacific to observe the Transit of Venus in 1769. The matter had first come before the Council of the Society in 1765 when Dr Thomas Hornsby, Professor of Astronomy at Oxford, urged it to take action; and at intervals in the next two years the Council discussed the matter. In February 1768 the King agreed to the Society's request for a grant of £4000, and by April the Admiralty was dealing with the question of an appropriate vessel and an appropriate commander.[25] The rest, as they say, is history: the vessel was that most famous of cat-built colliers, the *Endeavour*; the commander was James Cook. As preparations continued, so the novelty of the venture became apparent. To the necessary astronomers were added other civilians—the scientists Banks and Solander, the artists Parkinson and Buchan. New to Royal Navy expeditions, such supernumeraries had already sailed with Bougainville. It was they, rather than the modest figure of the unknown James Cook (unlike Byron and Wallis, a mere lieutenant, and a new one at that), who attracted attention. In all respects, the expedition seemed not to be part of the sequence of expeditions which ran from Dampier to Anson, Byron to Wallis. It was not in genesis an Admiralty venture, and had little if anything to do with affairs of state. If it had a precursor, then it was Edmond Halley's trio of voyages in the *Paramore* (1698–1701), fitted out by the Admiralty at the request of the Royal Society 'to improve the knowledge of the Longitude and variations of the Compasse'.[26]

Developments during the summer brought additions to the original plan, and these were reflected in Cook's instructions of 30 July. By now Wallis had been back almost three months, with official news of the discovery of Tahiti, and unofficial news of the possible sighting nearby of the southern continent. Tahiti first: a small, fertile island of known location, it seemed an obvious choice for an astronomical station. And so, under Wallis's name of King

George's Island, it appears in the instructions as the destination of the *Endeavour*. The separate, second part of the instructions left considerations of science, and returned to the more familiar themes of trade and navigation. From Tahiti Cook was to sail south, where 'there is reason to imagine that a Continent or Land of great extent, may be found'.[27] To some believers such as Alexander Dalrymple the population of the southern continent might be more than 50 million, its size greater than that of Asia, and 'scraps' from its trade enough 'to maintain the power, dominion, and sovereignty of Britain by employing all its manufactures and ships'.[28] There is no reference in Cook's instructions to the supposed sighting of this land-mass from the *Dolphin*, and Egmont later claimed that Wallis and his first lieutenant 'thought it most prudent on their Return, not to take Notice that they had Ever seen it at all'.[29] But Egmont had certainly picked up news of the sighting, and so no doubt had others more directly concerned with the *Endeavour* voyage. To combine the two objectives was a logical step, and committed the government to little additional expenditure. It was one which had been half-anticipated by Professor Hornsby in 1765 when he pointed out that in addition to carrying astronomers his proposed expedition might go on to more practical things, for it would be an 'object of attention to a commercial nation to make a settlement in the great Pacific Ocean'.[30]

This is not the place to assess Cook's achievement on his first voyage as he sailed through Polynesia, circumnavigated New Zealand, and the eastern coast of Australia; but we need to consider the reaction of the Admiralty on his return. The expedition, like its predecessors, was 'Secret', although the newspapers were full of detail (much of it garbled) about the voyage. Cook's instructions included a standard warning that at the end of the voyage he was 'to demand from the Officers and Petty Officers the Log Books and Journals they may have Kept, and to seal them up for our inspection, and enjoyning them, and the whole Crew, not to divulge where they have been until they have Permission so to do'.[31] Given the number of civilian supernumeraries on the *Endeavour* this effort to control news about the expedition was a forlorn hope. For more than one reason the new First Lord of the Admiralty, the Earl of Sandwich, was likely to encourage early publication. There were precedents, of course, for official or semi-official accounts, notably the popular and influential *Voyage round the World by George Anson* of 1748. If an authorised account was not published, then the way was left open for unofficial narratives, often conjured up by hack writers with an eye for the sensational. But there might be more dangerous contenders. On the final stages of the voyage Cook and Banks reacted sharply to the news from a French officer at the Cape about Bougainville's Pacific expedition. Banks wrote, 'How necessary then will it be for us to publish an account of our voyage as soon as possible after our arrival if we mean that our own countrey shall have the Honour of our Discoveries!'[32] Cook followed the same line of reasoning when he hoped that an account of his voyage and Wallis's would be 'published by Authority to fix the prior right of discovery beyond dispute'.[33]

'Published by Authority' was the key, and no doubt Sandwich needed no reminder of this. The French had been quick off the mark, for Bougainville's *Voyage autour du monde* was published in May 1771. It was followed by an enlarged second edition in 1772, and that year also saw an English translation of the first edition. In September 1771, two months after his return in the *Endeavour*, Cook wrote that he expected 'my Lords commissioners of the Admiralty will very soon publish the whole Voyage, Charts &ca'.[34] During the same month Sandwich asked Dr John Hawkesworth, a well-known man of letters, to undertake the task. Hawkesworth responded with enthusiasm: 'There is nothing about which I would so willingly be employed as the work you mention. I would do my best to make it another Anson's Voyage'.[35] The publication, it was clear, was to cover more than Cook's voyage, and when the three-volume work was published in 1773 its title revealed its scope: *An Account of the Voyages undertaken by the order of his present Majesty for making Discoveries in the Southern Hemisphere, And successively performed by Commodore Byron, Captain Wallis, Captain Carteret, And Captain Cook.*

An editor of literary rather than nautical expertise, Hawkesworth inserted reflective and philosophical passages, switched locations and opinions, and generally made frequent and sometimes substantive changes to the journals. The role of the Admiralty in all this is not at all clear. Hawkesworth wrote that his versions of each voyage were read to the respective commanders at the Admiralty, usually in Sandwich's presence, and that the manuscripts were then left with the officers for them to suggest alterations. Since this statement was published in the General Introduction of the *Voyages*, it is hard not to believe that this was broadly what happened. That it was not precisely what happened is shown by Carteret's fury at the misrepresentation, as he saw it, of the *Swallow*'s voyage, and by Cook's firm denials: 'I never had the perusal of the Manuscript nor did I ever hear the whole read in the mode it was written . . .'[36] The uproar over the work no doubt persuaded Cook and his successors to keep publication of their later journals out of the clutches of literary gentlemen, but there can be no doubting the impact and popularity of Hawkesworth's *Voyages*. As J. C. Beaglehole put it, 'for a hundred and twenty years, so far as the first voyage was concerned, Hawkesworth was Cook'.[37]

Cook did not read Hawkesworth's *Voyages* until two years after publication, for by 1773 he was in the Pacific again. His second voyage was the logical complement to what had been explored, and left unexplored, on his first. That it was his voyage this time, and not Banks's, was shown by the ill-tempered withdrawal of the naturalist after disagreements about which alterations should, and should not, be made to the *Resolution*. Cook's instructions, in all save the final flourish of their formal writing, were drawn up by himself. In other ways Cook's second voyage followed the precedents of the first. Again, there were naturalists (Johann Reinhold Forster and his son Georg), astronomers (William Wales and William Bayly), and an artist (William Hodges). The novelties of 1768 were becoming standard practice. And once again, the voyage took place in a context of international rivalry. The dispute with Spain over the Falklands had been settled, and the names given to the ships purchased for the voyage, *Drake* and *Raleigh*, were hurriedly changed to avoid upsetting Madrid. At least, the expedition was not cancelled, thanks to what Cook called the 'perseverance' of Sandwich as First Lord, and Hugh Palliser, Cook's first patron, and now Comptroller of the Navy. Cook continued: 'Had they given way to the general Clamour and not steadily adhered to their own better judgement the Voyage in all probability would have been laid aside'.[38] Some indication of the importance of

Sandwich here is given by his biographer, who points out that although in theory the First Lord of the Admiralty was subordinate to a Secretary of State, 'the instructions for Cook's second and third voyages—just the sort of operation big with implications for diplomacy which a Secretary of State needed to supervise—were issued by the Admiralty'.[39]

On his second voyage Cook disposed of the conjectural southern continent, reached closer to the South Pole than any man before him, and touched on a multitude of lands. To render a comprehensive account of this great voyage would be no easy task, and the winter of 1775–76 saw painstaking attempts by Sandwich and others to organise a joint writing enterprise in which Cook dealt with the voyage generally, and Forster was responsible for the scientific side. In the end, the attempt at a collaborative endeavour collapsed, and no fewer than three full-scale publications resulted: one each by the Forsters, father and son, and Cook's, published in 1777 as *A Voyage towards the South Pole, and Round the World*. It was an impressive work: two volumes, more than 700 pages, sixty-three plates. This time there was no Hawkesworth to 'brew' Cook's journal,[40] though Dr John Douglas, Canon of Windsor, was employed to smooth out some of the roughnesses of Cook's style. The continual redrafting of his journal on the voyage seems to indicate that Cook had a book in mind, that his journal's reading public would be a wider one than the Lords of the Admiralty. It would be, Cook wrote (perhaps with Hawkesworth's literary efforts in mind), 'a work for information and not for amusement'.[41] If there was a model, it might rather have been Captain Constantine John Phipps's *A Voyage towards the North Pole*, published in 1774, and heavy with scientific and technical appendices.[42] Cook was never to see his journal in print, for by 1777 he was again in the Pacific, on his final voyage.

With the fabulous southern continent fading from view, another phantom from the past had once more made its appearance, for in early 1776 Cook had been persuaded to take command of a new expedition to find the Pacific entrance of the Northwest Passage. The most effective pressure for a northern voyage came from members of the Royal Society. Its president, Sir John Pringle, was interested in questions of exploration, but it was Daines Barrington, a member of the Council of the Society, and friend of Sandwich, who was the main driving force. Between them Sandwich and Barrington agreed that when Cook returned from his second voyage an expedition would be fitted out for the northwest coast of America, while at the same time naval vessels would be sent to Baffin Bay to search for the eastern entrance of a passage.[43]

This double-pronged attempt constituted the most ambitious attempt yet undertaken to find the Northwest Passage, and raises the question of motive. The viewpoint of Daines Barrington was characteristic of the group of enthusiasts centred on the Royal Society. He was indignant that the Spaniards should regard news of the forthcoming expedition with suspicion, and thought they should 'be convinced that the English Nation is actuated merely by desiring to know as much as possible with regard to the planet which we inhabit'.[44] This attitude was not easy for the Spaniards to grasp. From Drake to Anson the English had appeared in the South Sea as predators. News of British interest in the North Pacific sent spasms of alarm through Spanish officialdom in Madrid and Mexico, already on guard against possible Russian incursions from the north.[45] Spanish suspicions may have had some basis, for hopes still remained of the commercial and strategic potential of a North-west Passage. The attempts by the British government to establish a base in the Falklands had shown its interest in securing an entrance into the Pacific; and it may have been more than a coincidence that the decision to send a naval expedition to look for the Northwest Passage was made in the same year (1774) as the enforced abandon-ment of Port Egmont. The discovery of a northern route to the Pacific might compensate for loss of control over the longer southern one. In the end Cook found no Northwest Passage, but his achieve-ment in charting long stretches of the American coastline from Nootka Sound to Bering Strait led directly to the opening of the region to European seaborne enterprise.

On his three voyages Cook had established the salient features of the Pacific. As James King put it, 'The Grand bounds of the four Quarters of the Globe are known'.[46] King helped with the writing of the official account of Cook's last voyage, whose preface remarked of this and the other published accounts: 'Every nation that sends a ship to sea will partake of the benefit; but Great Britain herself, whose commerce is boundless, must take the lead in reaping the full advantage of her own discoveries'.[47] Within three years of the publication of Cook's final voyage such a process was well under way. Ships sailed for Botany Bay to establish the first British settlement in Australia; Bligh and the *Bounty* left for Tahiti to collect breadfruit for the Caribbean plantations; and British vessels were on the northwest coast of America engaged in the sea otter trade whose potential Cook had revealed.

With the change, to put it crudely, from exploration to exploitation, came a change of agency. The Admiralty gave way to government departments concerned more closely with trade and colonies. In these years the ministry most involved was the Home Office, whose functions rather incongruously included oversight of Britain's overseas empire. There was also a change of personalities, for Sandwich resigned in March 1782 as the American war dragged to its close, and none of his immediate successors showed his interest in exploration. If there was a single guiding light in the new surge of oceanic endeavour which followed Cook's voyages then it was Sir Joseph Banks, not a minister at all, but even so a man of immense influence and energy. By now he was a baronet, President of the Royal Society, adviser of Cabinet ministers, and patron of the sciences on an international scale, but he never forgot that he had been Cook's sailing companion on the first voyage. In late 1780 James King, just back with the *Resolution* and *Discovery*, wrote to him, 'I look up to you as the common center of we discoverers'.[48]

Nowhere was this more evident than in the North Pacific, where the late 1780s saw a great stir of projects, though government was at first not much involved. The explorers were servants of trading companies: on land Peter Pond and Alexander Mackenzie of the Northwest Company, David Thompson of the Hudson's Bay Company; at sea George Dixon, Nathaniel Portlock, James Colnett and Charles Duncan of the King George's Sound Company. In Britain Banks and Alexander Dalrymple, hydrographer to the East India Company, began to put pressure on ministers to support further discovery expeditions to the northwest coast, and they established a close working relationship with the under-secretaries at the Home Office and Admiralty, Evan Nepean and Philip Stephens.[49]

All such plans and projects came to an abrupt halt when in February 1790 news reached London of the Spanish seizures of British ships and property at Nootka Sound the previous summer.

Among the initial reactions of the government was a decision to send a naval expedition to the northwest coast commanded by Cook's old shipmate, Henry Roberts. Its instructions from Grenville, the Home Secretary, and Nepean directed it to find out exactly what had happened in 1789, and then to establish a settlement as a counterpoise to Spanish claims in the region.[50] Those 'whimsical notions of exclusive rights' which had been tolerated in 1749 were now to be challenged. Approved by the Cabinet, the scheme was shelved as the situation deteriorated during the spring to a point where it seemed that general war with Spain was imminent.

Following the Nootka Sound Convention of October 1790 the expedition was reinstated, but with different instructions and a different commander. George Vancouver, who had sailed twice with Cook, and had been chosen as first lieutenant on the original expedition, was appointed commander of the *Discovery*, and the *Chatham* was provided as consort. Vancouver was set two tasks: to receive restitution of the land and buildings at Nootka seized by Spain in April 1789, and to explore the northwest coast to 60°N lat. for a navigable waterway through the continent.[51] If the Home Office loomed large in the direction of the expedition, Banks's association with it went well beyond the selection of the botanist, Archibald Menzies. At Grenville's request, Banks drew up detailed suggestions for the conduct of Vancouver's survey, and in separate instructions to Menzies told him to pay particular attention to the climate, soil and natural products of the northwest coast, in case it should at 'any time hereafter be deemed expedient to send out Settlers from England'.[52]

For all the obvious links between Vancouver's commission and Cook's third voyage, his expedition was a more workaday affair than that of his celebrated predecessor—or those to the Pacific of Lapérouse, Malaspina and Baudin. Apart from Menzies, there were no civilian specialists on board. Once on the coast Vancouver realised that to produce charts which would settle once and for all the question of a Northwest Passage in temperate latitudes he would have to carry out detailed surveys from his ships' boats. For three seasons the work was carried out with a grim doggedness as Vancouver and his men traced the intricate coastline regardless of whether Spanish or other expeditions had already been there. He saw his mission as one to prove Cook right, and those 'closet geographers', who still insisted on the existence of a passage, wrong. Vancouver's findings were in print by the late summer of 1798 when his three-volume account of the voyage was published. As was now customary, the Admiralty had made it clear to Vancouver soon after his return that it wished the details of the voyage to be made available 'for Publick information', and it paid for the cost of engraving the charts and views.[53] Significantly, some of these were lodged in 'Mr Dalrymple's Office', for in 1795 a Hydrographic Office had at last been established, with Alexander Dalrymple as the first Hydrographer.

If at the beginning of the decade Banks was prominent in the planning of Vancouver's voyage, at its end he played a similar role in the sending of Matthew Flinders on the *Investigator* voyage. Responding to appeals from New South Wales for a naval expedition to search for a passage into the heart of the Australian continent, Banks approached the government. To the Home Office he pointed out the possible benefits to trade, navigation and science— by now a familiar triumvirate—and in 1800 an expedition was approved. From the appointment of the commander to the equipment to be taken, from the naming of the vessel to the drawing up of the instructions, Banks was the moving force. It was altogether appropriate that Flinders, who had first come to Banks's notice when he was with Bligh on the second breadfruit voyage (and Bligh, of course, had been master on Cook's *Resolution*), took Cook as his model. Cook was 'the benchmark by which Flinders assessed himself and his achievements . . . the silent presence, the revered model who offered the key to success'.[54]

It was Cook and those who sailed with him who dominated the British voyages to the Pacific. As William Windham remarked on hearing of Bligh's remarkable open-boat voyage after the *Bounty* mutiny, 'But what officers you are! you men of Captain Cook; you rise upon us in every trial'.[55] They had graduated in the most demanding of training schools, and vanity, even a touch of arrogance, is excusable. Cook wrote of his chart of the North Island of New Zealand on the first voyage, 'I believe that this Island will never be found to differ materialy from the figure I have given it'.[56]

There is a sense of perfection, of permanence here, and this is reflected in the work of his successors. It is there in Vancouver's journal entry of August 1794, almost weary in its finality: 'I trust the precision with which the survey of the coast of North West America has been carried into effect, will remove every doubt, and set aside every opinion of a *north-west passage*'.[57] It is found again in Flinders's promise to Banks: 'My greatest ambition is to make such a minute examination of this extensive and very interesting country that no person shall have occasion to come after me to make further discoveries'.[58]

In the British naval discovery voyages of the later eighteenth century there was a striking discrepancy between resources committed and results achieved. A few small vessels had, for better or for worse, opened new worlds to Europe's gaze. The thirty years between the voyages of Byron and Vancouver had seen a dramatic expansion in the study of humankind and nature, revealed hitherto unknown areas for trade and settlement, and extended the boundaries of international rivalry. With hindsight, the pursuit of knowledge and all that followed seems relentless and logical. It is illustrated by a map of the Pacific showing the spider's web of Cook's tracks. Yet to see this activity as part of some government master plan would, I think, be a mistake. This is not to say that expeditions were not linked to wider national considerations, only that such considerations changed from time to time, and were not always the prime motivation. Still less is it possible to identify a single government ministry or department as the directing force. Chance, and the impact of individual personality, could be as important as the heavy weight of official policy.

In the promotion and organisation of the Pacific voyages of the eighteenth century, the dominant personalities were Anson, Egmont, Sandwich and Banks. With his circumnavigation of 1740–44 Anson had once more focused attention on the South Sea; but other commitments, other priorities, had prevented him from putting the plans for further ventures into effect. Egmont is the least known of the four, though Samuel Johnson's double-edged comment perhaps gives some insight into his character: 'a man whose mind was vigorous and ardent, whose knowledge was extensive, and whose designs were magnificent; but who had somewhat vitiated his judgement by too much indulgence of romantic projects and airy speculations'.[59] His period as First Lord of the Admiralty was brief, from 1763 to 1766, but during those years he set the process of Pacific voyaging in train; and although the Byron expedition looked back to an earlier age, that of Wallis was directed for the first time towards the great southern continent and its supposed potential. By contrast, Cook's *Endeavour* voyage reflected the scientific interests of the Royal Society. It became a discovery voyage almost by chance—through the coincidence of reports of a supposed sighting of a land-mass south of Tahiti reaching London as Cook was preparing to sail. From that mistaken conjecture, and from the presence on board of Joseph Banks, much was to follow. From 1771 to 1782 Sandwich was First Lord of the Admiralty, and his role was doubly important—in his promotion of Cook's second and third voyages, and in his insistence on full publication of the journals. After Sandwich, the torch of Pacific enterprise passed to his Fenland neighbour and friend, Sir Joseph Banks, not a minister but with more influence and a higher reputation than most ministers. His role is sometimes shadowy, often difficult to assess in precise terms, for much of what he did went unrecorded in official documents. Even so, for the first time there seems, paradoxically, to be some overall direction of British enterprise in the Pacific.[60]

The Spanish Yoke

British Schemes to Revolutionise Spanish America, 1739–1807

ALAN FROST

In the Paper of Ideas I had the Honour to lay before you in July, I mentioned that the Conquest of Mexico, or an Attack upon the Coasts of Chili and Peru, appeared to me to be Objects of the first Importance to the British Nation, in Case of a War with Spain; but lest this expression may be too General, I beg Leave on this Occasion, to say, that by *Conquest* I mean not, the Reduction of those Kingdoms to the absolute Dominion of Great Britain; but that by assisting the Natives with a Military Force, they may be enabled to throw off the Spanish Yoke, and resume their ancient Government, Rights, Privileges and Religion.

It is but reasonable to expect, that, exclusive of the Distress which Spain must experience from the Diminution of her Revenues in that Quarter of the World, the British may, for such an Act of Liberality to the oppressed Natives, secure to themselves a Preference in all Articles of Commerce from those extensive and opulent Kingdoms.

Sir Archibald Campbell to Pitt, 18 October 1790[1]

I N 1973, GLYNDWR WILLIAMS published an essay titled '"The Inexhaustible Fountain of Gold": English Projects and Ventures in the South Seas, 1670–1750'. In this, he examined the 'infinite variety of schemes . . . put forward to tap the silver lifeline of the Spanish Empire'. But as the materials Williams drew on amply indicate, simple conquest so as to gain control of bullion supplies was not the only, nor the most important, motive. Attached to the many schemes from Sir John Narborough's onwards was the idea that a firm British presence in the South Seas should enable the nation's merchants to establish an extensive trade in foodstuffs, woollen and other manufactured goods. Williams concluded his account with an analysis of Anson's 1740–44 circumnavigation and its aftermath in publication and in the promotion of fresh schemes, and with a look forward to the British exploration of the Pacific Ocean in the second half of the eighteenth century.

The scheming in the earlier period can now be firmly linked to that in the later one, so that it becomes clear that British thinking to diminish or destroy metropolitan authority in Spanish America in the interest of establishing a trans-Pacific trading empire continued into the nineteenth century. (In a particularly self-serving conceptualisation, the British commonly termed this authority the 'Spanish Yoke'.)

In the second half of 1739, the Walpole administration received proposals for three complementary actions about the Caribbean, in Spanish America and in the Pacific Ocean. A Mr Bladen urged the forming of a settlement on the coast of Darien. Hubert Tassell and Henry Hutchinson spoke up for a venture around Cape Horn into the South Sea, intended to form a base on Juan Fernández and to capture the Acapulco treasure galleon. And James Naish suggested an expedition through the East Indies against Manila. Each of these proposals had immediate strategic objectives; each also had in view longer-term trading benefits.[2]

In the end, a scarcity of resources dictated that only what became Anson's expedition went ahead, and, as is well known, Anson and a remnant of his crew returned with the contents of the treasure galleon. More importantly from the point of view of history, the commodore also returned with developed ideas of how Britain might strengthen its strategic and commercial position about South America and in the Pacific Ocean, particularly by establishing bases on one of the Falkland Islands and on Juan Fernández.[3]

Anson's views coincided with and were complemented by those advanced by John Campbell, in his much-enlarged version of John Harris's *Navigantium atque Itinerantium Bibliotheca* (1744–48). With the commodore's voyage a clear point of reference, Campbell urged, variously, that attempts be made to discover the supposed Northwest Passage from the Atlantic to the Pacific Oceans; that the discovery of New Holland and New Guinea be completed, with perhaps a colonisation of New Britain, for 'a great Trade might be carried on from thence through the whole *Terra Australis* on one Side, and the most valuable Islands of the *East Indies* on the other'. Perhaps, too, there should be an intermediate settlement made on the island of Juan Fernández, and another on 'the most Southern Part of *Terra Australis*', so as to take advantage of the 'Product and Commodities' of the south land, which must be 'extremely rich and valuable', 'because the richest and finest Countries in the known world lie all of them within the same Latitude'.[4]

Taking patriotic stances, both Campbell and Anson urged deliberate programmes of exploration to realise these possibilities. Campbell pointed out that, without efficacious sea routes, Britain might not easily develop its commerce; and he drew particular attention to the significance of a Northwest Passage:

> we might, very probably, reach, in six Weeks, Countries that we cannot now visit in twelve or fifteen Months; and this by an easy and wholesome Navigation, instead of those dangerous and sickly Voyages, that have hitherto rendered the Passage into the *South Seas* a thing so infrequent and ingrateful to *British* Seamen. If such a Passage could be found, it would bring us upon the unknown Coasts of *North America*, which we have many good Reasons to believe are very populous, inhabited by a rich and civilized People, no Strangers to Trade, and with whom we might carry on a very great and beneficial Commerce.[5]

We may now know that Anson set vigorously about mounting such a programme. On 19 January 1749, he 'signified' to his fellow Lords Commissioners 'His Majesty's Pleasure that Two Sloops should be forthwith fitted to be sent on Discoverys in the Southern Latitude'. The expedition was to have two distinct purposes: to explore in the southern Atlantic Ocean, particularly about the Falklands; and from Juan Fernández 'to proceed into the Trade Winds keeping between the Latitudes of 25 & 10 Sth & steer a traverse Course for at least 1000 leagues or more if they have an opportunity of recruiting their Wood & Water'. Spain's bitter protests then led the British to abandon the expedition; however, they did so asserting their 'right to send out Ships for the discovery of unknown & unsettled Parts of the World', specifically in the 'South Seas'.[6]

At the end of 1760, after Anson had first investigated the possibility of attacking Cadiz, the British Cabinet decided rather to move against Spain in its colonies. Anson met the Chairs of the East India Company on 29 December to inform them of the government's intention to attack Manila; and when Cabinet met on 6 February 1762, the ministers had a precise agenda to consider, viz.:

- Prosecution of the Spanish War, the Havannah & the Philippine islands
- The attack on Louisiana
- Buenos Ayres in connection with the Portuguese
- La Vera Cruz with a view to marching to Mexico.

Understanding that this was Anson's thinking, the ministers decided to mount expeditions against Louisiana, Havana and Manila.[7]

In a series of memorandums in the next months, Wright and Henry Ellis provided a plethora of information about the fortifications and personnel, the government and trade of Spain's far-flung colonies, and the mood of their inhabitants. As before, the immediate benefits of military victory were the lesser of their concerns. Always, they saw that the removal of the 'yoke' which metropolitan Spain laid so heavily on its colonial citizens should open wide trading vistas to enterprising British merchants. In his memorandum of 20 February, while he advised against a direct attempt on Havana, Wright did argue for the occupation of a harbour adjacent to Vera Cruz, from which a British squadron might interdict Spain's trade with Mexico. Later, he expanded his scheme to include the capture of Cuba, Florida and Louisiana, so that Britain might control North America from Florida west to Mexico.[8]

In addition, he proposed 'A Method . . . for the Entire reduction of the Kingdom of Chili and of obtaining the Dominion of the South Seas'. This grandiose scheme was to involve the establishment of a naval base on one of the Falkland Islands; the capture and fortification of Valdivia, which possessed the best harbour on the coast of Chile, and from which, with the aid of Indian allies, the inhabitants of Chile and Peru might be liberated, so that Britain might obtain command of commerce from Valparaiso to Acapulco.[9]

Expectations of what Britain would derive from the capture of Manila were similarly large. Between 8 and 12 January 1762, an unknown informant discussed this idea with Anson in considerable detail. What he proposed was, first, the capture of Manila; and second, the taking of the island of Mindanao. If both these objectives were achieved, then the British should establish a trading post on Mindanao or an adjacent island. The results of all this would be:

1) the cutting of 'all trade or intercourse betwixt the E. Indies & the Spanish American provinces in the So: Seas';

2) that 'the Spanish provinces in the So: Seas, both of So: & No: America may with great success be insulted & plundered, on the part of Gr. Britain';

and

3) that 'by the means of this Settlement, such a course of Trade may during the War be established from that Island, with China, Batavia, the coast of Coromandel Surat &c by the E. India Co: or free Merchants tradeing under its protection, as may be greatly beneficial to Gr. Britain: and which may be secured & improved after the conclusion of the peace'.[10]

Simultaneously, the Earl of Egremont sought the views of others. One wrote: 'Our possession of Manila will give our India Company a most convenient Magazine & Port to carry on not only their Trade to China, but enable them to Extend their Commerce all over that Part of the World'.[11]

The British did proceed against Havana and Manila. After a harrowing siege, British forces captured Havana in August 1762. The very heavy loss of life, mostly from illness, meant that the attempt on Louisiana could not be made. Much more easily, an expedition from India took Manila in October 1762, with its archbishop agreeing to pay a ransom of four million dollars in return for its not being sacked. News of Manila's fall did not reach Europe in time for it to become a pawn in the chess-game of peace.[12]

Britain ended the Seven Years' War in a situation much superior to any it had previously enjoyed *vis-à-vis* France and Spain. It had gained large new territories in North America and India, and smaller ones in the West Indies and Africa. It had decisively established its naval mastery; its strategists and navigators now much better understood the imperatives of maritime operations over very wide geographical ranges; and its merchant shipping capacity had risen from some 450 000 tons in 1755 to over 600 000 tons in 1763.

The ministers of the new administration knew that, if taken advantage of, these things might form the basis of a massive expansion of trade. In defending the proposed terms of peace at the end of 1762, the Earl of Shelburne made much of the connections between sea power and prosperity, and prosperity and the capacity to defend the nation and the empire. The terms, he urged, would leave Britain free to pursue commerce in a determined way. Not only would this increase the nation's wealth, but a greater volume of imports and exports would require more ships and sailors, and these would then become resources in any future conflict—'the northern [that is, American] Colonies increase Population & of course the consumption of our Manufactures, pay us for them by their Trade with Foreigners, & thereby giving employment to M[illion]s of Inhabitants in G. Britain & Ireland, & are of the Utmost consequence to the Wealth safety & Independence of these Kingdoms & must continue so for ages to come'.[13]

For all the successes of the Seven Years' War, though, in mid-1763 there remained three large impediments to Britain's realising this ambition of commanding the commerce of the world. It did not yet possess convenient sea routes to the South Sea and the Far East. It did not enjoy access to the markets of Spanish America, and therefore to the supplies of bullion so necessary for trade in Asia. And the Southern Continent, with all its fabled wealth, remained undiscovered. The quest to realise these purposes, which became intertwined, caused the British to embark on a set of activities which lasted into the nineteenth century.

THE STAGES BY WHICH the British decided to mount Commodore John Byron's exploring expedition to the southern Atlantic and Pacific Oceans (1764–66) remain exceptionally obscure. The best we can say is that the decision must have been taken sometime between mid-1763, when peace came, and early March 1764, when Byron wrote to Carteret telling him that he should hurry to town if he wanted to go on the voyage.[14] However, there are presently no clear answers to the questions of who precisely took the decision, in which forums, and why.[15]

However, it is now possible to identify Byron's expedition as a revival of that proposed by Anson in 1749, rather than as one conceived of *de novo* and reflecting the disinterested ideals of the Scientific Enlightenment. And what seems the likely context is offered by a long series of related memorandums in Egmont's papers. Written by Henry Hutchinson, these memorandums extol the advantages to be gained from establishing a secure presence in the South Sea. The chronology of these documents is problematic. Some of them are essentially identical to those which Hutchinson gave in to the government at the time of Anson's expedition. Indeed, all of them may have been first written in the 1730s, with Hutchinson subsequently updating them as a consequence of information obtained during the voyage, or later. What is the more significant, though, is that these papers were passed by Hutchinson's son to Egmont in the period between 2 January 1763 and 6 October 1765—that is, at the time that Britain mounted Byron's expedition and decided to colonise the Falkland Islands.[16]

Four of these papers are most relevant here. These are: 'Spaniards in the South Sea dread a War against foreign Princes & the Vice-Roys Power' (after December 1742); 'Passages from the North, to the South Sea of Importance' (20 August 1739); 'A Free Port in South America of Importance' (undated); and 'Colony in South America of Importance' (undated). Looking back wistfully to the grandiose scheme of settlement promoted, but never pursued, by the South Sea Company in the 1710s, Hutchinson envisaged grand possibilities. He argued that if there were a 'free' port on the western coast of the Americas, then it would become a focus of trade, with Indian groups and foreigners resorting to it. He saw few potential limits to this trade. Slaves might be brought from Madagascar as well as Guinea. 'All Sorts of [British] Manufactures and fabricks' might be shipped out, and sold for bullion. Then, 'we might hereafter if necessary, from this Colony carry on a Trade to China, & the East Indies, without carrying any Bullion out of Great Britain'. And discoveries might be pursued. He had heard there were, out in the Pacific Ocean, 'some Good Islands, which have been seen, and are often talkd of by the Spaniards in Peru, who say, through Policy, those Islands have not been sought after in a proper manner'. The reasons for this neglect, he had been told, was 'owing to the fear of their being discover'd to other Nations, which might probably induce foreigners to take & Hold such Islands, when they might probably molest the Trade carried on in the South Seas, & at some favourable opportunity offerd, might Declare War against Spain by making a well timed Descent on the Coast of Chili or Peru'.[17]

These purposes resonate in the Admiralty's instructions to Byron, and in his actions. He was first to search the south Atlantic for 'Land or Islands', Byron was told. Finding any, he was 'to make purchases, with the consent of [the] Inhabitants, and take possession of convenient Situations in the Country, in the Name of the King of Great Britain'; or if the lands were uninhabited, he was to take possession of them. He was to survey Pepys's Island and the Falkland Islands, so as to locate suitable harbours. Then, after wintering either at the former or at Port Desire on the coast of Patagonia, where he would be resupplied, he was to proceed into the Pacific Ocean, and sail north to New Albion. There, he was 'to search the said Coast with great care and diligence' for the entrance of a passage to the Atlantic. If, however, he found no signs of one, he was to proceed across the Pacific, and return to England through the East Indies and via the Cape of Good Hope.[18]

Byron did reconnoitre the Falklands, reporting favourably on Port Egmont on the western one. Notoriously, once in the Pacific Ocean, he made no effort to look for the Northwest Passage. Rather, he decided to 'make a NW Course til we get the true Trade wind, and then to shape a Course to Wtward in hopes of falling in with Solomons Islands if there are such, or else to make some new Discovery'—that is, he followed the general route specified by Anson for the abortive 1749 expedition.[19]

Byron accomplished little except the fastest circumnavigation of the world to that date. Nonetheless, British ministers seized avidly on his information about the Falklands. Cautioning his colleagues that the business was one of 'very great Moment & of the most secret nature', Egmont argued in Anson-like tones that Falkland's 'Island' was

> undoubtedly *the Key to the whole Pacifick Ocean.* This Island must command the Ports & Trade of Chili[,] Peru, Panama, Acapulco, & in one word all the Spanish Territory upon that Sea. It will render all our Expeditions to those parts most lucrative to ourselves, most fatal to Spain, & no longer formidable tedious, or uncertain in a future War.[20]

Cabinet decided to establish a base at Port Egmont, and in October 1765 Captain John McBride and a company of marines sailed to do so. On learning of this (as of Bougainville's settlement on East Falkland), Spain protested mightily, with Shelburne in the end telling Ambassador Masserano that

> the right of Navigation was so indisputably of our side, that I could not consent to talk seriously upon it. That if the Spaniards talking of their Possessions included the A[merican] & S[outh] Seas, and that our navigating them gave occasion to them to Suspect a War, I had no hesitation to say that I would advise one if they insisted on reviving such a vague & strange pretension, long since wore out, as the exclusive right of those Seas.[21]

It was in this atmosphere that in mid-1766 Egmont urged on reluctant colleagues a second exploring expedition to the southern hemisphere.[22] Wallis found Tahiti, and mistakenly thought he saw the coastline of *Terra Australis* to the south of it. Other voyages followed. On his first, Cook found no trace of the southern continent; however, he did circumnavigate New Zealand, chart the eastern coast of Australia, and sail through Torres Strait. On his second, he removed the speculative *Terra Australis* from the map, but also pursued an eastern, route from Europe to the central Pacific and, discovering many islands, learned how to navigate efficiently its southern half from Australia in the west to South America in the east. On his third, he learned how to navigate the northern half of the great ocean, and searched unsuccessfully for the Pacific entrance of the Northwest Passage. By 1780, even though they had relinquished the Falklands settlement, the British had acquired the broad geographical knowledge necessary to achieve the trading empire that Hutchinson, Anson, Egmont and the others had envisaged.

IT WAS WITH war again that the British sought to achieve the political circumstances necessary for the realisation of their dream. Late in 1776, after the revolt of the American colonies, Robert White presented to the North administration a plan for fomenting revolution throughout Spain's American colonies. In 1778 Captain Joseph Speer offered Sandwich his 'Plan for attacking the Spaniards in the West Indies'. Noting that 'the Native Indians and Creoles . . . are Enemies to the old Spain Spaniards, and have for many years past wished for an opportunity to shake off the Yoke', Speer asserted that the inhabitants of

> the great Kingdom of Mexico on being assured of Protection and free Trade, would revolt to a Man, and by settling this Government in the hands of the principal Creolians, Great Britain would receive the vast Revenue now collected for the King of Spain, besides opening a Trade by which all the Advantages of carrying our Manufactures and disposing of them for the Spanish Gold and Silver.

The next year, he enlarged his thinking to comprehend the securing of bases in Nicaragua, so as to gain control of the trade of the South Sea.[23]

Early in 1779, John Call put forward a similar scheme; and White renewed his in the middle of the year.[24] The time was now propitious. Between June and November 1779, the administration received a series of reports from John Hippisley, an informant in Rome, concerning civil unrest in Spanish America. There were then, Hippisley said, about 2000 expelled Jesuits in the papal precinct, many of them the scions of 'old Spanish settlers, who have intermarried with the principal American families'. Those from Mexico and Peru, particularly, 'to a man' bore 'implacable animosity to the Court of Spain'; and these 'might prove *essential instruments* in effecting a reduction of New Spain, having an entire influence on their countrymen, who universally, both in Peru and Mexico, are predisposed to revolt'.[25]

Towards the end of the year, the North administration was clearly thinking seriously about attacking Spanish America. There are in the Sandwich papers two memorandums, one in Sir Hugh Palliser's hand, the other in Sandwich's, which discuss the idea of sending a force from India across the Pacific Ocean, perhaps to attack Manila on the way.[26]

Simultaneously, the administration received a series of fresh proposals. From Major William Dalrymple, Sir John Dalling, the Governor of Jamaica, and others came schemes for 'obtaining possession of the River St John and Lake Nicaragua and opening through them a communication with the South Sea at Rija Legia, or elsewhere'.[27] From the major's brother, Sir John Dalrymple, came one of much vaster import. Longtime resident of Lisbon, enriched from trade, and having a keen eye, John Dalrymple was probably the author of the series of reports to Chamier in 1777 concerning the military and commercial circumstances of ports about the Mediterranean.[28] He also gave his attention to Spanish America and the Pacific Ocean; and here his thinking was informed by a surprisingly modern understanding of the world's fundamental geophysics. A generation later, in renewing his proposal to another administration, he wrote memorably:

> Ever since the world began a South land wind has blown from the Province of Chili to the bay of Panama. And ever Since the world began a north land wind has blown from the province of Mexico to the bay of Panama. So that the South of Chili and the north of Mexico command by the winds the intermediate Spaces of the Spanish possessions in the new Hemisphere an hundred leagues all along the Coast of America.[29]

In 1779, Dalrymple proposed a privateering expedition against Spain's shipping in and settlements on the shores of the South Sea. He began by acknowledging the difficulties of the western passage into the Pacific—it was dangerous, and might only be attempted at the height of the (southern) summer; because ships using it needed to refresh somewhere on the eastern coast of South America, the

Spanish usually had warning of their presence; and once round into the South Sea, maurauders had no feasible means of disposing of prizes. Pointing to the prevailing winds off the western coasts from Chile up to California, and to how 'from the bay of Panama, ships are carried to the East Indies by the great trade wind', Dalrymple saw that the eastern passage into the Pacific pioneered in part by Tasman in 1642 and then fully by Cook on his second voyage— that by Africa, across the southern Indian Ocean and via New Holland and/or New Zealand—was the key to warships ranging the western coasts of the Americas and to the opening of the vast ocean to British commercial activity. A small squadron of fast frigates, Dalrymple argued, might approach Chile unheralded along an easy route through the southern Pacific Ocean, plunder shipping and towns as it swept north, then recross the mid-Pacific to India or China. Commanders might sell prizes and goods, refit, and then cross the Pacific again.

Subsequently, Dalrymple suggested that the attackers might rather leave prizes and booty at the Galapagos Islands or New Zealand, and that he had now discussed the scheme with Wallis 'who first discovered Otaheite, . . . [who] tells me that he proposed to Lord Sandwich to send ships to pillage the South Seas, and to deposit the plunder at Otaheite, and from thence to return to plunder again'. What makes Dalrymple's proposal distinctive is, first, its grasp of the great wind and current systems of the Pacific Ocean; and second, its being the first attempt to put Cook's discoveries to strategic and commercial use.[30]

Dalrymple interested some wealthy Scottish merchants in his scheme, and continued to promote it with the administration. At the end of 1779, it was to involve a small squadron of warships and some 9000 troops sailing from England to attack the 'Spanish Settlements on the Coast of Chili, Peru, & Mexico [which] are at present in a very defenceless state, & the Naval force of the Spaniards there by no means sufficient to protect their trade'.[31] At the beginning of 1780, however, the administration came to favour an alternative put forward by Colonel William Fullarton. There were then protracted deliberations. By year's end, having obtained further information from (among others) Robert M'Douall and Arthur Phillip, who had served in the Portuguese squadron in Brazilian waters in the 1770s, the administration had settled on complementary ventures—the one to be led by William Dalrymple from Jamaica across the Isthmus of Panama; and the other, under Commodore George Johnstone's command, to be mounted via India, which should capture one of the Philippine islands, then 'proceed to some healthy spot in New Zealand, in order to establish means of refreshment, communication, and retreat'. From there, it was to cross to South America, where there was 'not one place from California to Cape Horn, capable of resisting such an Equipment'.[32]

Dalrymple's expedition came to terrible grief in the swamps of Nicaragua, while Johnstone and Fullarton, whose expedition was mounted in conjunction with the East India Company, were distracted into an abortive attack on the Cape of Good Hope—though not before M'Douall had landed a disaffected Jesuit at Rio de Janeiro. However, these failures are not as significant as the facts that the North administration attempted the ventures; and that the ministers did so in the belief that success would lead to long-term commercial advantage. The author of the Nicaraguan scheme among the Shelburne papers in the Clements Library saw that Reja Leja might be made 'the grand Emporium of Trade for all the pacific Ocean, which Trade, under proper management, could bear such impost to be laid on it as would create an amazing revenue'.[33] Fullarton thought that 'some advantageous Posts should be fortified, and terms of independence offered to the native Mexicans, Peruvians and Chilians'; and that if both these ends were achieved, 'the Trade of South America would be opened to our East-Indian Territories'.[34] Sir John Dalrymple foresaw a complete revolution in the system of Britain's overseas commerce if this were done, observing in March 1780 with considerable prescience:

England might very well put up with the loss of America, for she would then exchange an empire of dominion which is very difficult to be kept for an empire of trade which keeps itself. Instead of going round by the Cape of Good Hope her East India Trade would then be conducted by that isthmus [that is, of Panama] which would be another sort of passage in point of advantage than the northwest passage that we are all agog about. The run from England to the isthmus with the trade wind is six weeks; from the other side of the isthmus to the East Indies is two months. The present East India trade is loaded with a passage in which there is no stop and consequently no intermediate profit. But if their passage was by the isthmus their ships would take the West Indies and North America in their way and and give an intermediate profit. Such a communication would connect the trade of England completely together. In time of war there would be required only two great convoys, one to carry the whole trade between England and this side of the isthmus and the other to convoy the whole trade between the other side of the isthmus and the East Indies.[35]

THE FAILURE OF these ventures by no means diminished belief in the efficacy of the thinking which underlay them. In February and April 1781, Richard Oswald developed a vast scheme involving Britain's joining with Russia for a comprehensive move against the Spanish in the Americas.[36] In mid-1782, Oswald renewed his proposal to the Shelburne administration. The Prime Minister was interested, and had Grantham, the Foreign Secretary, convey the scheme to Harris, Ambassador at St Petersburg. Harris replied that there was no immediate prospect of getting the Empress to consider it.[37]

Nonetheless, Shelburne continued interested in the idea of attacking Spain in the Americas. In August and September, the administration received advice on how this might best be done from John Blankett (who had had some hand in the scheme of Cook's third voyage, and who was Shelburne's private agent) and Arthur Phillip. This interest was directly related to lack of progress in the negotiations for peace. Spain wanted Gibraltar back, but was offering what the British considered to be only inadequate exchanges. What the British wanted in return was significant territory in the West Indies, together with the right to trade 'with Spain & its Colonies on the same terms as France'.[38] In the autumn of 1782, Shelburne and his ministers saw the capturing of some of these colonies as the most effective means of breaking the impasse and of obtaining what they wanted. It is significant that they also had reports of insurrections in Chile and Peru at this time.[39] As Townshend reinstructed Oswald about 25 September, 'We shall incline to listen to the Proposal of attacking the Spanish Possessions in preference to the Dominions of France'.[40]

Towards the end of November, the administration proceeded to mount an expedition comprising three line-of-battle ships and a frigate, with Phillip in command of the *Europe*. Its full purpose is not entirely clear. It was certainly intended to attack Montevideo and Buenos Aires. Alternatively, or additionally, it might also have attacked the towns facing the South Sea. It also may have been carrying arms for the Creole and Inca rebels in Peru. The ships sailed in January 1783, but a storm ravaged them in the Bay of Biscay. Only Phillip proceeded on. He wrote plaintively to Townshend from Rio de Janeiro:

> the situation of the Spanish settlements are such as I always thought them . . . All the Regulars in Buenos Ayres Monte Video, and the Different Guards in the River of Plate do not amount to five hundred Men. No ship of the Line and only two frigates in the River . . . You will Sir, easily suppose how much I must be mortified in being so near & not at liberty to Act.[41]

STILL THE IDEA persisted. In proposing a colonisation of New South Wales in 1783 and 1784, James Matra, Sir George Young and Sir John Call each pointed out how it would facilitate an attack across the Pacific Ocean against the Spanish colonies, and thereby contribute to the liberation of Spanish America and the growth of British commerce.[42] The idea was also kept alive by a series of arrivals from Spanish America of persons claiming to be emissaries of disaffected Creoles. In 1783 Don Juan Antonio de Prado reached England, and enlisted Edward Bott's help to argue for an expedition to support the insurgency in Peru—though he and Bott also envisaged general insurrection, with the introduction of a constitution modelled on the English one.[43] In May 1784, Don Luis Vidal asked for the same sort of help for the rebels in New Granada.[44] In 1786, Francisco de Mendiola claimed to represent the cause of powerful interests in Mexico, who he said would conclude a commercial treaty with Britain in return for armed support.[45] Most enduring and persuasive of these dissidents was Francisco de Miranda, who reached London in February 1785 with a vision of creating a United States of Spanish America, and who was to seek British support for it at intervals over the next twenty years.[46]

And the Pitt administration certainly did not discourage Miranda. Pitt heard his advice on 14 February 1790, and three weeks later received very detailed accounts of South America from him.[47] As part of the response to the Nootka Sound crisis of 1790, in early May Lord Mulgrave presented the India Board with five options for schemes against Spain's American colonies:

- a squadron might sail from India and attack Manila, then cross the Pacific via the Hawaiian Islands;
- the squadron might bypass Manila, but take much the same course across the Pacific;
- the squadron might sail south from India, and refresh at New Holland or New Zealand before crossing the Pacific to South America;
- a squadron might sail from England via Brazil and round Cape Horn;
- one or other of these might act in conjunction with one sent against Nicaragua.[48]

The administration then sought further advice from Miranda, William Dalrymple and James Creassy. Creassy added the idea of a complementary expedition via the West Indies, 'to establish *and forever secure to great Britain* a Communication across the Isthmus of Panama'. 'By once getting a superior Naval power in the South Seas, and securing a safe conveyance across this important passage', he maintained, the British 'would become masters of the Spanish wealth' and 'the keepers of the keys of their treasure'.[49]

In June, General Sir Archibald Campbell assumed particular responsibility for advancing these schemes. In August, Miranda drafted a proclamation to be read to the liberated populations, announcing an interim government. The administration continued its planning right up to the moment that Spain gave way over Nootka Sound at the end of October.[50]

THESE GENERIC IDEAS reappeared at the beginning of 1797, after the British had captured the Dutch colony at the Cape of Good Hope. For six weeks, Henry Dundas, William Huskisson (Under-secretary at the War Office) and Evan Nepean (now Admiralty Secretary) worked on the details. One force would proceed from Europe against the River Plate settlements. Another would sail from the Cape against the settlements on the western coasts of South America. The force against the Plate settlements was to comprise three regiments; the one from the Cape, two regiments of 1000 men each, and about 180 cavalry- and 70 artillery-men. These latter were to be joined en route 'by 500 Men from Botany Bay, part to be recruited from the Convicts & the remainer from the Corps now there'.[51] Huskisson announced these details to General Craig on 21 January. Nepean drafted instructions to Admiral Pringle, Commodore at the Cape, on 26 January. A month later, Huskisson asked Portland, the Secretary of State for the Colonies, to draw up instructions for Governor Hunter at Sydney, which Portland did. But then news of reverses in Europe and the emerging expense of the ventures caused the administration to call them off at the beginning of March.[52]

In 1798, Miranda made another proposal for general liberation to Pitt. Robert Brooke, the Governor of St Helena, advised Lord Macartney, now Governor of the captured Dutch colony at the Cape of Good Hope, to attack the River Plate settlements. Robert Dundas advocated a move against Chile and Peru. Towards the end of 1799, having more information from Miranda and Captain James Colnett (who had explored up the west coast of South America a few years earlier), Henry Dundas again urged action on his Cabinet colleagues. In 1801, Colnett renewed his proposal, when he pointed to a distinct role for New South Wales. And General Sir Ralph Abercromby also succeeded in having Cabinet consider the idea.[53]

The ideas were abroad again in 1803–4. In November 1803, Home Popham told Sir Joseph Yorke that either outright possession or political penetration of South America 'must offer the greatest Commercial advantages, not only to this Country but to our possessions in India, by opening a direct Trade on each Side of the Continent, & drawing all the Wealth of Spanish America from our

Enemies, which has always been their principal support in every war with Great Britain'.[54]

Twelve months later, Popham instructed Pitt and Dundas, now back in power, at great length on the subject of the 'Emancipation of Spanish America', and on how best to gain possession of 'prominent points' in South America. He too argued for a two-pronged attack, the one against the Plate settlements to be mounted from Europe, the other against the ports on the western coast to come across the Pacific Ocean. Of this second attack, he wrote:

> I consider two points of descent as sufficient, one however might suffice but if the other can be accomplished it will have a great Effect upon the People to the Southward of Buenos Ayres. I mean in speaking of this which is on the coast of Chili to propose Valpariso, & if the force for that object could either be concentrated at, or taken from New South Wales, by new levies or otherwise, it would make this proposition perfect. The great force however for the Pacifick which I will propose to come from India . . .[55]

Two weeks later, William Jacob advanced yet another scheme for atttacking Spanish America. In December, Creassy once more renewed his 'great national Plan' for stopping Spain's access to bullion and enlarging Britain's trade by an occupation of Panama.[56] Pitt clearly attended closely to these proposals, for he summarised Jacobs's, with an allusion to Popham's: 'Valparaiso on the Coast of Chili—Force concentrated by New Levies or otherwise at New South Wales'.[57]

In 1806–7, after more than fifty years of agitation, the idea's moment finally came. In August 1806, Captain John Hunter told Northumberland that the 'proximity' of the New South Wales colony 'to the Spanish Settlements on the coast of Chili and Peru' made it important 'in a *Political* Point of View'.[58] In October, Sir John Dalrymple renewed his schemes; and in November, William Kent gave Banks a copy of his 1803 paper concerning Sydney's being 'an eligible place from which a Squadron could sail against the Spaniards on the Coast of Chile and Peru'. *Inter alia*, he observed:

Had Commodore Anson gone the Eastern Rout, where he would have met with constant fair Winds, although the distance is greater than that by the Westward, and although he would have had no such place to stop and refresh at as Port Jackson, there is little doubt he would have carried all his Squadron with him to the Coast of Peru, and might in that case have been able to fulfill the high expectation the Nation entertain'd of his Voyage.[59]

Heading the 'Ministry of All the Talents', Grenville then took up the idea of conquering Spanish America, when he and his advisers considered sending a squadron and 4000 men against the Spanish in Chile. After occupying Valparaiso and establishing control of the country, the expedition would set up a chain of posts across the Andes and link up with the force sent against Buenos Aires. He also proposed attacking Mexico from the east with 9000 European and black troops, and from the west with 5000 Europeans and Sepoys, and attacking Peru with a small force from the Cape of Good Hope and New South Wales.

The administration did not proceed with the Mexico scheme, but they did organise an expedition to attack Chile. In the process, the Marquis of Buckingham advised his brother to attend

> very particularly to the advantage of ordering Murray to carry Crawford's force direct from their *rendezvous* through Bass's Straits to refresh at New South Wales—Port Jackson; and to exchange their less active men for the seasoned flank companies of the New South Wales corps; and to take with them 100 convict pioneers, who will be invaluable, as seasoned to work in the sun.[60]

As this force was being mounted, Popham and Baird took part of the force that had recaptured the Cape of Good Hope across the Atlantic to Buenos Aires. There they had been forced to surrender. Learning this, the administration then ordered Murray and Craufurd to go direct to the River Plate, where a second debacle followed.

For the time being, these defeats ended British hopes of removing 'the Spanish Yoke'. This now had to await the Creole insurrections of the 1820s. Nonetheless, the attendant ideas of liberation and expansion of trade had held great force in British thinking for more than half a century.

As we end the twentieth century, there is much discussion of the prospects of the countries of the Pacific Rim forming a great trading bloc, with the emphasis on its trade being free. The views expounded by the British in the second half of the eighteenth century have therefore a striking modernity.

Alexander Dalrymple and the Hydrographic Office

ANDREW COOK

AT FIRST SIGHT THE establishment of the Hydrographic Office is simple to explain. The Order in Council creating the office of Hydrographer to the Admiralty was dated 12 August 1795.[1] Its preamble averred that there was a lack of reliable information available to ships of the Fleet to navigate safely in the waters where the demands of war might direct them. It was the availability of the data, not its quality, which was the first difficulty:

> On a cursory examination of the plans and charts which have from time to time been deposited in the office, we find a considerable mass of information, which, if judiciously arranged and digested, would be found of the greatest utility to Your Majesty's Service; but from want of a proper establishment for the execution of this duty, Your Majesty's Officers are in a great measure deprived of these valuable communications.[2]

The steps already taken by other European countries to create hydrographic offices were called as evidence. The responsibilities of such an office in Britain were equally clearly defined, in the proposal of the Admiralty Board:

that a proper person should be fixed upon to be appointed Hydrographer to this Board, and to be intrusted with the custody and care of such plans and charts as now are, or may hereafter be, deposited in this office belonging to the public, and to be charged with the duty of selecting and compiling all such information as may appear to be requisite for the purposes of improving the navigation, and for the guidance and direction of the Commanders of Your Majesty's ships, in all cases wherever any knowledge in this respect may be found to be necessary.[3]

Alexander Dalrymple, FRS, retired East India Company official, navigator and geographer, was offered the post with effect from the following day, 13 August 1795.[4]

This process of 1795 the official historians, and historians of marine cartography, take as the origin of the Hydrographic Office as it is known today. The Office has operated consistently since the time of Sir Francis Beaufort, ordering surveys, compiling results, and publishing charts, sailing directions, lights lists, and other aids to navigation for mariners. But this simple version of events hides the real story of what prompted the Board of Admiralty Commissioners to propose then as they did.

In his magisterial history of the Hydrographic Service, Sir Archibald Day placed the proposal in the context of war in Europe, of Pacific and Hudson Bay exploration, of communication with the East Indies, of sponsorship of Des Barres's collection of charts, the *Atlantic Neptune*, and more particularly of the wartime expansion of the Navy Vote in Parliament.[5] Before him, A. H. W. Robinson brought the appointment into his narrative of the coastal surveys of Murdoch Mackenzie and Graeme Spence, while explaining that the Order in Council gave the Hydrographer no control over the planning and execution of surveys.[6] Both Day and Robinson used selected documents from the boxes of Hydrographers' Correspondence in Admiralty records in the Public Record Office.[7] Day had the additional advantage of the draft of the first two chapters of the official history of the Hydrographic Office which R. T. Gould was persuaded to commence in unwelcome retirement in the 1920s. Gould drew the thread of history through the Dutch rutters and *The English Pilot* of the seventeenth century, and the London chart-sellers of the eighteenth century, the latter as publishers of the surveys commissioned by the Admiralty from, for example, James Cook in Newfoundland.[8] He derived some details from the straightforward biographical accounts in L. S. Dawson's *Memoirs of Hydrography* (1883–1885),[9] and both these authors, with Day, relied heavily on the office memoir drawn up by G. H. Richards, Hydrographer from 1864 to 1874, and printed in 1868.[10] Richards had focused on the absence of any express intention in the Order-in-Council 'to do more than to utilise the documents which already existed', and enumerated the official surveys which the Admiralty had ordered since 1750, overseas by Cook and Lane in New-foundland, Gauld on the Florida coast, Des Barres and Holland on the eastern seaboard of North America, Vancouver in the Pacific Northwest, and Thomas Hurd in Bermuda, and at home by the Mackenzies and Spence. He acknowledged in his introductory remarks his use of 'the fragmentary notes of one connected with the Department from its earliest days, and until lately living'. These notes survive in the Hydrographic Office archives,[11] and have been attributed to Michael Walker, engraver, who died in 1868.[12] Walker, who had joined the Hydrographic Office in 1809, was a son of John Walker, Dalrymple's assistant from 1796 onwards. These imperfect notes, apparently recorded (and with interpolations) by F. J. Evans, then Chief Naval Assistant to Richards, and later suc-cessor to Richards as Hydrographer, represent the earliest statement of the history of the Hydrographic Office.[13]

At the time of his appointment, Dalrymple was already retained, quarter by quarter, by the East India Company, 'to examine the ships' journals' and to publish such charts, plans and sailing direc-tions as he thought fit.[14] He had held this position since 1779, though he had been publishing harbour plans of the East Indies by subscription since 1774, and charts of the Bay of Bengal and of the waters around Borneo on his own account since 1769. He later claimed that he owed his Admiralty appointment to Earl Spencer, First Lord of the Admiralty from November 1794.[15] But the sequence of events which identified the position and the man to fill it owed much to the chain of Admiralty appointments in March 1795: Sir Philip Stephens rose from the Secretaryship to a seat on the Board, Evan Nepean (previously Under-secretary for War) became Secretary, and William Marsden was introduced as Second Secretary.[16] All three had long connections with Dalrymple, either through the Royal Society and the Royal Society Club, or (in Nepean's case) through the conduct of colonial business in the Home Office. Dalrymple was already undertaking an investigation for Nepean in February 1795, using East India Company ships' journals to compare journey times between England and the Cape by the Guinea Coast route, via St Helena, and by the westerly route.[17] More significantly, in May 1795, at Stephens's request, he was compiling a portfolio of material on the Scilly Isles, including an engraved chart and views and printed tide tables.[18] Though nothing is known to have survived of this exercise, except a composite from impressions of three plates forming the chart,[19] it is a reasonable conjecture that the Scilly Isles exercise was a 'test piece' for Stephens to use with the Admiralty Board in support of a proposal for the Office of Hydrographer. Dalrymple was not currying favour: in his letters to both Stephens and Nepean he criticised the Admiralty's habitual tardiness in paying accounts, and Marsden smoothed the matter only by offering to take the payment for the Scilly Isles work personally to Dalrymple's bankers.[20] The significance of these matters is that the papers concerning them, though dating from the months before the Order in Council, were filed by the Admiralty as 'Hydrographer's Correspondence'.

Dalrymple was the chosen candidate for the proposed office long before August 1795. Already on 10 June he was seeking the East India Company's approval of his acceptance of the contemplated appointment.[21] This was necessary because although he had been receiving an annuity, or pension, from the Company since April 1791, Dalrymple's quarterly remuneration by the Company for 'examining the ships' journals' had not ceased,[22] and he had gone on publishing charts and plans. He was aware that he would continue to owe the Company part of his time and declined the secretaryship of the Board of Longitude, which the Admiralty Board had originally intended the Hydrographer also to fill.[23]

Dalrymple was the obvious candidate because he had long since established the appropriate credentials. From a base of 'examining the ships' journals' at East India House, with the freedom to publish such materials as he might select, he had arrived at a position where he could expect to be consulted on the geographical and navigational aspects of East India Company policy. In London towards the end of the eighteenth century, this expertise was increasingly concentrated in the formal and informal groupings associated with Sir Joseph Banks as President of the Royal Society. Dalrymple was close to Banks, and to this circle of government officials and advisers, particularly through his regular attendance at the Royal Society Club dinners.[24] As a Fellow of the Royal Society, and after 1777 a member of the Royal Society Club, he regularly met and dined with many of Sir Joseph Banks' circle.[25] He was closely involved in the engraving of the plans and illustrations to accompany the publication in 1784 of the account of Cook's third voyage, including the documented disagreement over the publication of the chart of the northern Pacific Ocean.[26] In his *Case* for personal exemption from the proposed operation of a disadvantageous clause of Pitt's 1784 India Bill, he drew attention to the value of his advice to the East India Company Secret Committee on the passages to China; and he contributed, perhaps unsolicited, in 1786 a pamphlet to the public discussion on the desirability of a penal colony at Botany Bay or Norfolk Island, advocating St Helena instead.[27] Charles Cathcart, in correspondence with Pitt in 1788 over the embassy to China, enclosed a memorandum from Dalrymple discussing the merits of different routes for the embassy's ships.[28] Through his connection with Samuel Wegg, Governor of the Hudson's Bay Company, Dalrymple was involved in 1789 in plans for exploration on the northwest coast of America, and in February 1790 he submitted a paper recommending exploration by sea in place of the suggested overland expedition from Quebec.[29] News of the Nootka Sound crisis in 1790 stimulated the historian and geographer in Dalrymple to write two pamphlets dismissive of the Spanish claims to territory, and he published later in the year a historical account of early Spanish expeditions northward from California, illustrating his narrative with four plates of maps.[30] He was kept informed, unofficially, of the Privy Council examination of John Meares in February 1791.[31] In 1792 he was called on for advice on which harbours and islands off the Pacific coast of South America might be used as refuges for whaling boats.[32] John McCluer kept Dalrymple informed of the progress of his surveys in

New Guinea waters in 1791 and 1792 and subsequently in the Palau Islands, and Dalrymple transmitted information from McCluer's reports in letters to Henry Dundas as Secretary of State.[33]

The conventional view of historians of the Hydrographic Office is that when the Admiralty recognised in 1795 the deficiencies in its own expertise, it is not surprising that Dalrymple, with his background in East India Company hydrography, should have emerged from this group as a preferred candidate to examine and evaluate the chart materials accumulating there. Increasingly, Dalrymple was being used privately as an expert witness by government officials in the 1790s, and the picture is developing that the proposal to create the post of Hydrographer, and to appoint Dalrymple to it, was orchestrated by Stephens, Nepean and Marsden, the old and new secretariat of the Board of Admiralty. By regularising this process of consultation, they achieved the appointment of their friend and colleague to a position which allowed him access to, and authority to investigate, the rooms full of deposited surveys 'laid aside', which had been the stated concern of the Order in Council.

The demands of Dalrymple's new appointment were quite unlike those of his Company position. His first responsibility was the organisation of a hydrographic collection which had accumulated, until his arrival, in the care of a clerk.[34] At the age of fifty-eight, Dalrymple was immediately faced with the task of running an office with subordinate staff, a position quite different from the personal retainer by the Company which he had executed practically alone, and often at home and in his private library. He secured the appointment of Aaron Arrowsmith as his assistant, from 7 September 1795 at a salary of £100 a year, his own salary being fixed at £500 a year in the same month.[35] According to Gould's account a draughtsman was also employed at £50 a year.[36] The work of the new department was first to sort, classify and arrange the materials collected, and then to evaluate them so as to select and compile information for the use of ships. No specific mention was made of printing or publishing charts, though Dalrymple's preliminary approach to the East India Company had mentioned 'forming and engraving charts'.[37] Naval officers conventionally treated the surveys made in the course of duty as their private copyright, and many had their surveys published through the map trade in London. This practice was foreign to Dalrymple's East India Company experience, and he later assembled a list of such publications.[38] Surveys commissioned directly by the Admiralty Board from appointed surveyors, such as Mackenzie and Spence, were retained and formed the nucleus of the collection in the care of the appointed Admiralty clerk until 1795. It was the lack of a system for co-ordinating and compiling this information, and for disseminating it securely to ships of the fleet, that Dalrymple had first to address.

Investigative work without tangible product, though satisfying to Dalrymple, was less so for his assistant. Arrowsmith was already an established map and chart publisher by the early 1790s, and he lasted barely more than a year as Dalrymple's office assistant. The Admiralty papers are scanty for this period, but there is no suggestion that the parting on 10 November 1796 was not amicable. In 1795 and 1796, Dalrymple had been sending out draughtsman work, reduction and copying of charts, to John Walker, an engraver whom he had long employed for his East India Company charts, and Walker was formally appointed in Arrowsmith's stead late in 1796 or early in 1797.[39] The office complement remained unchanged for the next three years, while the reorganisation continued. The work continued to be wide-ranging: in 1795 and 1796 Walker had been working on charts and plans of the Spanish coast, the North Sea, the Cape of Good Hope, the Texel and Zuyder Zee, and the Bay of Panama and the Isthmus of Darien, besides completing the Scilly Isles views and plans. Dalrymple took in the charts and journals of the Entrecasteaux voyage, brought to St Helena by Lieutenant Rossel when the expedition broke up in Batavia, and he employed Rossel, then in exile, to compute the results of the observations on the voyage.[40] Dalrymple responded to a variety of questions referred to him by Nepean, advising him which of a collection of Danish charts and sailing directions might be copied for the Admiralty, recommending maps, charts and globes for the Portsmouth Naval Academy, and assessing deviations in the homeward course of the *Sphynx* from St Helena in 1799 for possible 'sinister motive' on the part of her commander.[41]

Dalrymple put his private collection and East India Company experience to Admiralty use in June 1798 when he advised Marsden on the navigation of the Red Sea, and on the passage time to the Strait of Babelmandel.[42] He furnished Commodore Blankett with a set of his charts, plans and memoirs relevant for the expedition of

Blankett's squadron, which sailed with orders to counteract any move by the French expeditionary force in Egypt towards India by sea. He invoiced the Admiralty for the published items, and for copying manuscript accounts and sets of views.[43]

Dalrymple's East India Company function was effectively separate from his Admiralty position, and he had less time to devote to it. It was inevitable, though, that there should be some cross-fertilisation between his two appointments. Dalrymple's elaborate assistance to Blankett's expedition came two years after Blankett had supplied Dalrymple with a series of new plans of southwest African harbours taken in HMS *Star* earlier that year, which he immediately engraved for the East India Company.[44] The Admiralty's growing interest in the Red Sea in 1798 caused Dalrymple to assemble and engrave a series of plans and views between 1798 and 1800, including much material which had lain unpublished since his own 1776 voyage in the *Swallow*.[45] The East India Company's publication of an isolated plate of views from Entrecasteaux's previous voyage in the *Résolution*, shortly after Dalrymple had received in the Admiralty the confidential deposit of the Entrecasteaux expedition material, was clearly not coincidental.

The first phase of work in the Admiralty Hydrographic Office, the organisation of the existing charts and plans, was completed early in 1800. Dalrymple later referred to it as the time 'when the Hydrographical Office was made efficient'.[46] Dalrymple and Walker had organised the materials sufficiently to be able to promise Nepean on 22 March a list of charts and plans in the Office 'fit to be engraved', in answer to a request from the Admiralty Board.[47] Nothing more advanced than using the London map trade for engraving and publication appears to have been envisaged by the Board, although in 1808 Dalrymple claimed, in a heated moment, that from its creation:

> an avowed Purpose of [the Hydrographical Office] was to publish accurate Charts for The Use of The Royal Navy, which purpose could not ever be carried into effect if MS Charts &ca. given into the Hydrographical Office were delivered to private Chart Sellers to be mixed with other Materials of unknown or doubtful authority.[48]

Nevertheless, when Dalrymple applied for a press to be installed in the Admiralty building in 1800, the Board's response was immediate and favourable.[49] On 31 March Dalrymple wrote to Matthew Boulton, who had supplied him with his private rolling-press in 1774, with his request, and with a wry aside on the delay of three years:

> It is in contemplation to establish a rolling Press at the Admiralty with Iron rollers 32 inches wide. It occurred to me that the Admiralty could be better & cheaper supplied by You than they could here; and I was desired to write to You on the Subject; I'll be much obliged to You to be so good as send me an answer as soon as you can conveniently; . . . as 3 Years having been lost in inaction They are now impatient to get to work and I suppose will expect in the 3 months to come as much work done as could have been executed in the 3 years.[50]

Dalrymple 'was desired to look out for Engravers &c.', and a press was in place later in the same year. The list of charts and plans 'fit to be engraved' has not survived, but it is generally accepted that the first plate printed at the Hydrographic Office was Moore's plan of the island Houat in Quiberon Bay, with a date of November 1800.

The establishment of a rolling-press necessitated changes in the complement of the Hydrographic Office: two plan engravers were employed, John Cooke and Isaac Palmer, both of whom had private businesses outside the Admiralty. Thomas Harmar was employed on piece-work rates as writing engraver, and these three, as well as the two draughtsmen James Andrews and Francis Higgins and the copper-plate printer Richard Baily, were superintended by John Walker on an increased salary as Hydrographical Assistant. Walker and Harmar had worked for Dalrymple on East India Company charts since the 1780s, and, with Palmer, now formed the nucleus of Dalrymple's new office.

The factors governing the selection of charts to be engraved and printed in the Hydrographic Office are not now known. A distinction was made early between charts to be engraved from manuscript surveys and charts to be copied from foreign printed sources. Dalrymple obtained authority to have charts in the latter category engraved outside the Office, as not being confidential in character.[51]

This demonstrates that there was often more work than the engravers could handle, and that the Hydrographic Office press was seen as a security press, not subject to commercial constraints. The capital cost, salaries and cost of materials were borne by the Admiralty, and there was no provision for selling charts: printed charts were issued as 'Ship's Stores', and required to be returned after use. In May 1803 Dalrymple proposed that multiple copies of unfinished proofs should be sent to ships for evaluation and correction, and some plates consequently never went beyond the proof stage.[52] With no contemporary catalogue of charts and no surviving register of plates from the first years of the press, assessment of output can be made only from an analysis of surviving impressions, supported by evidence from contemporary correspondence.

The 1801 plan of Alexandria was for some years thought to be the earliest Admiralty chart,[53] but it is legitimate to see the group of three plates of Alexandria as an office exercise in reducing, engraving and printing. Dalrymple had received from Sir Thomas Troubridge a chart of part of the coast of Egypt drawn by naval officers in 1798 and 1799, and from another source two French manuscript plans of Alexandria.[54] He had the two French plans engraved and proofed, and the detail from each reduced and inserted, so far as it went, into the Troubridge chart, which was engraved and proofed in turn. Then the area of the plate between Rosetta and Alexandria was erased and beaten up to receive a new outline and information on troop movements in March 1801 from an additional plan, and the plate proofed again.

The other charts of 1801 and 1802 have little in common: a group of three plates of harbours in southern Africa, two plans of Dutch estuaries, Mackenzie's Falmouth Harbour and Carrick Road, two plans of bays on Sardinia, a chart of Chios and Smyrna, and a Spanish coastal chart reprinted from Vincente Tofino's *Atlas Maritima de España* (1787) with a parallel British revision. The chart of part of the Spanish coast was engraved at the request of St Vincent;[55] specific authorisations to engrave (beyond the missing list of March 1800) are not known for the other plates. Late in 1801 Dalrymple demonstrated the capacity of the Hydrographic Office to function as a security press when, as part of the Admiralty's involvement with the surveys being carried out for Philip Gidley King as Governor of New South Wales, he had engraved a sketch from King of Bass Strait with the discoveries made in the *Lady Nelson*, sending proofs to Nepean in January 1802.[56]

Dalrymple had no authority to commission surveys, only to engrave charts from materials supplied by ships' officers, supplemented by manuscripts in the Hydrographic Office and by foreign printed charts. His best efforts therefore followed, rather than preceded, naval interest in particular areas—for example, the results by mid-1803 included a series of plans of Adriatic harbours from Robert Nellson and the continuation of a series of Sardinia anchorages. An exception was his successful advocacy in 1805 of a re-survey of Falmouth Harbour. After publishing Mackenzie's survey of Carrick Road in 1802, Dalrymple issued a plate from Manderson's survey in May 1805, and wrote to Marsden on 15 June with a sketch showing disagreements between Mackenzie's survey, two plans from Manderson's survey, and another by Lockwood, suggesting that Hurd could easily establish the reciprocal positions of the prominent points on his passage to the French coast.[57] Hurd was ordered to do this, and in 1807 or early 1808 Dalrymple had a plate in proof showing Hurd's new survey.

Dalrymple organised the publication of coherent series of charts for the south coast of England. By March 1800 he had identified surveys by Mackenzie missing from, or not yet present in, the Admiralty.[58] The lack of materials in the Admiralty for coherent chart series was a recurring theme of Dalrymple. In recommending to Nepean in 1796 the acquisition of a Danish survey of the Goodwins, he remarked that 'It is not very creditable to us that other Nations should be referred to for our own Coasts'.[59] The problem remained for Dalrymple throughout his tenure of office: in his report of 10 October 1807 he complained that 'It is a Disgrace to This Country that the Hydrography of our own Coasts is not accurately delineated'.[60] This was not an admission of inadequacy, but rather a reflection that he had no authority to order surveys and little control over the results. The surveying officers' habit of retaining their surveys, stemming from the time when no effective Hydrographic Office existed, was difficult to break, particularly when, like Graeme Spence, they regarded their work as a rolling programme of coastal survey. Dalrymple wrote to both Stephens and Nepean trying to elicit from Spence his surveys of The Owers and of the coast from Dungeness to Beachy Head.[61] Spence, also present in the Admiralty working up his surveys, continued to be a source of irritation to Dalrymple, who successfully objected to Spence's practice of altering Mackenzie's sailing directions for the north coast of Kent to match his own more recent observations.[62] Keeping track of privately published surveys by naval officers was also a continual problem: in October 1807 he produced a list of more than fifty such charts and plans, doubting whether the Admiralty could re-engrave them without infringing private copyright.[63]

Using Mackenzie's and Spence's surveys as a base, Dalrymple began two series of charts for the south coast, an inner series at 3.2 inches to 1 nautical mile for The Solent, Spithead and Southampton Water, and an outer series at 1.6 inches to 1 nautical mile to extend from the Thames Estuary to Sidmouth. These were the first charts for which Dalrymple used the larger (double-elephant) plate size which the Admiralty press could accommodate. In the first series proofs were circulated of the Southampton River and St Helen's Road sheets, dated 11 October 1802 and January 1805 respectively. The other two sheets of the Solent were also engraved to Dalrymple's specifications. Finished versions of the four sheets were published by Thomas Hurd from Dalrymple's plates in September and October 1808.

The second series, planned in twelve sheets, was more complex. Dalrymple issued the sheets for The Owers and the outer coast of the Isle of Wight in November 1804 and July 1805, and followed these with the Winchelsea to Beachy Head sheet in July 1807, the first two from Mackenzie's and the third from Spence's surveys. A chart of the Strait of Dover, though not to the series scale, was already engraved in April 1806 from materials in the Hydrographical Office, but Dalrymple had the Dover to Winchelsea sheet, the sheet for The Downs, and at least one of the two Thames Estuary sheets in preparation for his series shortly afterwards, chiefly from Spence's surveys. Similarly, at the western limit of the series, the three sheets spanning the coast between Blackwood Point, St Alban's Head, Abbotsbury and Sidmouth were in preparation from Mackenzie's surveys, 'nearly engraved in the Hydrographic Office'. The gap between Beachy Head and The Owers was to be filled by surveys in progress by James Murray in 1807, but Dalrymple was dissatisfied with the internal inconsistencies and lack of scale in Murray's manuscripts.[63] The two sheets from Beachy Head to Worthing and from New Shoreham to Selsey Bill were not engraved until Hurd reissued the whole series in 1811.[64] Dalrymple had begun a similar series for the coast from Plymouth to The Lizard, at the smaller scale of 1.25 nautical miles to 1 inch: this was published later by Hurd, who was himself surveying the intervening coast from Sidmouth to Plymouth in 1807.

To encourage the transmission of nautical information from ships of the fleet, Dalrymple designed (or revised) in February 1804 a 'Form of Remark-Book', with a covering letter which he clearly proposed should be sent by the Secretary with orders to ships.[65] This was to give guidance to ships' officers as to the kind of information required about ports visited under headings such as 'Situation', 'Directions for sailing into or out of Ports', 'Anchorages', and extending to 'Trade and Shipping' and 'Inhabitants'. Under St Vincent, the Admiralty Board sought to revive this system of reporting, but Dalrymple told Marsden in December 1806 that he had received only one such report in almost three years, 'and that One of a well known part of the Coast of England, in a exceptionable stile'.[66] Two Sardinia plans came from the master of the *Victory*, and Lord Nelson visited the Hydrographic Office at least once, with a report of a further shoal discovered in the Esquirques group between Tunis and Sicily.[67] But such exceptions Dalrymple could quickly enumerate: William Durban's plan of the Esquirques and of Lampedusa taken in 1802, Joseph Edmonds's 1801 chart of the Formigas rocks off Elba, and Beaufort's plans of Montevideo in 1807 were the examples he called most easily to mind. Of the officers serving in home waters during the early years of the Hydrographic Office, William Bligh was the most sympathetic to Dalrymple's aims. Dalrymple had engraved Bligh's sketch of Smith's Knowl, and his surveys of Dungeness and Walcheren, in 1803.

Bligh was sufficiently conversant with Hydrographic Office procedures to assume temporary responsibility for the office in the spring of 1804, when Dalrymple was ill for six weeks.[68] Later his plans of the Humber and of Dublin Bay were engraved, the latter only to a proof state.

To increase the number of charts available to the Navy, in June 1804 Dalrymple offered the Admiralty the use of his plates that had been engraved originally for the East India Company. At this time he priced his 52 charts, 57 views and 640 plans at £34 12s 6d a set or £3462 for 100 sets. Allowing just over £450 for the paper and printing costs to be borne by the Admiralty, he arrived at a figure of £3006 7s for 100 sets, but settled with the Admiralty Board for a payment of 1000 guineas.[69] One hundred copies of 44 charts and 380 plans were completed by Baily by August 1805, and the job was finished in October 1806.[70] By this means the Admiralty acquired 81 700 impressions, 100 each of 54 charts, 57 views and 706 plans, Dalrymple having included those plates (including the Strait of Malacca series) which he had published since June 1804. Only a few hundred of these impressions survive, mostly bound as atlases in the Admiralty Library, and the impressions stamped with the Hydrographical Office foul-anchor oval seal.

Dalrymple continued to produce charts of European waters for the Admiralty, though his capacity to respond to fleet needs was limited by the long preparation time involved. He furnished James Gambier's expedition to the Baltic with sets of commercially published charts and sailing directions in 1807, and included 56 copies of printed Hydrographic Office directions and 59 proof copies of Thomas Atkinson's chart of the Great Belt,[71] which serves to show the reliance still placed by the Admiralty on the London chart trade in 1807. Besides the three series he was known to have in progress, the south coast of England, the Channel coast of France, and the waters between the Isle of Wight and Hampshire, most of Dalrymple's charts were single-source harbour plans, such as those of the Humber and of Boston Deeps, and many of these were from foreign printed sources. He still did not compete with commercial publishers in providing small-scale coasting charts. In November 1807 Dalrymple furnished the Admiralty Board with a

'List of Plates engraved, engraving and of Charts and Plans prepared for Engraving in the Hydrographical Office', which, though it does not survive in the Board's correspondence with the Hydrographic Office, appears to have been one of the source documents for the evaluation of the Office operations which the new Chart Committee was to carry out early in 1808.[72]

The old order had gone from the Admiralty by 1807: Henry Dundas (as Viscount Melville) had been censured by Parliament, resigned as First Lord, and underwent impeachment in 1805; and Sir Philip Stephens's retirement from the Board in October 1806 ended an association which Dalrymple had valued for forty years. Sir Charles Middleton (as Lord Barham), Charles Grey, Viscount Howick, and Thomas Grenville passed rapidly through the post of First Lord, none remaining more than a few months. Lord Mulgrave's appointment as First Lord in April 1807 brought John Barrow back into the Second Secretaryship, a position which had changed with the ministry after Marsden's promotion to First Secretary on Nepean's departure in January 1804. When Marsden retired on grounds of ill-health in June 1807, to be replaced by William Wellesley Pole, the 'office memory' of Dalrymple's achievement since 1795 was erased. The Board, through Pole, had a different concept of the function of the Hydrographic Office, as an office for assessing the commercial product of the London map and chart trade, and as an agency for supplying 'bought-in' charts in wholesale quantities for fleet use. Dalrymple's working relationship with Pole soon deteriorated into frigid politeness, punctuated by explosions, as Dalrymple persisted that he was not qualified, nor his office equipped or funded, to carry out new functions arbitrarily required. He found himself bypassed by the new Chart Committee when he suggested an advisory body of naval officers to evaluate current charts.

The members of this 'New Guard' at the Hydrographic Office wished to see a much more rigorous evaluation of surveys and charts, and more comprehensive publication of results—that is, they and the Admiralty commissioners who appointed them wished to see the Office develop its 'service' role much beyond what Dalrymple thought appropriate or possible. This was to be the direction taken by the Hydrographic Office under Dalrymple's successors, when, in order to fill in the gaps, the Admiralty also mounted extensive new scientific surveys.

Soon this modern tide was flowing too swiftly for the old man to withstand. After quarrelling bitterly with the members of the Chart Committee and his superiors at the Admiralty, he was dismissed in May 1808. Three weeks later, he was dead.

An Empire of Science

The Voyage of HMS Herald, 1845–1851

JANE SAMSON

B Y THE 1840s, despite the earlier efforts of Captains Cook and Vancouver, much of the western coast of the Americas was still insufficiently charted by the Royal Navy. The North Pacific whale fishery, and the sea otter fur trade between the northwest coast and China, had drawn attention to the area's economic importance since the 1790s. The North West Company's operations had been moving westward from the Canadas, taking advantage of the Anglo-American war to found a fur trading base at Fort Vancouver on the Columbia River in 1813, and later amalgamating with the Hudson's Bay Company. Wars of independence in South and Central America had drawn the Royal Navy into closer involvement throughout those areas, and British support for the revolutionary governments had secured the use of a number of important harbours. The focus was moving steadily toward the Pacific, reflected in the shift from the old 'Brazils' or South America Station, to the new Pacific Station founded in 1837 with its headquarters at Valparaiso on the coast of Chile.

The Royal Navy's Hydrographic Office knew the importance of the Pacific region, and had dispatched a number of survey vessels there in the early nineteenth century, notably HMS *Blossom* under the command of Captain F. W. Beechey in 1825–28. Beechey was commissioned to lead another Pacific survey in 1836 with HMS *Sulphur* and *Starling*, but illness forced him to return to Britain, and in his absence, Henry Kellett (then a lieutenant) took command of *Starling*. Overall command of the expedition passed to Captain (later Sir) Edward Belcher in 1837. Further north the Estonian captain Otto von Kotzebue had surveyed the Bering Strait area for Russia in 1816. But probably the most famous surveyor in the eastern Pacific, and the one whose writings had the most influence on HMS *Herald*'s officers, was Captain Robert Fitzroy. HMS *Beagle*'s work in South America and the Galapagos Islands during 1835 had become legendary by the 1840s, and naturalist Charles Darwin's role had not yet eclipsed that of his captain.

Like most Pacific surveys after the age of Cook and his immediate successors, the 1845–51 *Herald* expedition is little known despite its extensive scope. The 26-gun frigate HMS *Herald* under Captain Henry Kellett, and the 6-gun barque HMS *Pandora*, commanded by Lieutenant James Wood, left Britain in 1845. Neither vessel had steam power; this would be the last major survey to be at the mercy of wind and tide. Fortunately both commanding officers were experienced surveyors. Kellett had served under Captain Fitzwilliam Owen in Africa, and Captain Belcher in Africa, South America, and China. Wood had been with Kellett in Owen's and Belcher's African surveys, and joined later hydrographic expeditions to the North Sea and California. These two men made ideal partners for the *Herald* expedition, and would revisit several areas familiar to one or both of them. After a brief survey at the Falklands, they mapped the west coast of the Americas from Guayaquil in Ecuador to what is now British Columbia in Canada, detouring three times to Bering Strait to assist with the search for Sir John Franklin's missing Arctic expedition. *Pandora* returned to Britain in 1849, but *Herald* was out for six years, returning in 1851.

There are several assumptions in the historiography of Victorian naval surveying which are challenged by an examination of the important *Herald* expedition, assumptions which have led some historians to neglect this subject. The first of these is the traditional distinction between 'purely' scientific expeditions and other naval activities. Barry Gough, whose work dominates the study of the Royal Navy's Pacific Station, has written that British warships visited the northwest coast 'mainly on scientific missions until 1840, and as instruments of British policy thereafter'.[1] This explains why scientific missions after 1840 are given such cursory treatment by Gough; his interest is the Royal Navy's support of imperial policy. Thus he mentions the *Herald* expedition only briefly, despite acknowledging its importance in exploring and promoting the harbour of Esquimalt as a potential naval base.[2] This seems particularly odd when we consider the fruitful researches of historians of the eighteenth-century Pacific; Alan Frost, David Mackay, Glyndwr Williams and others have published extensively on the connections between surveying, natural history and empire during the age of exploration.[3]

The accepted view of the nineteenth-century Hydrographic Office in general, and Hydrographer Francis Beaufort in particular, is in special need of revision. The definitive biography of Beaufort is still Alfred Friendly's *Beaufort of the Admiralty*, published in 1977. Friendly made extensive but highly selective use of the Hydrographic Archives, opening his chapter on 'The Admiralty Chart' with a quotation that suggests Beaufort was completely uninterested in the politics of empire-building. In a letter to Edward Belcher, whose erratic behaviour and frequent detours exasperated him, Beaufort wrote the following oft-quoted remarks: 'Your last letter is really all Hebrew to me: ransoms and dollars; queens; treaties and negotiations? What have I to do with these awful things; they far transcend my limited chart-making facilities . . .'[4] This letter actually says much more about Beaufort's impatience with Belcher than about Beaufort's attitude to survey work. Even the most cursory look at his letterbooks reveals a man deeply immersed in the politics and economics of empire, and this reflected attitudes at the Admiralty itself. Its orders to Captain Kellett at the beginning of the *Herald* expedition in 1845 began with an appeal to 'the general interests of navigation and geography', but also mentioned 'the interests of Her Majesty'. Many of Kellett's investigations would be covert: the Admiralty charged him in a set of confidential instructions to 'carefully avoid embarrassing HM Government by exciting any jealousy of your proceedings . . .' while cataloguing the territorial claims of independent, Mexican and American territories, and 'particularly noting all those places which may appear to have been recently inhabited either by the spread of the population from the interior or by foreign settlers'. Kellett was also to forbid his officers and naturalist to publish any account of the voyage until the expedition had returned home and the Admiralty had authorised an official narrative. *Herald*'s survey was not merely a chart-making voyage: the Admiralty had no intention of passing up an unprecedented opportunity for detailed intelligence gathering, and quite rightly regarded the expedition's movements and findings as politically sensitive.

Nineteenth-century hydrography deserves the same attention from historians of imperialism as the activities of great explorers. Early and mid-Victorian naval history seems curiously untouched by the vibrant academic debate that characterises earlier and later time periods. Indeed, some naval specialists seem to want to insulate their subject from recent developments in the historiography of science and empire, pitting naval history against the social sciences, cultural relativism, 'modern historians' and other forces of destruction.[5] Rather than engaging with current debates, naval history can appear reactionary, and sometimes apologist.

Perhaps the neglected links between Victorian hydrography and imperialism owe something to differences between nineteenth-century ideas of 'truthfulness' and 'fact' in voyage narratives, and modern idealism about professional objectivity and neutrality.[6] In the introduction to his reminiscences of the *Herald* expedition, *Euryalus; Tales of the Sea*, former midshipman William Chimmo made no apology for publishing his private journals: 'Truth needs none, and truth I intend to be the type of my book. It is not my intention to make a novel of it'.[7] Likewise naturalist Berthold Seemann declared, in the introduction to his *Narrative of the Voyage of HMS Herald*, 'Fact is the object I have aimed at throughout the following pages, on the strict adherence to which will rest their sole recommendation'.[8] But their writings show that these men presented their observations in a way that would serve British imperial interests. They saw no conflict between scientific observation and the imperial gaze, and thus no diminution of their truthfulness and honour as chroniclers. In short, these men wrote from a cultural background quite alien to our own and naval historians, anxious to treat their subject respectfully, have too often imposed upon it their own ideals of objectivity and scientific detachment.

Archival sources for the *Herald* expedition are erratic and scattered: another reason, perhaps, for its neglect. Captain Kellett's return to the Arctic shortly after the end of *Herald*'s voyage in 1851 prevented him (to his relief) from writing up the voyage. The task fell instead to the second naturalist, the Hanoverian botanist Berthold Seemann, who would write both the *Botany* and the *Narrative* of the voyage. Seemann claimed later that he relied mainly on his own journals and letters for the *Narrative*, complaining that he had only restricted access to Kellett's journals and none at all to Wood's.[9] We must weigh this against Wood's complaint, to Sir William Hooker, that Seemann never contacted him about the *Narrative*.[10] Either way, Seemann's task was a difficult one: stitching together a narrative from disparate sources of information when he had not been present himself at many of the events being described. His *Narrative of the Voyage of HMS Herald* is difficult to follow. Seemann's use of the first person throughout the *Narrative* makes it impossible to tell whether he was drawing on his own journal, or on those of Lieutenant Henry Trollope and Midshipman Bedford Pim, which he also consulted.

These problematic sources invite historians to take the broadest possible view of this voyage and to move beyond its formal hydrographic contribution. Examination of its political and scientific motives, and its natural history documentation, allow the *Herald* expedition to be set into a wider context. It is particularly important, for example, to note Beaufort's direct involvement with the organisation of the *Herald* survey. Barry Gough has claimed that it was inagurated by the Commander-in-Chief of the Pacific Station, Rear Admiral Sir George Seymour.[11] But Beaufort approached Kellett in 1844 to say that he hoped to send two ships to link up Belcher's surveys of ports 'and to complete the West Coast of America from Guayaquil up to the Arctic Ocean. Are you in the mind to accept of that extensive enterprise?'[12] It emerged that Beaufort had been very disappointed by some aspects of Belcher's survey work. Writing privately to Kellett, he said he was reluctant to say too much about this 'because cross things are sure to travel, and our friend's skin is rather thin', but it was clear that all the positions between 1° and 2° N on the coast of Ecuador were in error. Beaufort also worried about the unfinished state of many of Belcher's harbour surveys, hoping that Kellett would quietly complete them 'for his sake, for mine, and for the good of the service'.[13] The problem was actually much more serious than this; captains visiting the Oregon territory and Vancouver island in the 1840s were saying that all of Belcher's positions from Juan de Fuca Strait to San Francisco were beween 30' and 1° too far east.[14] For this reason, the Admiralty wrote to the Hudson's Bay Company headquarters in London to ask for copies of any charts the company had made of the Strait, so that the Hydrographic Office could copy them for Kellett's use.[15]

The *Herald* expedition sailed from Britain on 26 June 1845 and on 1 January 1846 left Valparaiso for the Galapagos Islands and its first detailed surveying operation. Both the Admiralty and Admiral Seymour were keen to decide whether the islands would make a good naval base; in other words, whether Britain should take possession of them, and Kellett had confidential instructions to survey the islands with an eye to colonisation.[16] Earlier naval visitors had described their anchorages and provisioning capabilities, and Kellett noted that although there was a good anchorage at the famous Post Office Bay on Charles Island, where water and provisions were plentiful, there was no easy way of getting water down to the beach. Other islands had better facilities for watering, but inferior anchorages. More serious than this was the lack of coal. Beaufort and Seymour had both read John Coulter's *Adventures in the Pacific* and its description of plentiful coal deposits on Chatham Island.[17] It is easy to see how Coulter's claims would complement both men's hopes for a British Pacific: 'these islands, California and the passage across the isthmus ought to belong to England; she could make better use of them than any other nation, from her immense and enterprizing maritime power'.[18]

But there was no coal, and Kellett's report concluded that 'As to whether they would be an acquisition to Her Majesty's Government or not I consider they would, in case of war, as a commanding position on the coast, but not otherwise, as I do not think they could

ever support themselves'.[19] Admiral Seymour, who was determined
to secure the islands for Britain if he could, sent Wood and the
Pandora back for further information in 1847. Concerned that the
government of Ecuador might object to such intense scrutiny of an
area under its influence, Seymour asked Kellett to require 'those
under your command, both on board the *Herald* and *Pandora*, not
to talk of the service on which the latter vessel is Employed . . .'[20]
This would not be the last 'secret mission' to involve the *Herald*
expedition, and it reminds us of how deeply science and politics
were linked in its operations. As for the Galapagos, Kellett's reference to their lack of self-sufficiency would be decisive; the British
government was worried about the expense of its existing colonies,
and without coal supplies the Galapagos had little to offer.[21]

Kellett left the Galapagos towards the end of January 1846
for Ecuador where a dreadful accident took the life of his first
naturalist. After a botanical excursion near the Bay of Atacamas on
27 January, Thomas Edmondston had returned to the ship's boat
with the others. Although the officer involved was never officially
named, it seems to have been Lieutenant Trollope who stumbled
into the boat in a heavy surf and caught his trouser cuff in the
trigger of a loaded rifle that had been left behind. Shaking his
clothing free, Trollope caused the rifle to fire, killing Edmondston
instantly. After a funeral aboard *Herald*, the naturalist's coffin was
buried near the scene of the accident, and later, Seemann named an
Ecuadorian evergreen shrub *Edmonstonia pacifica* in his memory.
Kellett reported to his commander-in-chief that 'the Expedition has
suffered much and all regret the death of this young man who
possessed abilities that would . . . have placed him amongst the
most celebrated of his profession'.[22]

After a long survey of the South American coast from Guayaquil
to the Bay of Panama, the two ships reprovisioned for an excursion
to Juan de Fuca Strait on the northwest coast of North America.
Vancouver had not surveyed much of the island that bore his name,
and later surveys like Belcher's had concentrated on the Columbia
River area where the North West Company had a post at Fort
Vancouver. Kellett's instructions to Wood for the long voyage north
remind us that, although it was the mid-nineteenth century, this
coast was still barely known. Kellett was dependent on Vancouver's

journal for clues about the seasonal winds, telling Wood that 'As this voyage has not been made by any one that I am aware of I cannot give you any idea what Meridian I shall run down or any rendezvous but Cape Flattery', the landmark entrance to the Strait of Juan de Fuca.[23] During the voyage the cooler temperatures revived the weakened crew of *Herald*, many of whom had contracted fever off the New Granadian coast, but the journey to the Strait took sixty-nine days, and by the time the two ships reached it, they were badly in need of fresh food.

The timing of *Herald*'s visit was not coincidental. Admiral Seymour had been preparing for war with the United States over the disputed Oregon Territory. Seymour's hopes for a British Pacific had prompted him to strengthen his forces and to suggest a British alliance with Mexico against the Americans. He hoped that Kellett's survey would reinforce British claims on the northwest coast, telling Kellett that his activities in the area would 'be very beneficial in the proceedings which may be taken by the Government to oppose the unjust pretentions of the United States'. He added that he was dispatching HMS *Fisgard* and the steam vessel HMS *Cormorant* to the Strait as well.[24] But the British government had no desire for war, and signed the Oregon Treaty with the United States on 15 June 1846, granting all territory, except for Vancouver Island, south of 49°S lat. to the Americans. Plans for the island's colonisation were already under way in London while Kellett was surveying it, and it would officially become a British colony in 1849.

It was as well that Seymour sent *Cormorant* to assist Kellett; *Herald* and *Pandora* were becalmed after entering the Strait and had to be towed into harbour at the new Hudson's Bay Company post of Fort Victoria. Kellett found that the Company was expanding its establishment there without experiencing the feared influx of American settlers, and by the time *Herald* left the area in September, Kellett reported to the British minister in Mexico that 'the Season seems too far advanced for [the Americans] to do so this year; by the next they will have heard of the Settlement of the question'.[25] Seymour was reassured by this, and by the receipt of tracings of Juan de Fuca Strait and ports on the eastern coast of Vancouver Island which *Cormorant*'s steam power had enabled her to make. These, Seymour believed, had 'contributed so much to develop the resources of Vancouvers Island'.[26] Hudson's Bay Company officials were equally impressed by the impact of the expedition's visit:

> The concentration of so large a Naval force in Pugets Sound has caused a great sensation in this Country, and on the whole produced a most favourable impression on the minds of the people, being considered by British Subjects as a guarantee that our Government is determined to maintain its rights . . .[27]

But further south, Kellett sighted the American flag at San Francisco, where an American warship was already in port and another expected. Men were busily fortifying the area and Kellett believed that if the Americans could retain it for six months 'it will require a fleet to turn them out of it'.[28] The American commodore had recently announced that amid the just-declared war with Mexico, the United States was seizing all of California.

This news must have disappointed Beaufort as much as it did Seymour; the Hydrographer had been impressed by Beechey's report on San Francisco's potential as a British naval base. This had prompted Beaufort to write to Kellett before the *Herald* expedition sailed, urging him to do some covert reconnaissance:

> When on the coast or in the ports of California let the Americans understand that your labours there are only links of the great chain of surveys which we are extending from Cape Horn to Behring's Strait and not from any selfish views respecting those regions. Nevertheless if you should put into [San] Francisco (a place in which I should hugely like to hoist our flag) examine the place quietly—correct and improve Beechey's Plan, which was done on a wretchedly small scale, and state your opinions of the importance of the place (in many points of view) to me in a separate letter.[29]

Kellett duly reported on fortifications and gun emplacements, but of course it was far too late. Sailing quickly past the area occupied by the Americans, Kellett recommended detailed surveying south of San Diego, reprovisioned at San Blas on the Mexican coast, and left for Panama. On the way he was dramatically and unexpectedly detained by a zealous Mexican official at Siguantanego, some 100 miles northwest of Acapulco.

Before setting out for Vancouver Island, Kellett had asked the British Vice-Consul in Mexico for advice about whether or not the Mexican government should be kept informed of the survey's movements. The Vice-Consul might have said no, or perhaps there had been no time to pursue the matter. Kellett's report on his capture indicates simply that he had assumed _Herald_ and _Pandora_ were too well known along the coast to need official protection or assistance from the Mexicans. Whatever the reason for it, this omission had serious consequences. The Vice-Consul must have known that the Mexicans had become increasingly unhappy with the presence of foreigners south of San Francisco, in what was then known as 'Lower California'. In 1840, Mexican officals at Monterey had imprisoned forty British and American citizens for alleged spying, and were only induced to release them after the appearance of the USS _St Louis_. After this incident, the Foreign Office and Admiralty recognised the need for a greater British naval presence on the Californian coast, and dispatched Captain Jenkin Jones in HMS _Curaçao_ with instructions warning Mexico against interfering with British subjects.[30] Under the circumstances, it seems foolish for the _Herald_ expedition to have surveyed Mexican territory without first doing everything possible to prevent misunderstanding. As it was, Commandante Amaro and his small detachment of troops confronted Kellett's survey party on the beach at Siguantanego, imprisoning Kellett and his men and refusing to release them unless ordered to do so by the Governor-General at Acapulco. Wood took _Pandora_ to obtain the necessary instructions, which included a severe reprimand for Amaro, and on 14 December _Herald_ and _Pandora_ both sailed for Panama. The whole incident was an embarrassment for the Mexican government and everyone concerned was grateful to Kellett for his restraint during the incident.

After meeting his new naturalist, Berthold Seemann, at Panama, Kellett resumed the survey of Guayaquil; the Admiralty had been particularly interested in whether there were facilities for the careening and repair of large ships at the island of Puna, or in the Guayaquil River itself. This gruelling work up the west coast of South America continued into the spring of 1848; in February Kellett reported to Beaufort that he was finding the coast between Garachine and Chirambira particularly difficult. This is now part of the coast of Colombia, which the Admiralty chart showed (mis-leadingly) as a relatively plain coast. 'It has cost me exactly double the time that I expected to have done it in', declared Kellett, 'and has been the most tiring and laborious piece of work I ever under-took'.[31] Seemann's *Narrative of the Voyage of HMS* Herald reveals the reaction to this demanding programme: he and some of the young gentlemen (particularly Pim) felt that Kellett should be doing much more to explore possible sites for a canal route to the Atlantic. South of Garachine *Herald* had surveyed a fine harbour where the local Indians told the captain that a series of rivers linked the two oceans. Wood and Kellett went inland to investigate, finding a river which seemed to be running in the right direction. But there the matter had to be left; the surveying schedule had already been severely delayed. Seemann was disappointed that the senior officers would not share their observations, nor indulge in the speculation that passed the time in the wardroom:

> It is with regret that I am compelled to confess that I possess no data which might enable me to pronounce an opinion on the feasibility of the scheme. Captain Kellett never spoke on the subject, probably because he was not certain whether the river that the party reached actually flowed into the Atrato, and that portion of his journal relating to Darien is unfortunately wanting . . .[32]

More disappointment was to come off Point Chirambira, where the expedition surveyed the mouth of the San Juan River. 'It is to be regretted that Captain Kellett was prevented from exploring this fine river', wrote Seemann, 'especially as it is known to approach the Atrato within a few miles, and, if reports may be relied upon, is actually connected with the latter by a canal, by means of which canoes pass from the Atlantic to the Pacific'.[33] Of the many rumours surrounding the canal issue, this one was probably true. During his explorations in 1799–1804, Alexander von Humboldt had inves-tigated several possible canal routes and one of his publications mentioned the existence of a canal already running between the upper waters of the San Juan River and the upper Atrato River. The route was only large enough for canoes, and this had apparently been confirmed by the explorations of Captain Charles Cochrane in 1824. The more zealous members of the *Herald* expedition hoped that Kellett and Wood would settle the mystery once and for all, and were frustrated when the captain pressed on with the survey instead. Writing in 1863 about Britain's lost opportunities in the Pacific, Pim declared:

> It is curious to reflect how studiously we naval men are taught 'how *not* to do it'; for example, during the surveying service of the *Herald* throughout the Bay of Panama and its vicinity, many opportunities occurred of exploring the land intervening between us and the Atlantic, and I can personally testify that there would have been no lack of volunteers . . . but our captain was far too careful an officer to risk going beyond his instructions . . . It is painful to think how other nations must have laughed at the noisy squabbles and indecision which have characterised our transit attempt.[34]

In reality, Kellett had been ordered to report secretly (as he did so often) to Beaufort and Seymour. The Hydrographer wanted a confidential report on 'What the U.S. are doing about their canal across the isthmus, and their turnpike road from Chagres to Panama'.[35] Kellett's discretion was as considerable as his scepticism about obtaining unbiased information amid the frenzy of speculation about British, French and American canal plans; a report to Seymour about Panama's capabilities as a port was cautiously positive, however.[36] Beaufort, for his own part, was already in touch with at least two of the companies raising money in London for the building of a canal route. His correspondence reveals that he played these two organisations off against each other with promises of vital hydrographical information. After Wood returned to Britain in 1849, Beaufort authorised him to give the Atlantic and Pacific Junction Company the benefit of his advice; the company's subscribers included, among others, the Governor of the Hudson's Bay Company, Sir J. H. Pelly, and Admiral Sir Charles Napier.[37]

Such mingling between men of science and politics was neither unusual, nor confined to naval circles. The push for improved trans-oceanic communications put the knowledge of 'men on the spot' at a premium. In the early 1850s Royal Engineer Captain Millington Synge was using his Canadian land survey experience to promote schemes for a transcontinental railway under British control. Synge found comfort in the fact that Captain Cook had surveyed on both coasts of northern North America, as though the great navigator's activities had a still-living destiny of their own.[38] For Synge, Pim, Seemann and many others, control of routes to the Pacific was the key; its rapidly expanding British strategic, commercial and settlement interests must not be allowed to give way to American influences. Beaufort's own entanglement in the canal projects of the 1850s simply show how deeply the Hydrographic Office's activities were linked with the leading political and economic questions of the day.

Meanwhile, during the summer of 1847, the Admiralty ordered Kellett to prepare to join the search for Sir John Franklin in the Arctic. Kellett and Beaufort had lobbied for time to complete at least the most important aspects of the *Herald* survey, but by 1848 it was time for *Herald* to head north. Kellett obeyed his orders with a heavy heart; it was difficult for him to break off such an important hydrographic programme. In private letters to Beaufort and Seymour, he begged them to reconsider, or at least to send *Pandora* rather than *Herald*. A continuous survey of the west coast of the Americas was 'the great object their Lordships had in view for my labours, should I not finish Guayaquil . . . it will entail on me another voyage to the Southward and a consequent great loss of time'.[39] Little did he know that *Herald* would be making three detours to Bering Strait.

Kellett salvaged what he could of the survey by sending *Pandora* north in May 1848 to complete work on the harbour of Esquimalt and other parts of Juan de Fuca Strait. *Herald*, meanwhile, was to meet HMS *Plover* at Panama before proceeding to Bering Strait. *Plover* missed the rendezvous, so *Herald* left without her on a 92-day passage to Petropaulowski on the Kamchatka Peninsula in northeastern Russia, reaching it on 7 August 1848. Scurvy broke out on this voyage, not for the last time, reminding us that this dread disease still plagued the Royal Navy in the middle of the nineteenth century. *Plover* did not appear at Petropaulowski either, so Kellett proceeded to Kotzebue Sound to anchor off Chamisso Island on 14 September. With the winter freeze-up approaching, Kellett could do little but ask the local Malemiut people for rumours of Franklin. The Malemiut told stories about white men travelling in the interior, and Kellett and the others happily believed that these must have been survivors of the Franklin expedition, not Russian traders or—as it turned out—figments of the imagination created by the Malemiut to please their preoccupied guests.

Herald was forced by the oncoming winter to leave Kotzebue Sound for Petropaulowski on 29 September, where *Plover's* whereabouts remained unknown. Scurvy broke out again on the 199-day passage to Mazatlan, where Kellett rested his crew before proceeding to Panama. By the time of *Herald's* arrival there on 20 January 1849, news of the California gold rush was bringing floods of prospectors to the Isthmus from Europe and the eastern United States. The 'forty-niners' completely overwhelmed the resources of the town of Panama, producing the first of many cholera epidemics. *Herald* left quickly to begin surveying the coast of what is now Costa Rica.

By April the ship was in need of provisions again, and Panama was still stricken by cholera, so after collecting mail and landing dispatches and collections to be sent to Britain, Kellett proceeded to Honolulu where he met Wood and the *Pandora*. Here Kellett received orders to make another trip to Bering Sound. He accepted his new duties, but privately he was in despair. He wrote to Beaufort expressing his misgivings about these repeated Arctic searches, was concerned about his health, and doubted that his own motivation was what it needed to be in order to sustain his officers and crew through another unwelcome Arctic voyage. Wood, too, wrote to Beaufort about the captain's state of mind, claiming that the Admiralty's apparent lack of interest in the survey's efforts over the past two years, and its sloppy organisation of *Plover's* contribution, had depressed Kellett. Once resolved to carry on, however, Kellett did so with a will. *Pandora* was ordered home and returned to Britain via Tahiti, Pitcairn Island and Cape Horn in November 1849.

Leaving Honolulu on 19 May, *Herald* returned to Petropaulowski to hear that the *Plover* had wintered just to the north of that settlement; her poor sailing qualities had put her too far behind to meet any of the scheduled rendezvous. The two ships finally met up in Kotzebue Sound in July. An expedition of the two ships' boats proceeded up the Mackenzie River in pursuit of rumoured white travellers; escorting them, *Herald* went further north than any European vessels on record: to 72°16′N lat. *Herald* surveyed Wainwright Inlet, looking for a safe place for *Plover* to winter, but finding it too shallow the captains settled on the usual Kotzebue Sound anchorage off Chamisso Island. Then, in the only moment of the voyage which recalled the discoveries made by Cook, Vancouver and the others whose journals the officers had devoured, *Herald* found some uncharted islands, apparently unknown to Europe, northwest of the Sound. It was too rough to anchor, so Kellett went with two boats to the newly named 'Herald Island' and took possession of it and nearby 'Plover Island' by hoisting the Union Jack and performing what Seemann called 'The usual ceremonies, in the name of her most gracious Majesty Queen Victoria'.[40] The boats made a second excursion, this time up the Buckland River, but still found no trace of Franklin. *Herald* left the Arctic in September, leaving Midshipman Pim behind to winter in *Plover*, and reached Mazatlan on 14 November. They found that cholera had spread there too, in the wake of the gold rush, and after a brief reprovisioning Kellett began a long survey of Lower California which lasted until June 1850. *Herald* then returned for the last time to Bering Strait, retrieved Pim, and noted that some 200 vessels of all nationalities were now scouting for Franklin during the whaling season.

After *Herald*'s arrival in the summer of 1850 there were more rumours of white men inland, and more long searches ending in disappointment. Finally Kellett received orders for home, and Chimmo recalled that 'The men almost jumped out of their clothes for joy'.[41] Scurvy had set in again, and the ship was literally falling apart. After refreshing at Honolulu, *Herald* returned home via Hong Kong and the Cape, where the continuing illness of so many crew members (including Pim) forced *Herald* to stay while the sick were hospitalised. Several had already died. This grim homeward voyage reminds us that shipboard conditions had changed little since the pioneering days of Pacific exploration; supplies of lime or lemon juice were erratic and of varying quality, leading to dependency on fresh fruit and vegetables to prevent scurvy. In addition, there was still a poor understanding of the relationship between hygiene and the prevention of infectious diseases. As Christopher Lawrence has pointed out, naval historians tend to overlook the issue of scurvy and other health problems in their accounts of the nineteenth-century Royal Navy.[42] *Herald*'s outbreaks of fever and scurvy had severely debilitated its remaining crew, and after returning at last to Britain on 6 June 1851, the ship immediately discharged fifty-two men to hospital. The *Herald* survey had accomplished much, in addition to its contribution to the search for Franklin, but at a cost in human life and suffering.

Let me offer some final comments on connections between science and empire. The official publications of the *Herald* expedition, especially Seemann's *Narrative* and *Botany*, explicitly link the collection of scientific data with the interests of British commerce, and it is clear from the Hydrographic Office's original orders that *Herald*'s natural history survey was to concentrate on particular areas and issues. The Governor of the Falkland Islands was struggling to improve agricultural and grazing yields; on the outward voyage, naturalist Edmondston was instructed to collect samples of grasses for the Royal Botanic Gardens at Kew.[43] The connection between Kew and the islands was already so strong that Governor Moody had named a peninsula near Stanley Harbour 'Hooker Point'. Edmondston was also required to report directly to the Colonial Office on his investigations of the Galapagos Islands, especially their rumoured coal deposits, even though the Galapagos group was not a British colony.[44] As the use of steam power by the navy and British merchant shipping grew, so did the need for ports of call with supplies of coal. Although those of the Galapagos proved non-existent, the coal fields of Vancouver Island were a prominent feature of Wood's 1847 report on *Pandora*'s investigations there and naval officers had already done much to stake Britain's claim to this important Pacific coast entrepôt.

Commercially marketable plants were of greater interest than the discovery of new species; chincona plants and their quinine derivatives were of particular interest. Daniel Headrick's *The Tools of Empire* links steam technology with quinine as the twin engines of European expansion in tropical areas in the nineteenth century, while Lucile Brockway's work outlines Britain's exploitation of indigenous knowledge in the discovery and harvesting of South

American chincona species.[45] The *Herald* expedition featured these themes: an important aspect of Seemann's promotion of colonisation in Ecuador was the ready availability of quinine. Admiring the 'high mountains, extensive meadows, and valuable Quina-forests' of the country, along with its temperate climate, mineral resources and fertile soil, Seemann concluded that 'Ecuador presents a vast field for enterprise' and was 'inhabited by so limited a number of whites, that about twelve thousand immigrants would effect surprising changes'.[46] This praise of Ecuador contrasts with Seemann's discouraging conclusions about the Arctic. 'In a commercial point of view' he had found 'no productions which would play a prominent part in the traffic of civilized nations', adding that 'should the country ever be inhabited by a civilized people, they will have to . . . exchange walrus-tusks, eider-down, furs, and train oil, for the spices of India, the manufactures of Europe, and the medicinal drugs of tropical America'.[47] To Seemann the Arctic would only be valuable after it became part of a global system of trade.

For Seemann, and so many other explorers and naturalists in the nineteenth century, the essence of civilisation was its control and exploitation of nature. Naval survey expeditions did far more than chart coastlines: they also mapped the progress of Europe's conquest of the non-European world, cataloguing the future of empire. Natural resources of value to Britain were given top priority, and the indigenous populations living near them were described as unfit custodians of their value in a global market. When read together with supporting material from a range of sources, the published accounts of the *Herald* expedition reveal just how deeply entwined were the issues of scientific investigation and imperial expansion.

John Lort Stokes and the New Zealand Survey, 1848–1851

R. J. B. KNIGHT

WHILE MUCH ATTENTION is given, and rightly, to the achievements of those who went first to new lands through uncharted seas, very much less attention is given, if any at all, to those who came second. At what point an explorer becomes a mere surveyor is difficult to define, but it can be measured by the respect, even in some cases the reverence, accorded by historians. John Lort Stokes, who surveyed 4300 miles of the New Zealand coast in HMS *Acheron* between 1848 and 1851, seems to have come second all his life. His longest period of service was as second-in-command of the *Beagle*; he was not the first choice to command the New Zealand survey, and although it was the Royal Navy's first overseas hydrographic survey by steam vessel, *Acheron* was not the first steam warship in New Zealand waters, and Stokes was ordered home before he could complete the work—this was done by Captain Byron Drury in the *Pandora*. Nor was he made Hydrographer of the Navy, being overtaken by his second-in-command on the voyage, G. H. Richards.[1]

Yet a comparison of charts of New Zealand before and after this survey clearly demonstrates that it was this one which made the difference. With some exceptions (for example the work of Dumont d'Urville in 1827), very little progress had been made since Cook, and our knowledge today of what the whalers, sealers and traders who sailed in New Zealand waters knew in the first forty years of the nineteenth century is hazy. One author has demonstrated that movements of some vessels were kept secret to protect commercial activities, and a comparison of charts published through the 1820s and 1830s by J. W. Norie and Company with those from Cook's voyages shows few differences.[2] On the other hand, the general chart of New Zealand published by the Hydrographer of the Navy on 3 March 1856 looks like a modern chart, based as it was on the 250 tracings sent back to the Admiralty by the Stokes expedition. Uneven and patchy clusters of soundings and long stretches of vague coastline are replaced by systematic and detailed information. A comparison of astronomically determined land coordinates, published in the *New Zealand Government Gazette* in 1852 after the *Acheron's* survey, with James Wyld's chart, published in 1834, shows the earlier positions of established ports to be inaccurate by three or five miles, while on the west coast Milford Haven and Port Mason are as much as ten and twenty-five miles too far to the east.[3] Captain Sir Everard Home, the captain of HMS *North Star*, in Cook Strait in 1843 found himself navigating out of volume two of Hawkesworth's account of the voyages of Captain Cook, a sixty-year-old publication.[4] Many of Stokes's charts were in use into the present century, and some charts in use today still acknowledge explicitly Stokes's contributions.

Stokes himself called the west coast of the South Island 'the terra incognita of New Zealand', but generally in his letters he refers little to these inaccuracies, letting his tracings speak for themselves. His findings in Cloudy Bay, though, he noted, 'differ very materially from the charts now in use', and when he found a safe harbour near D'Urville Island, he commented to Francis Beaufort that it was 'known only to the Maoris, which we claimed as a discovery'. Some of this work was, of course, done in exceptionally difficult weather, particularly in the waters off Stewart Island; he described this period of the survey as 'a successful, though boisterous and hazardous exploration'.[5] Some of the sketches in the collection show the *Acheron* at anchor in extreme conditions, and are no less telling than the dramatic oil painting in the National Library of Australia, done by Stokes's fellow surveyor, Richard Brydges Beechey, showing the ship straining at double anchors, topmasts struck, wallowing between huge waves.[6] However, it was Stokes's work on the east coast of the North Island, on the Cook Strait and on the harbours of the east coast of the South Island which made the most impact on the colony, and which was essential for its development, dependent as it was on coastal communication and transport; and it was the need of the colony to develop economically which was the main driving force behind the *Acheron*'s survey.

Yet little notice has been paid to this important naval effort, nor to Lort Stokes himself, nor to the impact of steam on the process of surveying in the notoriously difficult New Zealand waters, nor to the role which the Navy took in relations between the Maori and the colonial administration.[7] Stokes never wrote the book which he intended to write on his return, perhaps because of his disappointment at being recalled.[8] General naval and hydrographic histories see no reason to give Lort Stokes special attention, and only one, by Sheila Natusch, *The Cruise of the Acheron*, published in 1978, tells the story.[9] She records, very usefully, the location of the sources in the United Kingdom and New Zealand and the book is profusely illustrated from the many sketches that survive; but while she achieved a lively and interesting narrative, there is more to say in the post-imperial 1990s.

Much more insight can be gained from this episode into mid-century imperial attitudes and the motivation of those who made a significant contribution to the history of New Zealand. The first question which needs to be addressed is why the survey took place when it did. To support a hugely expanding British naval influence, there were many demands on the Hydrographic Office under Francis Beaufort in the 1840s. Twenty-six ships were working on surveys throughout the world between 1843 and 1846, many of them in the China Seas following the Opium Wars, and by 1841 six of the new steam paddle sloops were engaged in new surveys around the British coast.[10] The early years of the decade saw the introduction of ships powered by steam, for surveying was ideally suited to the small paddle-wheeled sloops which were the first naval vessels to use steam efficiently.[11] *Acheron* was ten years old by the time of the survey, displacing 750 tons, barque-rigged, with what was strictly an auxiliary engine, underpowered though of remarkable reliability, generating 160 horsepower through her paddlewheels.[12] Surveying techniques and methods had changed but little from Cook's time, but the use of steam enabled the science of hydrography to move up a step. Now a surveyor could use his ship in calm conditions, and being independent, by and large, of wind direction and strength, could produce more accurate soundings, and more quickly. Stokes himself had no doubt. At the end of the New Zealand commission, he wrote 'on comparing [*Acheron's*] progress with that of a sailing vessel, it may be fairly set down at the proportion of months for years'.[13]

New Zealand first became involved in the European geopolitical struggle when the French laid claim to land in the South Island after the Treaty of Waitangi (1840). In 1843 HMS *North Star*, serving on the East India Station, was dispatched to New Zealand when, in the words of her captain, the French 'laid claim to Banks Peninsular, which they clearly have no right to do'.[14] In Britain, there was a considerable though irrational concern that steam power could furnish the French with the means to invade speedily and this issue was at the centre of politics.[15] The Anglo-French *Entente* of 1841–46, never particularly *Cordiale*, came to a rapid end when the belligerent Palmerston succeeded Aberdeen as Prime Minister in 1846. Though the Pacific was never a priority of the British Parliament, there was enough evidence of possible future difficulties to bring New Zealand's needs up the administration's priority list. At about the same time as the abortive French attempt on the South Island, a French admiral had occupied Tahiti (in 1842). When the British Consul was arrested in March 1844 by a French captain, 'Britain then exploded in official and public fury', and normality was restored only 'after much negotiation and some talk of war'.[16] In 1847 Lord Auckland, as First Lord of the Admiralty, recommended the creation of a new Australian-New Zealand Division of the East India Station; this was done in 1848. Because of the Maori uprisings, the Division's officers were always instructed to give special priority to New Zealand, and they often wrote about 'The New Zealand Station', even though the squadron was technically based in Sydney. HMS *Havannah*, 22 guns, was the flagship, and Stokes transmitted regular reports to her captain, Captain Erskine. When Stokes was in New Zealand in 1850, he noted that a French corvette, the *Alcemene*, had left Sydney hurriedly on receiving news that relations between Britain and France were again difficult, and he expected to see the ship in New Zealand waters.[17] These were touchy times.

However, it was the appointment of Rear-Admiral Robert Fitzroy as Governor and Commander-in-Chief of New Zealand in September 1842 which signalled the start of some British government effort. Fitzroy, who had earlier commanded the *Beagle* surveying expedition, and Beaufort came to an arrangement to appoint 'a capable but amenable surveyor' to be responsible to the Governor, and paid by the Admiralty, with copies of the surveys to be retained in the colony.[18] It was the cheap option. Alexander Usborne was appointed and sent out, but the scheme failed and he had to come home, possibly because Fitzroy's short and unfortunate period as Governor ended in November 1845, after he had incurred the wrath of the New Zealand Company.[19]

Meanwhile, the Maori uprisings had brought British warships, HMS *Driver, Inflexible, North Star* and *Fly*, to New Zealand waters. A steady stream of letters was received by Beaufort from Captain Home, an enthusiastic supporter and a frustrated surveyor, and fretful of the lack of motivation in his masters and crew to make a contribution to surveying knowledge. In addition to sending Beaufort magnetic and astronomical observations, he sent a stream of criticism of information on the charts. He wrote in May 1844, for instance, 'I am anxious to visit Stuarts Island, but the weather is very bad and we have no good, or bad charts to go by.'[20] Beaufort still looked for resources, by now being cut back, but, possibly because of fears of the French, the Admiralty made a ship available. Beaufort offered it to a Lieutenant Edge, searching not only for a surveyor but also a diplomat: 'surveyors are scarce, especially when other qualities than the mere professional talent is required'.[21] By July 1847 Beaufort had rather decided on Stokes, who had his doubts about the feasibility of the project, doubts shared by Fitzroy, who wrote to Stokes in July 1847:

Probably the New Zealand Company now in the ascendant and Lord Grey—their patron—have been urging the Admiralty to add increased eclat to their colonising operations by enabling them to talk and write about the 'immediate survey under the direction of a naval officer of rank, talent and experience'!!! Be the immediate cause what it may, you know as well as anyone how valuable a good survey of those islands would be. But, my dear friend, would it be right for you to accept the offer in its present shape?[22]

Stokes was clearly worried, even six months later, about the difficulty of serving two masters; and Beaufort assuaged his doubts and encouraged him in a skilful letter: 'There are hard masters in the world who whatever is done think that something more might have been added, but I will pledge myself for Lord Auckland and all the Board, and indeed for all the country, that if you acquit your own conscience they will be amply satisfied'.[23]

Not only had Stokes, therefore, to serve the Admiralty, but he had to serve the colony. Since 1841 New Zealand had been a Crown Colony, administratively independent of New South Wales, although economically it was still very dependent on Australia. Its population more than doubled by emigration between 1842 and 1852 to some 20 000 Europeans. Though whaling had decreased, bulk agricultural products, grain, flax, tallow and timber, and from 1846, wool, required considerable tonnage. The number of vessels entered and cleared through the 1840s averaged between three and four hundred a year, measuring approximately 100 000 tons.[24] Bulk products needed a lot of tonnage and they needed navigational information badly.

Stokes therefore faced a dilemma. The older tradition of disinterested scientific surveying, so strong since Cook and upheld by Beaufort, was now to be steered and influenced by the political and commercial pressures of the colony; and the expedition accordingly found itself doing many things which would not have been in Beaufort's original conception of a strict hydrographic survey. Only four years before the expedition set off, Beaufort himself had not seen that it was important to chart New Zealand more precisely. Reviewing priorities, he recorded in the Hydrographic Office minutes:

Of New Zealand a consecutive survey would be very satisfactory, for though the principal points of settlement have, by successive corrections and improvements become tolerably well detailed, yet the intervals of coast are very doubtfully represented in the charts—and of the whole Southern Island we have nothing excepting Cook Strait. But perhaps it would be unwise to stimulate the roving disposition of the Settlers there by exploring too far in advance of them, but rather to let the tide of discovery keep pace with that of colonisation.[25]

The oil portrait done of Stokes in later life shows a broad and stolid figure, apparently at ease with himself, in spite of his disappointments. Unusually for a naval officer in the Victorian age, almost all of his active career had been spent at sea. He had spent the extraordinarily long time of eighteen years in the *Beagle*, from 1825 to 1843, cruising in the Straits of Magellan until 1830 and then on the world voyage with Darwin until 1836. Afterwards, when the *Beagle* sailed for Australia's northwest coast, the captain was invalided and Stokes took command. The first survey for which he was fully responsible was that of the Gulf of Carpentaria. He was a man with simple religious beliefs, and as numerous incidents from his *Beagle* days portray, was good in a crisis. He wrote well, and was much affected by the extraordinary scenery he saw. Ten years before, Phillip Parker King, who earlier surveyed the north and west coasts of Australia, dismissed Stokes as a 'steady, plodding old-fashioned fellow', but he soon came to appreciate Stokes's many sterling qualities, and one cannot but admire Stokes's resourcefulness and stoicism when his wife died from fever on the journey out from England to New Zealand. Yet this was a man who all his life also wanted to travel towards unknown horizons. In a rare moment of non-religious introspection, he wrote: 'It is impossible to define . . . the exact charm which particular minds find in the perils and adventures of discovery, whether on the shore or o'er the wave. Certain, however, it is, that scarce any motive of human exertion can compete with it in the powers of endurance it supplies to its votaries'.[26]

One facet of his character is that Stokes got on well with difficult men. His relationship with Fitzroy, in the *Beagle* and later, was good, and for much of his time in New Zealand he worked closely with the colonial administration under Sir George Grey, the 'strange, complicated man, whose real charisma and genius almost matched his flaws'.[27] It is remarkable how much Stokes and the *Acheron* served the colonial administration, and how priorities were set by Grey's demands. The most notable example of this was the surveying of the then lightly colonised South Island. Work was to be done in preparation for the Canterbury immigration, and in surveying Otago harbour so as to support the settlement there, which was not flourishing. Laying and maintaining buoys there, at the colonial government's expense, was also part of the bargain. A good deal of the survey was done by land expeditions, especially in determining the fixed points by astronomical positioning; but Stokes's men were ordered to take account of the fertility of the land.[28] Only once did Stokes seem to balk at Grey's requests. He resisted a request, passed on by Grey from a timber merchant by the name of Atkins, for a survey of the river Wairoa in Kaipara Harbour. He wrote: 'Not being aware that Mr Atkins, or other timber merchants, has any peculiar claims on the *Acheron's* services—I beg to say in reply that the survey of Kaipara and its tributary streams must take its turn'; though he added: 'I shall continue to bear in mind the probability of an increasing timber trade in that part of New Zealand . . .'[29] In return, Grey immediately made labour and colonial boats available, and, indeed, much of the inshore surveying was done by independent expeditions commanded by the *Acheron's* officers. Because of wind and swell, one of the colonial schooners, the *Albert*, was lost at the mouth of the Whangamta River, Bay of Plenty.[30]

There is no doubt how much Stokes cared about the development of New Zealand. He fretted at the lack of progress in the settlements in Otago, noting that only 300 of the 2400 allotments had been sold. He urged the use of convict labour to build roads and bridges to open up the country, 'which private enterprise can never achieve'. He continued: 'and however the feeling of Englishmen may at first revolt from association with men banished through their crimes, still I am convinced of the advantages of an almost unlimited supply of unpaid labour to an infant settlement depressed by pecuniary and other difficulties'. He went on to suggest that a penal settlement be established at the southern part of Stewart Island, to the west of Port Pegasus.[31] In one of his more reflective reports to the Admiralty, he foresaw the end result of his work.

After dark, we anchored in Cooper's Bay off its newly arisen port town, where a few lights and the hum of human voices broke the solitude and silence that formerly marked the spot. The morning light showed a good size village of wooded dwellings had sprung up in the short interval between our former visit—the nucleus of the future Lyttleton.[32]

Inevitably, the expedition had a great deal of contact with the Maori, for whom Stokes developed much respect. After the recent uprisings, he was at first extremely tentative. His orders to his officers when they went off in their independent expeditions illustrate his attitudes. He made it clear early in the voyage that they should 'sedulously endeavour to obtain the Maori local names'; and to Richards, who was off to the Bay of Islands, he wrote: 'You will have to proceed with caution and skill in order not to give offence to Maoris who are thereabouts exceedingly suspicious of Surveyors'.[33] Another order warned them to be 'careful of sacred grounds or tabooed . . . in short, you will make it your study to cultivate the friendship of this fine race of men as much as possible'. A year later he was reporting with confidence that apart from a small dissatisfied party on the north side of Taranaki, there was no sign of dissatisfaction. He wrote: 'and as the years roll on, the causes of the dispute will be gradually exhausted, and both races discover their truest interest to consist in mutual understanding'.[34]

In the South Island he became involuntarily caught up in land deals and acted as emissary for Grey, to whom he reported on 31 August 1850:

Many parties visited the *Acheron* under an impression that this purchase formed part of our mission. Before our departure they all appeared satisfied in Foveaux Straits and also at Otago, after marking in the chart the reserves they were desirous to retain to sell all the land from Otago to the Western Coast. Two thousand pounds would probably be cheerfully accepted as purchase money, one half of which I would suggest should be distributed at Otago and the remainder at Bluff, an arrangement which would secure their fair share to all interested parties.

On Grey's instructions, four months later he delivered the disappointing news that 'the Lieutenant-General did not intend to negotiate for the purchase of the remainder of the Middle Island'.[35]

Yet Stokes's optimistic view of improved relations between the settlers and the Maori was essentially that of a man standing on the quarterdeck of a powerful machine capable of overwhelming force. He lost no chance in pushing forward his view that it was steam that was the key to control, as he indicated in his long description to Beaufort in London of the impact on the Maori of Queen Charlotte's Sound of his arrival:

> As we steamed up this picturesque arm of the sea, several Maori whaleboats, which have nearly superseded the use of canoes, passed, hastening out of the quiet nooks studding its shores, to gaze in intent awe on a vessel moved by the unseen agency of steam. As we drew near the head of the Sound, two densely crowded boats pulled into mid-Channel to meet us. On passing them, the *Acheron* suddenly stopped. The effect on our Maori spectators was very startling. Terror or admiration appeared to take full possession of them, in a moment afterwards their wild shrieks echoed from shore to shore. The violent manner in which they then threw their arms about and the contortions of their features showed intense excitement . . . The impression created by the visit of HM Steamer will not be soon effaced and may be useful in confirming the belief already generally entertained elsewhere that the English can promptly furnish any turbulence, or outrage on their countrymen, however remote from the rest of government their settlement might be.[36]

Two weeks earlier he had sent his opinion to the Secretary of the Admiralty:

> The great awe and profound respect manifested for a Steamer by the Maori inhabitants, highly informs the suggestion of establishing this kind of navigation and not only dispenses with the presence of one man of war, but effects a further reduction in the Expenditure by enabling the Government to withdraw one regiment until New Zealand becomes a convict colony.

And to Grey, at the end of his commission, he wrote:

> the high respect mingled with fear entertained for a steamer is
> very great. We know, say they, that there are bounds to a sailing
> vessel . . . beyond which she cannot pass, but with a steamer we
> are never secure. I would suggest to your Excellency the policy of
> not leaving New Zealand without a steam vessel of war, for the
> next two or three years.[37]

In the end, it was Stokes's vision that British power should be
applied in New Zealand by the mailed fist disguised by a velvet
glove.

There was, however, one snag to the implementation of this
vision—coal was needed to fuel steam shipping. How to obtain this
commodity for the *Acheron* was a constant subject of Stokes's correspondence. Although the expedition made a good start with coal
stockpiled for previous visits by warships, Stokes had to ensure that
he was kept well-supplied from Sydney. In addition to the coal
depots at Wellington and Nelson, he built up a supply at Otago,
and he was proud of the economy he applied: 'the expenditure of
only 110 tons in a cruise of two months, resulted in the addition of
300 miles of [the survey of] the eastern and fertile part of that
island'.[38] At the end of his time in the *Acheron*, he noted that 4700
miles of coastline had been surveyed for the expenditure of only
1300 tons of coal. Coal was expensive—shipped at Sydney for
13 shillings a ton, it cost £2 10s a ton at Otago. The only real
answer was to find a supply of sufficient quality and quantity in
New Zealand, but Stokes's search for coal was unsuccessful. He
wrote at one point: 'a good supply of coal will also be indispensable
to that success of that grand scheme of colonisation now in
progress'. It was not until December 1850 that he made a comprehensive report to Mr Fox of the New Zealand Company and it was
'less favourable than I anticipated', even allowing for the fact that
the material came from surface seams. Taking coal from Newcastle,
New South Wales, as a measure, he carried out burning and
steaming tests on material from Massacre Bay (now Golden Bay),
Waikati River, Saddle Hill, Otago and Motunao on the Canterbury

Plains. None of these deposits was satisfactory, and Stokes concluded that five tons of Manuku wood were equal in efficiency to one ton of Newcastle coal.[39]

All this was cut short by an order from the Admiralty at the end of March 1851. Although Stokes had sent careful tracings of his surveys, and other data, regularly to the Admiralty, and though he considered that the *Acheron* was good for another three years of service, the ship was suddenly recalled. A cut in the Hydrographer's budget of £10 000 meant the curtailing of surveys abroad. The survey would be continued by HM Brig *Pandora*, 400 tons; and the officers of the *Acheron* were to return to England in the *Havannah*. Stokes was outraged and he drafted, but almost certainly did not send, a wrathful letter to the Admiralty:

> Every exertion has been used to carry on the two great principles of economy and dispatch, in reference to the service which I left England to conduct, with a full understanding . . . that I should be allowed to complete it. Under these circumstances, I may be allowed to express my annoyance & mortification at being suddenly suspended from my command, and, together with my officers, turned out of my ship at a moment's notice.[40]

A later letter, wisely, moderated the tone to one of mere regret.

Though *Acheron*'s survey was cut short, the *Pandora* under Captain Byron Drury continued the survey, particularly of Kaipara, Manukau and Kawhia harbours in the North Island, at a hugely slower pace. It was not finished until 1856. Ashore until his Channel Survey of 1859 to 1862, Stokes still harboured optimistic visions blending steam power with high imperial ideas. In a letter to Gladstone in 1858, pressing for a regular steamer service north of Australia via the Torres Strait, he wrote:

> Once nations can be brought within wire intelligence, when the great rulers of the earth can be brought to hold wire converse with each other, wars with their dreadful effects will cease, and peace with its many blessings followed by Civilisation and Christianity, will spread their bright and happy influence over the darkened spots of the Globe. Once a knot of enterprising people can be got to take root when there is a prospect of commerce, a

trade will soon spring up and a fresh tract be opened for British manufacturers. England cannot, I believe, have too many well selected and well established colonies; they are to her like the rigging of a ship.

Having a view from the centre, Gladstone responded:

I feel less sanguine than yourself, and I am disposed to shrink from the extent of duty, of highly arduous and honourable duty, which you would England to assume. . . I hesitate to admit the propriety of any indefinite or wide extension of our protectorate, by acts or by a policy of ours, to tribes not within our dominions by fresh assumptions with misgiving and even with dread. There is no country upon earth so charged with responsibilities as we are: and I am by no means sure that we are not more ready to undertake them than ready to meet them.[41]

In these two letters, the extremes of the imperial argument were joined. It may have been that Stokes's simple faith in empire had been unduly influenced by Grey, but it was a powerful and moti-vating one, and it is unsurprising that with such attitudes, Britain, according to one estimate, acquired annually on average 100 000 square miles for its empire between 1815 and 1865.[42] The *Acheron* survey reached no great heights, but people such as its naval officers not only measured the earth but also influenced people on it; and John Lort Stokes should be studied not only for his technical achievements, but also for his wider role in the history of empire.

A Warrant Officer in the Arctic

The Journal of George Ford, 1850–1854

WILLIAM BARR

ON THE MORNING OF 19 MAY 1845 HMS *Erebus* and *Terror* sailed from Greenhithe on the Thames, in search of the Northwest Passage, under the command of Captain Sir John Franklin.[1] In late July the two ships encountered the whalers *Enterprise* (Captain Robert Martin), of Peterhead, and *Prince of Wales* (Captain Dannett), of Hull, in Melville Bay. Captain Martin and his crew were the last Europeans to see any of the 129 officers and men of the two ships alive.[2]

The ships were provisioned for three years, and it was anticipated that they might have to winter at least once before they emerged from Bering Strait; hence there was no particular concern expressed in Britain when there was no word from the expedition in 1846. But by the spring of 1850, despite considerable and far-ranging searches, involving expeditions dispatched by the British Admiralty to the Arctic via both Bering Strait and Baffin Bay, as well as overland expeditions dispatched by the Hudson's Bay Company, not the slightest trace had been found of the missing expedition. In this critical situation the Lords of the Admiralty decided to send an expedition of two ships via the Strait of Magellan and Bering Strait, in an attempt to search for the Franklin expedition from the west.[3]

The ships were HMS *Enterprise* and *Investigator*. Command of the expedition and of *Enterprise* was entrusted to Captain Richard Collinson; in command of *Investigator* was Captain Robert M'Clure.

So far, three accounts of the voyage of HMS *Investigator* have been published. Captain M'Clure's own diaries were edited by Captain Sherard Osborn;[4] and the ship's surgeon, Dr Alexander Armstrong, published his narrative a year later.[5] Much more recently, an English translation of the journal of Johann Miertsching, the Moravian missionary recruited as Inuktitut interpreter, has appeared.[6] However, it is the unpublished journal of George Ford, the ship's carpenter, which provides the most detail about some of its mundane circumstances.

As a warrant officer, George Ford saw things from a very different perspective from those of the authors of the previously published accounts. Ford wrote his journal as an ongoing letter to his wife Mary (Polly), with daily entries. The first part of the journal (from 10 January 1850 to 8 June 1852), covering the voyage from Britain to the Arctic via Bering Strait and the first of two winterings, was written on eight large, loose sheets of paper, which Ford had folded in half and, presumably to save paper, had cross-written. Their legibility is reduced even more by the fact that the ink bled through rather badly. There are no journal entries for the subsequent period (from 9 June 1852 to 25 May 1853), covering the second wintering at Mercy Bay. It is not known whether Ford kept a journal for this period which has not survived, or whether he simply discontinued his journal-keeping, but the latter appears more probable. The fact that Ford had recourse to cross-writing for the early part of his journal would suggest that his paper supply was very limited, and that he abandoned his journal-keeping when it became exhausted. Resumption of the journal in June 1852 may have been because one of the officers, being forced to leave most of his possessions on abandoning the ship, donated the notebook to Ford in which the final part of the journal is written. This small notebook (whose entries are much more legible) covers the period from 26 May 1853 to 21 September 1854, when HMS *North Star*, in which Ford returned home, was approaching Ireland.

GEORGE FORD WAS BORN on 26 December 1821 in the village of Cleeve, in the parish of Yatton in Somerset, some nine miles south-west of Bristol.[7] When he entered the Royal Navy on 28 February 1841 he gave his usual residence as Bristol. He first signed on as caulker, serving aboard HMS *Scylla*,[8] then on 1 October 1845 he gained his carpenter's ticket, taking the examination at Devonport. At that time he was 5 feet 5 inches tall with light hair, fresh complexion, grey eyes and no distinguishing marks. Given his place of birth we can safely assume that he spoke with a Somerset accent. Thereafter he served as carpenter on board HMS *Raleigh, Ocean*, and the sloop *Contest*. On board the latter vessel he suffered two quite serious accidents. On 30 January 1847 he ran a chisel into the ball of his left thumb: 'The result has been a complete inability to flex the last phalanx of the thumb which is thus rendered nearly useless'.[9] This does not appear to have seriously inconvenienced Ford thereafter, however. But the other accident would give him recurring problems. On 7 May 1849 at St Helena, he was 'driving a bolt with a heavy mall to secure the cap of the bowsprit, when he sustained a hernia on the left side'.[10] He was immediately strapped into a truss and was given an occasional dose of castor oil; in a few days he was out of pain. Later, during his third Arctic wintering on board *Investigator*, at Mercy Bay, the ship's surgeon, Dr Alexander Armstrong, certified that Ford suffered a further hernia, this time on the right side, while 'employed in assisting to remove the after hatchway, preparatory to housing in for the winter'.[11]

Returning to Portsmouth in August 1849 Ford joined HMS *Illustrious*.[12] Then, less than a week later, on 27 August 1849, he was married to Mary Bartlett of Portsmouth at Portsmouth Parish Church by the Reverend John P. McGhie.[13] Then, only a few months later, on 28 December 1849 he joined HM Discovery Ship *Investigator*, fitting out for her Arctic voyage; his warrant as the ship's carpenter was dated 26 December 1849.[14]

ENTERPRISE AND *INVESTIGATOR* sailed from the Thames on 10 January 1850.[15] They were towed through the Strait of Magellan on 19–20 April, but on reaching the Pacific the two ships were separated in a freshening gale. They never made contact again. *Investigator*, by far the slower sailer of the two, reached Honolulu, the next pre-arranged rendezvous, on 1 July, to find that Collinson in *Enterprise* had arrived a week earlier, but, anxious not to lose the Arctic season, had sailed again for Bering Strait (the next rendezvous) the previous day.

Collinson chose the established (and allegedly safer) route round the west end of the Aleutians; M'Clure, also anxious to reach the Arctic (and having consulted whaling captains) took a short cut through the Aleutians and hence reached Bering Strait weeks before *Enterprise*. On encountering HMS *Plover* (Captain Moore) in Kotzebue Sound on 29 July and HMS *Herald* (Captain Henry Kellett) on 31 July, M'Clure learned that *Enterprise* had not yet arrived but, stressing that his orders instructed him to be in the Arctic by 1 August, and arguing that *Enterprise* must have passed northwards unseen, he pushed north on his own, thus ensuring that he would have an independent command for the remainder of the expedition.

Investigator rounded Point Barrow in early August, and taking advantage of shore leads pushed eastwards. By 21 August it was passing the mouth of the Mackenzie, by 30 August off Cape Bathurst, and by 6 September off Cape Parry. Heading northeast-wards it raised Nelson Head at the southern tip of Banks Island on 7 September. From here M'Clure pushed northwards along Prince of Wales Strait. On 17 September his ship was blocked by ice at the north end of that strait and, beset, began drifting back southwards. Its final winter quarters, beset in the ice, were located near Princess Royal Island in the middle of that strait.

In the spring of 1851 sledge parties explored the north coast of Banks Island, and the north, west and southwest coasts of Victoria Island. The ice, with the ship embedded in it, began moving in July 1851; *Investigator* drifted almost to the north end of Prince of Wales Strait again, but when it got free there was no sign of it being able to make any further progress in that direction. Hence M'Clure took it back south, rounded Nelson Head and pushed north along the west coast of Banks Island. Rounding Cape Prince Alfred into M'Clure Strait *Investigator* penetrated east to Mercy Bay but was forced to winter there again. In the spring of 1852 M'Clure led a sledge party across M'Clure Strait to Melville Island, where he left a

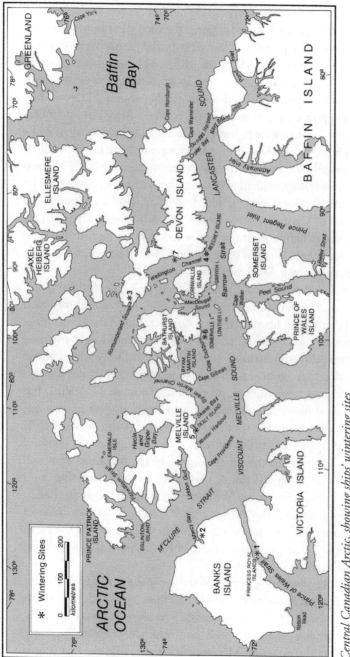

Central Canadian Arctic, showing ships' wintering sites

1 *Investigator,* 1850–51
2 *Investigator,* 1851–53
3 *Assistance* and *Pioneer,* 1852–53
4 *North Star,* 1852–54
5 *Resolute* and *Intrepid,* 1852–53
6 *Resolute* and *Intrepid,* 1853–54
7 *Assistance* and *Pioneer,* 1853–54

note at Winter Harbour. *Investigator* did not get free in the summer of 1852. On greatly reduced rations, the men went hunting whenever the weather permitted but despite this many were showing signs of scurvy by the spring of 1853. M'Clure made plans to dispatch forty of the less fit men in an attempt to escape from the Arctic; ten were to head south to the nearest Hudson's Bay Company post on the Mackenzie River (Peel's River Post, now Fort McPherson); thirty were to head east to Port Leopold to try to make contact with the whalers. Both parties were to leave on 15 April.[16]

Fortunately for all the expedition members, on 6 April a group of strangers was spotted approaching; this was a sledge party led by Lieutenant Bedford Pim, of HMS *Resolute*, wintering under the command of Captain Henry Kellett at Dealy Island. They had set off as soon as light conditions and weather permitted, in response to M'Clure's note left at Winter Harbour, which had been found by a sledge party from *Resolute* late the previous fall.[17]

After consultation with Captain Kellett, M'Clure decided that if twenty sound men volunteered to join him, they would stay with the ship, aiming to liberate her that summer. But in the event, fewer than twenty men volunteered and the *Investigator* was abandoned on 3 June; the crew trekked across the ice to Dealy Island where they took refuge on board *Resolute*. It and its steam tender *Intrepid* were liberated from the ice and got under way on 17 August, but made only limited progress eastwards before they were again beset, off Cape Cockburn, the southwestern cape of Bathurst Island.[18]

In the spring of 1854, on orders from Captain Sir Edward Belcher, who was in overall command of the squadron of which *Resolute* and *Intrepid* formed part, and himself wintering with *Assistance* and *Pioneer* in Wellington Channel, Captain Kellett abandoned *Resolute* and *Intrepid*; their crews, along with those of *Investigator*, hiked across the ice to Beechey Island, where the crews of all five ships sought refuge on board HMS *North Star*, which had been left there as a depot ship.

North Star had just got free of the ice in Erebus Bay in August 1854 when, no doubt to the relief of all those on board, two supply ships, *Phoenix* and *Talbot*, appeared. The shipless crews were distributed among all three vessels and returned safely to England. The officers and men of HMS *Investigator* were thus the first people to make the transit of the Northwest Passage. Admittedly they had travelled on board three ships and had covered two legs of the trip on foot across the ice, but they had travelled from the Pacific to the Atlantic Ocean along the north coast of North America.

THE MAJOR FEATURES of the voyage emerge quite clearly from Ford's journal, although the significance of some of the decisions and actions are perhaps not elucidated as fully as in some of the published accounts. On the other hand, as one might expect from a carpenter, Ford places particular emphasis on his area of professional expertise, namely repairs to spars, boats, and so forth.

For example, after a gale in the North Atlantic on 24 January 1850 carried away *Investigator*'s 'fore topmast, topgallant mast, royal mast, fore topgallant yard & crosstress, main topgallant & royal masts, topmast crosstrees and flying jibboom', Ford and his mates were kept busy 'repairing damages' for several days. Three weeks later, on 13 February, Ford noted: 'Carpenters employed making topgallant mast'; presumably they had dispensed with one of the topgallant masts in the interim (or had made do with a jury-rigged one).

On 15 May 1850, in the South Pacific, Ford recorded: 'Morning about 6 o'clock taken in a squall which carried away fore topmast, the crosstrees, jibboom & flying jibboom . . . that being the second time we were dismasted'. By evening the damage was largely rectified but next morning, 'on examining the spars I found that the main topmast was sprung from the accident the day previous. I went aloft & fished it'.

To make good this drain on the ship's spare spars, on 2 July, at Honolulu, Ford 'went on shore to select some spars for to make masts & yards that we were deficient through our accidents'. He does not specify whether this involved selecting trees to be felled, or selecting ready-made spars at a shipyard or lumber yard.

On at least one occasion in the Arctic, on 10 June 1851, Ford's duties took him away from the ship for a spell: 'I went with 3 men to Princess Royal's Island to repair our 1st whale boat as we leave her there'. The boat had been landed, as a security measure, in early March. Over the next three days Ford indulged in some hunting, apart from his work on the boat. Then, on the 13 June: 'Afternoon packed up & left for to return on board, having left on the island a 30 ft. whale boat with oars, sails, etc. for the use of any one that should require it (perhaps ourselves)'.

ONE OF THE MOST interesting aspects which emerges from Ford's journal is a shift in his attitude towards his captain. Initially Captain M'Clure had made a very positive impression on Ford. Thus on 6 June 1850, as the ship approached the Equator in the Pacific, he and the other warrant officers were grateful at being allocated a 'mess berth', that is, their own area for eating and relaxing, 'that was kindly given to us by our Captain'.

That fall, in Prince of Wales Strait, when a shore party led by the Captain had been cut off from the ship by a newly formed lead in the ice, Ford was a member of the party which went to the men's aid with two inflatable Halkett boats; with absolutely no suggestion of sarcasm Ford remarks that 'our gallant Captain' insisted on being the last to be rescued.

Similarly, on 2 November 1850, when M'Clure gave the assembled ship's company a report on his recent sledge trip across M'Clure Strait to within sight of Melville Island, thereby 'discovering' the Northwest Passage, Ford reports that the captain was given three cheers, and there is every indication that this reflected his genuine approval and admiration. These feelings appear to have been reciprocated. On Ford's birthday (26 December) M'Clure sent him a bottle of wine, 'wishing me many happy returns of the day'.

During the following fall, when *Investigator* was beset and in serious danger of being crushed by heavy, rafting ice, on 11 September 1851, off the north coast of Banks Island, M'Clure won Ford's unstinting praise: '& was it not for the good judgement of our gallant Captain & a strong ship we should not stand it a minute, as his cool, deliberate manner in hours of danger would win the heart of every well-disposed sensible man'. Throughout the second wintering, which the ship spent in Mercy Bay on the north coast of Banks Island, these positive feelings continued to be reciprocated. When Ford shot the first caribou of the season the Captain congratulated him and presented him with a glass of wine.

But at some point over the subsequent eighteen months, during the second enforced wintering at Mercy Bay, with rations getting scarcer, the hopes of getting the ship free steadily fading and, not surprisingly, nerves becoming frayed, what had clearly been a fairly warm relationship between a warrant officer and his captain evidently evaporated. Unfortunately we have no evidence as to whether this deterioration in relations was slow or abrupt, since there is a gap of twelve months in Ford's journal.

It was M'Clure's call for volunteers to stay with the ship in the spring of 1853 that first revealed that relations between M'Clure and his carpenter were no longer as warm as they had once been. Ford reported this incident (which occurred in June) in his journal on 25 July. He noted that in calling for volunteers the captain had stressed that:

> every man had done his duty, and if he would not volunteer we were to bear in mind it would be thought *no disgrace* whatever as we had done all that was expected of us but as it would contribute to the honor of our country to get the ship home, if 20 men on the examination from the doctor of the *Resolute* was found fit to stop they may volunteer, if not it would be no dishonor.

But when Ford was found fit but declined to volunteer, he found that the captain's tune had changed:

> I (knowing that all hands had agreed to leave & being the first asked) told him that under the present circumstances [I] would rather go home, he told me in a harsh tone I had deceived him & 'You can go, Sir. I'll not keep you' . . . On leaving the ship he addressed all hands saying that what they had done was barely their duty & that barely, as they were going to desert their ship & captain & repeated several times that all hands had barely, barely done their duty. He was happy to say all the officers came forward & volunteered except one & so he had written to the Admiralty about [it—] a pretty yarn to tell people about to undertake to travel & half-starved.

In August 1854, when *Phoenix* and *Talbot* reached Beechey Island, they brought mail, dispatches and newspapers, including the news of the outbreak of the Crimean War. In anticipation of getting a ship to participate in the war M'Clure invited his crew to 'join him

& brave the dangers of war as they did in the past, as he would give them all the first, best situations they could fill'. To which Ford adds the rather tart comment: 'The tune is altered now'.

THE 'REFUGEES' FROM *Investigator* reached *Resolute* and *Intrepid* on 17 June, to be welcomed and greeted with three cheers by the officers and men of those ships. *Investigator's* total complement of officers and men was accommodated on board *Resolute*; this cannot have been particularly convenient for either the hosts or the guests. Although initially very grateful, Ford quickly became disillusioned, and even bitter about the way he was treated, particularly as a warrant officer, accustomed to certain comforts and privileges aboard his own ship. On 2 July, two weeks after their arrival, Ford confided to his journal:

> Here we are, Mr N.[ewton], Mr K.[ennedy] & myself, no place to sit or wash or put our few cloths. But for the kindness of Mr Dean we should have no place to get a meal altho' we are all forced to work the same as this ship's company. I asked Mr Pim for a place to sit & wash yesterday. He told me I should think myself well off to be as I am, altho' Captn Kellett has told me that I shall have a place to sit & wash. Our treatment in this has been different to what we expected by the officers of her, & I pity poor Franklin's part[ie]s if they was found by them if they would get the treatment as we have. We have only our blanket bag & a buffalo robe to sleep on.[19]

Ford also claimed that the 'Investigators' were the object of the jealousy of the 'Resolutes', quite apart from the inconvenience and discomfort of their situation. On 18 July 1853 when the ships were still beset at Dealy Island he noted:

> I hope we shall get out & not stop another winter in *this* ship, as I have no place to sit, wash or anything & treated no better than if we were criminals. We should be very uncomfortable as we are here, being as there is jealous feeling towards us.

Reminiscing about their treatment on board *Resolute*, on 25 July Ford recalled:

On arriving on board the *Resolute* we was taken by the carptr
Mr Dean, whose kindness I cannot recompense, but no one
asked us if we wanted anything whatever. On the following day I
and my messmates was told we must work, which I have been
ever since. On asking Mr Pim if he could please to give us a place
to sit out of the way of people & put our clothes, he told me I
should think myself well off & I had better mind what I talked
about, threatening me if I spoke & I believe gave orders if any
of our men was heard grumble to report them to him. It's now
5 weeks & 3 days we have been never spoken to by any officer
except on duty. We have no place to sit down or wash & but for
Mr Dean's kindness no place to get our food. All that we have to
sleep on is a blanket and buffalo robe we brought with us in a
haversack. The men have been doing all the most servile work
while this ship's company does nearly nothing & part of them
officers' servants. We have never received the least extra to renew
our strength, nothing but barely the ship's allowance whilst the
travelling parties of this ship on returning got preserved milk,
Normandy pipins, etc., etc. & [there is a break in the text] of our
men has no place to sleep but on the chests; if they get wet they
are forced to sleep in their wet cloths. Our captn has never asked
us if we are comfortable or provided for since we have been here.
Our officers on board the *Resolute* is carousing in plenty of everything every day & never asks or cares about any one else as they
have all cabins. I wish I was out of this ship. A little in comfort is
better than a great quantity here.

The ships broke free when, along with the ice, they were driven out
to sea by a gale on 17 August. By the 27 August they were off the
east coast of Melville Island but Ford was still no happier with his
situation:

Today is the anniversary of my wedding & I am sorry to say I
shall spend it the most uncomfortably since I left home as I am
still situated the same. I am forced to mix with people filled
[with] jealousy & conceits and spend time day after day in a
place (for swearing, vulgarity, insults, brutishness) like a brothel.

By 20 September 1853 Captain Kellett had to acknowledge that his
ships were again beset, this time adrift in the open sea some twenty-
two miles off Cape Cockburn, the southwestern tip of Bathurst
Island. Soon thereafter, conditions for *Investigator*'s warrant officers
began to improve. On 3 October they were allocated a screened-off
area to sit; on 10 October they and the *Investigator*'s men were given
places to sling their hammocks in the hold, although these turned
out to be less than satisfactory quarters; and on the 12 October the
warrant officers messed separately for the first time.

But just as things seemed to be on the mend Ford received
another blow; his benefactor, Mr Dean, 'made a false report of me
alleging that I talked about him & threatened him on Sunday last
[16 October]'. And on 26 October came further disillusionment:
'The anniversary of our discovery [of the Northwest Passage] our
people kept up [that is, celebrated], but no encouragement here,
rather the reverse (jealousy); 2 of our men is now under punishment for it'. In contrast to this reaction to the overindulgence of
the 'Investigators', Ford noted that on 5 November, Guy Fawkes'
Day, 'Altho' a great number drunk no notice is taken of it but our
men are still under punishment. The 1 Lieut [Mecham] told
Macdonald he would take care he did not keep up another
"Norwest Day"'.

As some compensation, on 18 November the three warrant
officers were allocated a separate mess cabin (rather than just a
screened-off area). However, this was soon followed by a further
irritation. On 8 January 1854, the warrant officers' steward:

> was ordered out in the forenoon to exercise so that we shall have
> no one to get our meals for us. He is ordered to be out from
> 9 o'clock to 11 in forenoon & all the afternoon (whilst the
> gunroom steward, Anderson, never goes out at all, besides others
> of this ship's company).

Ford recorded the last of his complaints about the treatment on
board *Resolute*, concerning sleeping quarters and illumination, on
18 February 1854:

> The hold where we sleep is quite unhealthy as there is a dog kept
> continually down there, evacuating about under our hammocks

so that if we step out we step in that, & there has been a dead dog laying up stinking until a few days since.

As to illumination:

The capn gets 2 gall. of oil & 14 candles per week, the gunroom whale oil they require & the carpenter burns candles continually, whilst we can scarcely get enough to sit & get our meals by altho' out 6 hours a day & to bed at between 8 & 9.

It must have been some consolation to Ford that on St Patrick's day Captain Kellett (an Irishman) sent him a bottle of brandy.

Given the situation of the 'Investigators', and the fact that the rescuing ships were still in considerable potential danger, these criticisms may seem petty, the complaints of a warrant officer jealously trying to protect his privileges. But to Ford, at the time, these irritations clearly loomed very large. The real significance of his comments is that complaints are recorded nowhere else in the journals of the voyage, and it is important that the historian should be aware that these very human tensions existed on the wintering ships.

As indicated earlier, on Belcher's orders, Kellett was forced, reluctantly, to abandon his two vessels, although they were completely seaworthy, and to fall back by sledge on Beechey Island. Thus Ford was one of a party of twenty-three, led by Lieutenant William Haswell, which left *Resolute* with two sledges on 10 April. They reached *North Star* at Beechey Island on the 23 April, to be greeted warmly by the crew of that ship: 'In this ship we have a different reception to the *Resolute* as every one seems to try to assist and give us something what we stand most in need of'.

As WITH ALL the Royal Navy's Arctic expeditions, every attempt was made to augment the rations by means of hunting, and it is clear that Ford was one of the more avid, diligent and successful hunters on board *Investigator*. On 25 August 1851, on northwestern Banks Island, after Dr Armstrong, Ford and the bosun had fired at a musk ox and missed, Ford pursued it for about fourteen miles before reluctantly abandoning the chase—he found out the hard way that although usually appearing stolid and slow-moving musk oxen can run fast and far if necessary. On 19 January 1852, in the dark of the winter night at Mercy Bay, Ford spotted and chased two caribou, but lost them in the darkness and drifting snow. But on 28 January his persistence was rewarded when he not only shot a caribou weighing 87 lbs but, as previously mentioned, was congratulated by the captain and given a glass of wine, since this was the first caribou shot that winter. Of course Ford was not entirely motivated by altruism: small game (ptarmigan, hares, ducks, and so forth) belonged to the hunter who shot it (usually sharing it with his mess). Large game (caribou and musk ox) went into the common 'larder' although the head and 'pluck' (heart, liver, kidneys) were retained by the hunter.

That the bag from hunting became an important addition to a successful hunter's food intake may be surmised from Ford's lament on 22 April 1852 (at Mercy Bay):

> This is the place to feel the want of food. I feel sometimes [so] hungry that even when my belly is full I want more, which is through not being substantial food to keep up the body, as when I say 'belly full' it's only with tea or soup which we make in boiling our venison, not much better than water. It's here I have felt hungry & would turn from nothing that can be eaten.

As regards the importance of the large game to the common larder, in mid-May 1852 venison (caribou meat) was being served on three days per week, at a rate of 1 lb of venison in lieu of $\frac{1}{2}$ lb preserved meat per day. This would have contributed to the prevention of scurvy, as it was much more beneficial than the normal diet of salt meat and hardtack. During the first wintering, in Prince of Wales Strait, the bulk of the meat delivered to the ship was musk ox meat (the five animals killed by hunters from *Investigator* were shot during this first winter), hares and ptarmigan. By contrast, during the second wintering (at Mercy Bay) no musk oxen were killed and the bulk of the fresh meat came from caribou, hare and ptarmigan.

Table 1 reveals the significant contribution which George Ford made to the ship's total bag. He had reason to be proud of having killed one of the four polar bears shot, and five out of fifty-nine caribou. Even after Ford and his companions had hiked across

TABLE 1 George Ford's contribution to the game bag

	Bears	Musk oxen	Caribou	Hares	Foxes	Ptarmigan	Ducks	Geese	Eiders	Other birds
Victoria and Banks Islands (1850–52)										
Ship's bag	4	5	59	83	10	218	9	8	12	17
Ford's bag	1	1	5	4	1	2	2	4	10	
Melville Island (1853)										
Ship's bag	29		17	9		34	2	8	3	9
Ford's bag	2		2			13	1	8		7

The information for this table was taken from Ford's journal.

M'Clure Strait to take refuge aboard *Resolute* at Dealy Island, he continued to hunt. He was not involved in any of the musk ox hunts which, both at Dealy Island and later, off the southeast coast of Melville Island, supplemented the larder considerably, but he was still able to contribute two out of a minimum of seventeen caribou shot and thirteen out of thirty-four ptarmigan. It should be noted that Table 1 is based on the information contained in Ford's journal and may not be complete, especially with regard to the bag on Melville Island in the summer and fall of 1853, when hunting parties went ashore from both *Resolute* and *Intrepid*; Ford may not have been able to keep an accurate tally of the bag of the latter ship.

FROM HIS JOURNAL entries it is clear that Ford possessed a scientist's curiosity, despite his limited formal education. On being confronted with the striking phenomenon of the Smoking Hills on the west side of Franklin Bay, where plumes of smoke constantly billow from a number of spots in the coastal cliffs, on 5 September 1850 Ford noted: 'Afternoon discovered a volcano close to the water on fire, somewhere about the middle of the bay from which I obtained some of the lava'. The spontaneous combustion is in fact the result of oxidation of very fine-grained pyrite and organics, encouraged by periodic slumps and minor landslides, which continually expose new combustible material.[20] Nonetheless, Ford's guess that the phenomenon was somehow due to volcanic activity is certainly understandable.

On the north coast of Banks Island Ford was greatly intrigued by the fossil trees found there in the Beaufort Formation. On 20 August 1851 he noted:

> Mr Sainsbury discovered on shore a small mountain with trees covered in sand on its summit, about 300 ft high, some petrified into stone. We got one piece 6' 10" long, mean girth 3' 8". From what we can see & judge the trees must have grown there at some time & if so the climate must have been more temperate, as we have never seen within this Polar Sea a tree or branch 3 inches above ground. It would be impossible for anything to grow here.

Next day he investigated further: 'Evening I went on shore to the Mountain of Petrified Wood & collected a few specimens of it. I found large trees (some about 18 inches in diameter) & branches in regular layers on the top of the hills or mountains, like a stratified rock'. Fossil wood of two distinct ages is found in this area of Banks Island.[21] The petrified material is from the Iceberg Bay Formation of the Eocene Age (*c.* 45–60 million years), while fresher, un-petrified material is found in the Beaufort Formation, of Miocene age (10–20 million years). In either case, Ford's deduction that the climate was substantially milder than at present is well founded. Given its intriguing nature, it comes as no surprise that all three of the published accounts of the expedition also comment (at varying length) on this fossil wood.

Like most hunters Ford was a keen observer of the game he pursued. On 30 October 1850, when he helped in bringing aboard the five musk oxen (*Ovibos moschatus*) shot on Victoria Island, he noted: 'They are beautiful animals; . . . their hair upwards of 2 ft long; their shape is very much like the bison's, short legs & heavy fore quarters & small behind. The horns fall over the head & turn up out from the side of the head like a hook'. His accurate description of the king eider drake (*Somateria spectabilis*) (based on five he shot on Princess Royal Island on 13 June 1851) is as follows: 'handsome with a white breast, green head & on the beak a large red knob'.

Ford did make one important pioneer contribution, apparently on his own initiative. During both the winterings covered by his journal, at the beginning of every month he drilled holes in the first-year sea ice and measured its thickness. He appears to have drilled several holes and averaged the results. The recorded ice thicknesses are presented in Table 2. These are the earliest known measurements of the growth of sea ice from the Canadian Arctic, and possibly from any part of the Arctic.

FORD CAME IN contact with Inuit on only a few occasions during the voyage, all on the mainland coast in the summer of 1850, but his descriptions of these encounters are quite lively, informative and generally sympathetic. Here, for example, is his description of the first, a short distance east of Point Barrow, on 8 August 1850:

In the afternoon we were visited by several Esquimaux in their oomiaks (boats of skin). They appeared very friendly & willing to barter with their skins. Their token of friendship is extending

TABLE 2 George Ford's sea ice measurements[a]

	Nov	Dec	Jan	Feb	Mar	Apr	May	June	July
Princess Royal Island (1850–51)	–	2'6"	3'6"	4'9"	5'8"	6'5"	6'11"	7'0"[b]	4'9"[b]
Mercy Bay (1851–52)	1'6"	2'5"	3'8"	4'8"	5'5½"	6'4"	6'8½"	6'10"	–[c]

a Measurements usually taken on the first day of the month, but sometimes later; the latest was on 4 January 1851.
b Ice very rotten.
c No data; journal discontinued on 8 June.

both arms to about 45 degrees from a perpendicular & their manner of salutation is to rub noses, that is rub their nose against yours. In the lips of the lower jaw the men have two holes, one each side below the corner of the mouth, where they carry two ornaments, something like the stud of a shirt worn in England, one part against the gums and the other outside. Their women has the chin tattooed but no other mark. Therefore the men are easy distinguished from the women as their dress is nearly alike. They have a deer skin frock something like a sailor's with a hood to it come over the head as there was no other head cover. They have a pair of breeches of deer skin & moccasins. They wear two frocks & breeches each, the one next to the skin with the fur or hair inside & the outside with the fur out ... [We] gave the natives several presents, but no news of our missing countrymen. We were very fortunate to have Mr Miertsching, the interpreter on board, who understood the Esquimaux well.

ON SEVERAL OCCASIONS Ford commented upon amusing incidents which the other journalists either did not observe, or felt did not merit being recorded. Thus while *Investigator* was running down the Channel to Plymouth, on 14 January 1850:

In the morning began to blow heavily. We reefed topsails; in so doing a man fell from the main top on the keel of the dingy that was turned bottom-up in the pinnace. He got up, rubbed his behind & went to work unhurt, that being, I believe the third time he has fallen from aloft.

On 13 July 1850, in the North Pacific:

About 6 o'clock one of the new men on going aft to relieve the man at the wheel fell through Captain's skylight but luckily did not injure himself. Captain in his cot awakened frightened: 'Hello. What's the matter? What are you doing here?' Man also frightened, not knowing where he is, being half asleep when he fell: 'Going aft to the wheel, Sir'. Captain: 'Stupid fellow, to fall down here'. Man shaking. Walked away, always giving the skylight plenty of room after.

Over a year later, on 6 August 1851, when the ship was drifting with the ice in the northern part of Prince of Wales Strait, the captain was involved in another amusing incident recorded by Ford:

> Our Captain, whilst walking the quarter deck, observed to the Officer of the Watch that he felt he heard a grinding noise & felt the ship shake. Thinking a piece of heavy ice was forcing itself under our bottom, this officer & several others immediately began to look round the ship in order to ascertain from whence the noise proceeded, when behold, on looking on the port sponson there lay our worthy son of Vulcan fast wrapped in the arms of Morpheus, snoring, which proved the source of all the consternation. It made a fine joke for Jack to see his officers deceived in such a manner.

Later that month, on 25 August, off the north coast of Banks Island Ford reported a hunting accident which, while quite serious, could easily have been much worse, and had an amusing side to it:

> In the meantime our boatswain saw another [musk ox] & fired to draw my attention, being a long way off, & on reloading, having put in the powder & rested the muzzle of the musket against his belly whilst he was getting out a ball and shot, the gun went off & blew all his trowsers & all his cloths from the lower part of his belly & burned him very much, but luckily nothing more, as had the ramrod or shot been in the gun, it must have killed him. He is now confined to his bed in great pain.

THROUGH THE ENTRIES in his journal we learn something of Ford's character and personal life. For example, his love of music and the satisfaction and solace he derived from his flute emerge strongly from his journal. 'In the evening had a tune on the flute to pass the dull time away' is the first reference to this important aspect of Ford's life, on 29 January 1850, just a week after sailing from England. On occasion (as in the evening of 27 June 1851) he joined forces with Miertsching (guitar) and the sergeant of marines (octave, or piccolo) for a musical evening.

Another recurring, indeed continual, theme in Ford's journal is his love for his young wife Mary. As mentioned, they had been married less than five months before *Investigator* sailed from England. References to his thoughts turning to his young wife recur frequently throughout the voyage.

And finally Ford was sustained by his deep Christian faith. Regular readings from the Bible, and from a range of 'inspirational' works (which he commonly lists in detail in his journal) definitely helped him to survive the physical and mental hardships of four Arctic winterings and the abandonment of two ships in the ice.

NORTH STAR REACHED the Thames early in October 1854. On 8 October, along with all the other members of *Investigator*'s crew, Ford was ordered to report to HMS *Waterloo* at Sheerness, to act as a possible witness in the obligatory court-martial of Captain M'Clure for abandoning his ship. The court-martial ruled that M'Clure, his officers and men were all fully acquitted and that they deserved the highest commendations.[22]

Ford's subsequent appointments (as carpenter) were to: HMS *St Vincent* (Portsmouth), from 22 October 1854 until 30 January 1855; *Hogue* from 1 February 1855 until 23 May 1856; *Royal William* from 24 May 1856 until 2 June 1856; *St Vincent* again from 3 June 1856 until 30 June 1857; and *Ganges* from 1 July 1857 until 15 May 1861.[23]

The captain of the *Ganges*, James Fulford, noted that Ford:

> ... has conducted himself with sobriety and attention and always obedient to command. A most valuable officer, full of resources, and has made himself most useful in the ship, particularly at Vancouver Island, in planning and building stores and fitting up the hospital there, etc., besides being most efficient in every way in the ship. Mr Ford is the inventor of a most capital plan of a hawse plug which has been approved by the Admiralty and used with great success in the *Ganges*.[24]

For several years thereafter Ford was stationed at Portsmouth, having 'the supervision of all the repairs & fittings for the maintenance of the [steam] reserve & the management of the accounts connected therewith'. In this capacity he was stationed on board HMS *Formidable*, from 16 to 21 May 1861, HMS *Illustrious*, from 22 May to 15 July 1861, and HMS *Asia*, from 16 July 1861 to 26 July 1870.[25] At that time he retired on pension, largely due to poor health. On 19 December 1870 he wrote to the Secretary of the Admiralty, requesting some medical compensation:

> I most respectfully beg to forward copies of 2 certificates from medical gentlemen who attended me in a recent severe attack of paralysis, and to state that I have suffered very much from defective vision and general shock to my system since accompanying Captain W. C. Chamberlain (who could testify to the accuracy of my statement) at the trial of Steam Launch No. 7 at the end of September or beginning of October 1868 when it was blowing a very severe gale of wind, and I was for some hours exposed to the heavy wash of the seas, and as that circumstance combined with long and hard previous sea service in all parts of the world including $4\frac{1}{2}$ years in the North Pole under Sir R. MacClure has according to medical testimony been the chief cause of my present helpless condition; I would humbly submit my case for their Lordships favorable consideration with a view to their being pleased to grant me some remuneration and thus assist me in bearing the great and continual expense to which I am now part for medical and other attendance as I am quite unable to do the least thing for myself.[26]

On 27 December he received a reply from his former shipmate Dr Alexander Armstrong, now Director-General, with orders to present himself to the Royal Naval Hospital 'for resurvey'. The outcome of this examination is not known.

Ford died on 14 January 1877 at his home, 10 Brougham Road, Southsea. His estate was valued (on 2 February 1877) at £485 and 9 shillings (plus household goods worth £97 and 15 shillings). Soon afterwards his widow wrote to Dr Armstrong, requesting that she might be awarded 'the special instead of an ordinary pension', in the light of the fact that Ford had died due to 'extraordinary exposure' on duty, citing the hernias received in the Arctic and the reduced vision and paralysis resulting from his experience on board Steam Launch No. 7. On 8 March 1877 she was granted a pension of £25 per annum, backdated to 15 January. She herself died on 20 January 1909.[27]

GEORGE FORD'S JOURNAL of his participation in the Arctic voyage of HMS *Investigator* in 1850–54 represents an important contribution to the literature on the Royal Navy's search for the missing Franklin expedition. Since Ford's perspective is that of a warrant officer the picture which emerges of the events and conditions of the expedition is refreshingly different from that portrayed by existing published journals (namely those of officers, or of participants of approximately equivalent status). For example, we see a marked deterioration in Ford's opinion of Captain Robert M'Clure over time, in which the critical event appears to have been M'Clure's unwarranted and unfair censuring of Ford for his refusal to volunteer to remain with the ship in the spring of 1853. We are also treated to a warrant officer's view of the reception of the 'refugees' from *Investigator* by the complement of the host vessel, *Resolute*. Ford is extremely critical of the accommodations and living conditions with which he and the other warrant officers were provided. While this may appear petty, given the circumstances, it is enlightening (although not entirely surprising) to learn that such tensions arose between the two ships' companies.

Ford's journal probably reveals much more about the journalist than do any of the contemporary officers' journals from the Franklin search. We are presented with a picture of a man with a strong sense of humour; an avid hunter; a man with an enquiring scientific mind; a musician who derived considerable pleasure and solace from his flute; a man of deep religious convictions whose faith provided him with even greater solace; and a man who was sustained by his deep love for his wife. As one of the minor, yet crucial players in the drama of the Franklin search, here is a man who deserves to be better known.

PART

Encounters and
Transformations

The Hegemony of Laughter

Purea's Theatre

GREG DENING

P OWER AND LAUGHTER have an uneasy relationship. A history of
the fool would show that. But laughter is more subversive than
the assuaging double-plays of a fool. Laughter in the total institution of a British eighteenth-century naval vessel, the *Bounty* say,
was the way oppressed sailors maintained freedom and drew a
boundary around their personal space. The mocking laughter
of Polynesian islanders at the cultural absurdities of intruding
Strangers was a first step to resistance, and in a post-colonial world,
truly revolutionary. But laughter is an instrument of power, too.
Laughter distracts attention from more terrible things being done.
Laughter denies the integrity of other experiences. Laughter dis-
claims obligations to suffer differences. Laughter excuses amorality.
Laughter sets the stage for empire. Perhaps the story that follows is
too slight to bear such a judgement. Think of it as just a first step in
a history of the hegemony of laughter in the Pacific. Perhaps it
would be more convincing if it had more about cannibal jokes,
Kodak hula dances, market-place exhibitions of savages, mock
battles, international expositions, tricks on natives, the litter of
civilisations—and last laughs. They will have to wait.

PERHAPS ACROSS TIMES, across cultures, across genders the person is inaccessible. Perhaps it is only the *persona*, the mask, attributed to an individual by others that is accessible. That certainly is the case for Airoreatua i Ahurai i Farepua—'fortunately known also, and more commonly as Purea', the historian of James Cook's voyages, J. C. Beaglehole, wrote.[1] Beaglehole probably should have written, more commonly known as 'Oberea', 'Obadiah', 'Obariea', 'Obareea' as her English contemporaries called her. Indeed, 'Queen' Oberea —although it is difficult to write into the orthography of the word 'Queen' the satire and laughter that are resonant in it.

Anyway, the mask that is fitted to Purea's person comes to us from a variety of visitors to and observers of her native Tahiti. Samuel Wallis, Tahiti's 'discoverer', was the first to call her 'Queen'.[2] But an English public only saw Wallis's representations of her through the eyes of the erudite but naive Dr John Hawkesworth, and he had Wallis refer to Purea as 'my princess'.[3] That is when the laughing began. No one in the general public at the time would have seen the journal of the Master of the *Dolphin*, George Robertson. It was not published until 1948.[4] He, too, thought that Purea was 'Queen', but had some problems attaching this cross-cultural concept to the political relationships he saw, but only dimly understood.

By the time James Cook arrived in Tahiti, Purea obviously was not 'Queen' at all, though she had a presence that was a little mystifying. His companion in the Great Cabin of the *Endeavour*, Joseph Banks, had come prepared to liaise with 'Queen Oberea', but was a little disappointed at her large stature and age, and what he saw as her passing or past beauty. He quarrelled, near to duelling, with Jonathan Monkhouse over their shared sexual fancies. But while he slept naked, or near naked, with Purea in her canoe, he probably did not 'sleep' with her. On that famous night, which was a gift to London satirists, he had his breeches, shirt and waistcoat 'with silver frogs' stolen.[5] Banks's adventures with Purea, reported again by Dr Hawkesworth, made the English laugh and laugh, not just at Banks but at the absurdity of the idea that savages could be 'queens'.

By the time William Bligh, then the *Bounty* mutineers, and then Bligh again, came to Tahiti, and the Tahitian polity had come under the gaze of more direct observers such as James Morrison, Purea was dead. Morrison could see how her ambitions for her son, Teri'irere, had been foiled by the very families who came to power by the mutineers' muskets. Purea for Morrison was history, and history is, as we all know, as good a mask as any. 'Pbooraya', wrote Morrison, had no other child but Teri'irere, 'having killd all that came before him'. She was not so much 'queen' for Morrison, as *arioi* and bound by the rules of that exotic group to kill their children, or 'come out'.[6]

BEFORE PUREA WAS made history, though, she was made theatre. A remarkable trio made her so: John O'Keeffe, Irish playwright; John Webber, painter on Cook's third voyage; Philippe de Loutherbourg, stage designer extraordinaire. They combined to put 'Oberea' on the Covent Garden stage for the 1785 Christmas pantomime: 'Omai, or a Trip round the World'. Purea had long been an object of derision as 'queen'. Now the London Christmas audiences, including George III, could 'boo' her as sorceress, seeking to thwart the lovers Omai and Londina (the daughter of Britannia) in their attempt to become 'King' and 'Queen' of Tahiti.[7]

Purea became history again at the hands of a far more competent historian than James Morrison, Henry Adams. Disturbed greatly at his wife's suicide, thinking to leave all behind for a time, Adams went to the South Seas, much like Robert Louis Stevenson, with his artist friend, John La Farge. Bored by Tahiti, dismayed by Paul Gauguin whom they encountered there, in their last days they met up with a remarkably talkative old woman, Arii Taimai. She was a descendant of Purea's family. She had lived most of her life in the courts of Tahiti's kings and queens and was wrapped around with their webs of intrigue. Adams puts into her mouth words patently his own, but which, of all the things said about Purea, have become the most remembered: 'If a family must be ruined by a woman, perhaps it may as well be ruined thoroughly and brilliantly by a woman who makes it famous'.[8]

SO PUREA WAS fitted for her first mask, 13 July 1767. Well, probably 13 July. Wallis, grievously ill all through his stay at Matavai on Tahiti, with scurvy probably, but also with something 'paralytic', possibly arthritis, was amiss on details. According to Robertson it was a little later. It was, in any case, some three weeks after the terrible beginnings of Tahitian–English relations. The *Dolphin* had crept around the eastern and northern coast of Tahiti, its people looking for an anchorage. For two days they had looked in vain. Their encounters with the islanders had already been violent. The 'Dolphins' had killed some with their muskets when their large canoes threatened to overrun the launch in which the 'Dolphins' were making soundings, in order to find an anchorage. There were young girls on the beach, too, 'with their coats turnd up' doing a 'thousand antick tricks'. Most of the crew were deathly ill with scurvy. They did not know if they would make the thousands of miles still to go to Tinian unless they got refreshment. Then Matavai, in the lee of the trades and behind the reef, seemed providential. Its river split the point, later to be called Point Venus. The fright of running aground—but fortunately not piercing their experimental copper sheathing—only added to their worries. Their anxieties grew with the unfathomable behaviour of the islanders. Firstly, women on the prows of the canoes began performing their 'tricks'. The 'Dolphins' were 'gigling, some laughing and gaping at the wanton positions of the women'.[9] Then a shower of pebbles made them presume it was all an ambush and they fired their cannons full of grape. 'It would require the pen of Milton to describe', Robertson reported.[10] How many Tahitians were killed it is impossible to know. A strange silence descended on everybody about it. Joseph Banks said that when they tried to discover how many were killed, the Tahitians would only say, ten, twenty, thirty on their fingers, then some word they used for flocks of birds or shoals of fish, hundreds and hundreds.[11] Only once is it referred to in the *Dolphin's* various logs. An old woman, dressed in mourning, Robertson reported—mistaking the red *tapa* banyan cloth of the socially élite and the *arioi* for mourning costume—said that her three sons and her husband had been killed. She would accept no gifts. Indeed, she reversed the Englishmen's expectations, insisting that she not be given something by the English, but that she sacrifice something to them, a hog.[12] That was the *Maohi* way. The violent had to be assuaged in some way by sacrifice.

Purea had not been at Matavai on that terrible day. She came from her home at Papara on the other side of the island. She had come from the south by the western coast in her canoe. Parkinson made a drawing of this or a later canoe,[13] the one Banks would sleep in. Purea would use it as lodging in her travels. The 'Dolphins' had seen the flotilla arrive on 8–9 July, but did not realise that it had been Purea's entourage.

One of that entourage came aboard the *Dolphin* almost immediately. He was clearly assessing the lie of the land. 'Jonathan', the Dolphins called him. Tupaia was his real name. From the start he seemed more observant than any of the other islanders. He was very curious about everything on board the ship. He learned things by touching and handling, sometimes the hard way: that teapots held hot water, for example. That the Strangers had vessels capable of boiling water stirred the imaginations of the *Maohi*. A miniature portrait of a lady sent him into raptures, Wallis remarked.[14] Sensing that Tupaia was of superior rank, even a priest, the officers of the *Dolphin* fussed over him. They sat him down to dinner—a large dinner: broth of fowl, roast fowl, roast pork, roast yams, plantain, bananas, soft bread, biscuit apple pudding, apple pie, and a cup of tea. Tupaia mimicked the etiquette and was embarrassed when he got things wrong, like putting his fingers in the butter, or, as they invited, or rather, incited him to do, wiping his mouth on the tablecloth since he did not have a pocket handkerchief such as they used. Indeed he was a point of dispute among the officers, as some thought that savage's bad manners should not be tolerated.[15]

It was a brief visit, and his only one to the *Dolphin*, but it was an important one. They decked him out in a complete suit of clothing before he left and in this garb he went back to the beach where he delighted a large crowd in telling them what he had seen. Most importantly, he went back to Purea. Tupaia was Purea's advisor. 'Bedfellow', 'lover', 'companion' have been other descriptions. Tupaia, of course, became almost as famous as Purea, among scholars anyway. It was he who composed a map of the Tahitians' knowledge of the islands around them. Its extensiveness amazed James Cook and everybody since. It was he, too, about whom Banks had mused:

The Captn refuses to take him on his own account, in my opinion sensibly enough, the goverment will never in all human probability take any notice of him; I therefore have resolvd to take him. Thank heaven I had a sufficiency and I do not know why I may not keep him as a curiosity, as well as some of my neighbours do lions and tygers at a larger expence than he will probably ever put me to; the amusement I shall have in his future conversation and the benefit he will be of to this ship, as well as what he may be if anouther should be sent into these seas, will I think fully repay me.[16]

So Tupaia would go with the *Endeavour*. But he would die of fever in Batavia.

Tupaia was a priest of the island of Raiatea. He was a priest of the god 'Oro. 'Oro was the god of war and sacrifice. He had come to Raiatea on a rainbow and in the years just prior to the coming of the English 'Oro had begun to stir outside Raiatea. His place of worship was called Taputapuatea, 'Sacrifices from Abroad'. He was a fashionable god. The rituals of his worship were all about establishment, title and sovereignty. Purea was to learn of them and become involved in their metaphors of politics under the tuition of Tupaia. By the time the story of these events, begun by the *Dolphin's* arrival, were ended in Tahiti with the establishment of the Pomare dynasty as the 'kings' and 'queens' of Tahiti, there would be four Taputapuatea on Tahiti. They each would be placed on some headland opposite some break in the reef. Canoes bearing sacrifices would beach on the headland before the seaward pyramid of stone that was the depository of the bones, especially of the skulls, of the sacrifices. Between the seaward part of the temple and the landward section where the sacred treasures of 'Oro were kept, and the post-sacrificial feasts were held, there was a stepping stone. On this in-between stone, the *ari'i* who held the title of Taputapuatea would stand while sacrifices were made to him. This was where he would stand when he was invested with the insignia of his titles.[17]

The most important insignia of title was the feathered *maro*, red or yellow, *ura* or *tea*. These wraps were sewn with clusters of feathers representing sacrifices past. These feathered *maro* were the metaphors of *Maohi* politics. There were two of them, and, in all likelihood by historical surmise, with the coming of the *Dolphin*, there was about to be a third. They were the metaphor of politics but not necessarily the icon of power. The right to wear the *maro ura* or *tea* came from birth, and was managed by marriage. The power to rule was less ceremonial and a more manipulative balance of physical force and ceremonial title.[18]

Just a few years before the arrival of the *Dolphin*, Purea had made a dramatic entrance into these power plays and these metaphors of politics. A little time before 1767, perhaps only two years or eighteen months, she gave birth to her son Teri'irere. He was born of her marriage with Amo, although Amo need not have been her son's genitor. Purea must have been between thirty-five and forty years of age when Teri'irere was born. So he seems to have been a late arrival. He was her 'first-born', but not necessarily the first child born of her.[19] There are claims that there were nine other children. One cannot imagine that they came after Teri'irere. Perhaps they were the children disposed of when she was *arioi*, as Morrison suggested. The 'Dolphins' believed that she had no children at all, because her breasts were not as pendulous as other women of her age.[20]

We know that Amo and Purea's 'first-born' was an extremely valuable political asset. Purea, by being the sister of the chief of Fa'a'a, named Te Pau i Ahurai, and with other family connections, was among the highest ranked of *Maohi* women. Amo's name means 'Winker'. He was dubbed this after some characteristic of his son. Tevahitua i Patea, he would have been called more ceremonially. He was the tribal chief of Papara. When Amo's and Purea's lines and titles came together in Teri'irere, the boy was indeed a jewel in anyone's dream crown. From the *marae* (or sacred space) Taputa ara'i, he held the title Tui te ra'i i Taputauare'i; from To'orai, Aromaiterai i outa rau ma To'ora'i. In token of that Amo and Purea began to build at Papara the *marae* Mahaiatea, the largest stone structure in all Tahiti, an appropriate repository for what Purea and Amo clearly saw as the most significant *maro ura* of all, a symbol of the changed times the *Maohi* were about to experience. By that, Teri'irere would have the title Teri'irere i Mahaiatea.[21]

Tupaia came back to the beach at Matavai from the *Dolphin* clad in his suit of clothes. He persuaded Purea that she should go aboard

the *Dolphin* herself. This she did the next day, accompanied by six
men of 'superior rank', or so the 'Dolphins' thought. From the first
sight of Purea, the 'Dolphins' never had much doubt that she was
'Queen'. 'Well made', 'Muscular', 'very lusty', '5'10"' were some of
the phrases used about her. She 'had a majestic look and spoke with
authority and dignity to islanders who seem'd to be very submissive
to her', wrote Wallis.[22] Hawkesworth in his editing translated this
observation of the sailors into an 'easy freedom that always distinguishes conscious superiority and habitual command'.[23] Perhaps
they were trying to catch those characteristics that Neil Gunson has
described as those of 'Female Headmen', a sense that political
power and authority was bi-gendered.[24] Purea did, admiringly, or
so Robertson said, finger his bare legs and thigh and hairy chest and
tried to test his and her strength by picking him up. But Robertson,
not to be outdone in macho display, picked up her 200 lbs in one
arm and carried her around the cabin. She was without trinkets and
jewellery, they said, although they noted that she had taken out the
pearls in her ears to come aboard. Maybe the strangers' interest in
pearls had been reported to her and she was not going to give too
much currency to them. She wore 'petecoats' of white and yellow
and a gown of red. Robertson, thinking that they had killed her
husband, the 'King', a few weeks before, thought she was dressed in
mourning.[25]

Purea brought with her gifts of food enough to supply the ship
for two days. She was, they said, more curious than all the rest at
what she saw. The chefs' bright copper cooking pots and spit
especially fascinated her. She would not eat with them and left the
mess while her male attendants ate with the officers. They do not say
whether she donned the blue mantle and ribbands they gave her.
Wallis saw her back to the beach in his barge. On the beach she
gathered a large crowd seated in a ring around her. To them she made
a long speech which was heard without a whisper. The 'Dolphins'
could not know, of course, what she said, but she seemed at one
moment to be designating the captain and the officers as the
'princaple' people.

We, too, have to wonder what Purea said. There were plenty of
times in these first years when such a crowd would entertain
themselves with mimes of the gauche behaviour of the intruding
Strangers. This occasion on the beach with Purea seemed to have

been more serious than that. Perhaps it was the first occasion in which a person of authority could interpret to them what had happened. They surely needed some exegesis of it all. The English texts which we have are unlikely to dwell on the destruction and killings of the first days, although Robertson's fairly constant references to what he saw as signs of mourning suggest that there was more reaction than he was likely to reveal. One has to read between the lines. For example, each of the texts refers to lines of canoes flying white, red, yellow and, they say, blue streamers sailing out to the break in the reef to the west of where the *Dolphin* was anchored, and performing some ceremony there. The opening in the reef to the west was probably that opposite the *marae* which Robertson called 'Morai Point'. It would have been the site, Tarahoi, where the Taputapuatea of 'Oro would be established to hold the *maro ura* of the Pomares. There is a ceremony, described by Teuira Henry as occurring at Tarahoi, called *Raumatavehi*, by which a land destroyed by an enemy was made inhabitable again.[26] Henry called it a scapegoating ritual, Douglas Oliver calls it *ahuatai*.[27] Evil associated objects, and, if other Polynesian cultures such as the Marquesas can be cited, sometimes the dead were sent out to sea in open canoes through sacred passages in the reef. Who knows? Perhaps some of the gifts and trade goods, the musket- and cannon-balls, were sent back to the sea from which they came. Perhaps the silence about the destruction and the killings was a silence of presumption that retribution was at hand.

Perhaps Purea, now that she had performed some mediation between the islanders and the Strangers, was in a position to explain something of what happened the day after the killings. That day the Strangers had come ashore, erected a large pole and left a red streamer hanging from it. They had performed some rituals—or were they dances? No matter, the *Maohi* recognised the structured performances as something significant. Then the Strangers returned to their 'floating island'. The *Maohi* treated this streamer with all the care with which they treated red *tapu* things. They could not have known that by these ceremonies they had become possessions of His Majesty, King George III. They sent out an old man, perhaps a priest, to tell the Strangers how they understood it. He stood in a canoe, gesturing and chanting, making speech, offering in a plantain branch scapegoat sacrifices and signs of peace, or at least of settlement. Again, it is impossible to know for certain what it is that he was saying, but it is a reasonable guess that he interpreted the act of possession as a gesture of peace on the part of the Strangers, even of retribution for those killed. When he felt that he had explained to the Strangers how he understood it, he returned to the flag and again with gestures of reverence and sacrifice took it down and away. Next day the *Maohi* paraded the flag and processed with it towards 'Morai Point', Tarahoi, where there was a large collection of canoes, at least sixty of them, because that is how many the English later said they destroyed. The 'Dolphins' did not let the procession reach Tarahoi. They dispersed it with cannon shot which bounced over the landscape around 'One Tree Hill'. Then they landed and destroyed the canoes.

We do not know what happened to the flag immediately. Again it would be a fair guess to say that it was probably taken across to Papara and given to Amo and Purea. Perhaps the procession was the beginning of that movement. The next we hear of the flag is that James Cook sees it, then a little later William Bligh draws it as part of the *maro ura* which would have been invested on Amo and Purea's son, Teri'irere at the *marae* Mahaiatea.[28] This *maro ura*, with the red bunting of possession sewn into it, is the most remarkable document of the beginnings of these encounters between the English and the *Maohi*. We must necessarily return to it.

Purea does not appear at Matavai till at least a week after the killings and acts of possession. She has no title to be at Matavai, but at Ha'apape, whose boundaries adjoin the stream that divides Point Venus, she does. Her brother was married into the chiefly family there. The 'Dolphins' see her first not on board ship, but in a large house at Ha'apape which they call her 'palace'. They were mightily impressed by the 'palace'. Wallis has a plan of it in his log. He says it was 300 feet × 37 feet (Robertson, measuring it with his broadsword which might or might not be more accurate, says it was 320 feet × 37 feet). Some have said it was the *arioi* lodge *Atita* (Agitation). Others have said it was the *fare hau*, or council house, of the district.[29]

HARRISON, THE GUNNER, who was in charge of the provisioning trade that had been conducted on the beach all these days, and

Richard Pickersgill, the midshipman, were the first to see the 'palace', and, for that matter, Purea. They came upon the 'palace' filled with a thousand people of the highest rank. Although the accounts do not say it specifically, the people seemed to be both male and female. They were seated in an orderly fashion in a ring about Purea, who herself was seated on matting of the most elaborate sort. She had 'two very handsom Young ladys standing by her'. The assembly was being served a meal. The two young women served the food, which was cooked in the small houses around and was brought to them by 'servants'. Those served food would 'turn to the Sun', mutter some words and throw a little of their food aside. The assembly seemed to be served according to some ranking. When all had eaten, dishes with food of another sort were brought in. Purea invited Pickersgill and Harrison to eat with her, but they, for whatever reason, declined and enjoyed some fruit instead. Then the two young women began to feed Purea by turns, always from the right and with the right hand, always washing their hand in a basin of clean water before offering Purea another mouthful. Purea never touched her food with her own fingers. When she had eaten, the women then ate their own meal, 'attended by a Great many young Women'—it is that phrase that makes one wonder whether there were also women among the 'Grandes' who dined. Then all the 'servants' ate at some distance from the 'Ring'. The whole meal had been consumed in silence, although 'everyone appear'd cheerful and merry'. They had all carefully cleaned themselves before and after eating.[30]

We do not need to believe that these were the ordinary eating practices of Purea. Restrictions on self-feeding were likely to belong to special occasions. The most likely occasion for parents of the highest rank were in those eighteen months before their first-born child, inevitably of higher rank than them, had the *amo'a*, the 'freeing of the head', rituals performed. It is likely that Teri'irere, Amo and Purea's first-born was in the area, in one of those special houses for infants of the highest title and situated in or near his father's *marae*, Farehoi, at Ha'apape.[31]

Time belongs to those who experience it in their own way. This after all is not 13 July 1767 for the *Maohi*. This is some other date in the rhythm of their individual and cultural lives. It is they who have to adapt new experiences to their own understandings, to their own time. There are two polarities in the ways of explaining how this happens. The one says the adaptations are made in accordance with the structures of the mind already in place. In this view, the cultural mind accommodates experience to a template. The other says that human understanding is more universal than that and is dominated by more practical concerns of greed and power, anger and fear. In history, the confidence born of thinking that the historian knows the end of the story breeds a tonal character into the narrative. In the case of Purea, there is a tonal sense of glee in her presumed failure. There is a certain sense that Purea's history is of the 'monstrous regiment of women' sort. Purea's politics become the machinations of an ambitious woman, out of place, a 'hooty-tooty queen', the satirical verses will say, when Cook and Banks return home. And remember Henry Adams's account of her. 'Wink, wink', they seem to say as if the disaster that befell her was a consequence of her misplaced aspirations. Well, with a name like Amo in the equation, perhaps one should say 'wink, wink'.

'Wink, wink' seems to be the more politically correct view these days. Somehow to assert that the *Maohi* were seeing things through the filter of their cultural perceptions is considered to belittle them, as if they did not possess the realpolitik to see through the Strangers' behaviour, to see it for what it was, naked aggression and the pursuit of empire. Somehow the constructive cultural responses to a changed environment are seen as a denigration of the purity of a native culture.

Neither polarity works in relation to Purea, it seems to me, and neither of them sits well with our emerging understanding of the historical role of women of high degree. In fact, not many polarities at all sit well in understanding women in *Maohi* society, not *tapu* (sacred) and *noa* (impure), not male and female, not power and authority. Polarities are an outsider's invention. Polarities are like those maps that Pierre Bourdieu speaks of as the metaphor of culture made by outsiders. Insiders do not experience culture as a mapped way of living. Insiders experience culture as a process of practical visions. Insiders experience culture as a merging of all sorts of polarities.[32]

Before the 'Dolphins' left Matavai, they felt sure that they would be missed. Purea especially made them feel that way. The night before they left, 27 July, thousands slept on the beach at Matavai. Purea in the morning made all the *Maohi* retreat to the other side of the river on Point Venus and stayed alone on the black sand beach. She had experienced much that was new to her in these two weeks. She had even seen an eclipse of the sun through a darkened telescope, and saw herself how she could recognise people five miles away through the telescope. She appreciated the linens that were given her and easily accommodated the show of these gifts to the show of honour in wrapping the *Maohi* linen of bark cloth around her visitors. She even tried her hand at writing, catching the significance of these marks on paper if not their meaning. She wanted to sign a treaty, Robertson said, though how such a complex concept was communicated by sign and pidgin, he does not say. Anyway, Wallis pleaded a 'paralytic' hand and the treaty wasn't signed.[33]

Purea was faced with much that was new. She seemed to absorb it well. She mediated all these encounters with novelty to the *Maohi*. She was selective in what impressed her and in knowing their practical applications. Her greatest energy, it seems to me, was expended in merging the historic moment with *Maohi* cultural moments. Who knows how she interpreted the flag of possession or why it was incorporated into the *Maohi* symbols of sovereignty? But it is not impossible to think that she interpreted the valued red *tapu* insignia as a gesture of reconciliation, a buying off of the deaths the Strangers had caused. When the 'Dolphins' were leaving, they reported how Purea wanted them to delay—by 150 days, by fifty days, and then when it was certain that they would go in their own time, by three or four days. There were so many ways in which the events of these weeks had merged into the calendar of *Maohi* lives, that perhaps she was suggesting that they might have a dramatic ending—in an *amo'a* of her son, in an investiture of him at Mahaiatea.

Purea's story—Purea's history—is so coloured by all the delicious ironies of what in another time and another culture would have been called her 'machiavellian' ambitions that it is difficult to make a perhaps more subtle point. But let me try nonetheless. That there was social competitiveness in her actions there can be no doubt. The dynamics of Tahitian politics turned on that social competitiveness, as the kin-congregations of the different *marae* jockeyed for eminence through the whole island. Such competitiveness produced its own lore, its own rhetoric. So the story of Purea's downfall, though it sounds like court gossip, is likely to be roughly true. But not the whole truth. The whole truth is more likely to be that Purea mediated a moment of terrible social crisis for her people as much as used it for the advancement of personal political ambitions.

When James Cook arrived at Matavai in the *Endeavour*, 12 April 1769, it was immediately clear to him that something had changed in Purea's role or that the 'Dolphins' had it wrong when they dubbed her 'Queen'. When he made his famous tour of Tahiti in his launch, he came upon a most dismaying sight at Mahaiatea. He measured the dimensions of this, the largest structure in Tahiti, noted its dishevelled look and reported that it was surrounded by human bones and remains. These were not the remains of sacrifice. They were to his military eye the remains of battle. And so they were. They were the remains, probably, of many of those 'Grandes' who had assembled in Purea's 'palace' to be fed by her. They had been killed in a surprise attack by Purea's rivals for political eminence in Tahiti. They had been killed, in fact, by those powers that Cook was recognising as having emerged in Matavai and were to become the Pomare dynasty, the future 'kings' and 'queens' of Tahitian polity.

Purea, as the gossip, and in general the history, goes, devised a plan by which her son, Teri'irere, would be acknowledged as possessing the highest titles of all Tahiti. She imposed a *rahui*, a restriction on foodstuffs and festivals in preparation for his investiture with the *maro ura*. A *rahui* was more secular and political than *tapu*, even though it would be imposed with religious ritual. *Tapu* belonged to the deep cultural values of the *Maohi*. *Rahui* was more on the surface of things. The right and ability to impose a *rahui* was a question of negotiated politics.

Purea's right and ability to impose this *rahui* was challenged. Obedience to the *rahui* entailed some recognition by those who obeyed it of the pre-eminence of Teri'irere. First Purea's sister-in-law challenged it on behalf of her son by coming to visit Purea with the expectation of receiving all the honours of food and gift of an equal, thus breaking the *rahui*. Purea sent her away without acknowledging her. Then Purea's niece, known later as 'Itea, challenged on behalf of her brother. She too was repulsed, but this rejection took the quarrel out of the realm of symbolic actions to that of war, and became the occasion of a temporary alliance between those kin-congregations that bordered on Papara, the Taiarapu to the south and the Atahuru to the north. In the destruction of Mahaiatea that ensued, the Taiarapu took away the spoils of battle, the skulls and the property of those they killed. The Atahuru took away the spoils of politics, the *maro ura* and the paraphernalia of the god 'Oro. Purea's son was not deprived of his titles by that. It meant, however, that he would need to go to the *marae* Maraetaata in Paea to claim them and in that recognise the pre-eminence of Tu, the hope of the Pomare line. The *Bounty* mutineers would witness (as they also had facilitated) the investiture of Tu with the *maro ura* at the *marae* Tarahoi on 'Morai Point' near Matavai. The mutineers were obliged to submit to ritual procedures, such as only coming to Matavai by traversing the seaward section of Taputapuatea to the landward section, the general procedure for 'Sacrifices from Abroad'. Even twenty years after the arrival of the Strangers in Tahiti, the *Maohi* were controlling their entry as Purea had done, by putting it into *Maohi* time and space.

Purea and Amo had to flee for their lives to the mountains after the destruction of their *marae* Mahaiatea. They found refuge with their families at Ha'apape and F'a'a'a.

James Cook came to Tahiti under the apprehension that he might have to shed blood to do what he came to do, observe the Transit of Venus. His thinking was shaped by the fact of the violent overture of the English encounter with the *Maohi*. He was prepared for violence in two ways. He would construct a fort to protect his observatory and to control all trading and meeting with the *Maohi*. He would make an English space to control the relationships with the *Maohi*. Then, because he assumed that Wallis had met with some figure of sovereignty, a 'queen', he planned to control *Maohi* behaviour by taking her hostage if necessary. At the end of his stay, as he mused on the successes and failures of his visit, he felt fortunate that the only blood shed was that of the first *Maohi* thief. The *Maohi* had snatched a musket and was shot dead by the sentry at the fort.

Cook had attempted to take Purea hostage twice, however. The once unsuccessfully when a quadrant was stolen from the observatory; the other dramatically, and, he thought with poor consequences for English–*Maohi* relationships, when he held Purea and the other 'Grandes' prisoner until they saw to the return of two deserters.

What complicated his plans for hostage-taking was his uncertainty about who held sovereign power in Tahiti. It was very obvious to him that in whatever way Purea was 'queen' to Wallis, she could not be 'queen' to him. Tuteha, the founding father of the Pomare dynasty, was obviously now the political force at Matavai. Cook had to manage what he saw to be Tuteha's jealousies whenever Cook dealt with Purea. Purea, in fact, had only come to him when Robert Molyneux, who had been with Wallis, recognised her in a tent with others. She was 'very masculine', Cook said to himself. Sydney Parkinson, with a more artistic eye, said she was a 'fat, bouncing, good-looking dame'. Cook's first gift to her was a child's doll. He has a little laugh at her native simplicity and excitement in the gift by telling her—it is hard to know how—that the doll was a 'Picter of my Wife'. Purea's excitement seemed unbounded. She fastened the doll to her clothing and took Cook by hand this way and that among her people, exhibiting it. Because Tuteha seemed surly at this, Cook let him have a doll too. But in all this Cook got to know that Purea was 'head of only her family', but had 'no authority over the rest'. So it was no use taking her hostage, unless he took the others hostage too.[34]

When his two men deserted, Cook duped Tuteha and Purea on board the *Endeavour* and held them there. It 'struck general Terror through the island & the Prisoners ('tho very well Treated) was inconsoleable', Robert Molyneux reported.[35] Cook was to use this tactic frequently through the Pacific. In fact he would be killed in Hawai'i trying to use it. He never reflects on its morality, although in this first use of it he knows what it cost and who to blame. 'Thus we are likely to leave these people in disgust with our behaviour towards them, owing wholly to the folly of two of our own people' (that is, the deserters).[36]

It would take Cook three more visits to Tahiti to get a better understanding of *Maohi* politics, but he had two experiences with Purea which sharpened his learning curve. Late in his visit, 21 June, Amo and Purea brought Teri'irere to the fort. The boy, six or seven years old Cook thought, was accompanied by a young woman of about sixteen years of age. She was said to be Teri'irere's intended bride. What surprised everybody were the extravagant protocols that surrounded the boy. Everyone, including his parents, stripped to the waist and bowed deeply in his presence. Amo and Purea were very careful where he went, not allowing him into the English buildings and tents. Cook in this had his first lesson in the ways marriages funnelled honours and made the child more honourable than his parents. And Cook learned that in Tahiti authority and power could be separated.[37]

The other incident would earn Cook considerable opprobrium. Purea brought a boy of about sixteen years and a girl of about twelve years of age to the gateway of the fort, and there choreographed a public copulation. Cook, though he was somewhat scandalised, made his first effort at a little cultural relativism. It was 'more from custom than lewdness', he remarked. He noted that Purea did not disapprove. Indeed, she instructed the pair. The girl seemed unwilling. At a later date, and long after Purea had lost her reputation with an English public, William Wales said that Purea—'old demirep of quality'—obliged the pair to attempt copulation. They were both terrified and could not perform it. He added that the *Maohi* audience remonstrated with Purea about it. What was happening we are clearly never really going to know. Clearly it was theatre of some sort on the part of Purea. The stage of that theatre —the gateway of Fort Venus—cannot be random. The audience is the English rather than the *Maohi*. Purea had had, with both the *Dolphin*'s and the *Endeavour*'s visit, plenty of experience of the English preoccupation with violence and sex. Enough, perhaps, as later missionaries suggested more generally about the Tahitians, to be offended at the various indecencies of the English. Maybe she was enacting some Tahitian theatre of the grotesque. After all, the English were mimicked and mocked in dance and song on almost every island they visited. And that Sunday morning Purea and others had excitedly watched Divine Service and mimicked what they saw.[38]

JOSEPH BANKS WAS a man of multiple preoccupations, but certainly one of them was sex. He had undoubtedly come to Tahiti with the stories of the 'Dolphins' about its pleasures in his head. To judge by his pouting disappointment at Purea's indifference to him, he might have even come with dreams of liaisons with a 'queen'. 'Her eyes [were] full of meaning', he wrote in his journal. 'She might have been hansome when young but now few traces of it were left'. In any case, she had a 'gallant' which she made 'not the least secret of'. Banks first met up with Purea asleep in her canoe with this 'lusty young man of 25'. On Banks's arrival 'Her majesty put on her breeches' and clothed Banks in fine cloth. Being curious about these things he discovered that Tupaia, who had been 'her right hand man' in the *Dolphin*'s time, still did things like overhauling her canoe and advising her on matters of state. But he had lost his place to this new 'gallant'. Of course, Banks senses that Purea really wants him, but Banks is 'at present otherwise engaged' with another 'flame'. 'Indeed was I free as air, her majesty's person is not the most desirable'.[39]

It is operatic, indeed comic operetta stuff. And Banks would get his just deserts. He squabbled with Jonathan Monkhouse to the point of duelling over the same 'flame'. Then, on tour with Cook around the island and without his 'flame', Purea offered him a bed in her canoe. It was a hot night, so he 'stripped'. Purea took his clothes—breeches, shirt, a waistcoat with 'silver frogs'—his pistols and a powder horn. He must have slept well, for next morning everything was gone. (Cook, sleeping elsewhere, lost his white stockings the same night.) Making a 'motley appearance', Banks half in *tapa* cloth and English linen, was highly suspicious of Purea, or at least of her 'gallant' with whom she was supposedly at the time in some quarrel. Banks's relations with Purea cooled. She perceived it and was 'rather out of humour' that the exchanges which had somehow made them equal had ceased.[40]

Purea, if she had made the English the subject of her own theatre of the grotesque, was herself about to be made theatre of the grotesque over these several incidents with Wallis, Cook and Banks. Dr John Hawkesworth was paid £6000 to publish the journals of these various English expeditions to the Pacific. This was a fortune for such a publishing venture. Everybody thought that they could do something like that for £6000, and do it better than Hawkesworth. Hawkesworth, however, would die before he could enjoy his fortune, because of the criticism poured over him. His biggest mistake was to catch that tiny sense of cultural relativism that Cook had expressed and to enlarge it a little. He enlarged it by adopting a neutral attitude about things which no one would give him the right to be neutral about. There was no way that the public copulation could be deemed 'custom' and not 'lewdness'. There was no way in which a 'queen' with a tattooed backside cavorting with native 'gallants' could really be 'queenly'. And there was no way in which the multiple preoccupations of Banks in the exotics of botany and native culture could justify his obvious preoccupation with sex. So the pages of newspapers and reviews were filled with outraged criticism and satirical verse. 'Oberea' was a 'crafty, subtle, sunburnt strum'. 'Callst thyself a Queen?' And Banks, you turned King George's great scientific design 'to filthy farce/And search for wonders on an Indian's a . . . '[41]

One might have thought, given all our understanding of the *philosophes* and the ideas of the Noble Savage, that Purea's cultural innocence might have received some sympathetic treatment. But the theatre of the grotesque is more hegemonic than that. The theatre of the grotesque says that natives are not innocent at all. They are just like us, only worse. There is nothing to be learned from them. There is nothing to be changed in us. If they were innocent, they would not have been killed. Laughter blocks out guilt. There is no time between guffaws to think that things might have been otherwise.

It is hardly likely that these representations of Purea affected her life very greatly, although they surely affected the lives of many Pacific islanders. The captains who treated Pacific islanders outside the systems of justice and morality in which they bound themselves in the name of realpolitik always had the sense that their public at home would support them. No matter what voices of conscience were raised against them, these voices would not be loud enough to shake the 'madcap realism' of empire.

We lose sight of Purea after her perceived plots are seen to have failed. She seems to have died somewhere between 1775 and 1785. Amo outlived her. He was killed in 1793 in one last battle against his old enemies in Atahuru. He was killed, it was reported, by a musket fired by a Swedish beachcomber, Peter Haggerstein, who had deserted from the *Daedalus*.

No woman's reputation could survive the grotesqueries of the dozens of poetic attacks against her. By the time John O'Keeffe, the Irish playwright, wanted to portray her in his pantomime 'Omai', she had dropped in status from monarch to sorceress. The beginning and end of her story, so far as the English reputation of her is concerned, is marked by pictorial representation. The one is an engraving of her outside her 'palace' ceding Tahiti to Samuel Wallis, a make-believe cession that never happened. The other is of her in costume as the sorceress in the pantomime, as make-believe as the cession. Do not think, however, that make-believe is just make-believe.

Vancouver's Vision of Native Peoples

The Northwest Coast and Hawai'i

ROBIN FISHER

I T OFTEN SEEMS that discussion of first contacts and early cultural relations between Natives and Strangers is bedevilled by two countervailing tendencies. One of these is the penchant for large generalisations that can be applied to vast geographical areas and a host of Native cultures. In attemping to capture the big picture, some historians ignore subtleties of shading in favour of simple conclusions drawn in black and white. At the other end of the spectrum lies the notion that the past is so complex and the sources so compromised that it is not possible to discern any patterns. Since reason and evidence cannot bring us to any valid view of the past, historical interpretation is a matter of competing fictions or, worse, simply an illusion.[1] This essay takes its first cue from Nicholas Thomas's admonition to use specific accounts to look at local situations.[2] During his long voyage to the Pacific, George Vancouver wrote about his actions and reactions on the northwest coast of North America and in the Hawaiian Islands. It is clear that he felt very differently about the peoples and cultures of the two places. I wish to consider why he had these differing reactions and whether his account of them in any way connects with actual differences between the two sets of cultures.[3]

Centennial 'celebrations' of European voyages often provide the occasion for sweeping generalisations about the impact of those voyages on Native peoples. Much of this history is still written in terms of the clash of opposites and Native and Stranger quickly come to represent good and bad. Certainly this was the view in much of the writing in North America during the Columbus quincentenary of 1992. In a book titled *Stolen Continents*, which was on the best-seller list for months, Ronald Wright adopted a conceit that was far greater than anything imagined by Columbus. Wright presumed to see *The 'New World' through Indian Eyes Since 1492*. And what he saw were two cultures meeting in incomprehension with the inevitable result of violent encounters and the dispossession of the Native peoples.[4] In Canada the Native rights advocate, Thomas Berger, took the occasion of the Columbus carnival to write a book called *A Long and Terrible Shadow* in which he argued that the history of Native people in North America has been a straight downhill run from 1492 to the present day.[5] Few noted that 1992 was also the bicentenary of George Vancouver's arrival in North America and that his sojourn on the west coast was very different from that of Columbus in the east.

But the formulators of grand generalisations are seldom deterred by contrary evidence. While many scholars have become interested in the subtleties of power in contact situations, others still seem to assume that the mere arrival of Europeans established their hegemony. This view is perhaps implicit in Anne Salmond's concept of *Two Worlds*, as applied to the first meetings of Maori and Europeans.[6] It is certainly explicit in the recent academic fascination with the notion of the Other which emphasises the distinctions between people.

This dichotomous construct, of two completely different cultures meeting at an absolute line of contact, failing to communicate, and often resorting to violence, has a long and persistent history. The notion of the 'fatal impact' was popularised by Alan Moorehead and, to some extent, it goes back to the accounts of the European explorers themselves.[7] To have a fatal impact one must, of course, first have a noble savage, a perfidious European and the whole bundle of ideas that go with such naive distinctions. But when we look at George Vancouver's relations with the Native peoples of the northwest coast and Hawai'i, the past is not quite as simple as some would like to make it.

The reverse trend in recent scholarship holds that the past is never simple, but is always complex and contested, indeed almost unknowable. Postmodernists, who are frequently obsessed by truth, or at least the need to deny it, have mounted a major assault on the validity of the written record. The accounts of European explorers, so the argument goes, are so much a product of their own culture and assumed hegemony that they do not say anything of value about the cultures that they are observing. Thus European accounts of early contact situations become merely 'illusions of contact' and 'fabricated truths'.[8] The development of Native history has also potentially, and perhaps with good reason, diminished the authority of the written record. The ethnohistorical approach demands that we use oral and material sources in an effort to come to a more rounded history of Native peoples. But the results gained from these sources should be incremental and not a zero sum game based on replacing one set of sources with another. We can see from his written account that Vancouver reacted quite differently to the people and cultures of Hawai'i and those of the northwest coast, and we should then ask ourselves whether these differing reactions have any grounding in actual differences between these various cultures.[9]

George Vancouver came to the Pacific in 1791 in command of a Royal Navy exploring expedition. This was not his first voyage to the Pacific, for he had been on both Cook's second and third voyages. Now leading his own expedition, the primary objective was the northwest coast of North America. When he arrived on this coast, Vancouver's first task was to settle some outstanding details from the Nootka Sound controversy by negotiating on the spot with representatives of Spain for the restitution of any land and buildings formerly owned by British subjects.[10] His second, and as it turned out, more important, instruction was to chart the northwest coast of North America in order to establish, once and for all, whether or not there was a northwest passage between the Atlantic and the Pacific Oceans. For reasons largely beyond his control, Vancouver failed at the first task, but succeeded brilliantly at the second. He spent the three summers of 1792, 1793 and 1794 meticulously charting the western coast of North America from Baja California in the south to Cook Inlet in Alaska in the north. On the way north in 1792, and at the end of the first and second survey season on the coast, Vancouver visited the Hawaiian Islands. On the latter two occasions the expedition stayed for several weeks so that the ships could be repaired, supplies replenished and the men could gather their energy. With the coastal survey complete at the end of the summer of 1794, Vancouver returned to Britain in 1795 and wrote a detailed account of his expedition which was published, along with his superb charts of the coastline, a few months after his death in 1798.

Adding the period spent with Cook to his own voyage of four-and-a-half years, George Vancouver had probably spent more time in the Pacific and among its peoples than any other European of his generation. At the end of the instructions for his own expedition Vancouver was required, in addition to carrying out his primary tasks, to do all he could to avoid disputes with the Native people and 'to conciliate their friendship and confidence'.[11] Yet navigating the often turbulent waters of inter-cultural relations could be more hazardous than charting a coastline. Here there were no precise science or navigational instruments to guide the voyager, and experience on one section of coast did not necessarily help on another. Nevertheless, *Vancouver's Voyage* tells us as much about his view of, and relations with, the people of the Pacific as it does about the relatively straightforward task of mapping their coastlines. And it also leaves us with the question of why Vancouver reacted so differently to the Native peoples and cultures of the northwest Coast compared with his responses to the Hawaiians.

There can be no doubt that the Vancouver expedition was as much engaged in establishing cultural lines as it was involved in inscribing lines on the map. Early in the first season on the northwest coast, when the boat crews were operating out of Port Discovery on the Olympic Peninsula, there was a revealing moment. As they were working their way along Hood Canal, Vancouver and his crews went ashore to rest, eat breakfast and dry their equipment. A group of Native people landed a short distance away and walked along the beach towards Vancouver's party. They approached with confidence, were apparently unarmed, 'and behaved in the most respectful and orderly manner'.[12] But Vancouver wanted to control the encounter and prevent too much familiarity. As the Native people drew near, he had a line drawn in the sand between the two groups. He would not allow anyone to cross it without first requesting permission. Yet, as Greg Dening has shown us, lines in the sand, like the beaches upon which they are drawn, both define boundaries and invite crossings.[13] No sooner was the line drawn than trade began across it. Even though it turned out that the Native people did carry weapons, they exchanged their bows and arrows in a trade that was conducted in 'a very fair and honest manner'.[14] The line in the sand had provided the security needed to facilitate cultural exchange.

The first time Vancouver's crewmen went ashore at Waimea Bay on Kauai there was a similarly defining moment. The Hawaiian leader set aside two houses for the European guests and used his authority to disperse the large crowd that had gathered. He then had a line drawn in the sand around the dwellings over which none of the Hawaiians should cross.[15] The members of the expedition had mixed feelings about this boundary. Some of the junior officers and seamen were distressed that the Hawaiian women refused to cross it. But again the line was not strictly observed for long, and Vancouver's men were happier when the Hawaiian leader made sleeping arrangements for those who wanted them on the other side.[16] Vancouver himself was censorious of the ready availability of Hawaiian women at Waimea and, perhaps in a contrary mood, felt that their reception there 'was not of that hearty, friendly nature' that he was accustomed to in Tahiti.[17] Presumably Vancouver was not so comfortable with boundaries established by others. But one thing could not be denied: in Hawai'i, the lines of authority were very clear.

On the northwest coast, Vancouver's own boundary lines were both physical and mental. The expedition's first encounter with the Native people of the northwest coast was with a group of Tututnis who lived along the lower reaches of the Rogue River in southern Oregon. They paddled out to the passing ship, appeared to be open and friendly, and were interested in trade. Vancouver wrote a rather perfunctory account of their physical appearance and showed little enthusiasm for their presence. Not all crew members were as scathing as Thomas Manby who commented that: 'The eye received them with disgust: in stature small and in person filthy and stinking, we considered them the nastyest race of people under the Sun'.[18] The naturalist, Archibald Menzies, as he would do throughout the voyage, recorded a much more detailed ethnographic description of these people.[19] Yet this first meeting was hardly auspicious and it was not the prelude to close encounters of any kind on the northwest coast.

Vancouver kept some physical distance between his men and the people of the coast largely out of fear and the desire to avoid conflict. Before he left England, since his men would be frequently among Native peoples, he had ordered four extra field pieces and thirty-six more barrels of powder to be delivered to his ship 'for their better protection'.[20] His first encounters were with Native people who were friendly enough, and yet he constantly expected hostility and often exaggerated perceived threats. I assume that his mental distance came from lack of curiosity about the people of the coast. Unlike other European visitors of the time, he took little interest in detailed ethnography. During his first weeks back on the coast he drew on his earlier experience with Cook and compared all the Native groups to those of Nootka Sound. In spite of the point of comparison, he was slow to appreciate the diversity of languages, and therefore of cultures, even on the relatively short stretch of coastline between Puget Sound and the north end of Vancouver Island. He did not place much credence on Native testimony, even on simple points of geography. His scepticism arose from his notion that 'most Indians' paid 'little respect . . . to the truth, and were ready 'to assert what they think is most agreeable for the moment . . . although they could have no motive for deceiving us'.[21] And Vancouver was particularly struck by cultural features that were unusual and different from his preconceived expectations, once again emphasising the lines of distinction between the Native people and Europeans.

Even those among Vancouver's men who did look across the boundary lines, recognised the limits of their understanding. Archibald Menzies, who was both a more interested and a more perceptive observer, made up to some extent for Vancouver's lack of interest in the cultures of the northwest coast. Like Vancouver,

Menzies had been to the region before. He had spent the summers of 1787 and 1788 on the trading vessel *Prince of Wales* under James Colnett as it sailed up and down the coast in search of furs. Now that he was back with Vancouver, Menzies continued the practice he had begun on *Prince of Wales* of recording the encounters with Native people. His journal includes long and detailed accounts of the physical culture and observable characteristics of the people. When time permitted, he tried to understand the indigenous languages and he was quick to recognise that there were significant linguistic differences over short distances. Yet even Menzies was conscious of the limitations to his comprehension. While he had a great curiosity, he did not jump to quick conclusions for which there was little support.[22] At Port Discovery in May 1792, he came across the site of a large fire and what appeared to be human bones. It was the kind of evidence that led some to assert that the Native people were cannibals, but, for Menzies, such conclusions were 'without any rational proof that brings the least conviction to my mind'.[23]

Both Menzies and Vancouver, and also Peter Puget, were interested in the possibility that the population of the Native people was declining. Noticing large burial sites and deserted villages they began to speculate about causes. Menzies felt that on the southern coast the population seemed 'too small for such a fine territory'. So he wondered if a hunting way of life could not sustain large numbers of people. In addition to the impact of disease, he contemplated that of warfare, and considered the possibility that people had moved to be near the centres of trade. Though these were interesting hypotheses, in the end Menzies remained cautious about coming to conclusions. He had to admit that 'they could form no conjecture or opinion on the cause of this apparent depopulation which had an equal chance of proving fallacious from their circumscribed knowledge of the manners & modes of living of the Natives'.[24] During an expedition out of Birch Bay, Puget noted that he could not even assume that deserted villages were evidence of population decline as opposed to simple relocation of groups.[25]

More recent authors of works on population decline in the Strait of Georgia area would do well to emulate this caution. Even though

Vancouver's men clearly stated their reservations about the meaning of what they saw, the geographer Cole Harris uses their evidence to build up a case for a massive smallpox pandemic sweeping through the area in 1782.[26] It is often not so much the written historical record itself, but the way in which it is used by scholars, that brings it into disrepute.

The artistic record of the Vancouver expedition's time on the northwest coast is also of limited ethnographic interest. Vancouver's artists were midshipmen trained in drawing coastlines for navigational purposes. Most of their drawings, and therefore most of the engravings in *Vancouver's Voyage*, have little human interest. With a couple of exceptions, such as John Sykes's watercolour, 'View of Indian Village on Cape Mudge . . .', or the engraving of 'Cheslakee's Village' at the mouth of the Nimpkish river, there is little evidence of the presence of Native people.[27] The engravers for *Vancouver's Voyage* sometimes added a flotilla of Native canoes to the otherwise uninhabited drawings done by the expedition's artists.[28] But none of the visual record from Vancouver's voyage has anything like the ethnographic detail of John Webber's drawings and engravings from Cook's stay at Nootka Sound.

Though Vancouver and his men had limited ethnographic curiosity, he did recognise that charting the northwest coast involved more than hydrography. He arrived on the coast determined to avoid violence and he soon realised that his survey could not be carried out without the co-operation of the coastal people, or at least their tacit acceptance of his presence. His men were very vulnerable in their little boats and they depended to some extent on the local people for food. Vancouver's wish to avoid violence was not just a matter of self-interest, for he also believed that no Native people should lose their lives because of his expedition. Throughout the first and most of his second season on the coast, Vancouver maintained peaceful relations with its peoples. He assumed that he was the determining factor in avoiding violence, but the Native peoples had their own reasons for tolerating his presence. As well as charting the coast, Vancouver's men traded for furs on the side. At one village at the mouth of the Nimpkish River on the east coast of Vancouver Island, they acquired more than two hundred sea otter pelts.[29] This was a business that the Native people knew well and it could provide the basis for mutual and peaceful relations. Yet, even with this inducement, some Native groups wanted to limit contact with the newcomers. The Heiltsuks, for example, were interested in trade at the ships, but made it equally clear that they did not want the Europeans to land at their village. They wanted, it would seem, to be left alone rather than being the object of European curiosity.[30]

Late in the second and during the third season on the coast, perhaps because the trade goods had run out, there were violent skirmishes with the Tlingit. In one instance Vancouver and his boat crew were almost overwhelmed by a hostile group in Behm Canal. The explorers only got away by firing on the Native people and killing and wounding several. This conflict with the Tlingit had erupted, Vancouver believed, because 'that attentive wariness which had been the first object of my concern on coming among these rude nations, had latterly been neglected'.[31] From then until the end of the survey, the boat crews would avoid conflict by keeping their distance from potentially aggressive Native groups. But Vancouver still felt that the killings had marred his record on the coast. He had hoped to complete his work without firing a single shot in anger and was disturbed that he had failed.

When he was on the coast he was preoccupied with the difficult and often dangerous work of the survey. The coast seemed endless, the seasons imposed deadlines, so he was constantly on the move. After the first season, in order to reduce the risk of conflict, Vancouver himself rarely went on any of the boat excursions, and his ship, *Discovery*, was seldom anchored near a Native village. Most of the Vancouver expedition's contacts with the coastal people were brief encounters, as Native people paddled out to the vessels or when boat crews put ashore for a short respite. With the possible exception of Nootka Sound, Vancouver's men never stayed in one place for long enough to learn much about any one group. After a summer on the southern coast, Peter Puget reflected, while he was at Nootka Sound, that his contact with the people had been so limited that when he spoke of them it was 'more from conjecture and appearance than Real Information . . .'[32]

Along with many European observers, Vancouver thought that the people of the northern coast were more interesting and attractive than those to the south.[33] Yet, while his curiosity was quickened, there was much that he could not know. At some places on the northern coast he noticed Native women taking an active, and sometimes even a determining role in trading with his men. European males were often surprised by the power and authority of Native women on the northwest coast, but in the early contact years they were seldom able to go beyond observation to explanation. Vancouver wondered whether this was a matriarchal society but, like Puget, he concluded that he could not be sure, because 'the knowledge we obtained of their manners and customs, in our short acquaintance, was however too superficial to establish this or any other fact, that did not admit of ocular demonstration'.[34]

Yet even at Nootka Sound, where he had been with Cook, and to which he returned at the end of each survey season to negotiate with the Spanish, Vancouver found little to appreciate in Native culture. Vancouver's dealings were mostly with the Nuu-chah-nulth groups who lived on the west side of Nootka Sound. They had a major winter village at the head of Tahsis Inlet, and Yuquot, or Friendly Cove as it was known to the Europeans, at the opening of the Sound was one of their summer dwelling places. The ranking leader among these people was Maquinna, who had led them through the difficult years of European contact since his meeting with Cook in 1778.[35] As a diplomat, Maquinna was as skilled as any European who came to his territory, but he too was navigating in some difficult waters. While he had become both wealthy and powerful through his ability to manipulate the fur trade, at the same time the international rivalry over Nootka Sound threatened to undermine his leadership.[36]

Vancouver's relations with Maquinna got off to a bad start and did not improve much. When the Native leader first tried to come aboard *Discovery* he was stopped by the deck officer who did not realise who he was. This was a serious gaffe in protocol that had to be smoothed over by Bodega y Quadra, the Spanish commander, who had established a rapport with Maquinna. Particularly when they were among the Salish and Nuu-chah-nulth groups on the southern coast of what is now British Columbia, Vancouver and his men commented that they could not tell who were the leaders. There were chiefs by name, but they appeared to have little authority and there was little apparent subordination on the part of the people.[37] It was difficult, from a European perspective, to figure out the indigenous political system.

Yet even when Vancouver realised Maquinna's pre-eminence among his own people, he was unimpressed. Bodega arranged a visit to Maquinna's village at Tahsis Inlet. The two commanders were served a meal, followed by dancing and ceremony. Vancouver was unmoved by the ritual of the occasion, commenting when Maquinna danced with a mask that the presentation was 'ridiculously laughable'. Later, Maquinna and his retinue made a return visit to *Discovery*, and Vancouver dismissed them 'as the most consummate beggars I had ever seen'.[38] In September 1794, Vancouver once again visited Maquinna's village with the Spanish representative at Nootka Sound. They were given an effusive welcome and led to Maquinna's house where they were seated according to their rank. This time Vancouver was a less critical and more perceptive observer of the proceedings. Maquinna made a speech in which he apparently said that he was honoured by the visit, which he saw as the outcome of the peaceful relations that he and his people had maintained with the Europeans. When dancing followed, Vancouver still found the music 'as offensive to the ear' as the dancing was 'to the eye'. He did acknowledge the skill with which Maquinna changed masks, the enthusiasm of the performance, and the need, at least in the interests of diplomacy, to enter into the spirit of the occasion.[39] But he had little idea that he was being used as a pawn in indigenous politics as Maquinna capitalised on these European visits to his village to enhance his prestige.

Though there may have been moments of comprehension and communication, Vancouver left the northwest coast without having established close contact with any Native group or appreciating the strength and diversity of the coastal cultures. Throughout most of his three summers on the coast he did avoid violent encounters with the Native people: a point that went unnoticed during the Columbus quincentenary as instant historians made continental generalisations about the nature of early culture contact in North America. And yet, during his time on the northwest coast, Vancouver does appear as the stereotypical European explorer. He was there to pursue his own instructions and objectives, so his contact with Native people was limited by self-interest, and he found little to appreciate in their cultures.

VANCOUVER'S EXPLORATIONS were not, however, confined to the northwest coast. He visited the Hawaiian Islands three times during the course of his voyage. The first visit was in March 1792 as he sailed up the Pacific towards the northwest coast. Then at the end of the 1792 and 1793 survey seasons, as winter closed in on the coast and the storms began to rage, Vancouver sailed south to a gentler climate. On each of these occasions, the expedition spent about six weeks in Hawaiian waters, most of that time at Kaelakekua Bay. Vancouver had, of course, also been to Hawai'i with Cook.

As on the northwest coast, Vancouver's first contacts with the people of Hawai'i were not very promising. Kaelakekua Bay had its gloomy memories and during the events that led up to the death of Cook, Vancouver himself had been involved in a dangerous altercation with a group of Hawaiians.[40] Not surprisingly perhaps, he seemed edgy when he returned to the islands in March 1792. He was deeply suspicious of Kaiana, the Hawaiian leader who wanted to accompany him from the big island to Kauai.[41] Some incorrectly suspected him of having led an attack on the trading vessel *Fair American* in 1790 and Vancouver thought that he had planned attacks on other vessels.[42] Walking down the beach at Waimea on Kauai, Vancouver saw some fires that had been lit to burn off vegetation. He interpreted them as a sign of hostile intent and flew into one of his rages. Later, towards the end of the first survey season on the northwest coast, Vancouver learned that Richard Hergest, his close friend and commander of his supply ship *Daedalus*, had been killed, along with the astronomer, William Gooch, and another crew member, by a group of Hawaiians at Waimea Bay on Oahu.[43] From Vancouver's point of view there should have been no more reason to establish any relationship with the Hawaiians than with the Native people of the northwest coast.

Yet on his return visits, after spending time on the northwest coast, Vancouver found the Hawaiian welcome more to his liking. Particularly during his two sojourns at Kaelakekua Bay in early

1793 and 1794, Vancouver seemed like a different person. His lively and engaged accounts of both the Hawaiian Islands and the people contrast with his routine and often sombre commentary on the northwest coast. Obviously he was under less pressure in Hawai'i. He went there to restore both his men and his vessels, there was no great rush, and he was much more relaxed. Vancouver was just as judgemental in Hawai'i as he was on the coast, but in the south his judgements were much more positive. Vancouver and his men lived for weeks on the beneficence of the Hawaiian people who provided an abundance of hogs, fruit, vegetables and fresh water. He could not help but compare the openhandedness of 'these untaught children of nature' with the miserable reception he had recently received at San Francisco and Monterey from 'the educated civilized governor of New Albion and California'.[44] Though he did not ignore the harsh side of Hawaiian life, like many Europeans, he saw these people as archetypal Noble Savages, and favourable comparisons between Hawaiians and Europeans occurred to Vancouver more than once. 'A conduct so disinterestedly noble, and uniformly observed by so untutored a race', as he described their hospitality, 'will not fail to excite a certain degree of regret, that the first social principles, teaching mutual support and universal benevolence, should so frequently, amongst civilized people, be sacrificed to suspicion, jealousy, and distrust'.[45]

Clearly Vancouver responded to the people of the Pacific out of his own preconceptions. But there were other reasons for his different reaction to the Hawaiians and the Native peoples of the northwest coast. Some had to do with real differences between the cultures. Vancouver was much better acquainted with the language of the Hawaiians than he was with any one of the many languages along the northwest coast.[46] He was impressed with the Hawaiians because, like Europeans, they cultivated many of their resources. But the extensive fields and paddies contained by elaborate walls and dykes and the carefully constructed fish ponds were not figments of his European imagination any more than was their absence among the hunting and gathering cultures of the northwest coast.

In comparison with the west coast of North America, Vancouver also had no difficulty working out who the leaders were in Hawai'i.

Leadership was much more formalised and Hawaiian chiefs apparently had almost absolute power over their people. This much was readily evident to the European visitors. Indeed, the hierarchical nature of Hawaiian society was familiar enough to be described in European terms. On his departure from Kaelakekua Bay for the last time on 2 March 1794, Vancouver wrote a letter extolling the virtues of Kamehameha. He had established a close and apparently mutual relationship with the Hawaiian leader and, in this letter to be passed on to other European visitors, Vancouver wrote of his generosity and trustworthiness. Kamehameha's conduct had, concluded Vancouver in a significant phrase, 'been of the most princely nature . . .'[47]

Though they took a little longer to figure out, Vancouver also had some awareness of the relations between Hawaiian leaders. During the years between his first visit with Cook and his return in 1792 a few high chiefs were contending for control over the whole island chain. By the early 1790s Kamehameha was dominating the island of Hawai'i and his rival, Kahekili, held sway over the rest of the island chain. There was now a lull in the conflict as each prepared for the final assault on the other.[48] By his second visit with his own expedition in 1793, Vancouver understood the basic power dynamics on the islands and he deplored the extent to which Europeans and their weapons had become a factor in these disputes. He tried to bring Kamehameha and Kahekili together for peace negotiations, but, after years of fighting, neither side trusted the other enough to attend a meeting.

On his third and final visit, Vancouver anchored again at Kaelakekua Bay and continued to develop a very close rapport with Kamehameha. Vancouver was particularly interested in arranging a cession of Hawai'i to Britain, but he began by intervening in the Hawaiian leader's personal relations. He learned that Kamehameha was estranged from his favourite wife Kaahumanu. The chief could not initiate a reconciliation without loss of face, so Vancouver acted as intermediary. He contrived to have the two meet aboard *Discovery*. It was a risky move that might easily have incurred Kamehameha's anger. Fortunately the stratagem worked and the couple were reunited. Vancouver's intercession and Kamehameha's reaction indicated a high level of good will between the two. 'The domestic affairs of Tamaahmaah having thus taken so happy a turn', Vancouver wrote, 'His mind was more at liberty for political considerations; and the cession of Owhyhee to His Britannic became now an object of his serious concern'.[49] On the face of it, Vancouver quickly persuaded Kamehameha to agree to this, and then went on to convince the sub-chiefs of the various districts. At a ceremony on the morning of 25 February 1794, the Hawaiian leaders formally 'ceded' Hawai'i to Britain.

Whatever one makes of this 'cession' we can safely assume that Kamehameha had more on his mind than gratitude at being reunited with his favourite wife. The Hawaiian leader was, by all accounts, a powerful personality: as fearless in battle as he was shrewd and tough-minded in politics. Within a year of Vancouver's departure, Kamehameha would bring all the Islands except Kauai under his control. Later Hawaiian accounts make it clear that Kamehameha had no intention of ceding any land to Britain.[50] Throughout the discussions with Vancouver the Hawaiian leaders were clearly focused on the advantages for them. Kamehameha was partly interested in British protection from the depredations of other Europeans and more particularly in any assistance that would give him an edge in the final conflict with his rivals. Vancouver, at least publicly, continued to refuse to trade in firearms, but he did offer Kamehameha military advice and also had a small vessel built for him. Vancouver's support was a factor, though not the most important one, in Kamehameha's rapid rise to pre-eminence.

Vancouver's last visit to Kaelakekua Bay was characterised by a mutual relationship between two leaders as each pursued his own interests. Kamehameha was generous to the end, presenting Vancouver with huge quantities of supplies, and Vancouver wrote in glowing terms of the trustworthiness of Kamehameha and the hospitality provided by his people. There was an emotional good-bye between the two leaders when Vancouver sailed away towards the west coast of North America.

Not all of Vancouver's dealings in Hawai'i were so satisfactory to both the Hawaiians and the Europeans. As on the northwest coast, his visits to the islands sometimes led to violence and high-handed actions. He was, for example, determined to have retribution for the deaths of Hergest and Gooch. During a brief stay at Waikiki in

1793, three man alleged to have been involved in the murders were brought to *Discovery* where they were 'tried' and executed. The evidence of their guilt was scarcely conclusive, and it is likely that three unfortunates were served up by the Hawaiian chiefs to placate Vancouver. It also became clear that Hergest's own ill-considered behaviour had been a factor in the deaths at Waimea the previous year.[51] But violence and misunderstanding were only a small part of the story. On the northwest coast and in Hawai'i both sides kept conflict to a minimum. Limited contact may have limited Vancouver's vision of the people of the northwest coast, but even there conflict was also restrained by common interests. In Hawai'i there was real communication, at least at certain levels of the two societies in contact, as self-interest became mutual interest.

In his ethnohistorical work on the Huron and other Iroquoian-speaking groups of the St Lawrence lowlands, Bruce Trigger has suggested the concept of interest groups that cut across cultural lines as one way of getting to a more detailed understanding of the contact situation. While the actions of Native people must be interpreted in a cultural context, in North America early relations between Natives and newcomers seldom simply involved two teams lining up against each other. Neither culture was monolithic as each contained a diversity of interests. Rather than merely setting up cultural abstractions for comparative purposes, Trigger urges us also to pay attention to the common interests that groups developed in real historical situations. The proposition that indigenous people were able to deal rationally with the early European presence not only admits the existence of Native agency, but allows us to take into account that common humanity which transcends cultural differences.[52] The 'opposing teams' approach to contact situations tends to play down both the subtleties of particular circumstances and differences between situations.

Such an approach also calls into question facile generalisations that are grounded in the notion of absolute cultural differences and oppositions. In North America at least, recent anniversary commemorations of European contact have not resulted in a rethinking of the hard issues of history. Rather they have produced a shift from one simple-minded view to another. European explorers have been transformed from heros to villains, and their coming is seen as an unmitigated disaster for the Native people. As the past is called upon to serve the present, the distinctions between different times and places are lost in the big generalisations. If we must draw lessons from the past, we would do well to remember that, both in North America and the Pacific, there were fleeting moments as well as long periods of reciprocity and accommodation between Native peoples and the Strangers.

Recognising the distinctions between local situations does not, however, have to lead us to the conclusion that there are no patterns to be discerned through written and other sources. No doubt it is useful to be reminded that the accounts of Cook and Vancouver are versions of the past, or, if we must, 'models of truth', that 'are bound up with cultural relations of power'.[53] But most Pacific historians have known this since they first read Bernard Smith's *European Vision and the South Pacific*, which was published in 1960.[54] Some scholars are, in spite of themselves, very like the European explorers in the Pacific: they make much of announcing what the people there already know.

It is often argued that European accounts of Pacific peoples are merely constructs determined by European preconceptions rather than Pacific reality. This view has gained even greater currency through the recent descent into discourse.[55] It also tends to privilege the notion that Europeans and indigenous people in early contact situations met along lines of incomprehension. The next step in the argument is that historians, particularly when they rely on written sources, can do little to penetrate this initial confusion. By taking the example of George Vancouver's written account of his experience among Pacific people, I suggest that we do not have to slide down this slope. Vancouver's differing reactions to the people of the northwest coast and Hawai'i clearly had something to do with his own background and prejudices. But they also had much to do with actual differences between the northwest coast and Hawai'i: a set of distinctions on which *Vancouver's Voyage* was and is very revealing.

Whose Scourge?

~~~

Smallpox Epidemics on the Northwest Coast

CHRISTON I. ARCHER

[The Spanish], it should seem, are a nation designed by Providence to be a scourge to every tribe of Indians that they come near, by one means or another.

Nathaniel Portlock[1]

T HE DIMINUTIVE SMALLPOX VIRUS *variola major*, truly a most effective and maleficent killer of human beings, has been eradicated from the populations of the globe, so it is believed. Without vaccination to remind people of the intense itch and pain, not to mention the death and disfigurement that went with this terrible disease, more than ever smallpox has entered the historians' pantheon—the section dealing with holocausts, catastrophes, pandemic diseases, and 'virgin soil' epidemics. These apocalyptic events form the substance of popular books and of introductory history lectures. Everyone can share the horror of Queen Elizabeth I who is popularly but incorrectly thought to have lost her girlish complexion and her hair to smallpox.[2] And, as Alfred Crosby has stated, smallpox had 'seven-league boots'[3] in its capacity to ravage countries and to appear where it was least expected—or totally unknown. Without much corroborating evidence, it is claimed that the Inca emperor Huayna Capac died of pandemic smallpox, introduced by the Spaniards at the Caribbean coast, that quickly ravaged distant native populations well in advance of the sixteenth-century conquerors.[4] The Aztecs suffered even greater losses possibly to the haemorrhagic smallpox that served Hernando Cortés as his forces besieged their capital Tenochtitlán. The epidemic apparently killed off much of the leadership including aspirant emperor Cuitlahua, and within a few decades reduced a population of over 25 million people to a pathetic remnant of just over 1 million.[5] In Australia, during April 1789, the newly arrived English settlers at Port Jackson observed a smallpox outbreak that swept away the nearby Aboriginal population. Twentieth-century historians argue that this was a small part of a continental pandemic that penetrated Australia by way of Macassan trepang fishermen thousands of miles away from Port Jackson in the Gulf of Carpentaria.[6]

While it would be foolish to discount the remarkable capacity of smallpox to maim, blind and kill its victims, certain questions remain about the pathology of the disease and about its transmission through a region as large as the Pacific Ocean basin. Smallpox is passed only from human to human. The smallpox victim has the potential to begin a chain of infection that could affect millions of people. Aboard a ship or in a tightly knit tribal, family or clan organisation involving communal living, exhaled droplets circulated in the air or lodged upon utensils, clothing, blankets and bandages conveyed the virus to devastate a population. After an incubation period, generally from ten to twelve days, the disease ran its course in about three weeks. At first the victims would suffer from a splitting headache, intense back pain, chills, high fever of 40°C, intense sore throat and finally the skin rash that produced the well-known, excruciatingly painful pustules. Victims were most infectious from just before the rash appeared until the last scabs fell off. Blankets and clothing contaminated with pus or scab matter were effective vehicles for transmitting the virus.[7]

Although governments attempted to legislate for the isolation of patients and the incineration or burial of infected bedding and clothing, good order and almost military discipline were required in order for the regulations to be effective. Indeed, to avoid cumbersome quarantine laws and lengthy delays, on some occasions even naval surgeons attempted to conceal smallpox patients or attempted to pass off obvious symptoms as 'just a rash'.[8] Among indigenous populations that lacked previous experience of the disease, one can only imagine the revulsion and dread of those who witnessed the hideous disfigurement and the malodorous stench of victims who most often perished from infections caused by the absence of basic hygiene, food and liquids. Apparently healthy people fled to seek sanctuary elsewhere—and in the process they transmitted the infection. However, without onward linkages to other groups or the possible exchange of clothing and other contaminated items, smallpox was not a malevolent miasma or communicated like malaria or yellow fever through the disease vector *Anopheles* mosquito. Indeed, with its victims so ill they were incapable of travel, smallpox spread more slowly than some other infectious diseases, confining some epidemics to one region or district, where it burned out quite quickly.[9]

The scholarship on sixteenth- to eighteenth-century smallpox epidemics is impressionistic, being based upon quite limited hard evidence and few detailed statistical studies. Without adequate data (sometimes there are no records whatsoever), empirical research on the disease is difficult. Recently, a number of historians have begun to question long-accepted ideas about pandemic smallpox and to reinterpret the existing sources. Francis J. Brooks tackled the sixteenth-century Mexican disease catastrophe, concluding that during the actual conquest of the 1520s there was no evidence of a devastating pandemic.[10] Brooks argued that the native population collapsed later from labour exploitation, disruption of food supplies, and a devil's brew of different diseases that wiped out millions. After a first response of 'guarded sympathy' for Brooks's revision of the catastrophe paradigm, additional research and thought moved Robert McCaa into diametrical disagreement. He concluded that Brooks's revisionism stemmed from 'overlooked sources, misread texts, flawed reasoning, and false analogies'.[11] In McCaa's view, during the early epidemics Native caregivers and nurturers succumbed to smallpox alongside their patients. Without any assistance being available, the immobilised sick perished from hunger, thirst and exposure.[12]

This rather lengthy introduction illustrates some of the real difficulties for historians and epidemiologists confronted by a lack of evidence and a broad range of variables. Smallpox may have changed its pathology over time; it may or may not have been pandemic; and it may on some occasions have been misdiagnosed by untrained observers as chicken pox or even measles that left characteristic pockmarks upon victims. The present study examines the northwest coast of North America in the eighteenth century, where very limited sources have rendered obscure the history of smallpox transmission, the extent or existence of epidemics, and the presence or lack thereof of devastating continental pandemics. Despite the potential strategic value of this coast's being the western terminus of a possible Northwest Passage linked with the Atlantic Ocean, except for a few accidental voyages and a minor Russian presence, Europeans entered the higher latitudes of the northeast Pacific only after the mid-eighteenth century. There were three possible routes for smallpox transmission: the first was from Kamchatka by way of Russian expansion eastward along the Alaskan coast and by other European fur traders who sailed from Asia in the wake of Cook's 1776–80 voyage; the second was northward and westward by way of infected native carriers as part of a North American continental pandemic in the 1770s and 1780s; the third was by way of Spanish maritime explorers from Mexico commencing with the expedition of Juan Pérez in 1774, and of maritime fur traders of different nationalities who rounded Cape Horn, sometimes touching at Spanish-American ports.

While the sources on northwest coast smallpox epidemics are thin for the eighteenth century and reports of the disease came from isolated locations well off major trade routes, it is widely concluded by historians and anthropologists that Spanish explorers from Mexico in 1774, 1775 or 1779 were responsible for the smallpox decimation of Tlingit tribes in the region of Cape Edgecumbe (57°47′N lat.) near Sitka in today's Alaskan Panhandle. In 1787, the British sea otter fur trader Nathaniel Portlock visited Tlingit villages, observing abandoned houses, large unused canoes, and very few inhabitants.[13] At Cross Sound, Portlock met a girl of about fourteen and an old man, both much disfigured by deep pockmarks on their faces. Through signs, Portlock said that the man attempted to explain his own personal suffering and the 'torments' wrought by the contagion which had swept away much of his band, including ten of his own children. In a story that Portlock or his editors tailored to tug at the heartstrings of chronically anti-Spanish English readers, the native victim exposed ten strokes tattooed on an arm, one for each lost child. Since none of the younger children aged ten to twelve years showed any signs of pockmarks, Portlock dated the epidemic to the summer of 1775 when he knew that a Spanish expedition had been in close proximity. Since, like many British and American navigators, Portlock completely accepted the Black Legend concept of Spanish-Catholic barbarities, he assigned full culpability: 'as the Spaniards were on this part of the coast in 1775 [the Hezeta and Bodega y Quadra expedition], it is very probable that these poor wretches caught this fatal infection'.[14] Like other observers of the period, Portlock pointed out that complete lack of sanitation in the native settlements—stinking filth, putre-faction, fish guts, and 'beds of maggots a foot deep'—must have contributed to the transmission of disease.[15]

Twentieth-century historians accepted Portlock's remarks, thus establishing a Spanish origin for smallpox in the northwest coast region, and also advancing pandemic theory or at least illustrating that the dreadful disease reached the most isolated frontiers of European/Native encounter. Although English-speaking historians might be pardoned for their failure to read Spanish, it is quite remarkable that others who did turn to archival sources and printed journals also failed to question Portlock's allegations. The Spaniards made no reference to smallpox aboard their ships or signs of the disease in the Native populations. In fact, the only other reference to a Spanish origin for epidemic smallpox was from the American fur trader John Boit, who in 1791 mentioned in passing while at Nitinat on Vancouver Island, 'Twas evident that these Natives had been visited by that scourge of mankind the Smallpox. The Spaniards as the natives say brought it among them'.[16]

Despite this, however, in his prize-winning study *Flood Tide of Empire: Spain and the Pacific Northwest, 1543–1819*, Warren L. Cook determined that while smallpox did not accompany the 1775 expedition, the disease must have been present during the 1779 voyage. He noted that in 1779 there was an 'epidemic' reported aboard the Spanish ships at Bucareli Sound, Prince of Wales Island (55°40′N lat.). Cook was correct about the absence of smallpox in 1775 and wrong about the nature of the 1779 'epidemic'.[17] In 1983, James R. Gibson suggested the possibility of a Russian source for the disease, noting that a 1768–69 epidemic of smallpox in Okhotsk and Kamchatka killed off 60 to 70 per cent of the population and could have ravaged the Aleutian Islands.[18] It would seem a logical leap to have projected this epidemic to Unalaska and Kodiak Islands and onward round the Alaskan littoral to infect the Tlingits. However, Gibson presented as alternatives the 1774, 1775 and especially the 1779 Spanish expeditions—and then went on with flimsy evidence to state definitively, 'this outbreak spread at least as far south as the Chinooks of the lower Columbia'.[19]

In recent studies, anthropologist Robert Boyd identified pandemic smallpox during the 1770s that seems to have decimated many North American indigenous populations.[20] Boyd catalogued references by fur traders and explorers, speculating about overland transmission from Mexico, by sea from Kamchatka, westward from the North American interior, and by sea, along the coast, carried by the Spanish marine expeditions. Given the isolated nature of coastal outbreaks, the expeditions from New Spain, where it was known there had been smallpox epidemics, appeared to be the most likely source. Following careful consideration of the areas where smallpox seemed to be present, Boyd dismissed the idea that it was carried by the 1774 and 1779 Spanish expeditions, concluding that the 1775 one of Hezeta and Bodega y Quadra was the most likely carrier.

As Boyd and other scholars of epidemics recognised, solid evidence about demographic changes in native population levels prior to European contacts is in very short supply. However, if any Europeans on the coast possessed better information and continuity of contact than others, the Spaniards were those observers. Without developed competitive commercial motivations to distract them, knowledgeable about native societies, disciplined by naval regulations, and guided by special royal orders to observe like scientists, the Spanish officers and friars also enjoyed a continuity of visits from 1774–95 that included the occupation of a fort and settlement at Nootka Sound, in 1789–95. The explorers carried detailed instructions to investigate all aspects of Native cultures, including health. Finally, the Spaniards knew smallpox very well from their own culture and from contemporary observations of Mexican outbreaks.[21] If there was epidemic or pandemic smallpox scouring the northwest coast during this period, the Spaniards could not have missed reporting its impact.

Unlike the Spanish, whose exploration journals for a variety of reasons remained unpublished and hidden in archives, often until the late twentieth century, the British and American explorers and maritime fur traders were anxious to proclaim their successes. The published account of George Vancouver's voyage appeared to corroborate the evidence of pandemic continental smallpox. During his 1792 circumnavigation of Vancouver Island, Vancouver and his officers commented upon deserted villages in Puget Sound and the Strait of Georgia, scattered bones about native burial sites, the graves of many young children, and the telltale pockmarks of *variola major* among survivors. In Puget Sound, after observing a man whose scars indicated that he had recovered from a particularly severe case of smallpox, Vancouver noted,

> This deplorable disease is not only common, but it is greatly to be apprehended is very fatal amongst them, as its indelible marks were seen on many; and several had lost the sight of one eye, which was remarked to be generally the left, owing most likely to the virulent effects of this baneful disorder.[22]

A little later, following a boat exploration, Peter Puget stated that a group of Native traders 'In their persons seemed more robust than the generality of the inhabitants; most of them had lost their right eye, and were much pitted with the small pox'.[23] Although left-eye, right-eye blindness depending upon location added an odd element to these observations, this evidence of smallpox in Puget Sound appeared quite convincing. Having seen several Native men naked, Vancouver reported: 'their skins were mostly unblemished by scars, excepting such as the small pox seemed to have occasioned; a disease which there is great reason to believe is very fatal to them'.[24] Nevertheless, Vancouver was careful to qualify his evidence of Native depopulation and to propose additional scientific inquiry.

Despite Vancouver's own care to avoid terms such as 'demographic disaster' or 'pandemic', he had a quite acute sense of demography where the Native peoples of the Pacific were concerned. Like many other Enlightenment observers, Vancouver expressed deep concerns about a whole range of afflictions consequent upon the arrival of 'civilized' Europeans. Vancouver's recent editor, Kaye Lamb, described him as 'mildly obsessed by the idea of depopulation'.[25] While Vancouver's men appear to have observed the remnants of a smallpox epidemic, some historians have interpreted the reports of unburied bones, abandoned villages and depopulation as the normal consequences of the annual migration cycle, burial sites disturbed by animals, the disorder of native settlements, and the fact that the northwest coast peoples were highly aggressive and warlike. Robin Fisher dismissed theories about Native depopulation in the era of European explorations, identifying instead a 'guilt-induced mythology' disseminated by historians.[26] Nonetheless, Alfred Crosby used Vancouver's evidence to support his theories of pandemic outbreaks and depopulation well beyond the European frontier in North America to Puget Sound—'a part of the world then as distant from the main centers of human population as any place on earth'.[27] Recently, the geographer Cole Harris fleshed out Crosby's view, concluding that Vancouver and his men observed the remains of a continental pandemic of smallpox that in 1782 had crossed the mountains from the interior of the North American continent and advanced northward from the Columbia River valley to devastate a quite large and prosperous Native population in Puget Sound and around the Strait of Georgia.[28] Remarkably though, the Spanish explorers of this same region during 1791 and 1792 made no mention of pockmarked natives or of smallpox. With their base at Nootka Sound and extensive contacts with foreign fur traders as well as Natives, the Spaniards would have been aware of any demographic catastrophe among the Native populations provoked by smallpox. Even if the smallpox epidemics among the Tlingits of the Alaskan Panhandle in the 1770s and the peoples of Puget Sound and Georgia Strait in the early 1780s were unconnected, as Harris argues,[29] Spanish observers viewed both regions with sufficient regularity to perceive any impact.

Did Spanish naval officers during visits to Alaskan ports and the Strait of Georgia simply overlook or fail to mention signs of small-pox epidemics? If Vancouver scoured the Pacific Ocean as a scientific observer seeking evidence of disruptions and depopulation triggered by Europeans, this was not always the case with the eighteenth-century Spanish explorers. With the exception of Alejandro Malaspina, who most certainly represented the mainstream of Enlightenment voyaging, often the Spanish explorers were journeyman naval officers selected for northwest coast expeditions because they were available and not because they displayed special brilliance, scientific skill or imagination. They tended to think first of their own careers—how to earn promotions—and often wondered if assignment to Mexico's isolated west coast naval station at San Blas could do them the slightest good. Nevertheless, if the viceroys of New Spain ordered expeditions they did their best to fit out the sturdy supply vessels employed in coastal service to the California settlements, and assembled crews of Mexican mestizos and Indians who expressed little joy at the prospect of maritime adventures at high latitude where the climate was known to be cold.

In 1773, Viceroy Antonio María de Bucareli received orders from Madrid to dispatch a naval reconnaissance mission northward to evaluate the possible penetration of Russian maritime fur traders into North American coastal territories claimed theoretically by Spain. He ordered First Pilot Juan Pérez to take command. A career mariner who had served in the trans-Pacific trade to the Philippines and helped to supply the new California missions, Pérez was curious to determine the shape and resources of the North American continental littoral. From an intellectual perspective, his voyage to protect Spanish interest was a blend of old and new ideas. Scientific factors were important, but Spain would learn more about correct Enlightenment usage and language from James Cook and other foreign voyagers. Beyond orders to reach 60°N lat. and to take formulaic possession of the littoral, the thirty-two articles of Pérez's *Instrucción* focused upon the Native peoples and upon attracting them 'to the sweet, tender, desirable vassalage of His Majesty'. He was to commence a spiritual conquest that would expose them to the light of the Holy Gospel and raise them out of the shadows of idolatry.[30] To help achieve this great goal, the eighty-four men of the frigate *Santiago* included not only a ship's chaplain, but also Friars Juan Crespi and Thomas de la Peña of the Colegio Apostólico de Propaganda Fide de San Fernando de México, an élite missionary unit of the Church that had worked out effective systems to evangelise and to settle indigenous populations in the Sierra Gorda region of New Spain and most recently in Alta California.

The Spanish approach, reactionary though it may have been in some respects, compared with other voyages of Pacific exploration in that it required the careful collection of information about Native populations. The friars, Pérez, and his first officer Esteban José Martínez received orders to keep detailed daily journals and where possible to maintain accuracy by reading their entries aloud at night to the ship's officers. They were to describe Native peoples, their customs, way of life, numbers, systems of governance, religion, diplomacy and warfare, and usage of resources.[31] In order to obtain this information, Pérez received four cases of beads and trinkets to be distributed as gifts according to perceived ranks in Native culture, and he carried strong prohibitions against abuses or the use of deadly force except as a last resort to save Spanish lives. The viceroys of New Spain issued similar instructions to all successive expeditions.

To employ the exploration metaphor used by Greg Dening, the Spaniards were ready to cross the beach[32]—to intrude with all of their ideas and plans upon Native cultures of the North Pacific littoral. In fact, Pérez failed to locate a safe port for the duration of the expedition and those Haida and Nootka Natives who desired contact had to gather up their trade goods and paddle some distance off-shore in their ocean-going cedar canoes to initiate exchanges. The first of these took place on 20 July 1774, off the northern tip of the Queen Charlotte Islands, where Haida men and women rapidly overcame initial nervousness to celebrate ceremonies of peace, including gestures, singing in chorus that reminded some Spaniards of sea shanties sung in the Peruvian port of Callao, and standing erect in their canoes with their arms extended as in the shape of a cross. In another sign of peaceful intentions practised from Alaska to California, the Haidas cast feathers and bird down upon the surface of the sea.[33] Pérez described the men as being of good stature with well-built bodies and handsome eyes and faces. They wore their hair tied back like a wig with a tail like the custom of Spanish soldiers. Martínez exclaimed optimistically, 'This is a nation as white as Spaniards with blue eyes like the English, and brown hair almost with a blond cast more than any other colour'.[34] The Haidas approached the poop of the ship to receive beads, handkerchiefs and biscuit in exchange for their dried fish. Some seamen offered knives to purchase sea otter and seal skins, one sailor obtained a hat woven in different colours, and another traded for an attractive woven mat designed with intricate black and white squares. The natives offered to provide water and were enthusiastic even insistent in their invitations for the Spaniards to visit them ashore.[35]

The next day, while Pérez searched unsuccessfully in foggy conditions and treacherous currents for a safe port, the Haidas returned with trade as their prime objective. By mid-afternoon Martínez counted twenty-one canoes with over 150–200 Natives —including two large canoes crewed only by women accompanied by very young children. Crespi observed one canoe paddled by twelve women who controlled the vessel like the most dexterous seamen.[36] Martínez described the women as being as fair-skinned as Spaniards and very good looking except for the disfiguring labret, the wooden disk inserted into their lower lips that from a distance made them appear as if their tongues had been pulled out and left suspended.[37] They wore bracelets of iron, lead and copper and wore many metal rings on their fingers.

After renewed greeting ceremonies that included tambourine music, jingling, singing, and much good-natured shouting, the Haidas commenced trading mats, blankets and other items. The Spaniards were surprised to see many pieces of iron used for cutting edges, a half bayonet and part of a sword already in Haida possession. Martínez speculated that the metal possessed by the Haidas could have originated with the 1741 Russian expedition of Aleksie Chirikov which had lost two boats and crews not far to the north.[38]

Although most of the Native people refused invitations to board the ship, two men accepted, ate bread and cheese, and seemed to enjoy escorted tours. The officers attempted to question them and made many signs, but the Natives did not comprehend most meanings. They did indicate that the Spaniards should not sail further to the north where the people were evil and would shoot them with arrows. While the visitors were aboard, two seamen went into the canoes as hostages where they were welcomed with embraces, permitted their faces to be painted, and even danced. The Haidas accorded them signs of friendship placing a hand to their chests and behaving as if they were old friends.[39]

In their descriptions, the Spanish observers made no references to pockmarks or other signs of disease among the Haidas. Since many native men literally sold fur clothing off their backs until they stood stark naked, the prudish Spaniards could not avoid viewing them in their full glory. In their remarks, the officers and friars expressed great admiration for the physical condition of both men and women. With his lengthy Philippine experience, Pérez compared the Haidas to the Chinese traders who went to Manila to sell their merchandise.[40]

Prevented from finding a safe port because of contrary winds, heavy rain, thick fog, and dangerous currents, Pérez turned *Santiago* southward hoping to experience better luck. He was fearful of risking his vessel on a reef or of marooning his crew in some unknown bay; and to make matters worse, scurvy and other ailments had begun to reduce the efficiency of the crew. On 9 August, Pérez approached the coast once again, this time in the roadstead of Nootka Sound, later to become the entrepôt of trade and the site for Spain's most northerly Pacific outpost. Again, desire for metal and other trade items overcame the Natives' fear of the unknown visitors and they approached the ships day and night. The Spanish observers remarked on the differences in canoe design, clothing, and jewellery of these people, noting their hearty constitutions. Martínez exclaimed, 'they are robust and white as the best Spaniard as were the two women I saw'.[41] Surrounded by fifteen canoes crewed by about one hundred men and a few women, the Spaniards traded for a variety of items and recorded positive observations about the Natives—noting that the women did not ruin their looks with the labret.[42]

Even during this first Spanish voyage, it seems obvious from the detailed observations and medical records that the existence of smallpox aboard *Santiago* or of pockmarks on natives visiting from shore would have been noted in the journals. Aboard the ship, members of the crew suffered from the cold and damp of the northern climates. Pérez reported that not a man escaped rheumatic pains in his joints, headaches and colds, and some suffered severe nose and throat infections. By mid-August near the end of the voyage, the majority of the crewmen exhibited symptoms of scurvy and twenty had sores on their legs and in their mouths. Martínez blamed the bad water and salted provisions that with the cold climate 'fermented' the blood of crewmen. Despite the best efforts of the surgeon, Martínez criticised the Mexican mestizos who rejected preventative medicines and good medical advice. Some resisted swallowing their anti-scorbutic preparations, stating that they would rather die naturally than 'be killed by the surgeon and his medicine'. However, there is no mention of smallpox.[43]

THE MEDICAL RECORD of the 1775 expedition dispatched to accomplish what Pérez had left undone is fascinating, but despite the claims of some historians, it also indicates that smallpox was neither aboard the Spanish vessels nor mentioned in the detailed reports on the Natives visited from California to Alaska. Recognising the need for better-educated officers to command the Pacific expeditions, the Spanish Crown transferred six young men to Mexico including Bruno de Hezeta who commanded the expedition and *Santiago*, and Juan Francisco de la Bodega y Quadra who ended up commanding the schooner *Sonora*. Even as the two vessels sailed from San Blas in company with the California supply ship *San Carlos*, the surgeons were busy. The captain of *San Carlos*, Miguel Manrique, another of the young officers transferred from Spain, became totally deranged, insisted that his crew wanted to kill him, and locked himself in his cabin after first arming himself with six loaded pistols.[44] Neither copious bleeding nor medicines suppressed Manrique's madness and if anything the treatments left him even further possessed by his apprehensions, mania and fits of crying.[45]

Determined to fulfil their instructions to the letter, and to obtain fresh water, Hezeta and Bodega landed at 41°8′N lat. on the California coast which they named Puerto de la Trinidad (near today's Little River). They found a safe anchorage and traded with the Natives who offered sea otter pelts, deer skins, and other items in exchange for knives, iron barrel hoops, beads and other trifles. Hezeta landed Padres Benito de la Sierra and Miguel de la Campa, and an armed party to raise a cross, celebrate mass, and to fire off musket volleys proclaiming Spanish possession. Native observers fled from the din of gunfire, but soon returned to engage in trade. They appeared to be a peaceful people and there were few incidents during the nine days Hezeta's men spent in port. Although the women were modest in their dress, the men wore no clothing whatsoever during the heat of the day and only a fur cloak if the weather was cool. The Spaniards described them as being of medium stature, swarthy in colour, robust, and even corpulent. They were beardless and wore their hair long and loose.[46] Men and women tattooed their faces and bodies with patterns of lines and circles—like common seamen, said Francisco Mourelle—and pierced their lower lips from which they suspended their jewellery.[47]

The Spanish officers were surprised to find that, like the Haidas, these Natives possessed iron knives and other iron cutting implements. Hezeta questioned them at length on the origins of the metal and received the same answer from all, who indicated that it had originated in the north. Mourelle thought that the knives were made from pieces of old sabres and he noted that one was marked with an 'L'.[48] Like the Tlingits of Alaska, they suspended their knives, which were in wooden sheaths, from cords hung about their necks so that they could defend themselves in an instant. The Spaniards visited Native houses, examined their sweat lodges, and two seamen ran off to spend several days living with them, until hunger forced them to return.[49] Despite the detailed descriptions, no observer noticed any sign of pockmarks or other disease blemishes on the skin of these California Natives and the Spanish crews remained in robust good health.

The loss of seven men in an encounter with Natives near Point Glanville dampened enthusiasm for exploration just as scurvy commenced to ravage both crews. The surgeon aboard *Santiago*,

Juan González, recommended an immediate return to the south. By 23 July, he reported sixteen men seriously incapacitated and another twelve who exhibited early symptoms of scurvy. At first, Hezeta rejected his officers' advice to conclude the voyage, but on 2 August twenty-eight seamen were prostrate in their hammocks and another nineteen were sick although still able to function.[50] Hezeta turned for the coast at just over 49°N lat., around Barkley Sound, where some Natives dressed in cedar fibre clothing paddled off-shore to market their sea otter furs. The Spaniards commented upon their beautifully constructed bone inlaid canoes, their dexterity at navigating such narrow vessels in heavy seas, and Hezeta criticised their deceitfulness in commercial dealings. Several traded a canoe and some harpoons for a sword and other items—then attempted to flee without actually delivering their side of the bargain. Threatened with muskets, they changed their attitude instantly which made Hezeta suspect that they must have had previous experience with the effect of firearms.[51]

For Hezeta and his crew, the return voyage to Mexico was a nightmare of scurvy-induced disasters. Rather than heading for San Blas, he put into Monterey to await Bodega with *Sonora*. By this point, thirty-six men suffered severe scurvy and fourteen were ill with dysentery and other ailments. A seaman, Antonio Estevan, died before he could be moved ashore to a hospital tent and, on 1 November, Pérez, the commander of the 1774 expedition, died of complications resulting from scurvy.[52]

While Hezeta retreated south to California, Bodega rejected the idea of failure in his mission to achieve high latitude. The two ships lost company—probably intentionally—on 30 July after Bodega had obtained a cannon and additional munitions. On 16 August, after a punishing series of storms, *Sonora* reached 57°N lat. where Bodega sighted the snow-capped peak of Mount Edgecumbe, which he named San Jacinto. The next day, the expedition entered Bucareli Sound on Prince of Wales Island, a protected port that permitted the Spaniards to obtain water, firewood, and to cut the much needed new topmast. At this point, five seamen were suffering from scurvy with sores in their mouths, swollen knees, and paralysed legs that prevented them from manning daily watches.[53]

It was from this location that historians have Bodega's crew communicating smallpox to the Tlingits. In fact, the Natives were cautious, refusing to go aboard the schooner and for some time retreating to a strongly fortified house surrounded by a palisade of posts dug into the ground. Bodega and a small contingent landed nearby to erect a cross, raise a Spanish flag, and to take formal possession of the land. As soon as the Spaniards departed, the Tlingits went to the place and removed the cross to their palisade. Later, they raised a white banner beside their dwelling and explained through clear signs punctuated with shouts that the visitors must pay for any water and wood taken from Native territories. Bodega offered beads and pieces of cloth to placate them, but they rejected these gifts as utterly worthless. To back their claims to sovereignty, they brandished their long flint-tipped spears and iron knives, but the Spaniards replied with similar threats of their own while continuing to fill their water casks, withdrawing quickly without completing their task so as to avoid any outbreak of real violence.

Because of the limited contacts, the Spanish descriptions of the Tlingits were brief. However, Mourelle stated that they looked quite similar to the Natives of Puerto de la Trinidad in California except that they wore furs.[54] There was no smallpox in Bodega's crew, no mention was made that the Tlingits looked anything but physically robust, and there were no close contacts between the two sides that might have communicated *variola major*. Bodega attempted to sail even further north, but by now scurvy, which Mourelle blamed upon an infection transferred from the frigate *Santiago*, beset the entire crew. They turned south, recuperating for a month at Monterey where fresh vegetables, meat, and milk were made available by the Franciscan padres.[55]

THE 1779 EXPEDITION of Ignacio de Arteaga and Bodega y Quadra in the frigates *Princesa* and *Favorita* is the best-documented of the early Spanish northwest coast voyages. Following Cook by a year, Arteaga received orders to evaluate again Russian penetration of Alaska and to establish if a navigable Northwest Passage joined the Pacific Ocean to the Atlantic. Sailing from San Blas on 11 February 1779, he avoided coastal reconnaissance and headed directly for Bucareli Sound, where he arrived on 2 May. From the medical perspective, one artillery man, Antonio Uribe, died suddenly aboard *Princesa* on 18 April and was interred at sea and one other seaman fell ill and died shortly thereafter. Since the clothing and other effects of the two crewmen were auctioned and redistributed, as was normal procedure to provide a small fund for the families of the deceased, we may conclude that smallpox was not suspected.[56] Aboard *Favorita*, there were no deaths or reports of significant illness.[57]

Because the voyage north was shorter than anticipated (only eighty-one days), Arteaga decided to explore the region around Bucareli Sound for a month or so to allow time for the advance of warmer weather further to the north. The Tlingits responded favourably to the arrival of the floating emporia, scattering feathers from headlands and canoes, singing melodious songs, and standing with their arms extended. Although they refused to go aboard the ships for a few days, they accepted small gifts of biscuit, copper wire, buttons, brown sugar, and beads, responding with similar small trifles of their own and fresh fish. Some men carried spears, bows and clubs, and wore the distinctive Tlingit slat armour cuirasses, heavy hide mantle, gorget, and helmets carved in the form of ferocious beasts that Padre Riobo described as being 'like that of the ancients'.[58] Recalling the experiences of 1775, the Spaniards conducted many musket drills and trained themselves in defensive tactics during the voyage north.

Despite all precautions, however, the sojourn with the Tlingits was anything but peaceful. While there was active trade in hides, sea otter pelts, and even of sickly unwanted Native children,[59] the demand among the Natives for iron and European clothing combined with their aggressive assertion of ownership over the land, water, and all other resources to provoke numerous incidents. The Tlingits ripped down a large cross erected by the Spaniards, and during one of the launch expeditions dispatched to chart the complex waterways of the port they attempted to occupy exactly the same camp sites selected by the Spaniards. They threatened violence, tested their arrows, and by many signs made clear their sovereignty over the territory and its resources. Demonstrations of musket fire deterred them temporarily, but it was obvious that the Tlingits were a warlike people.[60] They stole everything that they could get away with—washed clothing set out to dry ashore, chisels, spoons, hoops, latches, nails, fixtures from the ships, and any other items that they could grab.[61] In what was an obvious show of power, the Tlingits assembled a flotilla of eighty-six canoes and over 1000 warriors, surrounded the frigates, and then set up camps to observe the Spanish anchorage.[62] When two sailors disappeared from a washing detail—slipping away on a lark to visit the natives voluntarily, as it turned out—the Spaniards took nineteen hostages and fired broadside warning salvoes crashing through the trees that accidentally killed at least one man.

If the 1779 expedition had harboured smallpox, there were many chances to communicate the virus to the Tlingits. Shortly after they arrived at Bucareli Sound, a ship's boy from *Princesa* died of unknown causes and was buried ashore at the foot of the Spanish cross. On 20 May, Arteaga and the majority of his crew aboard *Princesa* fell ill very suddenly, suffered wrenching pain, and at first appeared to be in very great risk of dying. Bodega's surgeon, Mariano Nuñez de Esquivel, feared plague and moved the sick ashore to a tent hospital made of sails where the change of location and 'freshness of the land' might help cure the mysterious ailment.[63] Two seamen, Manuel Domínguez and Felipe Sanauria, died, the latter after spending some time in the hospital ashore.[64] Fortunately, within a few days the remaining patients recovered fully and the 'epidemic' as it was described ended as quickly as it had appeared. Fearing attacks against the camp ashore, Arteaga withdrew the provisional hospital.[65] Although the causes of the illness were not established, the fact that it affected only one ship would suggest food poisoning—likely from the consumption of shellfish—and certainly not smallpox. Incipient scurvy was present in both vessels although it had not yet become debilitating.[66]

In their detailed descriptions of Native society, the Spaniards noted the fair skins and attractive faces of the Tlingits who, as Bodega reported, were 'arrogant, high-spirited, and generally inclined to war'.[67] Second Pilot Juan Pantoja said that they were of regular stature, some more swarthy than others, and physically very strong. As had been noted previously, the men wore their hair long and tied it in a tail 'like the most polished soldier'. They perforated the cartilage of their noses in which they wore metal pins and pierced their ears in three or four places to hang copper wire, coins, buttons and beads obtained from trade. Most painted their faces and bodies white, blue, black, and red, and on some days they plastered their heads with bird down. Like other coastal Natives, the men wore sea otter fur cloaks that hung to their waists and on cold days used another fur wrapper that covered them to their feet. As usual, the men caused the Spaniards some consternation since they wore no undergarments and cared not at all about modesty. The women were agreeable in looks, with rosy cheeks, and they tied their long hair in a single tress. Much more modest than the men, they covered themselves completely from neck to feet in a tunic of skins fitted at the waist. Nevertheless, positive descriptions turned negative as each Spaniard expressed revulsion at the labret, using phrases such as 'abominable to the sight', 'ridiculous', and 'an ugly imperfection'.[68] In older age, women's lower lips hung down against their chins making their speech blurred and indistinct.

If the Spaniards did not introduce smallpox, neither did they mention pockmarks disfiguring the Bucareli Tlingits. All observers commented about the robust good health of the natives, sometimes noting that scars on the men were the result of wartime combat rather than disease. Indeed, Bernardo de Quirós questioned several individuals about their healed wounds and they bragged that most had been caused by enemy daggers. Like other observers, Quirós noted that in addition to stone axes, some Tlingit men carried long iron knives, shaped something like European bayonets, which they suspended from cords hung round their necks. When necessary, they fixed the knives to long staffs to make very effective lances.[69] Enquiries about the origin of these iron knives carried by some women as well as men and about other metal implements in their possession produced no satisfactory answers. Without scientists or friars present, the officers failed abysmally in their efforts to make progress at recording accurate vocabularies of the Native language.[70] Bodega speculated that the Tlingits either mined their own iron, purchased bars from traders who came to visit them, or received neighbours who acted as merchant middlemen. The Spaniards questioned the Tlingits carefully on these possibilities, but failed to obtain any responses except gestures towards the mountains and other indications that they had traded previously with ships.[71]

However, the high level of artistic activity, the intricate fringed woven wool textiles in various colours and designs, the sophisticated offensive and defensive weapons and armour, sea-going canoes, and the skilled production of such items as painted carvings of canoes, wooden frogs that opened like powder boxes, decorated wooden boxes, flutes and whistles, figures of men, copper necklaces, bracelets, and other jewellery, illustrated a flourishing culture as yet undamaged by foreign contacts, epidemic smallpox, or any other devastating disease.[72]

The 1779 expedition pushed on to Hinchinbrook Island (named by the Spaniards Isla de Magdalena) searching for a Northwest Passage at Prince William Sound before heading westward to the entrance to Cook Inlet. The officers expressed amazement at the continued willingness of Natives—now in hide boats and kayaks—to seek trade far off-shore and to board the Spanish vessels without apparent fear. Unaware of Cook's visit the previous year, and convinced that the powerful initiative to seek trade opportunities exhibited by all coastal cultures must have predated any recent events, Arteaga speculated about possible previous contacts with Russian traders. Some Natives wore necklaces of glass beads and some boats flew red, white and blue flags. At Prince William Sound, five crewmen aboard *Princesa* suffered varying degrees of scurvy and five others were sick with other illnesses. On *Favorita*, there were two cases of scurvy and six other sailors suffering different medical problems. However, by the beginning of August, scurvy, 'an illness so contagious and rapid',[73] killed artillery man Juan Rivera and a seaman named Juan Severino. Following a junta of officers, Arteaga accepted majority advice to sail for San Francisco where he landed eighteen sick seamen to recover in provisional hospital tents.[74]

Having failed to discover Russian intruders or a Northwest Passage, Spain withdrew from North Pacific explorations for almost a decade. In the interim, of course, other nations, following the potential realised by Cook's men, opened the trans-Pacific sea otter fur trade. It was not until 1788 that the Spanish imperial government awoke once more to new rumours of Russian expansion along the Alaskan coast. This time, Esteban José Martínez led an expedition with the frigate *Princesa*, supported by Gonzalo López de Haro commanding the packet *San Carlos*. Although Martínez soon earned a bad reputation among the English for his arrest and detention of fur traders at Nootka Sound in 1789, he was a great admirer of James Cook and a man with a grand vision of a Spanish trans-Pacific Ocean trading empire. Sailing from San Blas on 4 March 1788, Martínez introduced a thorough programme aboard *Princesa* to wash the galleys, storage rooms, and holds regularly with sulphur and vinegar mixed with lime juice, to leave hatch covers off whenever possible for air circulation, and to fumigate the holds by burning gunpowder. To maintain the health of his men, he added bitter lime juice, sulphur, and vinegar to the ship's water supply. Unlike previous commanders, Martínez distributed cold weather clothing and extra lengths of heavy cloth to his seamen. When he arrived at Montague Island, he followed Cook's example of cutting greens such as wild celery and wherever possible relieving the monotonous diet of salt meat and biscuit, by purchasing fresh fish from the Natives and sending his men out to fish.[75]

Using Cook's chart and the less detailed Spanish charts of 1779, Martínez explored Montague Island and parts of Prince William Sound. The Natives now wore European beads, silver coins, French and English coats, and they shouted the names of Cook's ships. Hearing the boatswain's whistle, they shouted in English, 'All hands ahoy', and repeated words such as 'yes' and 'plenty'. They appeared robust and healthy, but the Spaniards could not even begin to comprehend their language and managed to recognise only a few words from Cook's vocabulary. When the officers attempted to pronounce such words, the Natives kept on talking without showing the slightest sign of recognition. While Martínez reported in detail about Native weapons, armour and kayaks, and commented at length about their trade and customs, he and his officers also recognised that by this date there had been many previous European expeditions in the region. On Hinchinbrook Island, the Spaniards found a partially completed house with four-well made windows that they learned later had been constructed the previous year by Russian fur traders.[76]

Heading west to Kodiak, Trinity, and finally Unalaska Islands, Martínez and López de Haro separated in foggy conditions and each reconnoitred the Alaskan coast. Natives who boarded the

Spanish ships now took off their hats and made the sign of the Cross. López de Haro proceeded to Three Saints Bay, Kodiak Island, where he met the Russian commander Evstrat Delarov, and toured the settlement. Martínez went to Trinity Island and on to Unalaska where he visited the trader Potap Zaikov and learned a great deal about Russian activities through his Hispanicised Ragusan (Croatian) translator Estéban Mondofía. Indeed, while the Spaniards were extremely duplicitous in their explanations and surreptitiously took possession of the land for Spain wherever possible in Russian territories, both sides exhibited friendship and relations were outwardly cordial throughout the visits. For their part, the Russians misinformed their Spanish visitors about their exact population in Alaska and reiterated ambitious schemes to move southward during 1789 to occupy Nootka Sound.[77]

In their sojourn with the Russians and Russianised Natives, neither Martínez nor his officers made any references to smallpox or to pockmarked Natives. However, it became obvious in Russian territories that the fur trading outposts exerted a significant impact upon the indigenous population. Several Natives approached the Spaniards to show small tribute receipts issued by the Russian authorities and they were very anxious to make certain that their documents were returned.[78] In their visits aboard the ships, Natives appeared to be overly docile and humble. They did not carry any weapons and often complained that Russian officials punished them severely with whippings. At Three Saints Bay, a Russian priest guarded by a watchtower and armed sentinels was observed preaching the gospel to a large group of adult Natives. Corroborating the indications of poor treatment were Russian defensive preparations at each post and numerous stories about chronic Native treachery.[79] Delarov showed López de Haro many healed scars on his officers and men caused by arrow wounds.[80] Zaikov told Martínez that three years previously the Natives of Cook Inlet had killed seven Russian fur traders and some Unalaska workers, forcing them to retreat entirely from the area. At Prince William Sound, attackers besieged a party of Russians who had been forced to winter over because of scurvy. Finally, Zaikov mentioned that during the past winter, 700 indigenous men of the island and coastal population, including some educated by the Russians, had perished from the cold and as the result of an epidemic.[81] Unfortunately this passing reference did not mention the nature of the disease. Since the Spaniards did not report pockmarked Natives, it seems unlikely that the epidemic mentioned was smallpox.

The Spanish officers made no mention of smallpox among the Natives of the Alaskan coast as far east as Unalaska Island until Martínez met Zaikov and described him as swarthy like a Spaniard, 'scarred by smallpox, with black hair, a well built body, and medium stature'. At least Martínez mentioned smallpox when he thought he saw its unmistakable pockmarks! Likely, the Russian commander had suffered the disease years before in Kamchatka where it was known to have been almost endemic. Although the 1787 winter epidemic indicated the possible extent of disruption in Native societies caused by the Russian fur traders, the Spaniards reported no continuing signs of poor health. They did question the Russians about iron weapons and tools among different coastal tribes that were of unique design and indicated evidence of trade networks that predated recent Russian, British, French and Spanish expeditions. Zaikov reported the wreck of a Japanese trading vessel in 1786 further to the west in the Aleutian Island chain from which ten male survivors had been sent to Siberia. He explained that iron salvage from this vessel had been traded eastward to Prince William Sound and that this plus the iron introduced recently by foreign expeditions accounted for the Native inventories. He said that the Russians never traded iron to the American Natives—only beads, tobacco, and other items in exchange for their furs.[82]

While this answer seemed plausible for the recent period, the Spanish observers expressed perplexity at the amount of iron and at the different specialised methods the Natives had devised to work and to utilise the metal. Despite Russian explanations, it appears that a trans-Pacific iron trade from Asia much predated the European presence and that earlier commercial connections could have communicated diseases. In this case, North America may not have been as isolated from Asian disease pools as many historians have believed. Based upon the detailed evidence in the journals and correspondence from the Spanish expeditions of 1774–88, we may conclude that these eighteenth-century visitors did not introduce smallpox to the northwest coast. In fact, given the nature of small-pox transmission, it would be more logical to suggest Russian origins since they could have imported the disease from Kamchatka through the Aleutian Islands.

With Russian warnings in 1788 about projected movements southward along the continental coastline, the Spaniards hastened to occupy Nootka Sound (which they did from 1789 to 1795), and they conducted many voyages of exploration within the region. While they introduced 'an incredible abundance of rats' at their Yuquot settlement at Nootka Sound and suffered disease deaths—especially during the wet winter months—from catarrh, rheumatic pains, flatulent colic, diarrhoea, dysentery with bloody stool, and scurvy,[83] their detailed dispatches made no reference to smallpox. Indeed, if *variola major* had been carried to the North Pacific by ship in this active period of the maritime fur trade, it should have appeared at Nootka, which during these years became the entrepôt for traders of different nationalities and origins.

For Mexicans and Spaniards alike, the cool rainy marine climate was 'insufferable' and most men survived their tours of duty only with the forbearance of 'an admirable spirit of resignation'. One post commander, Ramón Saavedra, described how in June 1794, when he raised his voice to shout an order, a great amount of blood poured out of his mouth. This terrified Saavedra and also the surgeon who proceeded to bleed him twice and to administer medicines. That winter, Saavedra fell ill again during a period when many members of the garrison suffered from scurvy.[84] In such a difficult climate, the Spaniards simply could not comprehend how the Natives, clothed only in sea otter skins and old European items, managed to retain their strong constitutions, good health and remarkable agility. In 1791, scientists with the expedition of Alejandro Malaspina also found absolutely no signs of diseases or ulcers among the indigenous population. Their only scars were the ubiquitous healed battle wounds that they bragged about and showed off with great pride. They consumed a diet mainly of fish and grease, lived in excessive filth, and in the Spanish view they were addicted to chronic laziness. Nevertheless, despite monoto-nous food and the cold damp climate, the Natives appeared to be immune to scurvy and all of them kept their teeth until the most advanced old age.[85]

The episodes of smallpox on the northwest coast in the 1770s and 1780s witnessed by Captains Portlock and Vancouver (assuming that they were correct in their diagnosis based upon pockmarks) appear to have been confined to limited population pockets rather than illustrations of a great pandemic that caused demographic damage among the entire indigenous population. Of course, small-pox epidemics did not sweep away all populations in a uniform manner and this essay treats only the coastal populations that in some instances were quite isolated from one another.[86] During the early period of contact with the Spanish explorers, the Native populations appeared to enjoy dynamic good health. Their pos-session of iron and attitudes towards the appearance of Strangers suggest evidence of visits by earlier maritime traders as well as a well-developed system of Native commerce up and down the North American littoral. The fact that indigenous peoples from California to Alaska did not view Europeans aboard sailing ships as returning gods such as Quetzalcoatl of Mexico or Lono of Hawaii, also supports this view.

If there was a much older trans-oceanic diffusion of iron from Japan, China, Korea or elsewhere in Asia, the indigenous North Americans may not have been as isolated from diseases as many historians and anthropologists have believed. While there is no hard evidence, it seems at least possible that limited outbreaks of smallpox—for example, the case reported by Portlock among some Tlingit bands—could have been introduced to the northwest coast Natives as an accidental tourist packed in cases or bales of old clothing that contained scab matter from Mexico, Asia or else-where. Given exactly the right conditions in a cool, dry and dark ship's hold, one wonders if under optimum conditions the virus might have survived the ocean voyage to infect a Native com-munity.[87] Certainly, by the 1790s, used clothing was a major item in northwest coast Native trade. In 1792, Secundino Salamanca reported that the people of the Strait of Juan de Fuca no longer wanted copper or Monterey conch shells and that old clothing was the best currency to use with them.[88] Spanish officers often noted that Mestizo and Native sailors from Mexico looked little different from the northwest coast Natives who appeared in cast off garments acquired from every trading nation. In dealing with the Tlingits at Yakutat in 1791, Antonio de Tova Arredondo, second officer aboard *Atrevida* with Malaspina noted: 'One saw [Natives] dressed in complete uniforms and some with great coats of fine cloth buttoned at the breast as in our usage and with the rest of the body naked'.[89]

Did smallpox find its way into a few of these sometimes burlesque recreations of European fashion? This might explain the appearance of the disease at isolated locations. If so, it would be ironic that European clothing with its symbolic meanings as well as its ability to protect against bad weather could have been the agent. It is clear that George Vancouver was correct in his general concerns about the dangers of the European presence in the Pacific world. Not only did the newcomers introduce iron, clothing and firearms, but they also brought diseases such as smallpox, and disrupted Native societies and traditional methods of subsistence. Already in 1788 when Martínez visited the Russians, their aggressive fur traders had interfered with and dislocated the indigenous populations of the Aleutian Islands and the Alaskan coastline. At Nootka Sound, where the Spaniards displaced the major whaling village at Yuquot with their fort and settlement, the Natives were most anxious that they should leave. By 1794, some bands pushed out of traditional fishing areas now occupied by the Spaniards were reduced to eating roots and some people suffered starvation during the winter months. Out of compassion for their suffering, the Spanish post commander provided them daily with a cauldron of cooked beans.[90] Together with the pressures of disruption and changes in their economy of subsistence, there was a devil's brew of different diseases including venereal complaints, measles, mumps, dysentery, influenza and typhoid. By the early nineteenth century epidemic smallpox did arrive to devastate further the indigenous peoples. As for the eighteenth-century pandemic among northwest coast Native cultures, the fragmentary evidence of an anti-Spanish Portlock and one apparently legitimate sighting by Vancouver appear to have fuelled the creation of a figment of historical imagination.[91] Confused by a paucity of information and possibly some quite localised outbreaks that may have been chicken pox, measles or other skin diseases, some researchers blamed the Spanish explorers for causing smallpox epidemics. In some cases, historians wishing to correct the record concerning the destruction of Native cultures following the intrusions of Europeans may have misinterpreted scant sources on demographic disasters or at least pushed later population declines back in time. Knowing that the smallpox scourge did eradicate many indigenous communities in the nineteenth century, it is tempting to inflate very thin evidence to explain later depopulation and other catastrophes. However, in the eighteenth century at least, smallpox epidemics do not appear to have caused major demographic disruptions among the Native peoples of the northwest coast.

The Career of William Ellis

British Missions, the Pacific, and the American Connection

ANDREW PORTER

I N MUCH WRITING about Britain's empire from the mid-eighteenth century onwards, there is a pronounced tendency to emphasise both a steady eastward shift in the central focus of imperial concern, and the overwhelming importance of India and Africa in the imperial system. The roots of this preoccupation are well known. The loss of the American colonies, the declining relative economic importance of the Caribbean, the expansion of British economic influence and military power in India are only a few of the most important. Their significance and interconnection have been explored in many different ways, from the mid-twentieth-century writings of Eric Williams and Vincent Harlow to more recent work by C. A. Bayly and Alan Frost.[1] In all this, however, there is a danger that alternative contemporary visions of the world may be overlooked.

A prime concern of Glyn Williams's scholarship has been to keep firmly in focus the importance to the eighteenth-century European mind of connections with North America and the Pacific. It is therefore particularly appropriate to use this opportunity to examine further the extent to which, for many people, an outlook shaped by a westerly perspective and the linkage of North American with

Pacific interests continued to overshadow alternative world views until well into the nineteenth century. The career of William Ellis, from his departure for the Society Islands in 1816 as a member of the London Missionary Society (LMS) to his resignation from the post of Foreign Secretary to the LMS in 1841, offers an interesting insight into just such a world view. It also reveals how, in a missionary setting, Pacific experience and American connections could influence developing responses to African or Asian problems as attention did at last turn slowly eastwards.[2]

Finally, in a world where Pacific historians, no less than other regional specialists, are liable to fragment their studies of missions by focusing on a single society or territory, Ellis's progress provides a useful reminder of the global awareness and international co-operation which imparted so much dynamism to missionary enterprise.

WILLIAM ELLIS WAS BORN in London in 1794. Trained as a candle-maker and then a gardener, he was encouraged to approach the LMS in 1814, and, on being accepted, was trained briefly, like other early luminaries of the Society, by David Bogue at the missionary academy in Gosport, Hampshire. After additional crash courses in printing and medicine, he left for 'the South Seas'— Tahiti—in 1816, with the increasingly common missionary accompaniments of a wife, new-born daughter and printing press.[3] When compared with the alternatives, cheaper and potentially more reliable passages were at times obtainable on convict ships as far as Port Jackson (Sydney) in New South Wales. As a result, Ellis, his wife and another missionary couple travelled for 200 guineas on the *Atlas*, leaving England at the end of January 1816, sailing via Rio de Janeiro, and reaching Port Jackson on 22 July.

Missionaries were sometimes unwelcome passengers. Although Ellis was at first pleasantly surprised at the civility he met, he soon found himself not only contending with sea-sickness but also living in fear of a convict uprising, abetted by the ship's crew, against the guards. He also faced the growing obstruction of a captain who refused either to feed him properly or to honour the terms of the passage agreement with the LMS.[4] Like many before and after him, Ellis was robust but also very much the innocent abroad, often an easy touch for any inclined to take advantage of him.[5] Accustomed to the open hospitality of English supporters' homes, he was horrified at the hefty bills for his four months in the home of 'Christian friends', the Hassall family, in Parramatta. The LMS Directors were no wiser as to the difficult local circumstances. They were highly critical of his costs, unsympathetic to the problems of finding and negotiating a passage to the islands, and scarcely appeased either by the news that he had secured a free passage to Tahiti or by his present to their museum of 'a flying Squirrel skin'.[6]

Ellis's time in New South Wales was largely spent assisting Samuel Marsden, at Parramatta, with services, itinerant preaching, printing and Sunday School teaching, activities which set something of a pattern for later LMS missionaries on their way out.[7] Eventually leaving Sydney in December, and spending Christmas week in New Zealand at the Bay of Islands, Ellis finally arrived at Eimeo (Moorea), close to Tahiti, Huahine and Raiatea in the Society Island group, on 13 February 1817 after a two-month voyage. This is not the place for a detailed account of Ellis's activity. Naturally, his early years were spent attending to the many staple tasks of a missionary's existence—growing food and surviving, learning the language, getting the press set up and a printing programme under way, preaching, teaching, and keeping his journal for regular dispatch home.[8] His family also grew, a son being born in 1820. From Moorea he moved to Huahine in July 1818, where he lived for most of the next four years, with occasional visits to Raiatea.[9] The scope and integration of missionary activities proceeded apace. Ellis and his colleagues became heavily involved in the work of translation and the drafting of local law codes. They were also, for instance, struck by the continual 'eagerness of the people for books'. This they encouraged not only for its own sake, as additional evidence of the progress of the Word and its civilising impact, but also as the basis of a barter trade. In any case anxious to encourage the local islanders to take up commercial pursuits, the missionaries also exchanged copies of the Gospels of Luke and Mark for coconut oil in the hope of finding a market to offset the mission's own expenses.[10]

Ellis's contacts with the world of American missionary enterprise were first opened in 1822. The previous year the Directors had sent

the Reverend Daniel Tyerman and Mr George Bennett as a deputation to review existing LMS activity in the South Seas and to
make recommendations for future expansion. With this in view,
and taking with them the by now experienced and fluent (at least in
Tahitian) Ellis, the two deputies set out in February 1822 to visit
the American mission at the Sandwich Islands (Hawai'i), intending
to return by way of the Marquesas where the LMS some years
before had failed to establish a mission. Having arrived under the
Reverend Hiram Bingham in April 1820, seven missionaries from
Boston were by this time occupying three stations, the most important of which was Honolulu on the island of Oahu.[11] In the end, the
LMS party never reached the Marquesas. Arriving at the Sandwich
Islands at the beginning of April 1822, a change of mind by their
ship's captain left them stranded there for four months.[12] One consequence of this enforced stay was that Ellis was invited to join the
Americans. With the approval of the deputation, he accepted and,
after returning briefly to Huahine to arrange his affairs and collect
his family, he reached Oahu again with several Tahitian teachers on
4 February 1823. There the Ellises lived until they left the Pacific
for Britain in September 1824.

Ellis's move was somewhat unorthodox. It not only presented
the London Directors with something of a *fait accompli*, but
involved the LMS in an area already occupied by another Protestant mission, and necessitated a complete change in the terms of
Ellis's engagement with the Society.[13] Only the presence of the
deputation made it thinkable and their backing was important in
securing London's approval.

The explanation customarily given for this turn of events hinges
on the linguistic difficulties being experienced by the Americans,
the rapidity with which Ellis adjusted to the local Hawaiian
language, the legitimacy given to Christianity by the presence with
the deputation of Tahitian teachers, and Ellis's personal popularity
with both the Americans and the local people and their leaders.[14]
At the time, writing to the Society, Ellis stressed the ease of co-
operation with the Americans and the readiness of the islands for a
great forward push by Christian evangelists. There was much talk
of Providence in action and the importance of the common
missionary endeavour.[15]

While these convictions should not be dismissed, other considerations strongly influenced the deputies in supporting the scheme. Urging confidentiality on the Directors, Tyerman explained that 'our most cogent reasons for stationing Mr Ellis here . . . cannot be given to the public'. He continued:

> Of the piety of the American missionaries we cannot speak too highly. Their conduct is truly exemplary, and so far as religion goes, their spirit and temper are admirable. The Lay-brethren are highly suited to their situations, and the wives of all are truly excellent women . . . But the two ordained missionaries under whom the whole is placed are seriously wanting in that ardent and enterprising zeal which is so especially necessary in a Missionary who goes to new ground, to excite attention, create events, and turn to good account occurring circumstances. They love to be at ease, and one would think they were seeking a snug sinecure, and having found it, they are content to remain in possession.[16]

American lethargy 'pained our minds beyond expression', and the deputies were therefore happy that Ellis should stay. In Tyerman's view, 'Mr Ellis has a pleasing method of ingratiating himself with the natives—the King and chiefs and all appear to be highly pleased with him—and finding that he can so soon speak their Language, they have formed a high opinion of his Talents, and very justly—he is indeed an excellent missionary'.[17] As for the Americans, despite their warmth towards Ellis, 'their modes of thinking and working are so different from ours' that the deputation anticipated difficulties to come. On this point the views of the LMS deputation were not so distant from those of Bingham; his memoirs suggest that he too was sensitive to differences, for instance, over such issues as the proper qualifications for missionaries.[18] However, Tyerman felt that in the end Bingham and his assistant, Asa Thurston, had had little choice in the matter, for not only did their own lay colleagues warm to Ellis by comparison with their own leaders, but local people were waxing enthusiastic for him in part from a dislike of the Americans.

As a ready friend to all the world, Ellis was in effect being encouraged as the best hope of rescuing the Americans from themselves, and was accepted by at least some of the Americans as a necessary buttress to their own credentials. Yet however fragile it might seem as a basis for fruitful co-operation, Ellis's presence proved a marked success. His experience, worn lightly, proved of great assistance to the American Board venture; despite the demands of his increasingly sick wife, which might easily have strained patience on all sides in the small missionary community, his tactful initiatives and willing co-operation were much appreciated. Bingham, with good reason to find his presence an irritant, was soon writing privately to the American Board of Commissioners for Foreign Missions in Boston that 'Mr Ellis is a man of the right stamp—I am happy to labor with him'. Bingham felt Ellis's absence when he left the Pacific, urged the LMS to support further joint plans rather than separate establishments, and continued to correspond with Ellis in the 1830s. Many years later he recalled how Ellis, 'peculiarly felicitous in his manner of communication with all classes, greatly won our esteem'.[19] The friendship was reciprocated. As Ellis told George Burder in London, 'the most perfect harmony and entire confidence exists between us, though brought together from such different spheres of action . . .'[20] When his wife's illness finally compelled the family to leave for home, there seems to have been marked sadness on all sides, and in his last surviving letter from the Pacific Ellis's sense of failure was confined to the hymn-book which he and Bingham had prepared together: 'I fear the brethren will never learn them to sing'.[21]

On leaving the Sandwich Islands in September 1824, Ellis found it necessary to take an American ship, the *Russell*, again benefiting from a free passage and sailing via Cape Horn to New Bedford, Massachusetts. He took with him 'large collections of natural and artificial curiosities' for the LMS museum as well as many drawings. By the time they arrived in New England, it was felt that his wife should have proper medical treatment and convalesce before they continued their journey to England. In this manner, therefore, the second phase of his encounter with America fell into place. Ellis spent four months there, visiting Philadelphia, Boston, New York and many other cities, preaching, lecturing and forming important friendships. Most notable among these was that with Rufus Anderson, who was about to become the American Board's

Foreign Secretary. Ellis's wife meanwhile recovered in the homes of American Board committee members.[22]

The suggestion that Ellis might make himself useful in this way came from the Board, and was accepted, as Ellis told his own Directors, 'from a sense of the great obligations I was under, a desire to advance in this country a cause common to both' while his wife benefited from a rest.[23] He was excited by the stirring of religious revival and enthusiasm which he experienced in many places in the eastern United States, and was enthused by the warmth of his reception. Everywhere, 'it has been highly gratifying to me to observe, in various classes, and particularly in religious society, such a friendly feeling towards England, and such a desire to cooperate with all associations of good men there, in ... promoting righteousness, peace and happiness among all the families of mankind'.[24] More than forty years later, Anderson paid generous tribute to the importance of Ellis's contribution to the work of the Board 'in many parts of the Northern and Middle states'.[25]

Writing from Huahine late in 1824, having just started on his return home, William Ellis had expressed his determination to do all he could in America and Britain to encourage the interest of patrons and friends in the evangelisation of Polynesia.[26] Just as in Boston, once back in Britain he was as good as his word, responding so vigorously to the Society's wish to make use of his experience in extensive tours through the kingdom, that they and their doctors began to fear for Ellis's health.[27]

In part his activity took the familiar form of speaking and writing about his years in the western Pacific. In fact Ellis left the region too soon ever to visit what from the late 1820s became the thriving LMS missions in other areas such as the Cook and Samoan Islands. Nevertheless, he gained a reputation not only as an expert on Polynesia, but also as the chronicler of the local 'progress' in Christianity and civilisation brought about by the missionary societies.[28] As he explained in the preface to his *Polynesian Researches*, his volumes showed the transformation of

the barbarous, cruel, indolent, and idolatrous inhabitants of Tahiti, and the neighbouring Islands, into a comparatively civilized, humane, industrious and Christian people. They also comprise a record of the measures pursued by the native governments, in changing the social economy of the people, and regulating their commercial intercourse with foreigners, in the promulgation of a new civil code . . . the establishment of courts of justice, and the introduction of trial by jury.[29]

There was, of course, more to this than a historical account of indigenous social and cultural change. Polynesian experience provided indisputable justification for the missionary movement: 'such facts as those presented to the world, in the recent history of the Society and Sandwich Islands, prove, that CHRISTIANITY ALONE supplies the most powerful motives, and the most effective machinery, for originating and accomplishing the processes of civilization'.[30]

Reiterated in many ways by missionaries everywhere throughout the century, this was at root a message designed to stimulate the interest and generosity of supporters old and new. At this time, however, it was also more than that. During Ellis's return voyage to Britain, considerable attention there was attracted by the visit of King Liholiho and Queen Kamamalu of Hawaii, their illness and deaths in London, and the official escort of their bodies and surviving retinue home to Hawai'i by Captain Lord Byron in HMS *Blonde*.[31] The saga not only revived widespread curiosity about the Pacific and Britain's presence there, but emerged as a focal point in the continuing and wider struggle between the missionary societies and critics of their role in British expansion. It was the interest of the LMS in Polynesia and of Ellis more particularly in Hawai'i which ensured that the argument was co-ordinated and taken up on both sides of the Atlantic.

Ellis had both prepared and checked his own Hawaiian journal with his American colleagues before leaving the South Seas, and en route he left a copy in Boston with a view to its publication in the United States. The interest it aroused during 1826 on its appearance in Britain undoubtedly owed much to the recent events, as did other publications at this time, especially the *Voyage of HMS Blonde*, based on material supplied above all by the ship's chaplain and officers.[32] The two volumes were the subject of a *Quarterly Review* article early in 1827 which forcefully criticised the missionaries, especially the Americans, as mischief-makers. Pursuing a common line of attack, the reviewer praised the achievements of the protestant Moravian Brethren's missionaries in linking civilisation and Christianity as against the 'amazing absurdity' of their counterparts in Polynesia, who 'have so little judgment, and are so little acquainted with the human heart, as to let their zeal out-run discretion on many occasions and in many shapes'.[33] The review attracted plenty of attention. Ellis and the Directors thought it had been written by Richard Charlton, the British consul for the Sandwich, Society and Friendly Islands (Tonga), who was regarded as no friend to missions. They immediately set about correcting the errors and misrepresentations they found in it, through the *Edinburgh Review*, the *Eclectic Review*, and a letter to the *Quarterly* itself which the Society then published. Ellis even visited Charlton's friends and relatives in Falmouth.[34] From Baltimore, one of the American Board missionaries, outraged by 'so many palpable falsehoods contained in so small a space of print', told Ellis of his own attempts to counteract the *Quarterly's* message in the local religious press.[35]

This 'battle of the prints' was to prove a persistent feature of the late 1820s and early 1830s. It is well-known how many of the missionary fraternity, from the time of the Demarara rebellion of 1823 through the Jamaica uprising of 1831, agitated increasingly to push the imperial government into action over slave emancipation. In the late 1820s in southern Africa, John Philip in particular fought for imperial intervention in defence of African rights. It is, however, important to recognise that the Pacific was equally caught up in this process of justifying the missionary task by appeal to its civilising impact, of exposing the brutality and selfish interests of so many of its white expatriate critics, and of winning support at home for evangelical enterprise, not least among Britain's social and political élites.

To this end, Ellis kept up his perpetual motion. He was to be found in the summer of 1827 cultivating Viscountess Lifford, Viscountess Powerscourt, Lady Lowton, Lady Westmeath, Lord Gosford and others during his prolonged Irish tour. Kept up to date by his own letters to and from the islands as well as those of the Society, he corresponded and dined with Lord Byron in his campaign to get Charlton removed from his official position. Byron's high opinion of Ellis was matched by his willingness to enter the dispute in public support of the missionaries.[36] Discovering for himself, as he itinerated, the extensive public attention, he emphasised that the LMS 'should not deprive itself of the high and continued interest on behalf of the Sand[wic]h Islands which prevails in this country . . .'[37]

His own *Polynesian Researches*, partly written in the midst of this hectic journeying, also contributed to the blending of persistent propaganda with enlightenment and edification. He was not alone in his satisfaction at its sympathetic reception in the *Quarterly Review*, where Robert Southey felt 'A more interesting book than this, in all its parts, we have never perused . . .' That Southey had his own conservative agenda in mind was evident from his closing suggestion, that as 'the missionaries desire that the great good which they have done should be rendered permanent, it behoves them . . . to procure for their church the best human security that can be obtained, by connecting it with the state.'[38] But the nonconformist Ellis was not to be deterred. Accepting an invitation from Southey, who had come to hear him speak at Keswick, he found him most hospitable and stayed long. That there was calculation mingled with pleasure is clear from his account afterwards to the Secretary in London. 'Not that I anticipate much from him individually but the circle in which he moves and the extent of his writings render it exceedingly desirable that he should be favourable. I have heard of several gentlemen to whom he had spoken favourably of the results of the Mission to Tahiti'.[39]

Contacts with the American Board in Boston were an essential part of this activity. Rufus Anderson not only welcomed copies of Ellis's notes and manuscripts, but in return supplied him with private information about the British consul from his own correspondents. He also sent details of the Board's own publishing plans as well as copies of publications.[40] A prime object of these exchanges was not only to share information but to maintain a common front. The two societies' common objectives would be greatly assisted because, as Anderson happily noted, 'In all the multiplied facts, which are mentioned directly and incidentally on both sides of the water, I do not find any discrepancy worth mentioning. In all the great points of fact and reasoning we agree perfectly, though writing 3000 miles apart, and with distinct sources of information'.[41]

After Ellis's own *Narrative,* among the most obvious early fruits of this co-operation was a London edition of the journal of the former American missionary, the Reverend Charles Stewart. Covering events in the Sandwich Islands from 1823 to 1825, including the return of the *Blonde,* and, according to Anderson, 'exceedingly and deservedly popular' in America, it was edited and extensively annotated by Ellis. Ellis used it in order to put paid for good to the *Quarterly Review*'s errors of the previous year, and also as a further move in the concerted effort to have Charlton replaced with a more amenable appointment.[42] Behind the scenes Ellis, Anderson and their colleagues continued to pool their information about atrocities carried out by British or American merchant seamen and naval personnel, as well as the details of ships involved and their owners, their intention being where possible to have employees disciplined. They recorded for each other details of their dealings with government and politicians. Anderson, for example, kept Ellis abreast of the Court of Inquiry into the abuses alleged against crew members of the American *Dolphin,* while Ellis recounted his contacts with Wilberforce, Sir Thomas Baring, and government departments as to the consulship and legislation against atrocities.[43]

The pattern of contacts Ellis had established in the 1820s, on the basis of first his own and then increasingly the two societies' common interest in the evangelisation of the Pacific islands, was naturally extended in the 1830s. The immediate occasion for this was the death of the Reverend William Orme, the LMS Foreign Secretary. Various successors were considered but eventually Ellis was himself persuaded to take the appointment. With the Home Secretary, the Reverend John Arundel, he attended his first meeting of the London Secretaries Association in December 1830; he accepted the position early in 1831, supposedly on a temporary basis until the May anniversary meetings, and was confirmed in it by the end of the year.[44]

In these circumstances, as he explained to Rufus Anderson when exchanging with him portrait drawings of the mission secretaries, he regarded their correspondence as ever more vital to their effective work in the field and to increasing or maintaining support at home. 'The better we understand each other', he wrote, 'the more effectually shall we be enabled to cooperate'. This was not just a routine pleasantry, and Anderson was in complete agreement.[45] Information exchanged was often inspiration shared. In Ellis's words, 'The accounts we continue to receive from your side of the Atlantic are very encouraging and give increased energy to our exertions here. Your *Herald* I look for with great anxiety and receive with much satisfaction'.[46] Exchanges of letters easily spilled over into mutual assistance with publication. Anderson and Ellis discussed the exchange of their own and others' manuscripts; the inclusion of material of particular interest to different audiences for separate British or American editions; how to outwit pirate publishers; how to obtain books on particular subjects from the other's country; and the steps each was taking to refute the calumnies of missionaries' critics.[47]

This was a continuous refrain, and although the outlook of both secretaries expanded along with their societies' operations, the counterpoint of the Pacific was frequently to be heard. The two of them shared a positive perception of Pacific islanders' capacities and a common diagnosis of the threats to their realisation. Their correspondence offered one means of co-ordinating a successful defence. While assisting in the LMS's Foreign Department in Spring 1831, Ellis put the finishing touches to his latest contribution to the continuing arguments surrounding the Sandwich and Society Islands. This was his vigorous *Vindication of the South Sea Missions*, brought out in response to the recent English translation of the Estonian Otto von Kotzebue's account of his world voyage which included serious criticisms of the missions, and had been published a few years earlier in German.

Kotzebue, whose voyage was supported by the Russians, admitted that the missionaries' work had had some beneficial effects, for instance in reducing theft and human sacrifice. However, he argued, Christianity had been spread and imposed throughout the islands by violence, in the course of which 'whole races were exterminated'. The missionaries, he said, now combined the roles of priests and rulers, and had secured an unlimited power over the

Tahitians, which they used in the most unscrupulous fashion. Ill-educated as the missionaries were, their religion had not surprisingly given birth to 'bigotry, hypocrisy, and a hatred and contempt of all other modes of faith . . . [attitudes] foreign to the open and benevolent character of the Tahitians'. The result of their efforts was a damaging and destructive style of life, hostile to learning lest this make the local people ungovernable but productive of a simmering discontent. Bingham's regime in the Sandwich Islands was only a shade less repressive than that of the LMS in the Society Islands.[48]

With a limited circulation in the original, Kotzebue's opinions and book had hardly seemed worth countering. Translated, and favourably noticed in one or two journals, the position looked more serious. As Ellis now explained, 'the account is made the vehicle of one of the most virulent and malicious, as well as unfounded, attacks upon the introduction and influence of Christianity in those islands, which it has yet had to endure'.[49] Not only did Ellis devote eight chapters to a point-by-point demolition of Kotzebue's veracity and reliability, but he also played a nationalist card, pointing out 'palpable indications of prejudice against the English government and nation'. For good measure he used the Appendix to hammer again the *Quarterly Review* article of 1827, and to correct 'misapprehensions' in Captain F. W. Beechey's otherwise well-regarded *Narrative of a Voyage to the Pacific and Beering's Strait*, which echoed Kotzebue and had recently been given currency in the *Edinburgh Review*. A copy went to Anderson hot off the press, and the Bostonian was still reporting to his friend two years later the 'good use made of your *Vindication*' in countering critics in the United States.[50] When next evidence of misrepresentations appeared, Ellis was quick to respond fully, and was ultimately able to tell Anderson of his success in getting corrections published in Prussia.[51]

Pacific affairs remained a perennial preoccupation. At intervals, Ellis and Anderson exchanged ideas about renewed expansion into the Marquesas and Washington Islands, anxious to avoid acting without the full knowledge and co-operation of the other. They continued their efforts to have Consul Charlton removed.[52] When later on, against the background of the French and Roman Catholic expansion into Tahiti, Ellis was commissioned to write the one-volume jubilee history of the LMS's first fifty years, there was much delay. This was only in part the consequence of his illness at the time, for Ellis appears unilaterally to have planned for a second volume, with consequent financial problems. Only the first was ever published, the need for another and the cause of delay evident in that thirteen of its nineteen chapters were entirely devoted to the South Seas. This same detailed attention was still evident in his correspondence with Anderson in the 1860s, and also led ultimately to his equally forthright defence of the Americans' Hawaiian mission in 1866.[53]

Information and inspiration, however, also went hand in hand with extended perspectives, and in his role as Foreign Secretary Ellis's outlook widened rapidly. Anderson and he discussed prospects and plans for extending their operations in Siam, Singapore, Malacca, and other Asian centres.[54] More generally, the 1820s and 1830s witnessed a growing appreciation among the missions, as among the wider humanitarian community, of the need for pressure behind the scenes to secure official protection both for themselves and for indigenous peoples in the face of the most serious threats. As already noted, his own early experience had included work with Samuel Marsden, whose concern for the Maori had just led him to establish the first Church Missionary Society settlement in New Zealand, at the Bay of Islands, in 1814. While at Parramatta with Marsden, he doubtless picked up information about the relations of Aboriginal people and settlers.[55] No one in Ellis's increasingly prominent and ultimately official position could ignore the steadily accumulating evidence—from South Africa, the West Indies, New South Wales and New Zealand, as well as other Pacific islands—of the combined threat to both indigenous societies and missionary activity posed by uncontrolled white expansion. These lessons of experience and acquired knowledge were also reinforced by theological understanding. Missionaries of Ellis's generation and their supporters shared the belief that humankind was descended from a single, original act of creation. In consequence, by divine fiat, people everywhere shared both a common nature and an essentially common history. For those with this world view, theology confirmed the lesson of Enlightenment rationality, that one common solution would apply wherever the identical problems seemed to arise. It was thus natural for Ellis to apply the lessons of Pacific and North American experience in African or other settings. In Hawai'i, he could have as 'the chief object' of his tour a survey of the religious state of the inhabitants of the island, just as he might have done in his home district of London.[56] Approaches based on a sense of cultural separateness, allied perhaps to convictions of racial distinctiveness, had yet to gain ground.

It is thus scarcely surprising to find Ellis in 1830 voicing a general concern that aboriginal tribes should 'be preserved and protected in the occupation of the land of their fathers'.[57] Over the next few years, together with the other mission society secretaries, Dandeson Coates of the CMS and John Beecham of the Wesleyans, he became steadily more involved with the political movements orchestrated by Thomas Fowell Buxton.[58] To a significant extent this was influenced by the extensive involvement of the LMS in southern Africa. Unlike his predecessor, Ellis was a warm supporter of John Philip, and was well aware of the extent to which Philip and the American Board since 1833 had begun to co-ordinate their missionary efforts in the Cape and Natal. He was not only in touch with Philip but also in close and frequent contact with both Buxton and Lord Glenelg during the disturbances there in the mid-1830s.[59]

The upheavals in southern Africa were naturally of shared concern to the LMS and the American Board. However, together with similar conflicts elsewhere between whites and indigenous peoples, they also raised general issues with enormous resonance for anyone acquainted with North America's history, as Ellis himself realised. British public concern culminated in the appointment of a parliamentary Select Committee on Aborigines in 1836–37, whose purpose it was to collect evidence and to review the problems of contact across the frontiers of British expansion. Inevitably Ellis and his secretarial colleagues were invited to give evidence. In preparing himself and to inform his thinking for the aftermath of the Committee's report, Ellis called on Anderson's help, asking him for advice on the history of North American Native relations with the white settlers. He wrote:

> The Aborigines of South Africa are exciting much attention. Are you acquainted with any work giving a correct and comprehensive view of the number and circumstances of the several tribes of Indians on the N[or]th America shores by [the] first settlers with an account of causes which have led to their extinction and suggestions on the best means of their preservation . . . I am desirous of obtaining all the information I can on the subject.[60]

It was a characteristic request, Ellis having always shown both that interest in books common in the largely self-taught, and a readiness to seek out the necessary sources to redress his own and colleagues' ignorance.[61] For his part Anderson, much preoccupied with the same problems, clearly understood the significance of the approach. He had already encouraged Dr Philip in his visit to England to give evidence to the committee:

> I see the same causes are in operation in South Africa, which are bearing so destructively upon the poor aborigines of our own country, and the same lamentable effects will follow, unless speedily prevented by the strong intervention of the national arm of justice. The cupidity of the settlers will move more rapidly than the benevolence of the churches. A thousand expedients will be successfully resorted to to deprive the natives of their lands; and if colonial legislation is not allowed to make slaves of these, war will be brought to exterminate them. To the disgrace of our country, such is the process rapidly going on among our Indians. May you and Mr Buxton and the other patrons of African rights in England, arrest the progress of similar evils among the negro and Caffre races of South Africa; for in their enormous cruelty and injustice, these fall not a whit behind the slave trade.[62]

Now, jotting down a long list of possibilities since (as he later told Ellis) there was no one work which would suffice, he proceeded to secure his Committee's consent to the purchase and dispatch of a dozen volumes 'with a request that they may be placed in the Library of your Society'. Together with additional suggestions of relevant works, Anderson's generous response gave Ellis much pleasure and was to the library's great benefit.[63] It was nevertheless only an example, although a particularly munificent one, of a constant process which was helping to build up missionary libraries on both sides of the Atlantic.

Although the American Board's gift did not arrive in time to affect the missionaries' evidence, their case to the Select Committee and even its own final recommendations were significantly informed by trans-Atlantic colonial experience. North America's own record, both north and south of the 49th parallel, was interpreted as providing more than sufficient proof that indigenous peoples and invading white communities could not be brought to adapt to one another unless the missions and Christianity were guaranteed a central place in the process of adjustment. North America's failure to date should not be repeated. Ellis also took the opportunity in his own evidence to use material drawn directly from American sources and experience in the Pacific, including his own recent correspondence with Hiram Bingham, still leader of the Hawaiian mission.[64]

Ellis had no doubt as to the value of discussing general missionary problems or dilemmas with Anderson. Some of the most serious had to do with their common, if sometimes touchingly naive, aversion to 'political' involvement. Both men regarded Roman Catholic missionaries as a dire threat to their societies' efforts, and were deeply resentful of their contribution to the eventual French seizure of Tahiti in 1842. For them, as for many other Protestant evangelicals, the Tahiti episode—'one of the most painful that has occurred in the annals of modern missions'—was especially shocking, being their first direct experience of 'Catholic aggression' and the revival under Pope Gregory XVI (1831–46) of the missionary enterprise of the Roman Catholic Church.[65] Just like the earlier onslaught of unscrupulous traders and whalers, now the Roman Catholic invasion gave point and added vigour to the societies' common front. However, for both secretaries the desire to exclude Catholics conflicted with their equally fervent wish to avoid supporting any infringement by the state of the principles of political and religious liberty. They agonised too over the implications for their principled avoidance of politics, of local rulers' wishes to take the missionaries' advice on matters of state.[66] At other times, Ellis pressed for ABCFM help in the LMS's attempts to curb the trade in spirits; he discussed the division of territorial spheres, the practical problems of recruiting unmarried females, and the desirability of medical missionaries.[67] Knowing of Ellis's close relationship with Anderson, LMS missionaries felt free to confide in Anderson and to use him as a safe post box for dispatches they feared might otherwise be interfered with en route, especially from the Pacific.[68]

THE PATTERN OF Ellis's life changed direction sharply at the start of the 1840s. Suffering from fits of depression, he was obliged to shed some of the Foreign Secretary's workload. For the year 1840 he was granted convalescent leave, and the Reverends Arthur Tidman and J. J. Freeman took over until his anticipated return. However, he never resumed full responsibility, and resigned in May 1841.[69] Living at Hoddesdon in Hertfordshire, where he eventually became an independent minister, he remained a member of the Board of Directors of the Society and closely in touch both with its affairs and with many of his earlier correspondents. This led to his particular involvement as a senior Director with overseas deputation work in the 1850s. He visited South Africa in 1855, and Madagascar twice in 1853–54, again in 1856–57, and once more in 1861–65. He died in 1872.

There is no room here to investigate Ellis's personal 'swing to the east' as marked by the African journeys of his later life. It has instead been my object to consider the manner in which an influential missionary, born as the modern movement began in the 1790s, came to approach the emerging Victorian world. Although William Ellis shared the evangelical sense of involvement in a global undertaking, persistent points of reference in his career were provided by his firsthand experience of evangelisation in the Society Islands and evangelical society in the eastern United States. These experiences influenced his reading, affected his friendships, shaped his views of those problems which beset missionary work, and provided the parallels with which he approached the missionary affairs of other territories. India and South—let alone any other part of—Africa did not provide the determinants of his outlook. In part this may be put down to a combination of generation and accidental circumstances. Many British missionaries inevitably lacked his opportunities and their outlooks were confined to a single limited field. However, one may reasonably suggest that there were also many like him for whom any 'swing to the east' was delayed until the mid-century. It was completed only in response to the opening of China to extensive missionary access after 1858, the decline of the West Indies as a missionary field, and the perceived need for redoubled missionary efforts in India after 1857. Yet even after that, the influence of American religious ideas and the capacity of the Pacific to divert metropolitan British attention remained very potent.[70] Ellis's career thus offers a useful counterpoise to the introspection of both 'area studies' and an imperial historiography centred too exclusively on India and Africa, by alerting historians to the continuing importance of a global outlook shaped by westerly perspectives.

Appendix

The books listed here are those roughly noted by Rufus Anderson on Ellis's letter dated 12 April 1837, 14/1, ABC. They have been identified as far as possible from the *Nineteenth Century Short Title Catalogue* (Avero, Newcastle-upon-Tyne, 1986–). Those marked § are the books Anderson recorded as actually sent, and include some not in the original list; those marked * are his further suggestions, in Anderson to Ellis, 4 October 1837, 2.1/1, ABC. Where several editions existed, it has not always been possible to identify the one obtained by Anderson.

The Library of the LMS at the School of Oriental and African Studies is in process of being catalogued; volumes from Anderson's lists so far recorded as still in its possession are marked CWML with the shelf mark.

* Adair, James, *The History of the American Indians: particularly those adjoining to the Mississippi, East and West Florida, Georgia, South and North Carolina, and Virginia etc.*, London, 1775.

§ [Archaeologia Americana] *Transactions of the American Antiquaries Society*, vols 1 and 2. Vol. 1 is in CWML, E.1/11, and at pp. 61–104 contains a reprint of an English translation of accounts of discoveries by Father Lewis [Louis] Hennepin, which was one of the books listed (see below).

Bancroft, George, *A History of the United States, from the discovery of the American Continent to the present time*, 1834.

§ Belknap, Jeremy, *The History of New Hampshire*, 3 vols, Philadelphia, Boston, 1784–92. Subsequent editions, Boston 1813, and vol. 1 only, Dover, New Hampshire, 1831.

Carver, Capt. Jonathan, *Travels through the Interior Parts of North America, in the years 1766, 1767 and 1768*, editions 1778, 1789, 1781, 1796.

* Charlevoix, Pierre Francois Xavier de, *Historie et description générale de la Nouvelle France, avec le Journal historique d'un voyage fait par ordre du Roi dans l'Amérique Septentrionnale*, 3 vols, Paris, 1744. Anderson gave the title in English, but I have not traced an English translation earlier than *History and General Description of New France* . . . trans. J. G. Shea, 6 vols, 1866–72.

Drake, Samuel Gardner, *Biography and History of the Indians of North America . . . also a history of their wars . . . likewise exhibiting an analysis of the . . . authors, who have written upon the first peopling of America*, 7th edn., Boston, 1837, CWML, E.3/27.

§ Drake, Samuel Gardner, *The Book of the Indians of North America, comprising details in the lives of about 500 chiefs and others the most distinguished among them*, Boston, 1833.

§ [Evarts, Jeremiah], *Essays on the present crisis in the condition of the American Indians, first published in the National Intelligencer, under the signature of William Penn*, Boston, 1829.

* Everett, Report to Congress on Indian Affairs (not identified).

§ Flint, Timothy, *Indian Wars of the West, containing biographical sketches of those pioneers who headed the western settlers in repelling the attacks of the savages, together with a view of the character, manners, monuments, and antiquities of the western Indians*, Cincinnati, 1833.

Gallatin's Wm. Lincoln (not identified).

§ Gordon, P., *The History of Pennsylvania from its Discovery by Europeans to the Declaration of Independence in 1776*, Philadelphia, 1829, CWML, E.4/53.

§ Haywood, John, *The civil and political history of the state of Tennessee, from its earliest settlement up to the year 1796, including the boundaries of the state*, Knoxville, Tenn., 1823. Anderson noted simply History of Tennessee in both his original note and his letter to Ellis; it is not known whether this volume and/or the following was dispatched.

§ Haywood, John, *The natural and aboriginal history of Tennessee, up to the first settlements therein by the white people, in the year 1768*, Nashville, Tenn., 1823. See note to previous item.

§ Heckewaelder, John Gottlieb Ernst, *A Narrative of the Mission of the United Brethren among the Delaware and Mohegan Indians, from its commencement in the year 1740 to the close of the year 1808*, Philadelphia, 1820.

* Heckewaelder, John Gottlieb Ernst, *History of the manners and customs of the Indian Nations*, new edn, rev., Philadelphia, 1826.

* Hennepin, Louis, *A new discovery of a vast country in America . . . With a continuation: giving an account of the attempts of the Sieur de la Salle upon the mines of St. Barbe, &c. the taking of Quebec by the English; with the advantages of a shorter cut to China and Japan . . . To which is added several new discoveries not published in the French edition*, 1st and 2nd edns, London, 1698; also 1699.

§ Hubbard, William, *A Narrative of the Indian Wars of New England*, Boston, 1775, further editions, 1801, 1802, 1803, 1814, 1839 etc.

* Hutchinson, Thomas, *The History of the Colony (Province) of Massachusetts Bay etc.*, 2 vols, Boston, 1764–67 (period 1628–1750).

§ Knowles, James Davis, *Memoir of Roger Williams, the Founder of the State of Rhode Island*, Boston, 1834.

Lewis, Meriwether, *Travels to the Source of the Missouri River and across the American Continent to the Pacific Ocean, performed by order of the Government of the United States in the years 1804, 1805, and 1806. By Captains Lewis and Clarke. Published from the official report . . .*, new edn, 3 vols, London, 1815.

Life of the Rev. John Eliot, Religious Tract Society, London, 1832. Anderson's hand is barely legible at this point but he seems to have had in mind a life by 'Frazer', so far unidentified but perhaps Francis, Convers, *Life of John Eliot*, vol. 5, J. Sparks Library of American Biography, 1834.

Long, Stephen Harriman, *Account of an expedition from Pittsburgh to the Rocky Mountains, performed in the years 1819 and '20, by order of the Hon. J. C. Calhoun, Secretary of War: under the command of Major Stephen H. Long*, 1823 (see British Library Catalogue under Edwin James, Botanist).

§ Macclung, John A., *Sketches of western adventure: containing an account of the most interesting incidents connected with the settlement of the West from 1755 to 1794*, Philadelphia, 1832, further editions 1838 etc.

* M'Coy, Isaac, *The Annual Register of Indian Affairs, within the Indian, or Western, Territory*, nos. 1 and 2, 1835, 1836.

* Marshall, Humphrey, *The History of Kentucky*, 2 vols, Frankfort, USA, 1824.

* Mather, Cotton, *Magnalia Christi Americana: or the Ecclesiastical History of New England, from its first planting in the year 1620 unto the year . . . 1698. First American edition, from the London edition of 1702*, 2 vols, Hartford and New Haven, Connecticut, 1820.

§ Morse, Jedidiah, *A Report to the Secretary of War of the United States, on Indian Affairs, comprising a narrative of a tour performed in 1820 under a commission from the President . . . for the purpose of ascertaining . . . the actual state of the Indian tribes in our country*, New Haven, 1822.

§ *Speeches on the Indian Bill* (originally listed as *Speeches in Congress*). Almost certainly Jeremiah Evarts (ed.), *Speeches on the passage of the Bill for the removal of the Indians, delivered in the Congress of the United States, April and May 1830*, Boston, 1830, CWML, E.3/37.

Transactions of the Historical and Literary Society of Philadelphia.

Colonised Lives

—— ——

The Native Wives and Daughters of
Five Founding Families of Victoria

SYLVIA VAN KIRK

T HE FUR TRADE HISTORY of the Pacific northwest is in many ways
a transborder story. Until the imposition of the border in
1846, most of the territory was known as the Columbia Department of the Hudson's Bay Company. The headquarters of this
district was Fort Vancouver, but a network of posts stretched far up
the coast into Alaska and was connected to posts in the interior by a
system of river routes and pack trails (as shown on page 216). The
role that Native women played in the fur trade and the extensive
family formation that resulted have been well-documented in
previous studies.[1] What I shall look at here is the experiences of the
Native women in five families who lived most of their lives at
various posts in the Pacific northwest and then settled at Fort
Victoria, capital of the Crown Colony of Vancouver Island which
had been created to forestall American expansion in 1849.

A look at a map of Victoria in 1858 (see p. 217) illustrates the
dominant position of the family properties of James Douglas,
William H. McNeill, John Work, John Tod and Charles Ross.
These men had all been officers of the Hudson's Bay Company. All
had indigenous wives, but of different tribal origins. Although all
these officers had toyed with the idea of retiring to Britain or

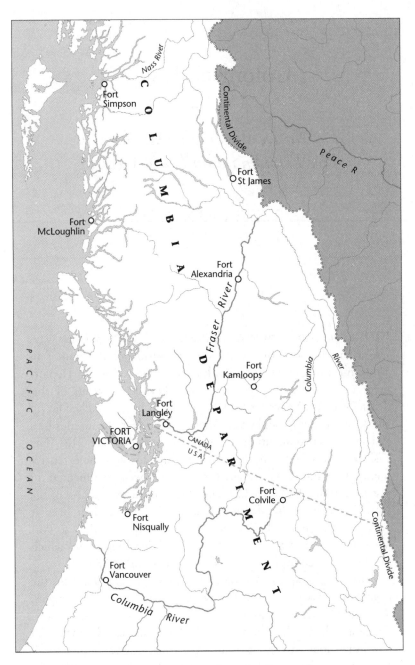

The Columbia Department of the Hudson's Bay Company

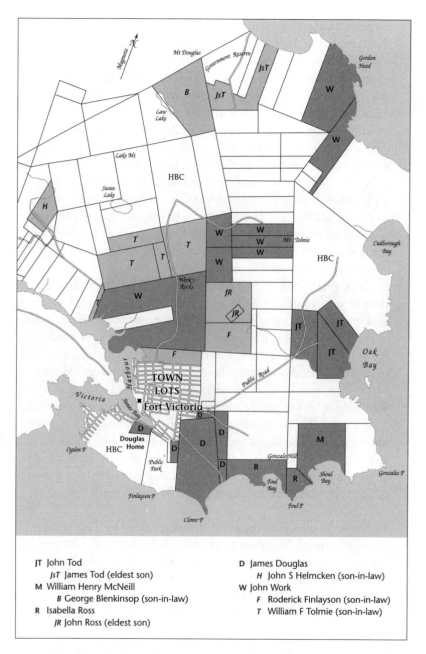

JT John Tod
   JsT James Tod (eldest son)
M William Henry McNeill
   B George Blenkinsop (son-in-law)
R Isabella Ross
   JR John Ross (eldest son)

D James Douglas
   H John S Helmcken (son-in-law)
W John Work
   F Roderick Finlayson (son-in-law)
   T William F Tolmie (son-in-law)

Victoria, 1858 (drawn from the Official District map)

eastern Canada, there were several reasons why they chose to settle their families at Fort Victoria. Coming from the élite of the fur trade hierarchy, these men had both the desire and the wherewithal to purchase the expensive estates which the Company made available. In Victoria, in geographically familiar yet 'civilised' surroundings, they hoped to maintain their social and economic standing by becoming part of the landed gentry, which was envisioned as the élite class in an agrarian colonisation scheme which was explicitly to replicate British social hierarchy.[2]

For the Native wives and children, however, adapting to life in colonial settler society as opposed to that of a fur trade post offered particular challenges. They were to be subject to an intensive programme of colonisation, designed to negate their indigenous heritage and to acculturate them to the norms and material culture of 'genteel' British society. As families with élite aspirations, there was little room for a middle ground, especially for the second generation: they could not build an identity which acknowledged the duality of their heritage. There were complexities in the intersection of the dynamics of gender, class and race. As wives and mothers, the Native women in these five families were to find their social roles severely circumscribed. Daughters, however, succeeded much better than their brothers in adapting to the colonising agenda of their fathers.[3] A fascinating window on the acculturation experience of these families is provided by the rich collection of portrait photographs which have survived in the British Columbia Archives and Record Service. Most of these photographs are from family albums and the images preserved for family posterity (and public consumption) emphasise adaptation to British material culture.

IN ORDER TO appreciate the social challenges faced by these families, it is necessary to sketch out their fur trade background.[4] All of the Native women had married young, their unions initially being contracted according to the fur trade marriage rite known as 'the custom of the country'. They produced large families, from seven to thirteen children, and the sex ratio was heavily weighted in favour of daughters.

Significant to the social hierarchy of colonial Victoria was the fact that the governor in its formative years was Chief Factor James

Douglas, whose wife Amelia was part Cree. Her mother Miyo Nipiy had married her father Chief Factor William Connolly at Rat Portage (south of Hudson Bay) in 1803, and they had lived at various posts throughout Rupert's Land, before moving to Fort St James (in northern British Columbia) in the 1820s. There in 1828 the promising young clerk James Douglas took his superior's sixteen-year-old daughter Amelia for his 'country wife'. The Douglases soon moved to Fort Vancouver where most of their thirteen children were born, but many did not survive to adulthood. When Douglas was given charge of Fort Victoria in 1849, his family consisted of his wife and five daughters. The only surviving son was born in 1851, followed by another daughter. Shortly after becoming governor, Douglas bought up large parcels of land and was one of the first to build a substantial home outside the fort. When Douglas was knighted in 1863 for his services to the colony, his wife gained the title of Lady Douglas.

Adjacent to the Douglas estate was that of the widow of Charles Ross. Ross only lived long enough to see Fort Victoria built in 1844. But he left his widow Isabella with the wherewithal to purchase her own estate, which made her the first woman to be an independent landowner in Victoria. The daughter of a French-Canadian *engagé*, Joseph Mainville, and his Ojibway wife, Isabella had travelled far from her aboriginal home and kin, after marrying Ross at Rainy Lake (now in western Ontario) in 1822. The Ross family numbered six boys and four girls, all of whom survived to adulthood.

The wife of Chief Factor John Work, who would become the largest landowner in the colony, was also the daughter of a French-Canadian *engagé* and a Native woman. Josette Legacé, whose mother was Spokane, grew up along the upper reaches of the Columbia River where she and Work were married at Fort Colville in 1826. A redoubtable companion, she and her growing family moved with Work to various stations in the Columbia Department, including a fifteen-year stint at the northerly post of Fort Simpson at the mouth of the Nass River. The three boys and eight girls all lived to adulthood and settled in Victoria. The Work estate in the Hillside area encompassed over 1000 acres. Work died in 1861, his widow outliving him by thirty-five years.

Although often referred to as Indian, the wives of the above men were all of mixed descent. Although these marriages cut across class and ethnicity, they are still representative of fur trade endogamy—the wives' fathers having been connected to the Company and the women themselves growing up within or near the fur trade posts.

In the other two families, the McNeills and the Tods, the marriages harkened back to the old fur trade alliances whereby officers married high-ranking Indian women whose connections were useful to advancing the husbands' commercial position. William H. McNeill was a Bostonian who first entered the Pacific coasting trading in the 1820s for the firm of Bryant and Sturgis, in competition with the Hudson's Bay Company. His first wife was Kaigani Haida from Northern British Columbia. Haida women were noted for their influential trading role and this alliance undoubtedly helped to make McNeill such a successful trader that the Company went to some lengths to lure him into its service in the early 1830s. There is no likeness of Mathilda, as she was known, but she was described as a large, handsome woman of dignified bearing. This long union produced twelve children, of whom seven girls and three boys survived to adulthood. The mother, however, did not long survive the birth of the last two, twin girls born in 1850. Thus it was a motherless family that McNeill settled in Victoria on a 200-acre estate which encompassed much of south Oak Bay. Eventually McNeill took a second wife: this time, a high-ranking Nis'ga woman who was an active trader on the Nass River in her own right. Formally married in 1866, Neshaki (or Martha as she was baptised) retired with her husband to Victoria in the late 1860s. There were no children of the second union, this being the only one of the five families in which there was a stepmother who had to develop a relationship with a close-knit, already partially grown family.

Chief Trader John Tod's marital life, which had been considerably more irregular than many of his fur trade contemporaries, had included an ill-fated marriage to an English woman in the 1830s. This wife, having gone mad, was placed in an asylum in England and Tod then returned to the far west where he took charge of Fort Kamloops. There in the early 1840s he took a new young 'country wife', Sophia Lolo, eldest daughter of an influential local chief Jean-

Baptiste Lolo *dit* St Paul and his Shuswap wife. In his retirement years on his estate in Oak Bay, Tod was thus surrounded by a young family, eventually numbering five boys and two girls.

In these families, the patriarchal role exercised by the British husbands and fathers was greater than usual because of their own cultural bias which had increasing impact on the shaping of family life. This is not to deny that in fur trade society, Native wives had brought their husbands valuable knowledge for the trade and even survival. There is ample testimony to the bonds of affection which developed, such as Work's writing: 'The little wife and I get on very well and she takes good care of myself and children'.[5] But there was also acknowledgement that Native wives, in spite of their fine qualities, were lacking in ladylike attributes. Work spoke of his wife as being 'simple and uninstructed'; Ross confessed that his wife was 'not exactly suited to shine at the head of a nobleman's table'.[6] That Indianness was not something to be celebrated is illustrated in Captain McNeill's poignant lament when his Haida wife died in 1850:

> My poor Wife . . . had been a good and faithful partner to me for twenty years and we had twelve children together . . . the deceased was a most kind mother to her children, and *no* Woman could have done her duty better, although an Indian.[7]

The Native wives were subject to a programme of Anglicisation along with their children, especially when the prospect of settlement loomed. Indeed as early as the 1830s at Fort Vancouver several of these couples had had to deal with the racist implications which accompanied missionisation. When the Reverend Herbert Beaver and his English wife arrived at the fort, Beaver castigated particularly the wives for living in sin and suggested that they be kept outside the fort gates. Douglas and other officers gallantly defended the honour of their wives and the morality of their domestic arrangements, but both Douglas and Ross sought to protect themselves from further insult by having their wives and children baptised and submitting to a Church of England marriage rite.[8]

As for the children, these fathers were active agents in the colonisation of their families; they never seem to have questioned the desirability of acculturating them to British norms and customs.

Though their private correspondence is filled with paternal concern for the welfare of their children, this was posited in terms of negating their Native background. It was never suggested that their First Nations heritage should be actively incorporated into their upbringing. At the fur trade posts, the fathers took an active role in the education of their children, introducing them to the basics of English literacy and to Christian observances such as Bible reading and prayers. The critical role of mothers in socialising children, especially daughters, was severely truncated. Although there is certainly evidence of maternal devotion, mothers were tutored along with children in aspects of British material culture. But the fathers continually worried about their children growing up at isolated posts without 'proper education or example'. In 1834, for example, John Work wrote to a retired friend, Edward Ermatinger: 'I have now here four fine little girls, had I them a little brushed up with education, and a little knowledge of the world, they would scarcely be known to be Indians'.[9]

It had never been as common to send daughters as it was sons to eastern Canada or Great Britain for education, but for all it proved was a risky and expensive business, even if they were entrusted to the care of relatives or friends. Thus fur trade officers were eager to place their children at the first school established at Fort Vancouver in the 1830s. When this venture failed because of the mismanagement of the Reverend Beaver, Douglas and Work both placed their daughters with American missionaries in the Willamette Valley. Others did continue to cherish the hope of sending their children back home. Charles Ross, for example, felt that his promotion to Fort Victoria would enable him to support the education of his three teenaged children (two sons and a daughter) in England. Although the children were initially reported as 'much improved', their progress was cut short by their father's untimely death. Relatives were soon expressing their dissatisfaction with the children, whom they found 'extremely indocile and addicted to habits incompatible with a residence in this country'. All three children were sent back to their mother at Fort Victoria in the fall of 1845.[10]

The transition from fur trade post to colonial Victoria presented particular challenges for the Native wives of the fur trade élite. While they have left us little direct record of how they felt, family correspondence and newspaper reports suggest something of the contours of their lives. Evidence indicates that the wives viewed settlement in Victoria as a more attractive alternative to being transported back to the alien environment of eastern North America or Great Britain.[11] Most of them had already proved their adaptability in moving with their husbands to various locations in the Columbia District, and had borne the loneliness which resulted from their separation from their own kin. As officers' wives, these women would have enjoyed a relatively privileged status within the forts; the move to colonial Victoria resulted in many changes. Materially, they now found themselves living on isolated estates in houses which attempted to replicate more completely a British lifestyle. Socially, in the colony, their status was threatened. However willingly they had responded to their husbands' tutelage, they were understandably at a disadvantage in providing social leadership and invidious comparisons were quick to be made.

High class status could not protect these wives and even their daughters from racist jibes. It rankled some incoming settlers that Native families should stand so high in the social hierarchy. Numerous remarks were made by visitors and even working-class British immigrants that the society of the new colony was rather deficient because some of its leading officials were married to Native women. Shortly after her arrival from England in 1854, Annie Deans wrote home disparaging Douglas—a man who had spent his life among the North American Indians and got one for a wife could scarcely know anything about governing an English colony.[12]

An analysis of these wives suggests that they had varying degrees of success in adapting to the prescriptions laid out for them. This had to do with their own aptitude, the degree of familial support and the role that they were expected to play. These social tensions were poignantly highlighted in the Douglas family, which because of its position was subject to particular scrutiny. Initially, Amelia Douglas kept in the background, partly because she didn't speak English very well. The social calendar was kept by her daughters and a Douglas niece who had come from Britain, but gradually Lady Douglas became comfortable in her role as the governor's wife. Douglas wrote proudly of his wife, after a New Year's levee in the early 1870s: 'Darling good Mamma was nicely got up and won all hearts with her kindness and geniality'.[13] When Lady Franklin visited Victoria in 1861, she was curious to meet the 'Indian' wife of the governor. She found Amelia to have 'a gentle, simple & kindly manner' and was fascinated that her native features were less pronounced than in some of her daughters.[14] However shy she might have been in her public role, family correspondence indicates that Lady Douglas was a strong maternal presence in her own household. Described as 'a very active woman, energetic and industrious', she supervised the domestic production of her household, which ranged from raising fine chickens to putting up fruits and preserves from the extensive orchard.[15]

By contrast, Josette Work seems always to have played an active role in the round of social entertainments, for which her home, Hillside House, became renowned in early Victoria. The following description of a New Year's celebration in 1861, by military officer Charles Wilson, was typical:

> There were about 30 at dinner—such a display of fish, flesh and fowl and pastry as is seldom seen. We danced until 12 & then all hands sat down to a sumptuous supper and then set to work dancing again until a very late hour . . .[16]

'The Works', he enthused, 'are about the kindest people I ever came across'. Indeed, Mrs Work earned the admiration of all who met her; even the American historian Hubert Bancroft acknowledged that 'in body and mind, the Indian wife was strong and elastic as steel'.[17]

Josette herself seems to have always been interested in adopting British fashion. A fine portrait of her, taken by S. A. Spencer, shows her every inch the Victorian matron—indeed at a glance she could be taken for Queen Victoria herself! During her long widowhood, she took an active role in the management of the family property. Very much the matriarch, she grieved over her sons' lack of success and premature deaths, but rejoiced in the widening family circle over which she presided, the result of her numerous daughters' successful marriages.

Josette Work and Amelia Douglas would have known one another from their earlier days at Fort Vancouver and they remained fast friends, comforting one another in family trials and social rebuffs. As the youngest Douglas daughter wrote in her reminiscences: 'Mrs Work was a most wonderful woman. She and my mother were the most loving friends and such rejoicing when Mrs Work came to pay us a visit. She stood by my dear Mother on many sad occasions'.[18] These women were able to retain some of their aboriginal ways and were noted for their kindness to incoming immigrant women, especially during childbirth and illness when their knowledge of native medicine was particularly helpful. Dr J. S. Helmcken, who married the eldest Douglas daughter, remembered that his mother-in-law had rendered an Englishwoman Mrs Yates much assistance during a difficult confinement, notably by urging her to adopt the native position of squatting down. Josette Work was well-regarded as a midwife, Helmcken crediting her with saving the lives of babies of which he had despaired.[19] When this remarkable Métis woman of the Columbia Department died at an advanced age in 1896, she was eulogised for 'her usefulness in pioneer work and many good deeds'.[20]

Most of the wives experienced widowhood, although it affected their lives quite differently. The most difficult was that of the Widow Ross, who struggled gamely to build a respectable life for her family, after her husband died prematurely in 1844. Buying her own estate was an unusual step for a woman in her position to take but she relied on the support of her eldest son John, who also purchased an estate in Victoria, and undoubtedly hoped the younger sons would help develop her farm. Documents from the 1850s reveal the Widow Ross actively involved in commercial transactions, selling farm produce and livestock, but by the late 1850s family troubles were brewing. Her younger sons were gaining a reputation around town for being wild, one running up such a debt that his mother publically disowned him.[21]

Perhaps the offer of assistance with managing the estate made Isabella Ross succumb to the attentions of a young suitor from Eastern Canada, one Lucius Simon O'Brien, whom she married in 1863. But the new stepfather was soon at odds with the family, as it quickly became apparent that he was intent on defrauding them. The conflict resulted in much unfavourable publicity. Isabella's distress resulted in her temporarily running away, an action which

O'Brien used to try to tarnish her character. While he had been willing to overlook race in marrying the landed widow, once his plans went awry, he was certainly prepared to play to racist stereotypes, publishing the following notice in the Victoria *Daily Chronicle* in April 1864:

> Whereas My Wife, Isabella, has left my bed and board because I will not support her drunken sons, nor allow her to keep drunk herself, and have a lot of drunken squaws about her, this is to forbid all persons, harbouring her, or trusting her on my account, as I will pay no debts she may contract.

A few days later, the youngest son William attempted to come to his mother's defence and charged that O'Brien was trying to swindle the family:

> His every act since his marriage has been to try to get everything from my mother, and turn us (the children) out of the house; . . . Will you do me and my mother the simple justice to publish this, as such a statement as O'Brien has made is calculated to injure both her and myself.[22]

When the family then began proceedings against O'Brien to prove that he was actually a bigamist, he apparently deserted up island where he came to an untimely end a few years later. Isabella, assuming that his abandonment was as good as a divorce, resumed the title of the Widow Ross. Through continuing family misfortune, Isabella found solace from other Native wives and also from the Anglican clergyman Edward Cridge who had welcomed these families into his congregation. Cridge used to make regular visits to Mrs Ross to read and pray with her. The McNeills were her closest neighbours but she also paid visits to old friends Amelia Douglas and Josette Work.[23] By the mid-1870s, when the last son remaining in Victoria died, the Ross estate could no longer be maintained and was sold off. In her last years, the Widow Ross was financially dependent upon Flora, her youngest daughter; Isabella ended her days in a little house on the grounds of the convent of the Sisters of St Ann, dying in 1885.[24]

The record is almost silent on the Victoria life of Sophia Tod. Tod himself, who carried on an extensive correspondence with former colleagues, does not mention her, although he comments extensively on his children. The most important document that remains is a striking portrait of her in European costume, which may have been taken at the time of her church marriage in Victoria in 1863. This photograph invites various readings but it seems to indicate an ambivalence about the constraints of Victorian dress and customs. Tod's property was quite isolated from the rest of the community and his wife seems to have been also; unlike some of the other Native wives, she had no previously established female social ties and she also had a young family to raise without the support of kin. Local legend implies that Sophia Lolo did not make a happy adjustment to life in Victoria; the Tod house, which is the only one of the original family dwellings surviving today, is reputed to be haunted by the ghost of an Indian woman.[25]

Martha (Neshaki), Captain McNeill's second wife, presents quite a contrast. As a high-ranking Nis'ga woman, she was used to an active commercial role, which she apparently continued in Victoria. In the 1860s, McNeill had constructed an imposing residence on McNeill Bay, to which Martha's Nis'ga kin were frequent visitors in addition to the McNeill siblings and their families. The Big House, which seems to have been a cross between a Scottish baronial hall and a Nis'ga longhouse, was home to the unmarried twins and their stepmother in the early 1870s.[26] A glimpse into their lives is provided by a unique little diary, chronicled by Rebecca, one of the twins, for several weeks in August and September 1875. This account underscores the importance of kin ties in the McNeill household; there were frequent comings and goings between the female members of the Big House and the homes of various McNeill children who had settled nearby. Again female ties had been formed earlier at Fort Simpson; in 1863, Martha had taken her stepdaughter Lucy on a trading expedition up the Nass River.[27] After McNeill died, however, it appears that Martha was closer to her own Nis'ga kin than to her stepchildren. Her will leaves the bulk of her portion of the McNeill estate to her own kin, but specifically requests that she be buried beside her husband in the Ross Bay Cemetery. It was left to a Nis'ga niece to see that wish carried out.[28]

A convert to Christianity, Martha was quite adept at travelling in both British and Nis'ga worlds. This would have been increasingly difficult for her highly acculturated stepdaughters. A stunning portrait of the five surviving sisters was taken by Victoria's famous woman photographer Hannah Maynard, likely around the time of their father's death in 1875. The as yet unmarried twins are standing at the back of picture. The three married sisters are seated: dominant on the right is Lucy, the eldest surviving sister. Mathilda, named for her mother, holds the family photograph album, while Fanny kneels by her side. With their elegant, if sombre, Victorian gowns and elaborate braided hairstyles, the picture exudes British gentility. At least the younger sisters would have directly benefited from the new agents of colonisation, combined in the church and school that the colony provided.

Schooling specifically for the children of the élite had been set up with the arrival of the first Anglican missionaries, Robert and Emma Staines, in 1849. The five families dominated the Fort Victoria school register in the first years; out of thirty pupils listed, there were four Douglases, five Works, three McNeills, three Rosses and two Tods, mostly girls.[29] The girls were being groomed for marriage with considerable emphasis on dress, deportment and ladylike accomplishments. An English observer in 1860, in complimenting the schoolmistress, emphasised the class bias and the previous deficiences in young ladies' education: 'Mrs Woods has some 30 girls of the higher class here . . . She is accomplished as well as highly educated we understand. Even girls engaged to be married, placed themselves under her & were much improved'.[30]

For the daughters, success within the framework of the colonial élite was, of course, marriage to a British gentleman. The older daughters in these families had already an established pattern of marriage to aspiring young officers in the Hudson's Bay Company. It was not lost on incoming young clerks that their prospects could be enhanced by marrying 'a big-wig's daughter'. There were a number of notable weddings at Fort Victoria in the early 1850s; Work's daughters Sarah and Jane married Roderick Finlayson and

George Ford, soon after his return from the Arctic

George Ford in later life

Two portraits of Amelia, Lady Douglas, showing her acculturation to her role as the Governor's wife

Josette Work as 'Queen Victoria'

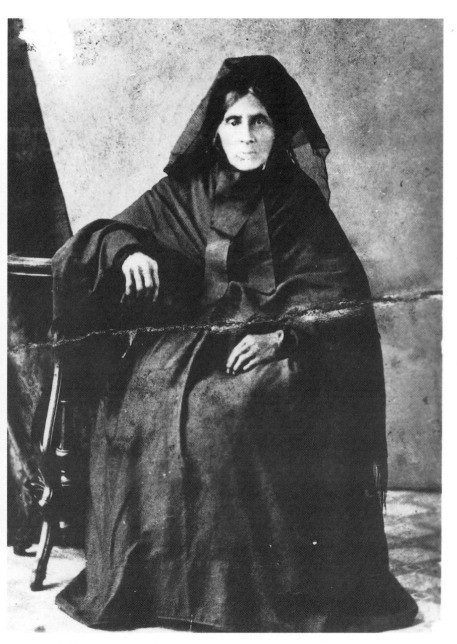

Isabella Ross in her widow's weeds

Sophia Lolo

The five surviving daughters of Captain W. H. McNeill and his Haida wife, Mathilda, c. 1875

(Left to right) *Douglas daughters Agnes, Jane and Alice; one of the earliest photos taken at Fort Victoria, 1858*

Studio portrait taken in London of Jane Douglas (seated) *and her younger sister, Martha*

Flora Ross, taken in the 1890s

The four surviving McNeill sisters in 1904; the woman in white is a daughter of Mathilda; she is holding her mother's cane

A page from Martha Harris's album, showing her mother and father and herself; Martha has done the pen and ink drawing

William Fraser Tolmie respectively, and then the governor's eldest daughter Cecilia married the Company doctor, J. S. Helmcken. The social networking among the women in these families was underscored when Lucy McNeill married Hamilton Moffatt in 1856, for her bridesmaids were Jane Douglas and Mary Work, who also soon married Company men.[31]

Advantageous as these marriages were, the social status of the younger sisters in the new world of the colony could not be taken for granted. A new element in the social scene was introduced with the arrival of the naval squadron at Esquimalt. The officers enthusiastically engaged in sponsoring balls and other entertainments, but could be quite scathing in ridiculing the young ladies' attempts to keep up with the latest English fashions. Charles Wilson's commentary in 1861 may have been kinder than most:

> Most of the young ladies are half breeds & have quite as many of the propensities of the savage as of the civilized being ... The ladies were nicely dressed & some of them danced very well, though they would look much better if they would only learn to wear their crinoline properly.[32]

Racism could indeed negate social aspiration. Although the younger Ross daughters featured at the balls given by the officers of the British Navy in the 1850s, they never attained the status they desired. According to Philip Hankin, they were very fine looking girls, but 'they had a great deal of Indian blood in them and were supposed to be only on the edge of society'.[33] That race could trump class is seen in what is reported to have been an exchange between the governor's daughter Agnes and a young midshipman at one of these balls. Miss Douglas demurred at his invitation to dance as being beneath her station, saying 'What would Papa say if I were to dance with a middy'; whereupon he haughtily replied, 'What would Mama say if I were to dance with a Squaw!'

In actuality, Agnes Douglas's station was such that she was to lead the way in a new trend in marriage patterns whereby the younger daughters began to marry British gentlemen attached to the colonial service. In 1862, she married a well-born recent arrival Arthur Bushby, who was clerk to Judge Begbie.[34] The weddings of the Douglas girls became increasingly elaborate affairs as did their education. These changes were epitomised in the experience of Martha, the governor's youngest daughter. Having been given the best education that the colony could afford, her father was gratified that: 'She plays well, sings, has a taste for drawing, is well read, writes a good hand and a nice letter'. But he sent her off to England in 1872 to 'get rid of the cobwebs of colonial training and give her the proper finish'.[35] A portrait taken of Martha and her married sister Jane Dallas in London, inscribed 'For dearest, darling Mother', illustrates how far the Douglas girls had come in both dress and deportment.

Nothing in early colonial Victoria capped the wedding of Martha, who after her return to Victoria married another colonial official, Dennis Harris, in 1878. The bride and her numerous attendants wore elaborate gowns, imported from Paris, and most of Victoria's notables were among the guests. This pattern of marrying colonial officials or merchant settlers was followed in the Work, McNeill and Tod families. In 1864, Fanny McNeill married bank clerk James Judson Young, who became provincial secretary, while in 1879 Rebecca married Thomas Elwyn who had served as Gold Commissioner. In the Tod family, the eldest daughter Mary married an American settler, J. S. Bowker, from San Juan Island while her younger sister married a successful merchant, J. S. Drummond.[36]

Certainly not all these marriages achieved the same class status. Of all the daughters in question, only the Ross girls were to marry Métis men. The eldest, Elizabeth, who had been sent to England for her education, married Charles Wren, a Métis who had immigrated from Red River to Oregon. After her death in 1859, he married a younger sister, Mary Amelia.[37] Flora, the youngest Ross daughter, is the only women in this study for whom marriage was not a critical factor in maintaining her status. In 1859, she married Paul K. Hubbs, an American settler who was described as 'a white Indian', but within a decade this marriage had dissolved.[38] Flora Ross went on to have her own career, becoming Matron of the Asylum at New Westminster. Like her mother, Flora Ross was a remarkable woman; the social respectability which is reflected in her portrait, taken in the 1890s, she had achieved in her own right.

By the 1870s, it was current local opinion that while the sons in these founding families had amounted to very little and certainly did not do their fathers' names proud, the daughters had achieved notable success. As John Tod remarked on one occasion about the Work daughters: 'It is rather remarkable that so numerous a family of daughters should have all turned out so well, their exemplary good conduct having gained the universal respect of all their neighbours'.[39] Indeed, in the late nineteenth century, several of the Work daughters, notably Sarah Finlayson and Jane Tolmie, lived an opulent lifestyle, their husbands having become two of the most wealthy and influential men in the city. At their mansion-like homes, 'Rock Bay' and 'Cloverdale', they were well known for their gracious hospitality.

Yet social success in early Victoria did not come without a price. Although she had become Lady Douglas, Amelia had not forgotten her Cree heritage and pined for the old days. A visitor in 1881 observed that she 'often expresses a desire to see the Indian country before she dies' and in spite of the fancy dishes presented at her table, 'she was more fond of bitter root, camas and buffalo tongue'.[40] Despite their marital and material success, the younger generation had the anxiety of living in an increasingly racist society —there was no guarantee that the stigma of native blood could truly be transcended. These attitudes were painfully underscored by the American historian Hubert Bancroft, who denounced miscegenation as 'the Fur Traders' Curse' in his *History of the Northwest Coast*, published in 1886. Imagine what the genteel families, who had entertained him so hospitably upon his visit to Victoria some years earlier, must have felt upon reading his denegration of their maternal ancestors:

I could never understand how such men as John McLoughlin, *James Douglas*, Ogden, *Finlayson*, *Work* and *Tolmie* and the rest could endure the thought of having their name and honors descend to a degenerate posterity. Surely they were possessed of sufficient intelligence to know that by giving their children Indian or half-breed mothers, their own old Scotch, Irish or English blood would in them be greatly debased, and hence they were doing all concerned a great wrong.[41]

For reasons that have nothing to do with miscegenation but resulted principally from a complicated intersection of racism and gender role expectations, the sons in the second generation were not successful in their fathers' terms; many, such as the Work and Tod sons, did not marry and died young. Leadership in the second generation in these families passed by and large to the white sons-in-law. Within the family circle, however, there was considerable loyalty and devotion shown to the widowed mothers, and kin ties were maintained by the daughters. Evidence that bonds were strong between the sisters in the McNeill family is highlighted by a very interesting picture, taken in 1904, which features four out of the five sisters from the portrait taken thirty years early. Again, Lucy Moffatt dominates the photo, obviously very much the matriarch of this part-Haida clan. Amelia Douglas and Josette Work remained the cherished centres of their families until their venerable deaths in 1890 and 1896 respectively.

But whatever the private family ties, as Christine Welsh so poignantly testifies in her film *Women in the Shadows*,[42] the practice of hiding one's native ancestry was an all too common response to the increasing racism of the late nineteenth and early twentieth centuries in the Pacific northwest and elsewhere. When they began to write family histories, male descendants made no mention of their distinguished maternal forebears, but rather played up the paternal Hudson's Bay Company connections. Simon Fraser Tolmie, who became a premier of the province, fondly reminisced about growing up on the family estate 'Cloverdale', but he hardly mentioned his mother and omitted all reference to his remarkable Work grandmother. In his family narrative of 1924, Donald H. McNeill was at pains to emphasise that his grandfather had been the first white settler of south Oak Bay; he did not acknowledge that he was descended from high-ranking Haida and Tongass women.[43]

It is significant that the only person to attempt to preserve an aspect of her native heritage was the most acculturated Douglas daughter, Martha. When she was at school in England, her father had chided her for telling her mother's Cree stories—the world must not know that her mother was a Native. But in 1901, Martha

Harris published a little book of native history and folklore, which did include her mother's stories. In her preface she lamented the destruction of First Nations heritage but only obliquely did she claim this as her own:

> As a little girl I used to listen to these legends with the greatest delight, and in order not to lose them, I have written down what I can remember of them. When written they lose their charm which was in the telling. They need the quaint songs and the sweet voice that told them, the winter gloaming and the bright fire as the only light. Then were these legends beautiful.[44]

PART

Reflections

The Great Map of Mankind

~

The British Encounter with India

P. J. MARSHALL

*T*HE GREAT MAP OF MANKIND: *British Perceptions of the World in the Age of Enlightenment* was published under the names of P. J. Marshall and Glyndwr Williams in 1982. With the arrogance of would-be imperial potentates, we divided the world into two spheres. I must confess responsibility for the chapters on Asia.

Were I to try to write the Asian chapters now, they would inevitably be rather different from those that appeared in 1982. I would have to take account of new findings and of new approaches to the subject in the widest sense. Since 1982 scholarship about the British in Asia has moved on, while there has been a huge outpouring of writing that has raised fundamental questions about how 'the West' has perceived and indeed continues to perceive and to represent other societies. Even so, I have no intention of inflicting rewritten chapters on my long-suffering co-author, nor do I wish to offer him a vindication of them or even an apology for them, well-merited as that would be. A collection of essays in his honour does, however, give me an opportunity of reflecting on how fifteen years of scholarship and debate have altered interpretations of that part of the Asian chapters in which I have an especial interest, the British involvement with India.

India played a dominant part in the Asian chapters of *The Great Map of Mankind* for the obvious reason that by the second half of the eighteenth century the British were more deeply involved there than in any other part of Asia. The wave of conquests that began with the acquisition of the Bengal *diwani* in 1765 gave British people both the opportunities and the incentive to find out about their new subjects and to formulate theories about them. A number of individuals, Warren Hastings and William Jones conspicuous among them, were deeply engaged in such inquiries. Jones's translations and his Discourses to the Asiatick Society of Bengal, over which he presided, Charles Wilkins's version of the *Gita*, Nathaniel Halhed's Bengali Grammar, and Henry Thomas Colebrooke's Vedic studies were their most notable achievements.

My chapters in *The Great Map of Mankind* were predominantly about the written word. I concentrated on writing that sought to describe and to interpret the peoples of India, their way of life, their social and political institutions, their religious beliefs and their history. Since 1982, however, sources that did not feature much in *The Great Map of Mankind* have been used for exploring British notions about India. Attention is now given to the way in which India was represented, not only in descriptive and analytic writing, but in verse and in fiction. The visual record of India left by eighteenth-century British people has also been extensively reproduced and analysed and there have been studies of British awareness of Indian music.

I did not pay much attention to poetry or novels with Indian settings or to the first attempts to translate Indian literature into English because I believed that literary orientalism was little more than the ignorant adaptation of supposedly exotic forms as a vehicle for satire or moral tales.[1] Such a view has not worn well. The engagement of literary scholars with 'colonialism' is a major development since 1982. For the early nineteenth century, oriental themes are now seen not as superficial decoration but, in reflecting the anxieties generated by the possession of empire in Asia, as a major preoccupation of British Romanticism.[2] Serious critical attention is now given to the limited body of British imaginative writing about India produced in the late eighteenth century, such as the novel *Hartly House, Calcutta*, or the nine hymns to Hindu deities of Sir William Jones, and to Jones's translation of *Sakuntala*.[3] Literary scholars have also turned their attention to material that historians would in the past have claimed as their exclusive territory, to reveal, as one has recently put it, 'narrative structure, style, images and tropes'.[4] The most sustained attempt to apply literary analysis to what might be conventionally regarded as a major 'political' source for British interpretations of India are the chapters in Sara Suleri's *The Rhetoric of English India* that deal with the Indian speeches of Edmund Burke.[5]

My sections of *The Great Map of Mankind* made little use of visual material. This deficiency now looks particularly glaring, since the art of the Raj has begun to attract the same kind of attention that is given to its literature. Well before 1982 there had been authoritative studies, such as Mildred Archer's *India and British Portraiture 1770–1825*,[6] of the work of the large number of professional British artists, some thirty painters in oils and twenty miniaturists, who went to India in the late eighteenth century to paint portraits. They included men of the eminence of Johann Zoffany, Arthur William Devis and Ozias Humphry. Portraits of European sitters dominate their work, but it is about much else besides. Indian sitters were the main subjects when British painters offered their services at Indian courts. Europeans commissioned portraits of their Bibis or Indian mistresses. Indian figures appear in profusion in the densely peopled scenes that Zoffany in particular delighted to portray, as in *Colonel Maudaunt's Cock Fight* or *The Embassy of Hyderbeck to Calcutta*.

A number of artists were also interested in depicting Indian 'types'. They evidently believed, as William Hodges put it, that painting should be 'connected with the history of the various countries' and should 'faithfully represent the manners of mankind'.[7] In 1792 Devis invited proposals for a series of prints which he published to illustrate 'the arts, manufacture and agriculture of Bengal'.[8] At about the same time the Belgian François-Balthazar Solvyns began an even more ambitious project, which he intended to be a comprehensive series of studies of castes and occupations to be found around Calcutta.

Eighteenth-century British artists depicted landscapes as well as people. Hodges, who had painted in the South Pacific on James

Cook's second voyage, was the first professional artist to work specifically on landscape in India during a stay from 1780 to 1783. He was followed by the intrepid Thomas and William Daniells, whose tours during a seven-year residence took them far beyond the frontiers of British influence. Both Hodges and the Daniells published their work in books of engravings, the Daniells reaching a very wide audience with their six volumes of aquatints called *Oriental Scenery*. Hodges and the Daniells established models for depicting Indian scenes that were to be imitated for a hundred years or more by amateur artists, such as army officers on campaigns or lady travellers who had acquired the accomplishment of drawing. The work of such people has been described as 'a unique artistic achievement; at no other time has one country been so extensively and minutely observed by artists from another'.[9]

The urge to accumulate and record knowledge about India was the stimulus not only for Europeans to depict landscapes and people, but for them to give commissions to Indian artists. Sets of Hindu deities and of figures in the dress and with the tools appropriate to their caste or occupation were painted in what has come to be called a 'Company' style, that is in the artistic traditions of cities such as Delhi, Lucknow, Patna, Murshidabad or Tanjore, modified to take account of European taste, as in the use of perspective or of more sombre colouring. Landscape was apparently deemed to be beyond the competence of Indian artists, but their depictions of natural history were much admired. Some British people acquired large collections of paintings of birds and animals, fruit and flowers.[10]

Indian paintings were collected as well as being commissioned. Collectors seem primarily to have been interested in the subject matter of the paintings. They looked for illustrations of religious beliefs, of Indian history, or of types of people. The greatest of all the early collectors, Richard Johnson, had served in the Residencies at Lucknow and at Hyderabad under Warren Hastings, which enabled him to acquire both Mughal and Deccani paintings. He was especially interested in pictures that illustrated Indian music, but he evidently derived aesthetic pleasure as well as instruction from what he called the 'exquisite specimens of the art in its best age' in his collection.[11] Collectors of fragments of Hindu sculpture, or those who studied engravings made from sketches of sculpture done by artists who had visited temples, seem to have been concerned primarily with what they could deduce from them about India's past, but some commentators also began to recognise their aesthetic qualities. William Robertson considered some Indian temple sculpture to be 'finished with an elegance intitled to the admiration of the most ingenious artists'.[12]

In the British community in India there were enthusiastic connoisseurs of music, trying to keep up with changing tastes at home. Some developed a taste for Indian music. Female singers from north India were especially patronised. Their songs were transcribed into European musical notation and were performed either in the original language or in translation.[13]

IN THE LAST fifteen years, western representations of non-European peoples, whether in what purported to be factual analysis with which *The Great Map of Mankind* was concerned, or in novels or verse, or pictorial depictions of them and of the lands in which they lived, or attempts to reproduce their music, have all come to be analysed with a new rigour.

The tone was of course set by Edward Said in his *Orientalism* of 1978, the arguments of which need no extended recapitulation. For him the way in which Europeans have represented any part of Asia has been an integral part of their exercise of power over it. They have endowed themselves with a definitive knowledge of Asia to reveal an Asian Other, different from and inferior to Europe. The work of generations of scholars, writers and artists has reinforced the ideas of difference and inferiority and has therefore served the cause of European imperial domination.

Said's shafts were primarily aimed against those who had written about the Middle East in the nineteenth and twentieth centuries. He was not much concerned either with India or with the eighteenth century, although he saw this as a formative phase for what became later 'Orientalism'. Late eighteenth-century 'Europe came to know the Orient more scientifically, to live in it with greater authority and discipline than ever before'. In particular, scholars claimed a new mastery of language, while artists and poets 'restructured the Orient by their art and made its colors, lights and people visible through their images, rhythms, and motifs'.[14] In another passage, he traced 'modern Orientalism' to the 'secularizing elements' of the eighteenth century with its universal principles for comparing societies and civilisations.[15] Said was somewhat dismissive of Sir William Jones. 'To rule and to learn, then to compare Orient with Occident: these were Jones's goals, which, with an irresistible impulse always to codify, to subdue the infinite variety of the Orient to "a complete digest" of laws, figures, customs, and works, he is believed to have achieved.'[16]

Such approaches were specifically applied to India by Ronald B. Inden in his *Imagining India* of 1990. The late eighteenth century is again important by implication for him because of the rise of what he calls the 'Anglo-French imperial formation' that was to dominate the nineteenth century. India was no longer seen as a region distinguished from Europe by religion, but by its failure in secular terms, above all by its failure to match the west in scientific rationality. Western scholarship displayed India as emotional, irrational, mystical, politically incapable and ultimately, to many commentators, as feminine; the West by contrast was practical, progressive, politically mature and ultimately masculine.[17]

The links between British scholarship and depictions of India and the exercise of colonial power are studied in some of Bernard S. Cohn's essays. The grammars and translations from Indian languages of the late eighteenth century were the first steps in a British 'programme of appropriating Indian languages to serve as a crucial component in their construction of a system of rule'. Through such knowledge they could 'assess and collect taxes, maintain law and order, and . . . identify and classify groups within Indian society . . . The vast social world that was India had to be classified, categorized and bounded before it could be hierarchized' and made governable.[18] In another essay Cohn deals with British artists who in their sketches and watercolours depicted Indian scenes through the conventions of the European picturesque, and thus 'made India into an object to be appropriated, made accessible and understandable through a cultural screen constructed by and for the British . . . The subject Indians were to be increasingly objectified by their British rulers in terms created by a continuous dialectic of how the British saw India and Indians, thereby constructing a reality to which the Indians were made to conform'.[19]

The same point has been made about the literary adaptations and attempted translations. They are acts of 'cultural appropriation'. 'The literary traditions of the East are at once conflated and commodified, turning into a kind of exotic item imported to enhance European traditions.'[20]

Thomas Metcalf's recent *Ideologies of the Raj* again stresses the importance of the later eighteenth century as the starting point for British colonial discourse about India:

> Secularized notions of the 'modern', and the 'civilized', emphasized at once the difference, and the inferiority, of non-European societies ... As the British endeavoured to define themselves as 'British', and thus as 'not Indian', they had to make of the Indian whatever they chose *not* to make of themselves.

Metcalf acknowledges the sense of 'wonder and of curiosity' of men like Jones. Yet he believes that what he calls 'the Orientalist project ... was clearly fitted to the needs of Europe. Classification always carried with it a presumption of hierarchy'.[21] For Metcalf, as for so many other writers, to depict, list or classify is to exercise authority over the object depicted, listed or classified.

Such arguments have not gone uncontested. 'Orientalism' is a term that had specific connotations in British-Indian history long before Said's polemical use of it. In 1969, for instance, David Kopf published a book called *British Orientalism and the Bengal Renaissance*. For Kopf, western Orientalism was not a body of knowledge imposed upon the east to establish domination over it. On the contrary, it was the means by which Indians recovered their own past and by doing so were able to modernise their culture for themselves. British Orientalists and Bengali intellectuals worked together 'to promote social and cultural change in Calcutta'.[22] Kopf has been robust in his denunciations of what he calls 'the partisans of Said who have taken upon themselves the ominous task of consigning British Orientalism—which they hate but do not understand—to the chopping block in a deconstructionist reign of terror'.[23] Jones still arouses fervent loyalty. His biographer and the editor of his letters insists that: 'None of his activities suggests that his research was ever motivated by a desire to keep India a colony, or that he was an ideological agent of Western imperialism seeking to exploit native peoples and their resources. Rather, he was the people's protector . . .'[24] To the historian of the Bengal Asiatick Society, Jones was 'the first scholar from the West to look at the East without a Western bias . . . He was unlike other scholars, who studied those subjects that helped them to know the people of the colonies better so that they could administer them more efficiently . . .'[25]

There can be no meeting of minds between those, on the one hand, who deny the colonial premises and sense of cultural superiority which inevitably impinged on the thought of even Sir William Jones, or those, on the other, who apply 'Orientalist' analysis in a crude way, insisting that all western representations of Asia were shaped by the needs of 'the colonial project' and that all claims to western knowledge about Asia were fabrications of an Other.

There seems to be little to choose between such rigid oversimplifications. The debate has, however, generally moved on. Analysis of colonial discourse now tends to modify earlier assertions about the cultural power of Europe to shape the world. Eastern voices are now heard as well as western ones in this discourse. Sara Suleri urges that 'the rhetoric of the British Raj' should not be understood in terms of 'domination and subordination as though the two were mutually exclusive terms'; the fixity of the dividing lines between them should be broken down.[26] At the same time, historical studies are providing much new evidence of the complexity of the cultural encounters in late eighteenth-century India. Two themes are emerging strongly. In the first place, generalisations about 'the British' or 'the colonial project' seem to have little validity. Even the small number of those who seriously engaged with things Indian showed a wide diversity of outlooks and had their own 'projects'. In the second, the role of Indians in shaping the notions of Europeans about India is becoming more and more apparent. Thus the representations produced in the name of Europeans, be they translations, interpretative essays, paintings or transcriptions of music, are being seen less as European orientalist constructions than as the product of both European and Indian influences.

THERE WAS NO uniformity of outlook among the British élite in India. The educational upbringing of the numerous Scots was different from that of the English. Individuals varied from the hard rationalism, later to somersault into millenarianism, of Nathaniel Halhed,[27] to the political radicalism and deism of William Jones, or the seemingly authoritarian political beliefs combined with religious ecumenicism of Warren Hastings. Certain generalisations are, however, possible about the British side of the encounter.[28] Those who participated in it were almost all of high social standing. To obtain a position in the Company's service, above all in the civil service and most especially in the Bengal civil service, where fortunes were thought to be most easily made, required powerful family influence. Army officers were likely to be less well connected, but they were still usually drawn from families of some political consequence. Men from such families went to India with high ambitions, most obviously to make money, but also to win a reputation. They were conscious that they were entrusted with a great new national asset and hoped for due recognition of their achievements as administrators or soldiers. A number were also aware of opportunities to win fame as men of learning or literary taste by relaying knowledge of India to the public. Robert Orme, who had chosen to make a career for himself as the historian of British India, assured Warren Hastings that 'the Educated World has received with the greatest satisfaction' the *Code of Gentoo Laws*, and that 'the valuable present you are making to learning and reason' would ensure that Hastings's name would be remembered by Philosophy's disciples.[29]

The education of the most aspiring members of this élite was likely to have given them certain assets in encountering cultures other than their own; but it also probably channelled their responses in certain fixed directions. Because of their age, few of those going to India had degrees from either English or Scottish universities, but a number of the young English had been educated in the public schools like Westminster, Harrow or Eton, while the Scots might have attended lectures at either Glasgow and Edinburgh, even if they had not taken degrees. Most would have acquired some linguistic facility from prolonged exposure to Greek and Latin. A classical education also shaped their literary taste and left them with a respect for the ancient and an expectation that civilisations, with the conspicuous exception of that of modern Europe, would decline from a golden age in the remote past.

There is also evidence that some at least of the young men who went to India had learnt to think speculatively. They were given to theorising about the world and its peoples. Their approach to India was generally to see it as a society comparable to others rather than as part of an exotic, mysterious Orient. Its society, religions, history or art could all be fitted into what were deemed to be universal patterns. Knowledge of India would extend knowledge of what was called 'the natural history of man', but it would not pose any fundamental challenge to accepted ways of explaining the world.

The standards of comparison by which India was judged were essentially secular. Societies were assessed by their capacity to maximise human well-being and to stimulate material progress. India generally failed by these criteria. Constitutional government on the British model was calculated to produce improvement; Asiatic despotism negated it. Most who held such views were also likely to have been at least nominal Christians, but to have judged Christianity in terms primarily of its rationality and its beneficial social effects. They defined other religions in terms with which they were already familiar, as having priesthoods and a set body of doctrine expounded in scripture, and they judged them too as much by secular criteria as by the extent they deviated from revealed Christian truth. Religions that instilled good conduct, as supposedly 'philosophical' Hinduism was thought to do, were commended. With notable exceptions like the young Charles Grant, few would have counted themselves Christian 'enthusiasts'; 'fanaticism' in other religions, as reputedly in Islam, was unreservedly condemned. On the other hand, outright free-thinking, as in the case of Halhed, seems to have been rare. By the end of the century, any tendency to views that were religiously or politically subversive was being firmly repressed by Wellesley.

Intellectual ambition was more than matched by cultural ambition, especially in Calcutta, where the rich spent profusely on houses, gardens, horses and carriages, paintings, musical instruments and books. 'The Civilized World', a Calcutta newspaper wrote in 1791:

> affords no similar instance in the rise and culture of the arts, and to such perfection as Calcutta this day affords—the mechanical arts, which depend on the luxuries of society, and the tangibility

of fashion are arrived to the summit of perfection; 'In splendour London now eclipses Rome'. . . and in similar respects, Calcutta rivals the head of the empire.[30]

The arts so assiduously cultivated in British-Indian settlements were of course European ones, but to explore the arts and learning of India and to present them to the wonder of polite society throughout the western world was regarded as a task befitting the rich and sophisticated communities of the British-Indian settlements. The foundation of the Bengal Asiatick Society, matching learned societies in other cities, was a very conscious act of civic pride by the British in Calcutta.

FOR ALL THE confidence and apparent self-sufficiency of the eighteenth-century British in India, they were part of a regime that depended on Indians at every point: Indian soldiers in their armies, Indian servants in their households, Indian bankers and agents in their businesses, Indian clerks and executive officers in the government departments. Most fundamentally, the eighteenth-century British depended, as is amply demonstrated in C. A. Bayly's most recent book, on Indian sources of information.[31] Virtually every Englishman had his Indian counterpart, who relayed information to him and mediated between him and Indian society. Those who sought to gather knowledge turned to the learned, to pandits and Muslim maulvis.

The importance of such men in how Europeans interpreted India is now fully recognised. It is possible to see their role as the victims in the appropriation of knowledge by colonial power, and to argue that 'The fathers of orientalism in India furthered colonial centralization by subordinating the Indian intelligentsia to English epistemological authority'.[32] Relationships generally seem, however, to have been more complex than mere subordination. With the decline of indigenous patronage, the service of the Company or of individual Europeans certainly became attractive. Learned Indians, like their British counterparts, took the Company's shilling, receiving offices with salaries or revenue grants. Though there is still much to know about their roles within this framework, it seems clear that pandits and maulvis could advance their own agendas as well as complying with those of their employers, even if what they contributed might subsequently be heavily overlaid with European assumptions.

The pandits employed by the British in Bengal have been the subject of illuminating studies by Rosane Rocher.[33] She shows how their Puranic learning and the Enlightenment assumptions of their employers converged.[34] The pandits purveyed material both for the needs of the Company, that is the sources for legal texts, beginning with Halhed's *Gentoo Code* and extending to Jones's and Colebrooke's *Digest of Hindu Law*, and to satisfy the curiosity of individuals about religion, history or literature. Such material enabled Wilkins to produce his *Gita*, and Jones to make his reconstructions of Indian history, write his essays on the Hindu deities and translate *Sakuntala*. Even in their legal work, the pandits were more than mere accomplices for British purposes. The interpretations of Hindu law that emerged in the late eighteenth century do indeed seem to embody characteristic 'Orientalist' assumptions, such as those about the superiority of ancient texts, emanating from a golden age, to corrupt contemporary practice. Yet, as Professor Rocher shows, these were the beliefs of the pandits as well as being the expectations of their masters. Jones no doubt imposed many conceptions of his own on his version of *Sakuntala*, but perceptive critics still recognised that it reflected an aesthetic different from theirs: 'We must not expect the unities of the Greek theatre; we must not measure it by our own standard of propriety . . .'[35]

The British needed the services of learned maulvis as well as of Hindus. As with the pandits, Muslim scholars rendered service to the colonial state for reward, but also received patronage for what went beyond state needs narrowly defined. Supposedly authentic translations of Islamic law were commissioned for the use of the Company's courts. The Company also took the first step in patronising Muslim education with the endowment of the Calcutta Madrassa in 1781. Hastings took pride in the fact that scholars and students were being drawn to his foundation from all over India. For him the Madrassa was much more than a school to train future government law officers. He believed that he was winning the esteem of Muslims for himself and for the British in general as patrons 'of the growth and extension of liberal knowledge'.[36] As their influence extended beyond Bengal, the British also acted as patrons of learned men in northern Indian cities. Such people certainly rendered important political services, but individual

Europeans, like Richard Johnson, the great collector of books and paintings, also acted as patron of poets and historians. In the treatises they wrote for the British, Islamic authors often took the opportunity to give their employers not only useful 'colonial knowledge' but instruction as to the proper behaviour expected of rulers in the Mughal tradition.[37]

In the visual arts Europeans could at last dispense with Indian intermediaries and their linguisitic skills and accumulated knowledge. 'Company paintings' by Indian artists reflected the influence on them of European aesthetics, but there is little if any evidence of European artists being influenced by Indian aesthetics in return in this period. From the arrival of William Hodges in India, landscapes were sketched or painted for the most part within the established conventions of the 'picturesque' as it was being interpreted in contemporary Britain, by which the artist sought to catch a higher truth than simply reproducing the apparent reality that confronted him. The case for seeing the picturesque as some kind of colonial appropriation of the Indian landscape therefore has some force. As has been pointed out, however, if the picturesque was a distorting lens through which to envisage India and Indians, it was not a lens fashioned for particular colonial purposes. The hold of the picturesque on contemporary taste at home ensured that it would exercise a similar domination in India, where metropolitan taste in the arts was keenly followed.[38]

Music, of which the British communities in India were so fond, could also be performed in private houses and increasingly in public theatres or assembly rooms without any concessions to things Indian. Some Europeans were, however, keen to incorporate Indian music into their repertoire. It is clear that interest in north Indian 'Nautch girls' went beyond the lubricious one so often identified. They were admired for their art. Although there were new sources of Indian patronage for them in Calcutta and at the Lucknow court, they also sought employment from the British. Efforts were made to transcribe their songs for performance by English singers. What became known as 'Hindostannie airs' were widely admired. Characteristically, Hastings was interested in them. He employed 'a little band' with three singers and was said to sing 'the Hindostannie Airs perfectly well' himself. He insisted that they should not be treated as westernised fantasies. 'I have always protested', he wrote, 'against every Interpolation of European Taste in the Recital of the Music of Hindostan'. Versions of the airs were eventually published in Britain.[39]

WERE I WRITING *The Great Map of Mankind* now I would try to give a fuller picture of the British encounter with India than I offered in 1982. I would endeavour to show that a group of British people engaged with India on a wider front than I then recognised. I would discuss poetry, novels, painting and music as well as translations, interpretative essays and descriptive accounts. In general, British people in India strike me now as even more remarkable than I then thought them to be for their exuberant high living, their determination to endow their settlements with all the amenities of sophisticated urban life at home and the willingness of at least a few to incorporate things Indian into their cultural ambitions, by becoming collectors, patrons and interpreters of India to the curious in Europe. They were of course the paid servants of a colonial regime and duly collected information for their employers, but their ambitions took them well beyond their official duties into literary projects of their own. Their dependence on Indians, pandits, maulvis, Muslim historians, artists and singers, is now even clearer than it was in 1982.[40] Knowledge about such people and about their relations with their employers is still sketchy, but, thanks to recent scholarship, it is surely impossible to regard them as no more than passive victims from whom Europeans could extract material at will to fulfil their own orientalist designs.

The Great Map of Mankind recognised that there were 'connections between assumed knowledge of the world and the growth of British power and influence'.[41] Since 1982, there has rightly been a much sharper awareness of the colonial context of all kinds of western statements about the non-European world. By the second half of the eighteenth century statements about India could not but be coloured by awareness of the extent of British domination. Yet within this all-pervasive framework of colonial dominance, individual British people still pursued all sorts of intellectual projects of their own devising and depended on the co-operation of Indians to carry them out. These Indian 'assistants' were partners, if ostensibly junior partners, in the projects and left an indelible mark on them.

Exploring the Pacific,
Exploring James Cook

DAVID MACKAY

F OLLOWING A HIGHLY SUCCESSFUL conference at Simon Fraser
University in British Columbia in April 1978, a distinguished
group of historians, art historians, anthropologists and scientists set
sail on a small vessel to visit the place of Captain James Cook's
landing 200 years before in Nootka Sound on Vancouver Island.
The party included Glyn Williams, who had delivered a paper
at the conference titled, 'Myth and Reality: James Cook and the
Theoretical Geography of Northwest America'. This was a return
to the territory he had explored in his first major work, *The British
Search for the Northwest Passage in the Eighteenth Century*.[1] The
Simon Fraser paper had shown how the prosaic Cook, the master
of the matter-of-fact, had been uncharacteristically lured into
mistakes by the theoretical geographers Müller and Stählin.

In spite of this geographical lapse of judgement, during his
period at Nootka Cook had managed to produce his usual, well-
documented description of the Sound, its flora, fauna and its
peoples. The detail of the account was such that subsequent traders
and explorers felt confident in using it as a base: so confident that
in 1790 it became the subject of a dispute between England and
Spain which almost led to war. Relationships with the Indian

inhabitants were cordial and business-like during the sojourn of the *Resolution* and *Discovery*. Trade was successful and although there were a few tense moments over missing pieces of equipment, violence was contained and cordial and reciprocal relationships were sustained throughout the visit. The landscape of the region impressed and the vessels had no difficulty replacing their tired masts and spars as the Sound consisted 'of high hills and deep Vallies, for the most part cloathed with large timber such as Spruce fir and White Cedar'.[2]

It is still clothed with conifers. The conference-goers of 1978 left from the lumber town of Gold River at the head of the Sound. The sides of the steep slopes running down to the water were in places being cleared by forest workers and the logs worked down to the shore to be towed away to the mill. For those on board the boat, and I suspect for Glyn Williams himself, this was a reverential journey to one of the more famous sites where Cook had landed. Unfortunately the boat on which the party travelled was not able to land its passengers. The Nuu-chah-nulth people of Vancouver Island were in dispute with the Provincial Government over land rights and the extraction of lumber. The origins of their dispute went back many years—200 in fact—and those who sought to tread in the footsteps of Captain Cook, and were attending a conference to celebrate his achievements, were not at all welcome. For two centuries James Cook had been a central source in the European documentation and interpretation of the eighteenth-century Pacific. In 1978, in Ship Cove, Nootka Sound, the Pacific was reinterpreting the experience of James Cook.[3]

This would not have been the first occasion on which Captain James Cook had lost his historiographical innocence or been identified as an agent of European appropriation, but given the presence of those who had gathered to celebrate the bicentenary of his achievement, it did have a certain poignancy. Since 1978 linkages between the voyages of Cook and contemporary political issues have become more common and academics have occasionally entered the fray or been asked to comment in the media on the historical significance and accuracy of particular interpretations of the past.

In Hawai'i there is a tradition stretching to the first half of the nineteenth century which portrays Cook as a figure of oppression.

This view was perpetuated by American missionary writers and identified by Beaglehole in his 1964 article, 'The Death of Captain Cook'.[4] In 1989 Haunani Kay Trask, a Hawaiian academic visitor to New Zealand, introduced some additional elements to this and accused Cook of being a tuberculose, syphilitic racist, responsible for the deaths of thousands of her countrymen. In this version he was at the vanguard of the fatal impact. She offered the almost blasphemous opinion that when the Hawaiians killed Cook at Kealakekua Bay on St Valentine's Day in 1779, they were doing the peoples of the Pacific a considerable service, since the great navigator had been the spearhead and symbol of European encroachments. Although this visit raised something of a stir in New Zealand, it was significant that at the time the focus was principally on the tuberculosis and venereal disease, and the argument did not carry through to the question of whether Cook should be viewed in the same way—as a scourge—by the Maori. A few years later, however, the Cook monument at Gisborne, where the explorer made his first New Zealand landfall, was toppled from its perch by protesters.

The issue arose with even more potent symbolism when the *Endeavour* replica visited New Zealand in 1996. A sub-tribe of the Gisborne region wished to prevent a visit to that port, observing that the blood of their ancestors had been spilled on the beach in October 1769 when they were fired on by the crew of the *Endeavour*. Another group which had been relatively hostile to the former were eager for the visit. Eventually, after detailed discussion and an expiatory ceremony on the decks of the replica, the visit went ahead, clearing the way for an immensely popular voyage around the country. The emerging indigenous view of Cook and the traditional European one were constructively reconciled.

In other parts of the Pacific Cook also has a place in political beliefs and mythology. The Aboriginals of the Botany Bay region are highly conscious of the part which the navigator played in the subsequent settlement of their lands. Among some peoples, history has reinforced mythology to assign Cook a malevolent role. The Noonkanbah people of the Kimberley region of northwestern Australia live many thousands of miles from Captain Cook's landfalls on the eastern coast of Australia, although the great navigator would have been only about 180 miles from them when he sailed past Timor in September 1770. Like all Aboriginals, they have a rich oral tradition and Cook features in their mythology rather ingloriously as a malevolent figure who killed their ancestors and took their land. Kolig points out that 'the Cook myth certainly gives expression to a notion of injustice, couched in the Aboriginal conceptual framework. The myth is reactionary to alien dominance and heavy-handed patronage that violates the pride of tradition-conscious Aborigines'.[5] He has become for them the powerful symbol of European depredations.

It is hardly surprising that Cook should eventually have ended up in the sights of nationalist movements and those seeking self-determination for their people. It is not simply that he revealed the Pacific world to Europe, thereby facilitating later exploitation and settlement. It is also the fact that in his own century and in ours he has been portrayed in a heroic mould; representing a fine, stoic, stern but also compassionate agent of empire. Indigenous figures who have the potential to contribute to national identity have been set aside in his favour. Webber's history painting of the death of Cook was in the mould of Benjamin West's *The Death of General Wolfe* or J. S. Copley's *Death of Major Pearson*. All are manifesting heroic qualities at the moment of death. In the case of Cook the painting shows a virtually defenceless explorer who was an agent of peace and human understanding. The 1794 print, *The Apotheosis of Captain Cook*, after Webber and de Loutherbourg, represented the allegorical elevation of Cook as hero, revealing the artistic peaks to which this reached.[6]

The modern biographical tradition encapsulates these strains. From Kitson in 1907 to Villiers to the most recent biography by Hough, Cook is portrayed as the finest type of Englishman and certainly the greatest eighteenth- century explorer of any nationality.[7] In *The Exploration of the Pacific*, first published in 1934, J. C. Beaglehole provided a sketch which was to shape appreciations for the next forty years: 'Of such a man legend inevitably grew. To the peoples of the Pacific, whether they recognized in him the aspect of deity or not, he was and remained a fabulous figure, alike in the power he personified and in his benevolence'.[8] The concluding remarks are illuminating:

Yet one thinks of Cook, not only as him who would always be in the eyes of that immortal Frenchman 'the first of navigators', or as the scientist for whose safety the governments of France and Spain took such honourable thought, but also as the tall smiling figure who on the beach at Ship Cove, in Queen Charlotte's Sound, threw trifles for naked Maori urchins to scramble for, laughing and fearless, till his pockets were empty. For the rest, the map of the Pacific is his ample panegyric.[9]

The monumental biography published posthumously in 1974 was more temperate, less effusive. The deficiencies were noted; the frailties of the second and third voyages outlined; the lapses of judgement were recorded. The passions, the temper tantrums were described. The relationships with Pacific peoples were not portrayed in such glowing terms or with such paternalistic images. Brutal punishments of islanders, some of which shocked the crew, were described. Inevitably, appropriately, the admiration and respect generated by a lifetime's acquaintanceship shone through and the biography ended with the now famous quotation from the venerable Maori chief Te Horeta, *e kore tino tangata e ngaro i roto i te tokomaha*, a veritable man is not hid among many.[10] In a sense this does seek indigenous complicity in the apotheosis.

The most recent biography, by Richard Hough, is a decided step back in time, and in its admiration of Cook it manages to be both patronising and ignorant about Pacific peoples. In effect the biographer rarely gets off the deck and in contrast to the great navigator the islanders are caricatures with the ironic names which Banks applied to them carried over into the narrative without any attempt to establish their true identities. Cook's spellings of Tahitian names are the accepted ones, although a dip into Beaglehole's footnotes would have provided corrections. Hough preferred to see Tahitian and Maori as accidental partners in culture contact whose actions are baffling and unworthy of analysis. Pacific Island behaviour is viewed consistently through the lens of European experience and expectation. Hough is particularly uncomfortable in dealing with New Zealand and Maori. Two of his chapters are entitled 'These People are Much Given to War', and 'Horrors of Grass Cove'—a reference to the killing of some of the *Adventure*'s crew in Queen

Charlotte Sound. Cook's rather philosophical attitude to cannibalism is disapproved of and hints of the ignoble savage abound.

Not surprisingly such portrayals of Cook fail to endear him to the Native peoples of the Pacific, many of whom are involved in issues of self-determination and land rights. In both Australia and New Zealand the issue of Cook's planting the flag and claiming the land for his sovereign has become a lively one. Until the 1990s it could be argued that the Treaty of Waitangi of 1840, rather than early contacts, had been the focal point for debates about the impact of Europeans upon the Maori. From a strictly historical point of view this had some benefits, as it enabled the evaluation of past figures in terms of the conditions of their own times, rather than from the rather contentious problems of the present. From the point of view of resolving conflict, it also had enormous advantages. Since the 150th anniversary of the signing of that Treaty the activities of Europeans prior to 1840 have come under closer scrutiny, including those of James Cook.

The New Zealand case raises another issue about Cook's position in relation to the indigenous peoples of the Pacific. The reception of the *Endeavour* replica in New Zealand in 1996 was extraordinary —a level of attention unmatched in the other ports it visited in Australia, South Africa and England.[11] This is an interesting indicator of the status and significance Cook has in the nation's historical consciousness. He has an iconic power and without doubt is visually the most recognisable historical figure associated with the country. The almost regulation, even hackneyed, image is that of the Nathaniel Dance portrait of 1776 which until recently appeared as the watermark on paper notes, guaranteeing the integrity of the currency. It is also used in advertising, school publications and is reproduced in various stages of degradation on the billboards of hotels, motels, schools, fast food outlets and numerous other institutions. The strong, sculptured face represented in that portrait is a more familiar image than the likeness of any past politicians, governors-general, military leaders or, most significantly, Maori chiefs. Cook's name graces streets, parks, suburbs, schools and other private and public institutions. Given that he spent less than a year of his life in the country this is a remarkable achievement.

How has this status been achieved? No doubt part of the answer lies in the fact that the written history of the country is short and before World War I New Zealanders of European origin looked back to Britain for their great historical figures, as the history was in many ways seen as a continuation of that of the mother country. No pre-European history was recognised or valued. There is also a dearth of plausible *Pakeha* (white) alternatives to Cook. Inland exploration was carried out by missionaries and settlers and the distances covered were not great. Unlike the United States, South Africa and some South American and Asian countries there are no liberation heroes since there has been no war of independence to gain self-government. The Westminster system of government imported from Britain has produced political stability but it has not thrown up leaders who have plucked national heartstrings.

From a more positive perspective there is a sense in which Cook embodied the pioneer virtues, qualities and skills required in developing a newly settled land. Adaptability, resourcefulness, endurance and doggedness—these have pre-eminently been seen as his attributes and were also the things required on the colonial frontier. He was a private man of few words, who kept his own counsel. Physically, he was a big, raw-boned individual, the epitome of the pioneer or frontier type in *Pakeha* terms. While he had mastered the theory of navigation and was adept at handling new technology, his genius was of a practical, methodical kind. He brought a new level of scientific and technical exactitude to surveying and navigation, and in that way symbolised the triumph of the new industrial age in which New Zealand was colonised. His intellect was characterised by pragmatism, or common sense of a high order. This quality has comforting resonances given the popular self-image of the New Zealander as a Jack-of-all-trades; able to fix anything with binder-twine and number-8 wire.

It is also significant that Cook was a self-made man, who had eschewed comforts and the easy road to success and pushed himself to the top largely by his own efforts. Hard work, dedication and application, rather than friends in high places, marked the road to distinction. In the egalitarian climate of colonial New Zealand such a background was highly respected and served as a model to younger generations.

In a more direct way Cook defined and labelled the New Zealand landscape. In a seaborne country his name and imprint is ever visible. On his first voyage, as the second European visitor to the land, he outlined its shape by remarkable running surveys from the ship. Although there were a couple of prominent mistakes, and the South Island is belted in rather tightly around the waist, this was a quite outstanding achievement by the hydrographic standards of his own and later ages. The resulting chart, in various reproduced formats is ubiquitous in New Zealand educational institutions, libraries and other public buildings.[12] There were as well charts of particular parts of the coast, and of harbours and bays, which were to be of enormous value to subsequent navigators. Some of these charts, such as that of Queen Charlotte Sound, are of such a degree of accuracy that they were used well into the nineteenth century.

One obvious and permanent by-product of this industry was that Cook named more New Zealand coastal landmarks than any other person before or since, and his own name is attached to two of the most significant geographical features as well as to many minor ones. Accompanying these charts were coastal views and plans by Cook and his crews which described and defined the New Zealand terrain, capturing its often rugged features with great clarity. In terms of the imagination and geographical conception, then, Cook had taken Tasman's squiggle on a map and turned it into the recognisable national shape of today. It is highly significant that one powerful component of Maori self-determination is the reclaiming of the landscape through the restoration of original place-names.

This point can be taken still further. Cook and his artists presented New Zealand to the European world and were responsible for the initial projection of New Zealand on to the European imagination. They were struck by the grandeur and beauty of the landscape, which they found both romantic and elemental. Spöring's and Parkinson's drawings of rock outcrops in Tolaga and Mercury Bays gave the earliest hints of this but the most dramatic impact came with the work of William Hodges on the second voyage. His magnificent oils created an impression which has endured to the twentieth century: towering mountains, great torrents of falling water; lush forests and humankind dwarfed by the elements. Johann Forster, never lavish in his praise, paid tribute: 'The Scenery of the country was bold & worthy of the Pencil of a *Salvator Rosa*, all the Sides of the hills were steep, rocky, & on all the little slopes & small terraces or Settlements covered with fine shrubs, of various kinds . . .'[13] Fortunately for that voyage Hodges was a more than adequate substitute, and the images he created influenced the landscape painting traditions of New Zealand up to World War I, and it is still the stuff of tourist brochures.

Another achievement of Cook's voyages was the beginnings of the scientific history of New Zealand. The *Endeavour* and *Resolution* were superbly equipped for the task of evaluating the natural history of the countries they visited, and the storehouse of botanical and zoological art and of preserved specimens brought back from New Zealand fully reflected this careful preparation. The accuracy and beauty of the natural history drawings, and the comprehensiveness of the collections are staggering.

Cook and his fellow travellers amassed an enormous written, visual and material collection relating to the world of the Maori. Cook's journals, and those of others on his ships, are rich in their references to the culture, physiognomy, language and economy of the Maori. In general the Maori were viewed as a noble, ingenious, artistic, brave, open but often warlike people. Although Cook recognised their many tribal divisions he was nevertheless disposed to search for a paramount chief or king to whom all would owe allegiance, obliging them to conform to recognisable European political forms. His descriptions of the social and cultural differences from one part of the country to another were sharp and perceptive, among other things seeking to account for the variations in prosperity between the southern tribes and the richer ones of the North Island.[14]

In general New Zealand terms, the legacy of the first voyage was an account of the Maori traditional society before the period of full-scale European impact. The same point can be made for many of the islands of the Pacific, including Hawai'i. From a Polynesian perspective there is only oral history testimony to set against it. The journals of the subsequent voyages began to reveal the consequences of culture contact in their concern for such things as prostitution, venereal disease, political change and the effects of provisioning on fragile and limited economies. Cook lamented the harmful effects which European contact was having and he detected a decline in Maori morality over the period of the three voyages. He saw this as a universal curse which Europeans imparted to indigenous peoples; 'what is more to our Shame civilized Christians, we debauch their Morals already too prone to vice and we interduce among them wants and perhaps diseases which they never before knew and which serves only to disturb that happy tranquillity they and their fore Fathers had injoy'd'.[15]

In practice relations with the Maori were often fraught with tension, suspicion and wariness on both sides. His instructions enjoined Cook to avoid bloodshed, and he struggled to follow this. Nevertheless there were deaths on the first two voyages. In the policy he developed for dealing with indigenous peoples there was no pretence of a trust built up between equals, for it was based on superior power, but in practice, and in terms of his age, it was relatively humane, and he struggled to abide by it. Nevertheless it is scarcely surprising that Maori today should view his record in a different light. It is also understandable that they should vigorously challenge his status in New Zealand national identity. The pioneer period has passed. The bulk of the New Zealand population, Maori and *Pakeha* now live in cities. The nation proclaims the values of biculturalism. Should it continue to have as its national icon an Englishman who spent only 328 days in New Zealand waters?

While much of the discussion about the role of Cook in a New Zealand and in other national contexts has been in a political arena, or the popular press, in 1992 it was provocatively injected into academic discourse with the publication of Gananath Obeyesekere's *The Apotheosis of Captain Cook*.[16] The core of Obeyesekere's thesis focused on Hawai'i and the question of whether during the Makahiki festival the Islanders took Cook to be a physical manifestation of the god Lono. Historians and anthropologists, most notably the Chicago anthropologist, Marshall Sahlins, Obeyesekere argued, had perpetuated an imperialist myth. Although this had reached what Obeyesekere regarded as absurd heights in the case of Hawai'i, he spread his net widely and found similar lapses in the western historiography of the rest of the Pacific. Generally Obeyesekere denied that Pacific Island peoples had held Cook in great regard, much less believed him to be a god. For them to accept Cook in such a way would have been a denial of their essential rationality. It was Europeans and European historians who were responsible for the apotheosis of Cook. 'This "European god" was a myth of conquest, imperialism, and civilization—a triad that cannot be easily separated.'[17] Less rational and more superstitious than Hawaiians, they were the myth-makers and as such were like Cook himself, agents of western imperialism, ethnocentrism and violence. Revealing a striking ignorance of the historiography of England in Cook's own day, Obeyesekere claimed a unique discovery: 'One of my basic assumptions is that mythmaking, which scholars assume to be primarily an activity of non-Western societies, is equally prolific in European thought'![18]

This argument was extended to New Zealand and the terms in which Maori regarded Cook. Taking as his text the quote from Te Horeta, cited earlier, Obeyesekere explained how this was plucked out of context from oral tradition and given mythical status by Europeans. The Maori, like the Hawaiians, were too rational a people to subscribe to such a notion. The writings of a number of New Zealand historians were selectively pillaged to illustrate the process of European myth-making.[19] Rather sadly the New Zealand section displayed an anthropological ignorance of the culture the author sought to champion. The book took on the status of an apotheosis of the rational savage, or in the words of Marshall Sahlins, established the Hawaiians as 'consistently practicing a bourgeois rationality'.[20]

The Apotheosis of Captain Cook received a mixed reception: initially warm but then increasingly subject to hostile reviews in scholarly journals. The most devastating onslaught came in the form of Sahlins's rejoinder, *How Natives Think: About Captain Cook, For Example.* The critics have identified the manner in which Obeyesekere played fast and loose with his sources and with the words of anthropologists and historians. However, it would be a pity if the rather sloppy history, and what Sahlins dismisses as 'pidgin anthropology', obscured the wider significance of the issues Obeyesekere sought to grapple with. His work was an anti-imperialist caricature of Cook and his biographers. That it was by a non-Pacific Islander claiming a privileged universal nativism which denied Maori and Hawaiian alike their own religious, imaginative and cosmological uniqueness lent a rather eccentric twist to the analysis. For what the Sri Lankan-born anthropologist did on behalf of Pacific Islanders was to attempt to interpret or landscape western culture and beliefs from an indigenous point of view. From a Pacific Islands perspective it is surprising that it was so long in coming.

This is almost a reverse of the process which the Cook voyages initiated more than 200 years ago. Cook had interpreted the Pacific and the documentary record he compiled provided the rich source material which historians, anthropologist and natural historians have used to reconstruct the people and environment of his day. The knowledge of these 'original cultures' was part of the privileged intellectual tradition of Europeans.[21] It was inevitable that in time this process would be to a degree turned on its head and the Pacific would come to interpret Cook and his biographers.

To GET A SENSE of the power of that privileged documentary tradition it is worth scanning the context and content of the record. As a recent study has observed, the eighteenth-century Briton had an insatiable thirst for narratives of travel: a thirst which pre-dated the voyages of Cook.[22] Although this was part of a broader taste for the exotic which encompassed foods, textiles, household goods, art, architecture and landscape gardening, the market for books on discovery was driven by particular forces. It matched Britain's increasing imperial confidence in both military and trading terms. As its sea power extended, and that of European rivals receded, interest in expanding the scope of that power and dominion increased. Given the extent of the Spanish, Portuguese and Dutch seaborne empires it seemed appropriate that Britain should be at the vanguard of opening up new territories.

This rampant imperialist theme was often explicit in collections of voyages, such as those of the mercantilist John Campbell in his 1744–48 edition of John Harris's *Complete Collection of Voyages and Travels*.[23] The potency of the call was evident in the account of his voyage which Anson sanctioned: 'Since as our fleets are at present superior to those of the whole world united, it must be a matchless degree of supineness or mean-spiritedness, if we permitted any of the advantages which new discoveries, or a more extended navigation may produce to mankind, to be ravished from us'.[24] Such writings were a call to greater extension of maritime power but to properly fulfil such objectives it was not only necessary to discover new lands but also for the voyagers to bring back accurate information about the climate, natural products and peoples as well.

The fact that demand for such narratives was also strong in Europe indicates that there were wider forces at work. As philosophers speculated about the history, nature and future of humankind they reached outward for comparative examples to illuminate their work. The popularisation of the Lockean idea that 'In the beginning, all the world was *America* . . .', that the level of civilisation was determined by the manner in which experience and environment shaped natural man, gave rise to the notion that by looking outwards to societies which had not yet attained Europe's level of civilisation the development of Europeans themselves could be traced. On Cook's second voyage, J. R. Forster put these ideas into a Pacific context:

> Mankind is therefore to be considered in various situations, comparable with the various ages of men from infancy to manhood; with this difference only, that men in their collective capacity ripen but slowly from animality, through the stages of savages and barbarians into a civilized society, which has again an infinite variety of situations and degrees of perfection.[25]

Just as they saw in the history of their own societies evidence of the doctrine of general progress, so by looking at other societies philosophers were able to scrutinise aspects of cultures at an earlier stage of development. A number of British writers from Locke onwards articulated this theme in a variety of ways. In Cook's own time it was most forcefully represented in the figures of the Scottish enlightenment such as Adam Smith, John Millar, William Robertson, Adam Ferguson and Lord Kames. The 'four stages' theory was its most schematic representation.[26] Natural curiosity about other peoples was therefore augmented by the self-reflective possibilities categorisation made possible.

It is apparent that Cook's voyages to New Zealand fitted into an established tradition and did not initiate one. Equally, it is indisputable that his voyages and the narratives based upon them raised the genre to new heights. Historians must be careful not to confuse modern editions of the voyages, themselves benchmarks for this type of literature, with the eighteenth-century accounts. Nevertheless the richly annotated Beaglehole editions of *Cook's Journals* were only possible because of the scale and detail of the original material. Even before the first published account appeared expectations were raised by the equipment and personnel of the *Endeavour* voyage. Perversely, the controversy evoked by the Hawkesworth edition, with its extraordinary editorial licence, helped to define the standard and served to highlight the demand of the educated public for high standards of accuracy. Given the choice between a polished, over-written, literary account and the lightly brushed but veracious words of a blunt seaman it was apparent that the informed public preferred the latter.[27]

It is also significant that although many other explorers had preceded Cook into the Pacific and brought back accounts of its peoples, none had done it so comprehensively or in quite the same intellectual and cultural context. The timing of the voyages opened Pacific Islanders up to a level of ethnographic and anthropological scrutiny which was entirely new. Interest in the customs, religion, material culture, social organisation and political systems of Pacific peoples was intense and the results of observations were placed in an interpretative framework which had wider philosophical purposes. Pacific Islanders became in a sense intellectual constructs, as noble savages or otherwise, and Mai, promenading through the streets of London, or Ahutoru through the streets of Paris, provided comforting, empirically based assurances that European thinkers were on the right track.

The published journals carried a startling authority so that even the Hawkesworth account of the first voyage, heavily criticised though it was, survived as the principal official source of anthropological information.[28] The pervasive effect of Cook's voyages was such that they shaped perceptions of the Pacific and its peoples for almost a century. One reason for this was that Cook's reputation was so revered in his day that his voyages provided a mandatory template for subsequent expeditions. They set the pattern in terms of the proper objectives of exploration and the type of men, ships and equipment which were required to carry them out. The commanders of vessels had to be skilled in the precise, scientific aspects of surveying and seamanship. They had to maintain the sort of seaboard regimen of diet, antiscorbutics, exercise and discipline which were found to be vital for such long voyages. A full and exact record of the voyage had to be maintained in journals kept up to date daily.

Not surprisingly those who followed Cook in this respect were frequently those who had served on his ships—Bligh, Vancouver and Roberts for example, all highly talented navigators. The proper ships for this work were not fast naval frigates, as had so often been the case in the past, but practical, capacious flat-bottomed boats which were sturdy, flexible and easy to repair in remote parts of the world. These vessels had to be equipped with the proper navigational instruments, journals and charts, stores and victuals according to the precedents set by Cook. Any respectable voyage of discovery had to include reputable scientists who were able to document the voyage from a natural historical point of view and convey the results of their endeavours back to London. For more than forty years Joseph Banks directed this activity as the *eminence grise* behind scientific voyaging and the custodian of the Cook model.[29] As has been argued elsewhere there was a belief implicit in the empirical method as it was extended to new lands. The environment could be exactly described and understood, but it could also in a sense be reordered. Indigenous place names, descriptions and categories did not fit usefully into European patterns and therefore the whole of the natural world had to be systematised, analysed and rendered in European terms. Control over nature, the colonisation of exotic flora and fauna, was a necessary preliminary to exploitation.[30]

Not only the leaders of state-sponsored expeditions felt obliged to follow the Cook example. The fur traders who voyaged to the northwest coast of America and some whalers also thought to follow his example. James Strange, about to head off to the northwest coast to gather sea otter furs in his vessels *Captain Cook* and *Experiment*, impressed on Joseph Banks the scientific merits of the voyage: 'I wished to avail myself of the Knowledge which in every Branch of Science, so Eminently distinguishes You, in that Station you hold with so much credit to yourself & Advantage to the Publick'.[31] The expeditions of Malaspina, Lapérouse and Baudin revealed the way in which national competitiveness could reinforce this tradition.

The intellectual context for this in scientific terms was the empirical tradition which could be traced back to Bacon, and the ethnographic interpretative tradition which was best represented by the leading figures of the Scottish Enlightenment. The Baconian tradition argued that scrupulous accumulation of data, close observation, consistent and universal systems of classification and analysis, and hypothesis based on reliable experiments would reveal the natural world in a true fashion, stripped of mysteries and fantasy. These were the expectations imposed on the scientists who travelled on Cook's ships and some of the subsequent voyages to the Pacific. As Bougainville had observed, 'geography is a science of facts'.[32]

Given the acknowledged precision which the scientists on the voyages brought to their study of natural history, there was no need to doubt the veracity of their accounts of indigenous peoples encountered during the voyages. There was a powerful curiosity about other cultures which possessed Cook, his officers and the scientists on board. Where did the Polynesians come from? What was their relationship to the peoples of Asia and Australia? How much contact was there between the islands and when were they settled? What were the similarities between these peoples in terms of language and culture? What were their religious beliefs and their systems of government? How advanced in European terms was their material culture and scientific knowledge? And hauntingly throughout the Pacific, and specifically in New Zealand, did cannibalism exist and what were the reasons for it?

The journals of Cook, Banks and Forster are replete with their observations on Pacific Islanders as they strove to come to terms with these questions. All three were highly systematic in their descriptions. As the vessels sailed from a territory, Cook and Banks wrote general observations which followed a standardised sequence of coast and landscape, natural productions and the physical social and cultural attributes of the population. Cook's physical descriptions covered size, skin colour, hair type, health and hygiene, bodily adornment, clothing, food, housing, material culture, manufacturing processes, language, social and sexual mores, religion, warfare and political structures. Attempts were made to rank or classify peoples and to find explanations for the particular place of any people according to the great map of mankind. J. R. Forster was the most systematic of these observers, almost two-thirds of his *Observations made during a Voyage round the World* being concerned with the origins, description and classification of Pacific Islanders. The resultant division into two main groups corresponding to Polynesians and Melanesians was largely based on environmental forces, linking the analysis into the works of the Scottish 'four stages' theorists.[33] The European comparisons often concluded in philosophical comments about the well-being or happiness of each culture and reflections about the particular virtues of simple, as opposed to civilised, societies. Banks wrote of the Aboriginals, for example:

> Thus live these I had almost said happy people, content with little nay almost nothing, Far enough removd from the anxieties attending upon riches, or even the possession of what we Europeans call common necessaries: anxieties intended maybe by Providence to counterbalance the pleasure arising from the Posession of wishd for attainments, consequently increasing with increasing wealth, and in some measure keeping up the balance of hapiness between the rich and the poor. From them appear how small are the real wants of human nature, which we Europeans have increased to an excess which would certainly appear incredible to these people could they be told it.[34]

Glyn Williams has explained the interconnection between this primitivist view of the Aboriginals and the similar, often quoted statement by Cook.[35] Such statements became indistinguishable from the close, empirical observations about climate, plants and customs which preceded them and carried equal authority when translated into the published accounts. Cook's opinions of the people of the Pacific blended observation and opinion in a subtle way which gave the latter a weight and authority. European knowledge of Tahitian, Maori and Hawaiian developed from an archetype provided by the great explorer and nineteenth-century impressions became an annotation on this base. The voyages in this way revealed Pacific peoples to Europe and in their documentation they provided the texts by which they would continue to be measured and evaluated through to the present day.

This evaluation has not been unvaried. Since the publication of Beaglehole's *The Exploration of the Pacific* there have been dramatic changes in the way in which European writers have used the Cook materials to reconstruct the eighteenth-century Pacific. In many respects this process began with the works of Beaglehole. The introductory materials on Polynesian history and the close textual annotation relating to Pacific Islanders, their language, culture and ethnography placed them on the stage, if not centre stage, in the portrayal of the voyages.[36] Since then Cook's relationship with the peoples of the Pacific has become an expanding preoccupation of those working in the field of eighteenth-century exploration. The volume which emerged from the 1978 conference on *Captain James Cook and his Times* in Vancouver included one chapter on the role of indigenous people in the voyages. When the same editors organised a similar conference fourteen years later to mark the voyages of George Vancouver the resultant volume included seven such papers.[37] General works on the exploration of the Pacific such as Lynne Withey's *Voyages of Discovery* have as their central focus Cook's relations with Pacific Islanders.[38]

Another dramatic change has been the entry of new players into the scholarship of eighteenth-century exploration. Journals which have been scrupulously edited and reconstructed and pored over for the light they shed on geographical knowledge, the art of navigation, the health and personalities of the discoverers, the application of scientific knowledge to the oceans, people and natural history of new lands, and European strategies and intentions are now treated as problematised texts by scholars working in a postmodern mould, often divorced from historical context. Principally from Departments of English, these scholars have deconstructed the texts of Cook and other explorers, illuminating the mentality of the writer and reader but not reflecting significantly on the world of Pacific peoples. More challenging has been the work of anthropologists and historian-anthropologists who have combined close textual analysis of eighteenth-century accounts with later European reports on Pacific Islanders and their insights on indigenous beliefs and customs. Prominent among such writers are Greg Dening and Marshall Sahlins.[39]

No doubt from the perspective of Pacific Island peoples there remains a reflective dimension to such analyses which seems rather self-indulgent. The Pacific is still a sounding board for the understanding of European experience. Further, from a nationalist perspective, in countries such as New Zealand, unsure of the meaning and legitimacy of their European experience, the status of the great explorer in the national mythology offends. It may be, as Obeyesekere claims, that historians have contributed to such national myth-making. The Pacific is still in the process of discovering Captain James Cook.

The Works of
Glyndwr Williams

'Arthur Dobbs and Joseph Robson: new light on the relationship between two early critics of the Hudson's Bay Company', *Canadian Historical Review*, vol. 40, 1959, pp. 132–6.

'An Eighteenth-century Spanish investigation into the apocryphal voyage of Admiral Fonte', *Pacific Historical Review*, vol. 30, 1961, pp. 319–27.

The British Search for the Northwest Passage in the Eighteenth Century, Longman, London, 1962.

'Captain Coats and exploration along the East Main', *The Beaver*, vol. 294, 1963, pp. 4–13.

'Introduction' to *Northern Quebec and Labrador Journals 1819–35*, Hudson's Bay Record Society, London, 1963.

'East London Names in Hudson Bay', *East London Papers*, vol. 7, 1964, pp. 23–30.

The Expansion of Europe in the Eighteenth Century: Overseas Rivalry, Discovery and Exploitation, Blandford Press, London, 1966.

'James Clouston's journey across the Labrador peninsula in 1820', *The Beaver*, vol. 297, 1966, pp. 4–15.

'Commodore Anson and the Acapulco galleon', *History Today*, vol. 17, 1967, pp. 525–32.

Editor, *Documents relating to Anson's Voyage round the World 1740–44*, Navy Records Society, London, 1967.

'John Scroggs' and 'William Stuart', *Dictionary of Canadian Biography*, vol. 2, 1701–40, University of Toronto Press, Toronto, 1969, pp. 604, 614–16.

Editor, *Andrew Graham's Observations on Hudson's Bay 1769–1791*, Hudson's Bay Record Society, London, 1969.

'Highlights of the First Two Hundred Years of the Hudson's Bay Company', *The Beaver*, special issue, 1970, Winnipeg.

'The Hudson's Bay Company and its critics in the eighteenth century',

Transactions of the Royal Historical Society, 5th series, vol. 20, 1970, pp. 149–71.

Editor, *Peter Skene Ogden's Snake Country Journals 1827–29*, Hudson's Bay Record Society, London, 1971.

Editor, *London Correspondence Inward from Sir George Simpson 1841–2*, Hudson's Bay Record Society, London, 1973.

With J. E. Flint (eds), *Perspectives of Empire: Essays presented to Gerald S. Graham*, Longman, London, 1973.

'"The Inexhaustible Fountain of Gold": English Projects and Ventures in the South Seas, 1670–1750', in John E. Flint and Glyndwr Williams (eds), *Perspectives of Empire*, Longman, London, 1973, pp. 27–53.

'Europe Overseas', part III of *Civilisation: Journey to the Modern World*, C.R.M. Books, Del Mar, California, 1973.

'John Bean', 'William Coats', 'John Longland', 'Christopher Middleton', 'Thomas Mitchell', 'William Moor', 'John Potts', 'John Rankin', 'Joseph Robson', 'Francis Smith', 'George Spurrell', 'Edward Thompson', 'John Wigate', *Dictionary of Canadian Biography*, vol. 3, 1741–1770, University of Toronto Press, Toronto, 1974, pp. 39, 127–8, 406–7, 446–50, 453–4, 471–2, 533–4, 544, 561–2, 594, 598–9, 624–5, 663.

With W. S. Cumming and D. B. Quinn, *The Exploration of North America 1630–1775*, Elek Books, London, 1974.

Editor, *A Voyage round the World by George Anson*, by Richard Walter and Benjamin Robins, Oxford University Press, Oxford, 1974.

'Governor George Simpson's Character Book', *The Beaver*, vol. 306, 1975, pp. 4–18.

Editor, *Hudson's Bay Miscellany 1670–1870*, Hudson's Bay Record Society, London, 1975.

'Andrew Graham and Thomas Hutchins: Collaboration and Plagiarism in Eighteenth-Century Natural History', *The Beaver*, vol. 308, 1978, pp. 4–14.

'The puzzle of Anthony Henday's journal, 1754–5', *The Beaver*, vol. 309, 1978, pp. 40–56.

'"Savages Noble and Ignoble": European attitudes towards the wider world before 1800', *Journal of Imperial and Commonwealth History*, vol. 6, 1978, pp. 300–13.

'Charles Clerke', 'James Cook', 'Thomas Hutchins', 'James King', 'William Wales', *Dictionary of Canadian Biography*, vol. 4, 1771–1800, University of Toronto Press, Toronto, 1979, pp. 155–6, 162–7, 377–8, 412–13, 757–8.

'Seamen and Philosophers in the South Seas in the Age of Captain Cook',

The E. G. R. Taylor Lecture for 1978, *Mariner's Mirror*, vol. 65, 1979, pp. 3–22.

'Myth and Reality: James Cook and the Theoretical Geography of Northwest America', in Robin Fisher and Hugh Johnston (eds), *Captain James Cook and His Times*, Douglas & McIntyre, Vancouver, 1979, pp. 58–80.

'Alaska revealed: Cook's explorations in 1778', in A. Shalkop (ed.), *Exploration in Alaska*: Captain Cook Commemorative Lectures, Cook Inlet Historical Society, Anchorage, 1980, pp. 68–87.

With P. J. Marshall (eds), *The British Empire before the American Revolution*, Frank Cass, London, 1980.

'Epilogue' in C. M. Judd and A. J. Ray (eds), *Old Trails and New Directions: Papers of the Third North American Fur Trade Conference*, Toronto University Press, Toronto, 1980, pp. 309–19.

With Sarah Palmer (eds), *Charted and Uncharted Waters: Proceedings of A Conference on the Study of British Maritime History*, National Maritime Museum, London, 1981.

'"Far more happier than we Europeans": Reactions to the Australian Aborigines on Cook's Voyage', *Australian Historical Studies*, vol. 19, 1981, pp. 499–512; reprinted as 'Reactions on Cook's Voyage', in Ian and Tamsin Donaldson (eds), *Seeing the First Australians*, Allen & Unwin, Sydney, 1985, pp. 35–58; and under original title in Susan Janson and Stuart Macintyre (eds), *Through White Eyes*, Allen & Unwin, 1990, pp. 51–64.

With P. J. Marshall, *The Great Map of Mankind: British Perceptions of the World in the Age of Enlightenment*, Dent, London, and Harvard University Press, Cambridge, MA, 1982, and Heibonsha Ltd., Toyko, 1989.

'The Hudson's Bay Company and the Fur Trade 1670–1870', *The Beaver*, special issue, 1983, Winnipeg.

'Andrew Graham', *Dictionary of Canadian Biography*, vol. 5, 1801–1820, University of Toronto Press, Toronto, 1983, pp. 362–3.

'Peter Skene Ogden', *Dictionary of Canadian Biography*, vol. 8, 1851–1860, University of Toronto Press, Toronto, 1985, pp. 660–3.

'George Atkinson', *Dictionary of Canadian Biography*, vol. 6, 1821–1835, University of Toronto Press, Toronto, 1987, pp. 15–16.

'Il dominio dei mari', in *La disgregazione dell'Ancien Regime*, Banca Nazionale del Lavoro, Milan, 1987, pp. 491–500.

'Alexander Roderick McLeod', *Dictionary of Canadian Biography*, vol. 7, 1836–1850, University of Toronto Press, Toronto, 1988, pp. 569–70.

'English and Aborigines: the first contacts', *History Today*, vol. 38, 1988, pp. 33–9.

'The First Fleet and After: Expectation and Reality', in Tony Delamothe and Carl Bridge (eds), *Interpreting Australia: British Perceptions of Australia since 1770*, Sir Robert Menzies Centre for Australian Studies, London, 1988, pp. 24–40.

With Alan Frost, *Terra Australis to Australia*, Oxford University Press, Melbourne, 1988.

'New Holland: The English Approach', in John Hardy and Alan Frost (eds), *Studies from* Terra Australis *to Australia*, Australian Academy of the Humanities, Canberra, 1989, pp. 85–92.

'Islands and Continents', in C. A. Bayly (ed.), *Atlas of the British Empire*, Hamlyn, London, 1989, pp. 57–61.

'The Pacific: Great Unknown', in *Mutiny on the Bounty 1789–1989*, National Maritime Museum/Manorial Research plc, London, 1989, pp. 19–34.

'The Achievement of the English Voyages, 1650–1800', in Derek Howse (ed.), *Background to Discovery: Pacific Exploration from Dampier to Cook*, University of California Press, Berkeley, 1990, pp. 56–80.

'English Attitudes to Indigenous Peoples of the Pacific', in John Hardy and Alan Frost (eds), *European Voyaging Towards Australia*, Australian Academy of the Humanities, Canberra, 1990, pp. 133–41.

With John Ramsden, *Ruling Britannia: A Political History of Britain 1688–1988*, Longman, Harlow, 1990.

'Canada at the British Conquest, 1763', and 'Exploration and Exploitation of the Pacific', in Andrew Porter (ed.), *Atlas of British Overseas Expansion*, Routledge, London, 1991, pp. 38–40; 57–60.

Consultant Editor, *The Times Atlas of World Exploration*, Harper Collins, London, 1991.

With William H. Goetzmann, *The Atlas of North American Exploration*, Prentice Hall, New York, 1992; and University of Oklahoma Press, Norman, 1998.

'Introduction' to *William Hack, A Collection of Original Voyages [1699]*, Scholars' Facsimiles & Reprints, Delmar (NY), 1993, pp. 9–21.

'Myth and Reality: The Theoretical Geography of Northwest America from Cook to Vancouver', in Robin Fisher and Hugh Johnston (eds), *From Maps to Metaphors: The Pacific World of George Vancouver*, University of British Columbia Press, Vancouver, 1993, pp. 35–50.

'Anson at Canton, 1743: "A Little Secret History"', in C. H. Clough and P. E. H. Hair (eds), *The European Outthrust and Encounter: Essays in Tribute to D. B. Quinn*, Liverpool University Press, Liverpool, 1994, pp. 271–90.

'Buccaneers, Castaways, and Satirists: The South Seas in the English Consciousness before 1750', in Jonathan Lamb et al. (eds), *The South*

Pacific in the Eighteenth Century: Narratives and Myths, Eighteenth-Century Life, special issue, 1994, pp. 114–28.

'"The Common Centre of We Discoverers": Sir Joseph Banks, Exploration and Empire', in R. E. R. Banks, B. Elliott, J. G. Hawkes, D. King-Hele, G. Ll. Lucas (eds), *Sir Joseph Banks: A Global Perspective*, Royal Botanic Gardens, Kew, 1994, pp. 177–91.

'Explorers and Geographers: An Uneasy Alliance in the Eighteenth-Century Exploration of the Pacific', in Donna Merwick (ed.), *Dangerous Liaisons: Essays in Honour of Greg Dening*, Melbourne University Press, Melbourne, 1994, pp. 95–114.

With William Barr (eds), *Voyages to Hudson Bay in Search of a Northwest Passage 1741–1747*, vol. 1, *The Voyage of Christopher Middleton 1741–1742*, Hakluyt Society, London, 1994; and vol. 2, *The Voyage of William Moor and Francis Smith 1746–1747*, Hakluyt Society, London, 1995.

'"To Make Discoveries of Countries Hitherto Unknown": The Admiralty and Pacific Exploration in the Eighteenth Century', Caird Lecture for 1995, *Mariner's Mirror*, vol. 82, 1996, pp. 14–27.

With Alan Frost, 'The Beginnings of Britain's Exploration of the Pacific Ocean in the Eighteenth Century', *Mariner's Mirror*, vol. 83, 1997, pp. 410–18.

Editor, *Captain Cook's Voyages 1768–1779*, The Folio Society, London, 1997.

'George Vancouver, the Admiralty and Exploration in the Late Eighteenth Century', in Stephen Haycox et al. (eds), *Enlightenment and Exploration in the North Pacific 1741–1805*, University of Washington Press, Seattle, 1997, pp. 38–48.

The Great South Sea: English Voyages and Encounters, 1570–1750, Yale University Press, New Haven and London, 1997.

'The Second Age of Discovery: The Opening of the Pacific', in John B. Hattendorf (ed.), *Maritime History*, vol. 2, *The Eighteenth Century and the Classic Age of Sail*, Krieger Publishing, Malabar (Florida), 1997, pp. 1–43.

'The *Endeavour* Voyage: A Co-incidence of Motives', in Margarette Lincoln (ed.), *Science and Exploration in the Pacific: European Voyages to the Southern Oceans in the Eighteenth Century*, Boydell Press in association with the National Maritime Museum, Woodbridge, 1998, pp. 3–18.

'The Pacific: Exploration and Exploitation', in P. J. Marshall (ed.), *The Oxford History of the British Empire, 2: The Eighteenth Century*, Oxford University Press, Oxford, 1998, pp. 552–75.

Abbreviations

~◦~

Archival documents

ABC	Archive of the American Board of Commissioners for Foreign Missions, Houghton Library, Harvard University
AGNM	Archivo General de la Nación (Mexico)
AGI	Archivo General de las Indias (Seville)
Estado	Sección de Estado
AHN	Archivo Histórico Nacional (Madrid)
BCARS	British Columbia Archives and Records Service (Victoria)
Add. MS	Additional Manuscripts
BL	The British Library (London)
Add. MS	Additional Manuscripts
BNM	Biblioteca Nacional (Mexico)
Bodleian	Bodleian Library (Oxford)
North	North papers
BRL	Birmingham Reference Library
Boulton	Boulton papers
Clark	Clark Library, UCLA
Clements	William L. Clements Library (Ann Arbor)
Shelburne	Shelburne papers
CWM	Archive of the Council for World Mission, School of Oriental and African Studies, University of London
SS	South Sea correspondence
Home	Home Correspondence
HBCA	Hudson's Bay Company Archives (Winnipeg)
A	London Correspondence
B	London Inward Corrrespondence
Huntington	Huntington Library (San Marino)

STG	Grenville Family papers
HM	Papers of George III
HOA	Hydrographic Office Archives (Taunton)
IOR	India Office Records
B	Court Minutes
D	Committee of Correspondence
E	Home Correspondence
F	Board of Control Records
G	Factor Records
H	Home Miscellaneous Series
L/P&S	Political and Secret Department
KML	Karpeles Manuscript Library (Santa Barbara)
Ford	George Ford papers
Kew	Library of the Royal Botanic Gardens, Kew
Banks	Banks papers
MN	Museo Naval (Madrid)
NLA	National Library of Australia
NMM	National Maritime Museum (Greenwich)
LBK	Kellett papers
SAN	Sandwich papers
MID	Middleton papers
STK	Stokes papers
NHM	The Natural History Museum (London)
DTC	Dawson Turner Collection
PRO	Public Record Office (London)
ADM	Admiralty
CO	Colonial Office
FO	Foreign Office
HO	Home Office
PC	Privy Council
PRO	Public Record Office
SP	State Papers
T	Treasury
WO	War Office
RH	Rhodes House (Oxford)
British Empire	British Empire Manuscripts
RS	Royal Society (London)
SLNSW	Mitchell Library, State Library of New South Wales (Sydney)
Bonwick	Bonwick transcripts
Brabourne	Banks papers

SRO   Scottish Record Office (Edinburgh)
  GD   Gifts and Deposits: Melville papers
Sutro   Sutro Library (San Francisco)
  Banks   Banks papers
UBC   University of British Columbia Library
               (Vancouver)
  Manby   Thomas Manby Journal

Published primary sources

Anson's Voyage   Richard Walter and Benjamin Robins, *A Voyage
                          round the World by George Anson*, ed. Glyndwr
                          Williams, Oxford University Press, Oxford,
                          1974.

Banks's Journal   J. C. Beaglehole (ed.), *The Endeavour Journal of
                          Joseph Banks, 1768–1771*. Trustees of the Public
                          Library of New South Wales in association with
                          Angus & Robertson, Sydney, 1962.

Byron's Journal   R. E. Gallagher (ed.), *Byron's Journal of his
                          Circumnavigation, 1764–1766*. Hakluyt Society,
                          London, 1964.

Campbell's   John Campbell (ed.), *Navigantium atque
Navigantium*   Itinerantium Bibliotheca: or, a Compleat
                          Collection of Voyages and Travels*, 2 vols, London,
                          1744–48.

Carteret's Journal   Helen Wallis (ed.), *Carteret's Voyage Round the
                          World, 1766–1769*, 2 vols, Hakluyt Society,
                          London, 1965.

Cook's Journals   J. C. Beaglehole (ed.), *The Journals of Captain
                          James Cook on his Voyages of Discovery*, 3 vols,
                          Hakluyt Society, London, 1955–1969.

Forster's Observations Johann Reinhold Forster, *Observations made
                          during a Voyage round the World*, London, 1778.

Forster's Journal   Michael E. Hoare (ed.), *The Resolution Journal
                          of Johann Reinhold Forster, 1772–1775*, 4 vols,
                          Hakluyt Society, London, 1982.

Hawkesworth's Voyages   John Hawkesworth (ed.), *An Account of the
                          Voyages undertaken by the order of his present
                          Majesty for making Discoveries in the Southern
                          Hemisphere*, 3 vols, London, 1773.

Morrison's Journal	O. Rutter (ed.), *The Journal of James Morrison*, Golden Cockerell Press, London, 1935.
Robertson's Journal	Hugh Carrington (ed.), *The Discovery of Tahiti*, Hakluyt Society, London, 1948.
Vancouver's Voyage	George Vancouver, *A Voyage of Discovery to the North Pacific Ocean and Round the World*, ed. W. Kaye Lamb, Hakluyt Society, London, 1984.

Frequently cited modern studies

Captain James Cook and His Times	Robin Fisher and Hugh Johnston (eds), *Captain James Cook and His Times*, Douglas & McIntyre, Vancouver, 1979.
The Great Map of Mankind	P. J. Marshall and Glyndwr Williams, *The Great Map of Mankind: British Perceptions of the World in the Age of Enlightenment*, Dent, London, and Harvard University Press, Cambridge, MA, 1982.
The Death of William Gooch	Greg Dening, *The Death of William Gooch: A History's Anthropology*, Melbourne University Press, Melbourne, 1995. (This work was first published as: *History's Anthropology: The Death of William Gooch*, University Press of America, Lanham, 1988.)
From Maps to Metaphors	Robin Fisher and Hugh Johnston (eds), *From Maps to Metaphors: The Pacific World of George Vancouver*, University of British Columbia Press, Vancouver, 1993.
Islands and Beaches	Greg Dening, *Islands and Beaches: Beaches Discourse on a Silent Land: Marquesas, 1774–1880*, Melbourne University Press, Melbourne, 1980.
Perspectives of Empire	Glyndwr Williams and J. E. Flint (eds), *Perspectives of Empire: Essays presented to Gerald S. Graham*, Longman, London, 1973.
Visions of Empire	D. P. Miller and P. H. Reill (eds), *Visions of Empire: Voyages, Botany, and Representations of Nature*, Cambridge University Press, New York, 1996.

Notes

Introduction

[1] Greg Dening, 'Past Imperfect', *The Australian's Review of Books*, April 1998, p. 5.

Williams: 'To Make Discoveries of Countries Hitherto Unknown'

This essay was first delivered as The Caird Lecture, at the National Maritime Museum, Greenwich, on 24 May 1995; and was then published in the *Mariner's Mirror*, 82 (1966), pp. 14–27. It is reprinted here by permission.

[1] *An Account of several late Voyages & Discoveries to the South and North, Towards the Streights of Magellan, the South Seas . . . By Sir John Narborough, Captain Jasmen Tasman, Captain John Wood . . .*, London, 1694, p. 10.

[2] Dampier's correspondence with the Admiralty is in ADM 2/1692 (no folio numbers), PRO; the main documents are printed in John Masefield (ed.), *Dampier's Voyages*, E. Grant Richards, London, 1906, vol. 2, pp. 325–30.

[3] The events of the voyage are described by Dampier in his two-volume work, *A Voyage to New Holland*, London, 1703, 1709.

[4] William Barr and Glyndwr Williams (eds), *Voyages to Hudson Bay in Search of a Northwest Passage 1741–1747*, London, Hakluyt Society, 1994–1995, vol. 1, pp. 51–2.

[5] Ibid., p. 56.

[6] See Glyndwr Williams, ' "The Inexhaustible Fountain of Gold": English Projects and Ventures in the South Seas, 1670–1750', in John E. Flint and Glyndwr Williams (eds), *Perspectives of Empire*, Longman, London, 1973, pp. 46–8.

[7] Middleton's instructions are printed in Barr and Williams, *Voyages to Hudson Bay*, vol. 1, pp. 86–9.

[8] *Campbell's Navigantium*, especially vol. 1, pp. 65, 325, 328, 331–2, 364–5.

[9] See Howard Fry, *Alexander Dalrymple (1737–1808) and the Expansion of British Trade*, Frank Cass for the Royal Commonwealth Society, London, 1970, p. 225.

[10] Add. MS 43423, fo. 81, BL.

[11] SP 94/135, fo. 271, PRO.

[12] Ibid., fo. 267v.

[13] *Carteret's Journal*, vol. 2, p. 309.

[14] *Byron's Journal*, pp. xxvii–viii.

[15] Ibid., p. 3.

[16] Ibid., p. 161.

[17] Add. MS 47014C, fo. 122, BL. I am grateful to Professor Alan Frost for drawing my attention to this set of Hutchinson documents.

[18] *Byron's Journal*, p. 161.

[19] *Carteret's Journal*, vol. 2, p. 302.

[20] *Byron's Journal*, p. 105.

[21] *Robertson's Journal*, p. 4; *Carteret's Journal*, vol. 2, pp. 311–12.

[22] On all this see *Carteret's Journal*, vol. 1, pp. 105–7; vol. 2, pp. 312–14.

[23] Ibid., vol. 2, pp. 310; and see the Cabinet papers in Shelburne, vol. 161, Clements.

[24] See *Robertson's Journal*, p. 4.

[25] See Fry, *Dalrymple*, pp. 16–21.

[26] Norman J. W. Thrower (ed.), *The Three Voyages of Edmond Halley in the Paramore 1698–1701*, Hakluyt Society, London, 1981, pp. 268–9.

[27] 'Introduction', *Cook's Journals*, vol. 1, p. cclxxxii.

[28] Alexander Dalrymple, *An Historical Collection of the several Voyages and Discoveries in the South Pacific Ocean*, London, 1770–1771, vol. 1, p. xxix.

[29] See *Carteret's Journal*, vol. 2, p. 312.

[30] See Fry, *Dalrymple*.

[31] 'Introduction', *Cook's Journals*, vol. 1, p. cclxxxiv.

[32] *Banks's Journal*, vol. 2, p. 249.

[33] *Cook's Journals*, vol. 1, p. 479.

[34] *Cook's Journals*, vol. 2, p. 295.

[35] John L. Abbott, *John Hawkesworth: Eighteenth-Century Man of Letters*, University of Wisconsin Press, Madison, 1982, p. 144.

[36] *Carteret's Journal*, passim; *Cook's Journals*, vol. 2, p. 661.

[37] 'Introduction', *Cook's Journals*, vol. 1, p. ccliii.

[38] *Cook's Journals*, vol. 2, p. 9.

[39] N. A. M. Rodger, *The Insatiable Earl: A Life of John Montagu, Fourth Earl of Sandwich 1718–1792*, Harper Collins, London, 1993, p. 221.

[40] Boswell's own account of a conversation with Cook included his remark to the explorer that 'Hawkesworth has used your narrative as a London tavern-keeper does wine. He has *brewed* it.' In Charles Ryskamp (ed.), *Boswell: The Ominous Years, 1774–1776*, Heinemann, London, 1963, p. 309.

[41] *Cook's Journals*, vol. 2, p. 2.

[42] See Ann Savours, '"A Very Interesting Point in Geography": The 1773 Phipps Expedition Towards the North Pole', *Arctic*, vol. 37, 1984, pp. 402–28.

[43] For the genesis of Cook's third voyage, see Council Minutes, vol. 6, pp. 214, 216, 220, 227, RS; and Sandwich to Barrington, 12 March 1774, SAN F/36/4, NMM. See also Howard T. Fry, 'The Commercial Ambitions Behind Captain Cook's Last Voyage', *New Zealand Journal of History*, vol. 7, 1973, pp. 186–91.

[44] Daines Barrington, *Miscellanies*, London, 1781, p. 472.

[45] See Charles E. Chapman, *The Founding of Spanish California*, Macmillan & Co., New York, 1916, pp. 376–80; Warren L. Cook, *Flood Tide of Empire: Spain and the Pacific Northwest 1543–1819*, Yale University Press, New Haven, 1973, pp. 85–93.

[46] *Cook's Journals*, vol. 3, pp. 1436.

[47] John Douglas, 'Introduction', in James Cook and James King, *A Voyage to the Pacific Ocean*, London, 1784, vol. 1, p. lviii.

[48] DTC, vol. 1, p. 304, NHM.

[49] See Fry, *Dalrymple*, ch. 8; David Mackay, *In the Wake of Cook: Exploration, Science and Empire, 1780–1801*, Croom Helm, London, 1985, chs 3 and 4.

[50] These instructions are paraphrased in W. W. Grenville to Phillip, March 1790, *Historical Records of Australia, Series I*, Library Committee of the Commonwealth Parliament, Sydney, 1914, vol. 1, pp. 161–4.

[51] See *Vancouver's Voyage*, vol. 1, pp. 283–6.

[52] Add. MS 33979, fo. 75v, BL.

[53] *Vancouver's Voyage*, vol. 1, p. 226.

[54] David Mackay, 'In the Shadow of Cook: The Ambition of Matthew Flinders', in John Hardy and Alan Frost (eds), *European Voyaging Towards Australia*, Australian Academy of the Humanities, Canberra, 1990, p. 108.

[55] Quoted in *Cook's Journals*, vol. 1, p. cxxii.

[56] Ibid., pp. 275–6.

[57] *Vancouver's Voyage*, vol. 4, p. 1390.

[58] Mackay, 'In the Shadow of Cook', p. 108.

[59] Samuel Johnson, *Thoughts on the Late Transactions Respecting Falkland's Islands*, London, 1771, quoted in Barry Gough, *The Falkland Islands/ Malvinas: The Contest for Empire in the South Atlantic*, Atlantic Highlands, London, 1992, p. 8.

[60] For more on Banks in this role see H. B. Carter, *Sir Joseph Banks 1743– 1820*, Natural History Museum, London, 1988; Mackay, *In the Wake of Cook*; Glyndwr Williams, '"The Common Centre of We Discoverers": Sir Joseph Banks, Exploration and Empire', in R. E. R. Banks, B. Elliott, J. G. Hawkes, D. King-Hele and G. Ll. Lucas (eds), *Sir Joseph Banks: A Global Perspective*, Royal Botanic Gardens, Kew, 1994, pp. 177–91.

Frost: The Spanish Yoke

[1] Campbell to Pitt, 18 October 1790, FO 95/7/4, fo. 481, PRO.

[2] Glyndwr Williams, '"The Inexhaustible Fountain of Gold": English Projects and Ventures in the South Seas, 1670–1750', in John E. Flint and Glyndwr Williams (eds), *Perspectives of Empire*, Longman, London, 1973, pp. 45–6.

[3] *Anson's Voyage*, pp. 91–102.

[4] *Campbell's Navigantium*, vol. 1, pp. 331–6, 399.

[5] Ibid., vol. 1, p. 399.

[6] Admiralty Board, Minute, 19 January 1749, ADM 3/60, PRO; Sandwich to Bedford, 14 April 1749, Add. MS 43423, fos 81–2, BL; Bedford to Keene, 5 June 1749, SP 94/135, fos 271–2, Keene to Aldworth, 29 June 1749, SP 94/135, f. 330, PRO.

[7] Court of Directors, Minute, 30 December 1761, B/77, p. 251, IOR; Cabinet Agenda, 6 January 1762, PRO 30/47/21, PRO. And see the King to Bute, 6 January 1762, in David Syrett (ed.), *The Siege and Capture of Havana 1762*, Navy Records Society, London, 1970, p. 3; and Newcastle to Hardwicke, 10 January 1762, Add. MS 32933, pp. 179–82, BL.

[8] Wright to Bute, 20 February, 10 and 30 April, and 2 and 12 June 1762, North b.6, fos 74–8, 85–90, 90–103, 124–45, 152–61, Bodleian; Ellis to Egremont, 15 January 1762, PRO 30/47/14/4, fos 240–5, PRO.

[9] Wright, 'A Method propos'd for the Entire reduction of the Kingdom of Chili and of obtaining the Dominion of the South Seas', North b.6, fos 59–71, Bodleian.

[10] [Anon], 'Rough Sketch of an Expedition to M[anila], &c. &c. mentioned to Lord A[nso]n on the 8th, 11th & 12 inst. Janry 1762', British Empire S1, fos 157–8, RH.

[11] [Anon], Memorandum, undated but c. January 1762, PRO 30/47/20/3, fos 1–2, PRO.

[12] See Syrett, *Siege and Capture*; and Nicholas Cushner (ed.), *Documents Illustrating the British Conquest of Manila, 1762–1763*, Royal Historical Society, London, 1971; and Nicholas Tracy, *Manila Ransomed: The British Assault on Manila in the Seven Years War*, University of Exeter Press, Exeter, 1995.

[13] Shelburne, Memorandum, undated but 1763, Shelburne vol. 165, pp. 320–1, Clements.

[14] *Byron's Journal*, p. xxi.

[15] Anson had died on 6 June 1762, to be succeeded as First Lord of the Admiralty by Halifax (19 June to 31 December 1762), George Grenville (1 January to 22 April 1763), Sandwich (23 April to 9 September 1763) and Egmont (10 September 1763 to 9 September 1766). What seems most likely is that, as Glyn Williams points out, Egmont took up Anson's role as promoter of schemes to explore the Pacific Ocean and to develop trade between Europe, the Americas and Asia.

16   The papers are in Add. MS 47014C, BL.
17   Hutchinson, 'Colony in South America of Importance', Add. MS 47014C, fos 121–2, and 'A Free Port in South America of Importance', Add. MS 47014C, fos 126–8, BL.
18   Lords Commissioners of the Admiralty, Secret Instructions to Byron, 17 June 1764, *Byron's Journal*, pp. 3–8.
19   Ibid., p. 89.
20   Egmont to Grafton, 20 July 1765, in ibid., p. 161.
21   Shelburne, Memo, undated, but *c.* 25 September 1766, Shelburne vol. 161, item 20, Clements.
22   Egmont, Note written in Molyneux's journal, undated but between 20 May 1768 and 20 March 1769, Add. MS 47106, BL.
23   J. S. Speer to Sandwich, undated, SAN F/30/87, 88, NMM. In the Calendar, these papers are dated to 1781 and 1782. However, textual evidence suggests that they were written as France and then Spain joined in the war—that is, 1778–79.
24   See White to Campbell, 25 October 1790, PRO 30/8/120, fos 58–60, PRO. Call's proposal has not yet been found; however, he refers to it in later correspondence: 'I formed a Project early in 1779 which I communicated to Lord North for an Expedition to the South Seas, to give countenance and support to the Inhabitants of Chili and Peru, by Assistance of Arms, ammunition and Troops from India; that these Provinces or Kingdoms might be enabled to fulfil their disposition and throw off the Spanish Yoke'—Call to [Pitt?], undated but 1785, HO 42/7, fo. 50, PRO.
25   Hippisley to Loughborough, 18 June, 7 July, 4 August and 28 November 1779, in *Memoirs and Correspondence of Viscount Castlereagh*, London, 1848–53, vol. 7, pp. 260–7.
26   Palliser, Memorandum, SAN F/22/53, and Sandwich, 'Thoughts upon an expedition to the S. Seas', 'Nov: 1779', SAN F/22/52, NMM.
27   Germain to Dalling, 4 January 1780, *Report on the Manuscripts of Mrs Stopford-Sackville*, Historical Manuscripts Commission, London, 1904, vol. 2, p. 282, and related correspondence in vol. 1, pp. 153–9.
28   [Anon], 'Military Memoranda of Spain &c', SP 94/254, fos 287–304, PRO.
29   John Dalrymple to Grenville, 20 October 1806, STG vol. 141 (2), Huntington.
30   See John Dalrymple, 'Account of an intended Expedition into the South Seas by private Persons in the late War', and related correspondence, in *Memoirs of Great Britain*, new edn, London, 1790, vol. 3, pp. 284–314; and Dalrymple to Germain, 1 February 1780, *Report on the Manuscripts of Mrs Stopford-Sackville*, vol. 1, pp. 153–8.
31   [John Dalrymple, et al.], memorandum, undated but *c.* December 1779, SAN F/22/97, PRO. For a summary of the history of Fullerton's

scheme, see Alan Frost, *Arthur Phillip, 1738–1814: His Voyaging*, Oxford University Press, Melbourne, 1987, pp. 107–9.

[32] Fullerton, 'Proposal of an Expedition to South America by India', 3 June 1780, L/P&S/1/6, IOR.

[33] [Anon], Memorandum, undated, Shelburne vol. 146, fo. 80, Clements.

[34] Fullerton, Memorandum, 3 June 1780, L/P&S/1/6, IOR.

[35] William Dalrymple to Germain, 1 March 1780, *Report on the Manuscripts of Mrs Stopford-Sackville*, vol. 1, p. 159.

[36] See R. A. Humphreys, 'Richard Oswald's Plan for an English and Russian Attack on Spanish America, 1781–1782', *Hispanic American History Review*, vol. 18, 1938, pp. 95–101.

[37] Oswald, 'Minutes relative to the Situation of England in the present War', 26 June to 1 July 1782; 'Summary of Objections and Queries regarding the Contents of these Papers', 3 July 1782; 'Supplement to the Preceding Papers', 5 July 1782, Shelburne vol. 72, items 26, 27, 28, Clements; and Oswald to Shelburne, 12 July 1782, in Lord John Russell (ed.), *Memorials and Correspondence of Charles James Fox*, London, 1857, vol. 4, pp. 256–7. Grantham to Harris, 27 July 1782, FO 65/7, Harris to Grantham, 9/10 and 16/27 August 1782, FO 65/8, PRO.

[38] Middleton to Shelburne, 25 September 1782 (draft), MID 2, NMM.

[39] See [Anon.], 'Carta do Rio de Janeiro em 20 de Junho de 1781', FO 63/2, [Anon.], 'A true and impartial Account of the present State of Peru', 30 July 1781, FO 63/3, and [Anon.], 'Intelligence enclosed in a Letter from John Staples Esq'. dated Rio de Janeiro, 3ᵈ June 1782, received by him from Captain M'Douall', PRO 30/8/345, fo. 105, PRO.

[40] Townshend, Draft Instructions to Oswald, undated but 24–25 September 1782, HM 25760, Huntington.

[41] Phillip to Townshend, 25 April 1783, H 175, fo. 237, IOR. For a description of the expedition, see Frost, *Arthur Phillip*, pp. 114–17.

[42] For a description of these schemes, see Alan Frost, *Convicts and Empire*, Oxford University Press, Melbourne, 1980, pp. 10–28.

[43] Bott, Memorandums, 6 and 21 December 1783, 7 April 1784, PRO 30/8/345, fos 29–36, 37–42, 43–4, PRO.

[44] See V. T. Harlow, *The Founding of the Second British Empire, 1763–1793*, Longmans, London, 1952, 1964, vol. 2, p. 643.

[45] Memorial, 10 November 1785, PRO 30/8/345, fos 45–6, PRO.

[46] See W. S. Robertson, 'Francisco de Miranda and the Revolutionising of Spanish America', in *Annual Report of the American Historical Association for 1907*, Washington, 1908, vol. 1, pt xii, pp. 189–539.

[47] See Miranda to Pitt, 8 September 1791, PRO 30/8/345, fos 53–6, PRO.

[48] Mulgrave, Memorandum, undated but *c.* May 1790, PRO 30/8/360, fos 87–93, PRO.

49 See L. B. Kinnaird, 'Document: Creassy's Plan for seizing Panama, with an introductory account of British designs on Panama', *Hispanic American Historical Review*, vol. 13, 1933, pp. 46–78.

50 Campbell, 'Ideas regarding a War with Spain', July 1790, and to Pitt, 18 October 1790, FO 95/7/4, fos 501–3, 481–5, PRO; Miranda, Proclamation, 3 August 1790, and to Pitt, 8 September 1791, PRO 30/8/345, fos 48–51, 53–6, PRO.

51 [Anon], 'Cape of Good Hope & Coast of South America', WO 1/178, fo. 53, PRO.

52 The relevant papers are in WO 1/178, fos 103–94, PRO.

53 Miranda to Pitt, 16 January 1798, PRO 30/8/345, fos 69–70, PRO; for Brooke, see Harlow, *Founding*, vol. 2, pp. 650–1; 'Proyecto para tomar posesión del reino de Chile por las armas de su Majestad Británica', *Revista Chilena de Historia y Geografía*, vol. 63, no. 4 , 1929, pp. 63–75; Colnett to St Vincent, 22 March 1801, ADM 1/5121/22, fos 643–4; for Miranda and Dundas, see Harlow, *Founding*, vol. 2, pp. 653–4; for Abercromby, see *Memoirs and Correspondence of Viscount Castlereagh*, vol. 7, pp. 269–73, 286–8.

54 Popham to Yorke, 26 November 1803, PRO 30/8/345, fos 81–7, PRO.

55 Popham to Pitt and Melville, 16 October 1804, WO 1/161, fos 39–66, PRO.

56 Jacob to Pitt, 26 October 1804, PRO 30/8/345, fos 93–105, PRO; Creassy to Sheffield, 6 December 1804, Banks P1/1, Sutro.

57 Pitt, Memorandum, undated, PRO 30/8/196, fo. 88, PRO.

58 Hunter, 'Memorial respecting New South Wales', Bonwick 5745/1, SLNSW.

59 John Dalrymple to Grenville, 20 October 1806, STG 141(2), Huntington; Kent to Banks, 5 November 1806, Brabourne A78/3, fos 284–7, SLNSW.

60 Buckingham to Grenville, 15 October 1806, *Report on the Manuscripts of J. B. Fortescue, Esq., Preserved at Dropmore*, London, 1892–1927, vol. 8, pp. 435–6.

Cook: Alexander Dalrymple and the Hydrographic Office

1 Order in Council, 12 August 1795, PC 2/144, pp. 51–3, PRO. The text is printed by G. H. R[ichards], *A Memoir of the Hydrographical Department of the Admiralty 1868*, London, 1868, pp. 31–2; and reprinted by Sir Archibald Day, *The Admiralty Hydrographic Service 1795–1919*, HMSO, London, 1967, pp. 334–5.

2 Ibid.

3 Ibid. For a summary of earlier survey work under Admiralty auspices, see A. H. W. Robinson, *Marine Cartography in Britain*, Leicester University Press, Leicester, 1962—especially ch. 6, 'The Birth of Official Hydrography', pp. 96–102.

[4] Admiralty, Endorsement ('Established to commence from the 13th Aug. 1795'), 22 February 1797, on Dalrymple's account of 'Disbursements in the Hydrographical Office', 20 February 1797, ADM 1/3522, PRO. For more details, see Andrew S. Cook, *Alexander Dalrymple (1737–1808), Hydrographer to the East India Company and to the Admiralty, as Publisher: A Catalogue of Books and Charts*, (PhD dissertation, St Andrews, 1993), from which much of this paper is drawn.

[5] Day, *Admiralty Hydrographic Service*, pp. 11–22.

[6] Robinson, *Marine Cartography*, pp. 102–12.

[7] Admiralty, Correspondence with Hydrographer's Office, 1795–1823, ADM 1/3522–3, PRO.

[8] R. T. Gould, *A History of the Hydrographic Department of the Admiralty*, typescript [1923], MISC 4, Parry Papers 1, item 2(g), HOA. Gould completed only two chapters of the planned work, a sketch synopsis of which survives at the same reference.

[9] L. S. Dawson, *Memoirs of Hydrography*, H. W. Keay, Eastbourne, 1883–85, vol. I, pp. 25–9.

[10] R[ichards], *Memoir*, pp. 1–7.

[11] [M. Walker, with additions by F. J. Evans], 'H.O. History of, MSS', manuscript [1868?], MISC 4, Parry Papers 4, item 2(h), HOA.

[12] Day, *Admiralty Hydrographic Service*, p. 31.

[13] The suggestion in Walker's notes that the post of Hydrographer was offered first to James Rennell has so far defied corroboration. When applying, in India, for a pension in 1776, Rennell proposed himself for an apparently similar exercise, the examination and selection of geographical and hydrographical materials in India House for the East India Company. See Andrew S. Cook, 'Major James Rennell and *A Bengal Atlas* (1780–1781)', *India Office Library and Records Report for the Year 1976*, London, 1978, pp. 5–42, particularly p. 15.

[14] Court of Directors, Minutes, 1 April 1779, B/94, p. 627, IOR. Dalrymple's East India Company practices are dealt with in Cook, *Alexander Dalrymple*, ch. 4.

[15] 'When Earl Spencer first intimated to me the intention of appointing an Hydrographer to the Admiralty and did me the honour to think me a proper Person for that Office I observed to His Lordship that I was flattered by his opinion . . .' Dalrymple to Pole, 23 December 1807, ADM 1/3522, PRO.

[16] J. C. Sainty, *Office-holders in Modern Britain, IV: Admiralty Officials 1660–1870*, HMSO, London, 1975.

[17] Dalrymple to Nepean, 27 February 1795, ADM 1/3522, PRO. This correspondence dates from before Nepean's formal appointment as Secretary to the Admiralty.

[18] Dalrymple to Stephens, 28 May 1795, ADM 1/3522, PRO.

[19] Admiralty Collection, Vf.2/21, HOA. This curiosity consists of impressions of three small plates of parts of the Scilly Isles, overlapping

in coverage, but cut to join, and mounted with blank paper pieces (watermarked 1801) and borders added by hand, to form a mock-up chart. The borders of the three constituent plates were done to Dalrymple's specifications, their small size suggests that they were done in Dalrymple's East India Company period before he had access to a large-plate press, and the date watermark on the mounting paper contributes to this attribution.

20 Dalrymple to Stephens, 28 and 29 May 1795, to Nepean, 21 July 1795, and Marsden to Wright, 27 July 1795, ADM 1/3522, PRO.

21 'It is in the contemplation of the Lords Commissioners of the Admiralty to establish an Hydrographical Office for forming and engraving Charts &ca. for the use of the Navy; when I was informed of This, I was also told that They did me the honour to think me a proper Person for the charge of the Office proposed: I replied that altho' I was highly flattered by this preference, I could not undertake It, without your Consent: at the same time I did not doubt of Your concurrence; as there were few parts of The World, in which the Navigation of your Ships might not, at least eventually, be interested, by more precise information than The Publick at present possess: and, consequently, that Their Lordships intention, in my favour, was rather an extension, than contradiction, to the duties of that Employment I now hold in The Company's Service'. Dalrymple to Court of Directors, 10 June 1795, E/1/92, p. 101, IOR. The Court consented on 17 June to Dalrymple's request. See Court Minutes, 17 June 1795, B/121, p. 277, IOR.

22 These payments to Dalrymple were neither a salary of office nor a pension, and required a formal resolution of the Court of Directors each quarter before the issue of a warrant for payment. Once the system of quarterly payments of £125 by warrant was established in 1781, these resolutions occur regularly in the Court Minutes until March 1808. See B/146, p. 1455, IOR. These payments are not to be confused with his annuity payments, nor with the advances made to Dalrymple on account for his chart compilation and engraving expenses.

23 Dalrymple to Earl St Vincent, 9 September [1803?], ADM 1/3522, PRO.

24 Despite occasional illness and absence from London, Dalrymple attended almost 700 of the 950 weekly dinners between his election and the end of 1795, an attendance rate of 73 per cent. His pattern of attendance did not significantly alter thereafter.

25 Dalrymple was elected on 31 July 1777 with Musgrave and Roy, Royal Society Club, Dinner Book 6, RS.

26 Tony Campbell, 'A Cook Mystery Solved', *The Map Collector*, 32, 1985, pp. 36–7.

27 *Case of Alexander Dalrymple, Esq.*, London, 1784; *A Serious Admonition to the Publick on the Intended Thief-Colony at Botany Bay*, London,

1786. The pamphlet embodies Dalrymple's letter of 13 July 1785 to the Court Directors, in answer to their request for his opinion.

[28] Dalrymple to Cathcart, 20 July 1787, enclosure in Cathcart to Pitt, 25 July 1787, PRO 30/8/121, fos 225–8, PRO.

[29] 'Mr Dalrymple's opinion on the Route across the Continent of America', 2 February 1790, CO 42/72, fos 249–56, PRO. This, and Dalrymple's other contributions in this context, are discussed by David Mackay, *In the Wake of Cook: Exploration, Science and Empire, 1780–1801*, Croom Helm, London, 1985, pp. 49, 84 and 90–1.

[30] *The Spanish Pretensions Fairly Discussed*, London, 1790; *The Spanish Memorial of 4th June Considered*, London, 1790; *An Historical Journal of the Expeditions, by Sea and Land, to the North of California*, London, 1790.

[31] 'Mr Dalrymple begs to caution Mr. Dundas not to mention any thing to indicate that Mr Dalrymple knew the particulars of the Examination of Lieut Meares before the Privy Council'—Dalrymple to Dundas, 12 March 1791, MS 43/7, NLA.

[32] 'Memoir concerning Places of Refreshment for the Whale Ships in the South Seas', 14 April 1792, ADM 1/4156, PRO.

[33] See Dalrymple to Dundas, 2 November 1792, MS 43/12, NLA.

[34] Order in Council, 12 August 1795, in Day, *Admiralty Hydrographic Service*, pp. 334–5.

[35] Admiralty, Note of 22 February 1797, ADM 1/3522, PRO; and Day, *Admiralty Hydrographic Service*, p. 334, no. 1.

[36] Gould, History of the Hydrographic Department, ch. 1, p. 11.

[37] Dalrymple to Court of Directors, 10 June 1795, E/1/92, p. 101, IOR.

[38] Dalrymple to Pole, 10 October 1807, ADM 1/3522, PRO, pp. 13–14.

[39] Dalrymple had to write to Nepean on 18 May 1797 to arrange for the payment of Walker's second quarter's allowance. In Dalrymple's 20 February account of disbursements, entries for fees to Walker for reducing and copying cease after 7 November 1796. See ADM 1/3522, PRO.

[40] Dalrymple gave a receipt for the charts and journals on 9 November 1795. For the copy of this list and receipt kept in the Hydrographic Office, and bearing Marsden's subsequent receipts of 17 August 1796, see the paper of the same title in ADM 1/3523, PRO. Dalrymple supplied a certificate of Rossel's employment on 25 August 1799. See ADM 1/3522, PRO. For the circumstances of the 'deposit' of Entrecasteaux's charts in 1795, see Hélène Richard, *Le Voyage de D'Entrecasteaux à la Recherche de Lapérouse*, CTHS, Paris, 1976, pp. 210 and 215–16.

[41] Dalrymple to Nepean, 24 March 1796, ADM 1/3522, PRO.

[42] Dalrymple to Marsden, 17 June 1798, ADM 1/3522, PRO. Dalrymple called on his own experience in the *Swallow* in 1776 and 1777 in the Red Sea.

43 Dalrymple, Report, 19 June 1798, with lists of charts, plans, views and accounts, ADM 1/3522, PRO.
44 Dalrymple to Spencer, 21 February 1797, MS 43/17, NLA.
45 Mocha Road (7 June 1798), Red Sea (July 1798), Red Sea views, plate 2 (30 November 1798), Red Sea views, plate 3 (7 February 1799), Red Sea views, plate 1 (November 1799), and Red Sea Ports (17 November 1800).
46 Dalrymple to Pole, 23 December 1807, ADM 1/3522, PRO.
47 Dalrymple to Nepean, 22 March 1800, ADM 1/3522, PRO.
48 Dalrymple, Memorandum, 26 April 1808, enclosed in Dalrymple to Melville, 29 April 1808, GD 51/2/399/1, SRO.
49 Dalrymple to Nepean, 22 March 1800, ADM 1/3522, PRO.
50 Dalrymple to Boulton, 31 March 1800, Boulton Papers, Letter D29, BRL.
51 Dalrymple to Nepean, 27 May 1803, ADM 1/3522, PRO.
52 Ibid.
53 See Day, *Admiralty Hydrographic Service*, pp. 20–1.
54 See Dalrymple, *Memoir concerning the Hydrographical Map of Part of Ægypt*, London, 1801, p. 1.
55 Dalrymple to Marsden, 16 May 1805, ADM 1/3522, PRO.
56 Dalrymple to Nepean, 15 January 1802, ADM 1/3522, PRO. The chart 'Bass Strait' (undated, but 1802) is in the Mitchell Library, SLNSW.
57 Dalrymple to Marsden, 15 June 1805, ADM 1/3522, PRO.
58 Dalrymple to Nepean, 22 March 1800, ADM 1/3522, PRO.
59 Dalrymple to Nepean, 24 March 1796, ADM 1/3522, PRO.
60 Dalrymple to Pole, 10 October 1807, ADM 1/3522, PRO.
61 By October 1807 Dalrymple was able to say that 'Those parts of The Coast of England which were surveyed by the two McKenzies and Mr Spence, are engraved, or are engraving in the Hydrographical Office; and That recently surveyed by Lieut. Murray'—Dalrymple to Pole, 10 October 1807, ADM 1/3522, PRO.
62 Dalrymple to Marsden, 17 January 1804, ADM 1/3522, PRO.
63 Dalrymple to Marsden, 7 May 1807, ADM 1/3522, PRO.
64 These were published in *Charts of the English Channel*, London, 1813.
65 Dalrymple to Nepean, 6 February 1804, enclosing a proof of the 'Form of Remark-Book' (which had been previously discussed between Dalrymple and Nepean, though no correspondence survives), ADM 1/3522, PRO.
66 Dalrymple to Marsden, 23 December 1806, ADM 1/3522, PRO.
67 Ibid.; Dalrymple to Nelson, 31 August 1805, Add. MS 34930, fo. 319, BL.
68 On 10 May Bligh requested payment of an invoice from William Cary for mathematical instruments for the Office. Dalrymple was back in post by 25 May, ADM 1/3522, PRO.

[69] Dalrymple to Marsden, 13 June 1804, ADM 1/3522, PRO.

[70] The copper-plate printer was to print from Dalrymple's plates 'as expeditiously as the Current Business of the Office will allow'— Dalrymple to Marsden, 23 August 1805, ADM 1/3522, PRO.

[71] 'A List of Charts sent to Lord Gambier and not returned', 7 December 1807, ADM 1/3522, PRO.

[72] Dalrymple to Pole, 14 November 1807, ADM 1/3522, PRO. The enclosure is not present.

Samson: An Empire of Science

[1] Barry M. Gough, *The Royal Navy and the Northwest Coast of North America, 1810–1914*, University of British Columbia Press, Vancouver, 1971, p. xiv.

[2] Ibid., pp. 104–5. A recent study by Andrew David, *The Voyage of HMS Herald*, Melbourne University Press, Melbourne, 1995, examines the scientific investigations of *Herald*'s later South Pacific expedition under Captain Henry Mangles Denham, but the book provides little historical context.

[3] For example, Alan Frost, 'The antipodean exchange: European horticulture and imperial designs', in David Philip Miller and Peter Hanns Reill (eds), *Visions of Empire: Voyages, Botany, and Representations of Nature*, Cambridge University Press, Cambridge, 1996, pp. 58–79; David Mackay, *In the Wake of Cook: Exploration, Science and Empire, 1780–1801*, Croom Helm, London, 1985; and Glyndwr Williams, '"The Common Centre of We Discoverers": Sir Joseph Banks, Exploration and Empire in the late 18th century', in R. E. R. Banks, B. Elliott, J. G. Hawkes, D. King-Hele and G. U. Lucas (eds), *Sir Joseph Banks: A Global Perspective*, Royal Botanic Gardens, Kew, 1994, pp. 177–91.

[4] Alfred Friendly, *Beaufort of the Admiralty: The Life of Sir Francis Beaufort, 1774–1857*, Hutchinson, London, 1977, p. 255.

[5] Examples include John Bach, *The Australia Station: A History of the Royal Navy in the South West Pacific, 1821–1913*, University of New South Wales Press, Sydney, 1986 (see pp. 46, 69); and Harry Morton, *The Wind Commands: Sailors and Sailing Ships in the Pacific*, Conway Maritime Press, Greenwich, 1975 (see pp. 385, 388, 390).

[6] I have discussed this in the South Pacific context in *Imperial Benevolence: Making British Authority in the Pacific Islands*, University of Hawaii Press, Honolulu, 1998.

[7] William Chimmo, *Euryalus; Tales of the Sea, a Few Leaves from the Diary of a Midshipman*, London, 1860, p. iii. The authorship of this book is in dispute. Flora Burns, in her article 'HMS *Herald* in search of Franklin', *Beaver*, Autumn, 1963, pp. 3–13, claims that *Euryalus* was a republication of Midshipman Bedford Pim's published journal, *Leaves*

from the Diary of a Midshipman (1852). I have not been able to trace a copy of the *Leaves* in order to check Burns's claim. In a note at the end of her article, she adds that *Euryalus* might have been a collaborative publication between Pim and Chimmo. I have referred to it as Chimmo's book in order to maintain consistency with the British Library classification of the version I consulted.

8   Berthold Seemann, *Narrative of the Voyage of HMS* Herald, 2 vols, London, 1853, p. xi.

9   Seemann, *Narrative*, vol. 1, p. ix.

10 Wood to Hooker, 11 November 1852, English Letters 1850, vol. 30, p. 672, Kew.

11 Gough, *The Royal Navy and the Northwest Coast*, p. 104.

12 Beaufort to Kellett, 4 November 1844, Letter Books, vol. 12, HOA.

13 Beaufort to Kellett, 24 May 1845, Letter Books, vol. 13, HOA.

14 In 1845 Captain Gordon of HMS *America* was relying on Vancouver's chart of the area. See Gordon to Admiralty, 22 October 1845, in Admiralty to Foreign Office, 13 February 1846, FO 5/459, PRO. Also see Courtenay to Hornby, 15 November 1848, in Hornby to Admiralty, 28 November 1848, ADM 1/5589, PRO.

15 Admiralty to Pelly, 13 April 1844, A 8/3, HBCA.

16 'Herald, Capt. H. Kellett' LBK 61, NMM. Two undated letters from early 1848 refer to these instructions. See LBK 61, fos 10–11, 13, NMM.

17 Beaufort to Kellett, 14 January 1848 and Letter Books, vol. 15, HOA; Seymour to Kellett, 10 July 1847, LBK 61, NMM.

18 John Coulter, *Adventures in the Pacific*, Dublin, 1845, p. 148.

19 Kellett to Admiralty, undated but 1846, LBK 61, NMM.

20 Seymour to Kellett, 2 August 1847, LBK 61, NMM.

21 John Hickman, *The Enchanted Islands: The Galapagos Discovered*, Anthony Nelson, Oswestry, Salop, 1985, pp. 97–8.

22 Kellett to Seymour, 27 January 1846, LBK 61, NMM.

23 Kellett to Wood, 20 April 1846, LBK 61, NMM.

24 Seymour to Kellett, 4 March 1846, LBK 61, NMM.

25 Kellett to Bankhead, 25 November 1846, LBK 61, NMM.

26 Seymour to Kellett, 27 February 1847, LBK 61, NMM.

27 Ogden and Douglas to the Governor and Committee of the Hudson's Bay Company, 28 July 1846, B 223/b/34, HBCA.

28 Ibid.

29 Beaufort to Kellett, 16 July 1846, Letter Books, vol. 14, HOA.

30 Gough, *The Royal Navy and the Northwest Coast*, pp. 44–5; Thomas to Admiralty, 28 December 1841, ADM 1/5512, PRO.

31 Kellett to Beaufort, 24 February 1848, LBK 61, NMM.

32 Seemann, *Narrative of the Voyage of HMS* Herald *During the Years 1845–51*, London, 1853, vol. 1, p. 221.

33 Ibid., p. 228.

[34] Bedford Pim, *The Gate of the Pacific*, London, 1863, pp. 181–2.

[35] Beaufort to Kellett, 16 May 1848, Letter Books, vol. 15, HOA.

[36] Kellett to Seymour, 27 April 1847, LBK 61, NMM.

[37] Miscellaneous Letters and Papers, Misc 24, folder 5, HOA, contains a number of letters showing these connections and machinations. The reference to Wood is in Haldon (Company Secretary) to Pelly, 6 May 1850, in Haldon to Beaufort, 26 June 1850, ibid.

[38] Millington Henry Synge, *Great Britain One Empire*, London, 1852.

[39] Kellett to Seymour, 10 July 1847, LBK 61, NMM.

[40] Seemann, *Narrative*, vol. 2, p. 116.

[41] Chimmo, *Euryalus*, p. 298.

[42] Christopher Lawrence, 'Disciplining disease: scurvy, the navy, and imperial expansion' in Miller and Reill (eds), *Visions of Empire*, p. 97.

[43] Beaufort to Kellett, 24 May 1845, Letter Book, vol. 13, HOA.

[44] [Edmondston], *The Young Shetlander*, pp. 282–3.

[45] Daniel R. Headrick, *The Tools of Empire: Technology and European Imperialism in the Nineteenth Century*, Oxford University Press, Oxford, 1981, pp. 17–82, and Lucile Brockway, *Science and Colonial Expansion: The Role of the British Royal Botanic Gardens*, Academic Press, New York, 1979, pp. 101–12.

[46] Seemann, *Narrative*, vol. 1, p. 202.

[47] Seemann, *The Botany of the Voyage of HMS Herald Under the Command of Captain Henry Kellett . . . During the Years 1845–51*, London, 1852–57, vol. I, p. 21.

Knight: John Lort Stokes and the New Zealand Survey, 1848–1851

I must acknowledge great assistance in the writing of this paper from Dr Jane Samson, and also from Ms Sara Joynes of the Australian Joint Copying Project. The project's detailed indexes has made examination of the Hydrographic Office's papers possible.

[1] See Marsden Hordern, *Mariners are Warned! John Lort Stokes and HMS Beagle in Australia 1837–1843*, Melbourne University Press, Melbourne, 1989.

[2] Brian Hooker, 'Finding Port Nicholson: a new look at European discovery and naming claims', *Mariner's Mirror*, vol. 79, 1993, pp. 179–91. The same author's unpublished paper, Early Surveys in New Zealand Waters, concludes that 'by the middle of the 1840s partial surveys had been carried out in most harbours and virtually all coastlines were laid down in charts with a fair degree of accuracy'. Some of this information must have been available to Stokes. I am grateful to Mr Hooker for a sight of his paper.

[3] Printed in Sheila Natusch, *The Cruise of the Acheron: Her Majesty's*

Steam Vessel on Survey in New Zealand Waters, 1848–51, Whitcoulls Publishers, London, 1978.

4 Home to Beecher, 3 December 1846, H 844, HOA.

5 Stokes to Beaufort, 30 September 1849, to Erskine, 25 June 1850, STK 13, NMM.

6 Reproduced in Natusch, *Cruise of the* Acheron, p. 141.

7 It is notable that John Bach, *The Australian Station: A History of the Royal Navy in the South West Pacific 1821–1913*, New South Wales University Press, Sydney, 1986, does not mention Stokes.

8 *The New Zealand Pilot*, 1st edn (1856), was compiled by F. H. Richards and F. J. Evans, officers under Stokes on the expedition. Stokes read a paper on the voyage to the Royal Geographical Society on 20 February 1851, and some botanical and zoological papers also came out of the voyage.

9 See also J. O'C. Ross, *This Steam Coast: The Story of the Charting of the New Zealand Coast*, Reed, Wellington, 1969.

10 C. J. Bartlett, *Great Britain and Seapower, 1815–1853*, Clarendon Press, Oxford, 1963, p. 153; also G. S. Graham, *Great Britain in the Indian Ocean, 1810–1850*, Oxford University Press, Oxford, 1967; G. S. Ritchie, *The Admiralty Chart: British Hydrography in the Nineteenth Century*, Hills & Carter, London, 1967, p. 197.

11 R. O. Morris, 'Surveying ships of the Royal Navy from Cook to the computer age', *Mariner's Mirror*, vol. 72, 1986, p. 390.

12 *Acheron* was 150 feet in length, measured on the gun deck, with a generous beam of 32 feet 9 inches and a maximum draft of 18 feet. It was built at Sheerness Dockyard and launched on 23 August 1835. Its two-cylinder, side-lever engine was built by Seaward at Millwall on the Thames and was relatively underpowered, with 1 horsepower to 4.24 tons. It was sold in Sydney in 1855. See John Fincham, *A History of Naval Architecture*, London, 1851, reprinted Scolar Press, London, 1979, p. 332; D. K. Brown, *Before the Ironclad; Development of Ship Design, Propulsion and Armament in the Royal Navy, 1815–60*, Conway Maritime Press, London, 1990, pp. 52–60, 110; and D. K. Brown, *Paddle Warships*, Conway Maritime Press, London, 1994, pp. 20–2.

13 Stokes to Beaufort, 2 June 1851, STK 13, NMM.

14 Everard Home to Beaufort, 25 July 1843, H 872, HOA.

15 See Bartlett, *Great Britain and Seapower*, pp. ix, 129–31; Andrew Lambert, *The Last Sailing Battlefleet: Maintaining Naval Mastery, 1815–1850*, Conway Maritime Press, London, l991, pp. 10–11.

16 Paul W. Schroeder, *The Transformation of European Politics, 1763–1848*, Clarendon Press, Oxford, 1994, p. 767.

17 Graham, *Great Britain in the Indian Ocean*, pp. 436–7; Stokes to Grey, 26 November 1850, STK 13, NMM.

18 See Minute, 12 April 1843, Minute Book no. 4, HOA. Beaufort's very detailed instructions to Usborne, 13 June 1843, are in STK 24, NMM.

19 Beaufort to Fitzroy, 1 July 1844, Letter Book no. 12, HOA. Beaufort cites his charts of New Zealand as 'constructed . . . from insulated scraps and inadequate authorities all which you might very strongly put to Lord Stanley'. Since Stanley was Secretary of State for the Colonies, pressures to bring the Usborne scheme to a halt may have come from the Colonial Office.

20 Everard Home to Beaufort, 3 May 1844, H875; Good Friday, 1844, H874; 7 March 1845, H877; 18 February 1846, H879; 8 March and 16 May 1847, H880, HOA. For an earlier and better-known visit see Jane Samson, 'The 1834 cruise of HMS *Alligator*: the Bible and the Flag', *The Northern Mariner*, no. 4, 1993, pp. 37–47.

21 Beaufort to Edge, and to Fitzroy, 30 April 1845, Letter Book no. 13, HOA.

22 Fitzroy to Stokes, 7 July 1847. This important letter is now in the possession of Gerald J. Ellott, to whom I am indebted for permission to quote from it.

23 Beaufort to Stokes, 14 January 1848, Letter Book no. 15, HOA.

24 Muriel F. Lloyd Prichard, *An Economic History of New Zealand*, Collins, London & Auckland, 1970, pp. 41, 58–9.

25 Beaufort, Minute, 2 November 1844, Minute Book no. 4, HOA.

26 See Hordern, *Mariners are Warned!*, pp. 3–5, 143, 188.

27 James Belich, *Making Peoples: A history of the New Zealanders from Polynesian Settlement of the End of the Nineteenth Century*, Allen Lane, The Penguin Press, London & Auckland, 1996, p. 190.

28 Stokes to the Sub Collector of Customs (Otago), 16 June, and Report to Grey on the fertility of the South Island, 31 August 1850, STK 13, NMM. These detailed inland surveys were in marked contrast to Beaufort's instructions of 1843: 'The topography of the adjacent country need seldom [be recorded] to any great distance from the shore; get the positions of villages or populous districts, and any remarkable objects which can be seen from seaward be inserted'. 13 June 1843, STK 24, NMM.

29 Stokes to the Colonial Secretary (Auckland), 17 January 1850, STK 13, NMM. The harbour was eventually surveyed by the *Pandora*.

30 Stokes to J. W. Smith (second master of the *Acheron*, who also commanded the *Albert*), 21 January 1850, STK 13, NMM. It was lost because of the wind and the swell at the mouth of the Whangamta River, Bay of Plenty.

31 Stokes to Captain Cargill, 26 December 1850, STK 13, NMM.

32 Stokes to Beaufort, 2 September 1850, STK 13, NMM.

33 This policy on names, in fact, followed Beaufort's ideas: 'It would be more beneficial to make the name convey some idea of the nature of the place, or still better to adopt the native appellation, than to exhaust the catalogue of public characters or private friends'—Beaufort to [?], 3 June 1843, STK 24, NMM.

34 Stokes to J. W. Smith, 4 December 1848, and to F. H. Richards, 4 May 1849, STK 12; Stokes to Beaufort, 25 June 1850, STK 13, NMM.

35 Stokes to Grey, 31 August, and to Maori Chiefs, 19 December 1850, STK 13, NMM.

36 Stokes to Beaufort, 30 September 1849, STK 13, NMM.

37 Stokes to the Admiralty Secretary, 18 September 1849, STK 12; to Grey, 22 May 1851, STK 13, NMM. We see here the ingredients of the Royal Navy's 'self-assigned moral guardianship', analysed by Jane Samson, in *Imperial Benevolence: Making British Authority in the Pacific Islands*, University of Hawaii Press, Honolulu, 1998.

38 Stokes to Beaufort, 2 June 1851, STK 13, NMM. Stokes also claimed that only 500 tons were purchased specifically for the survey.

39 Stokes to Erskine, 7 May, 25 June, 10 September 1849, STK 12; to Erskine, 1 October 1849, and to Mr Fox (Wellington), 20 December 1850, STK 13, NMM.

40 Stokes to Beaufort, 2 June 1851, STK 13, NMM. Stokes estimated that the *Acheron* would only need one more year to complete the survey; and his pride was clearly hurt, for he wrote: 'Surely their Lordships cannot expect me to serve in so small a vessel'.

41 Stokes to Gladstone, 15 July 1858, Gladstone to Stokes, 30 August 1858, STK 52, NMM. For a detailed account of the previous British attempts at northern Australian settlement at Melville Island and Port Essington, see Graham, *Great Britain in the Indian Ocean*, pp. 402–33.

42 See Paul Kennedy, *The Rise and Fall of the Great Powers: Economic Change and Military Conflict from 1500 to 2000*, Random House, New York, 1987, p. 155.

Barr: A Warrant Officer in the Arctic

I am extremely grateful to David Karpeles of the Karpeles Manuscript Library, Santa Barbara, CA, for giving me access to the George Ford Papers, for permission to quote from them and to reproduce the photographs of Ford, and for his hospitality. I transcribed Ford's journal during an administrative leave from the University of Saskatchewan in January–February 1990; I am indebted to the University for that leave, and for a travel grant to permit me to spend the necessary time in Santa Barbara. Finally I wish to thank Keith Bigelow for drafting the map.

1 See R. Cyriax, *Sir John Franklin's Last Arctic Expedition: A Chapter in the History of the Royal Navy*, Methuen, London, 1939.

2 A. G. E. Jones, 'Robert Martin: a Peterhead whaling master in the 19th century', *Scottish Geographical Magazine*, vol. 85, 1969, pp. 196–202.

3 R. Collinson, *Journal of HMS Enterprise, on the expedition in search of Sir John Franklin's ships by Behring Strait, 1850–55*, London, 1889.

4 S. Osborn (ed.), *The Discovery of the North-West Passage by HMS*

Investigator, *Capt. R. M'Clure, 1850, 1851, 1852, 1853, 1854 . . . from the logs and journals of Capt. Robert le M. M'Clure,* London, 1856.

5   A. Armstrong, *A personal narrative of the discovery of the Northwest Passage; with numerous incidents of travel and adventure during nearly five years' continuous service in the Arctic regions while in search of the expedition under Sir John Franklin,* London, 1857.

6   L. H. Neatby (trans. and ed.), *Frozen ships: The Arctic Diary of Johann Miertsching 1850–1854,* Macmillan Company of Canada, Toronto, 1967.

7   Ford, KML.

8   Ford Certificate Book, KML.

9   Ford, KML.

10   Ibid.

11   Ibid.

12   Ford Certificate Book, KML.

13   Ford, KML.

14   Ibid.

15   These and subsequent details of the ships' progress are taken from Collinson, *Journal;* Osborn, *Discovery;* and Neatby, *Frozen Ships.*

16   Osborn, *Discovery.*

17   These and subsequent details about the *Resolute* and its crew are taken from G. F. McDougall, *The eventful voyage of HM discovery ship Resolute to the arctic regions in search of Sir John Franklin and the missing crews of HM discovery ships Erebus and Terror, 1852, 1853, 1854,* London, 1857; and E. F. de Bray, *A Frenchman in Search of Franklin: De Bray's Arctic Journal 1852–1854,* (trans. and ed.) W. Barr, University of Toronto Press, Toronto, 1992.

18   These and subsequent details concerning Belcher and his ships are taken from E. Belcher, *The last of the Arctic voyages; being a narrative of the expedition in HMS Assistance, under the command of Captain Sir Edward Belcher, C.B., in search of Sir John Franklin during the years 1852–53–54,* London, 1855.

19   Mr Newton was the ice mate, Mr Kennedy the acting boatswain and Mr Dean the carpenter of the *Resolute.*

20   See W. H. Matthews and R. M. Bustin, 'Why do the Smoking Hills smoke?', *Canadian Journal of Earth Sciences,* vol. 21, 1984, pp. 737–42.

21   Information from Dr Jim Basinger, personal communication, September 1997.

22   'The late arctic expedition', *The Times,* 18 October 1854, p. 8.

23   Ford, KML.

24   Ibid.

25   Ibid.

26   Ibid.

27   Ibid.

Dening: The Hegemony of Laughter

1 J. C. Beaglehole, 'Introduction', *Cook's Journals*, vol. 1, p. clxxxiii.
2 Samuel Wallis, Entry for 18 July 1767, 'Logbook and Sketchbook of Captain Samuel Wallis', Safe 1/98, SLNSW.
3 *Hawkesworth's Voyages*, vol. 1, pp. 248–62.
4 *Robertson's Journal*.
5 *Banks's Journal*, p. 292.
6 *Morrison's Journal*, p. 172.
7 Greg Dening, 'Possessing Tahiti', *Archaeology of Oceania*, vol. 21, 1986, pp. 103–18, tells the story of the pantomime and its relationship to Tahiti.
8 Henry Adams, *Memoirs of Arii Taimai*, Privately printed, Paris, 1901, p. 40.
9 John Gore, Entry for 24 June 1767, Logbook of HMS *Dolphin*, 21 August 1766–October 1767, B1533–B1534, SLNSW.
10 *Robertson's Journal*, p. 154.
11 *Banks's Journal*, p. 307.
12 *Robertson's Journal*, p. 194.
13 Rudiger Joppien and Bernard Smith, *The Art of Captain Cook's Voyages: The Voyage of the Endeavour 1768–1771*, Oxford University Press, Melbourne, 1985, p. 118, drawing I.56.
14 Wallis, Entry of 9 July 1767, Logbook, SLNSW.
15 *Robertson's Journal*, pp. 187–8.
16 *Banks's Journal*, pp. 312–13; R. and K. Green, 'Religious Structures of the Society Islands', *New Zealand Journal of History*, vol. 2, 1968, pp. 66–89.
17 Greg Dening, *Mr Bligh's Bad Language: Passion, Power and Theatre on the Bounty*, Cambridge University Press, New York, 1992, pp. 177–238.
18 Roger Rose, 'Symbols of Sovereignty. Feather Girdles of Tahiti and Hawaii', *Pacific Anthropological Records*, vol. 28, 1978, pp. 1–69.
19 See Douglas Oliver, *Ancient Tahitian Society*, University Press of Hawaii, Honolulu, 1974, p. 1200.
20 Wallis, Entry of 27 July 1767, Logbook, SLNSW.
21 Oliver, *Ancient Tahitian Society*, p. 681.
22 Wallis, Entry of 27 July 1767, Logbook, SLNSW.
23 *Hawkesworth's Voyages*, vol. 1, p. 241.
24 Niel Gunson, 'Sacred Women Chiefs and "female headmen" in Polynesian History', *Journal of Pacific History*, vol. 22, 1987, pp. 139–72.
25 *Robertson's Journal*, pp. 205–6.
26 Teuira Henry, *Ancient Tahiti*, Bishop Museum Bulletin 48, Honolulu, 1928, pp. 319–20.
27 Oliver, *Ancient Tahitian Society*, p. 121.
28 *Cook's Journals*, vol. 3, pp. 202–3; William Bligh, Drawings, Mitchell Library PXA565, fo. 18, fo. 19, fo. 52, SLNSW.

29 Wallis, Entries for 13 and 22 July 1767, Logbook, SLNSW; *Robertson's Journal*, p. 213; Henry, *Ancient Tahiti*, p. 74.

30 *Robertson's Journal*, pp. 203–5.

31 Oliver, *Ancient Tahitian Society*, pp. 441–2.

32 Pierre Bourdieu, *Outline of a Theory of Practice*, Cambridge University Press, Cambridge, 1977, pp. 1–2.

33 *Robertson's Journal*, p. 211.

34 *Cook's Journals*, p. 526.

35 Ibid., p. 563.

36 Ibid., p. 116.

37 *Banks's Journal*, p. 293; *Cook's Journal*, pp. 103–4.

38 *Cook's Journal*, p. 96.

39 *Banks's Journal*, pp. 266–7, 279.

40 *Banks's Journal*, p. 282.

41 Dening, 'Possessing Tahiti', pp. 112–13.

Fisher: Vancouver's Vision of Native Peoples

1 For a scathing critique of these tendencies see Keith Windschuttle, *The Killing of History: How a Discipline is Being Murdered by Literary Critics and Social Theorists*, MacLeay Press, Sydney, 1994, particularly pp. 136–8.

2 Nicholas Thomas, *Colonialism's Culture: Anthropology, Travel and Government*, Princeton University Press, Princeton, 1994, p. ix.

3 The central question in this essay was raised for me by Glyn Williams during his concluding remarks at the Vancouver Conference on Exploration and Discovery at Simon Fraser University, Vancouver, BC, in April 1992. The question is an important one and I hope that he sees some value in my attempt to answer it.

4 Ronald Wright, *Stolen Continents: The New World Through Indian Eyes Since 1492*, Viking, New York, 1992.

5 Thomas R. Berger, *A Long and Terrible Shadow: White Values, Native Rights in the Americas 1492–1992*, Douglas & McIntyre, Vancouver, 1991.

6 Anne Salmond, *Two Worlds: First Meetings between Maori and Europeans 1642–1772*, Viking, Auckland, 1991.

7 Morehead's book was first published in 1966, came out in a Penguin paperback in 1968, and continues to appear in popular editions. See Alan Moorehead, *The Fatal Impact: The Invasion of the South Pacific 1767–1840*, Hamish Hamilton, London, 1987.

8 These phrases come from Jennifer S. H. Brown and Elizabeth Vibert (eds), *Reading Beyond Words: Contexts for Native History*, Broadview Press, Peterborough, 1996. The first is a section heading on p. 1; and the second is from Daniel Clayton's chapter, 'Captain Cook and the

Spaces of Contact at Nootka Sound', p. 120. Clayton is particularly anxious to attribute assertions of 'truth' to other scholars in order to facilitate his dismissal of their work.

9 Thomas, *Colonialism's Culture*, p. ix.

10 For an account of the Nootka Sound controversy, see Alan Frost, 'Nootka Sound and the Beginnings of Britain's Imperialism of Free Trade', in Robin Fisher and Hugh Johnson (eds), *From Maps to Metaphors*, pp. 104–26.

11 Vancouver's instructions, 8 March 1791, *Vancouver's Voyage*, p. 286.

12 Ibid., p. 524.

13 Greg Dening, *Islands and Beaches*, pp. 3, 157–61.

14 *Vancouver's Voyage*, pp. 524–5; Peter Puget, Log, Entry of 18 May 1792, ADM 55/27, fo. 91, PRO.

15 There is some discrepancy in the accounts of this incident. Vancouver said that it was a line of stakes driven into the ground, while Thomas Manby wrote that the boundary was a line in the sand. See Entry of March 1792, Manby, p. 57, UBC.

16 See ibid.

17 *Vancouver's Voyage*, p. 462.

18 Entry of 24 April 1792, Manby, fo. 70, UBC.

19 Archibald Menzies, Entry of 24 April, 'Journal of Vancouver's Voyage, 1790–1794', Add. MS 32641, fo. 109, BL.

20 Vancouver to Phillip Stephens, 7 January 1791, ADM 1/2628, PRO.

21 *Vancouver's Voyage*, p. 551.

22 For a detailed discussion of the relationship between Menzies and Vancouver, including the comparison between Vancouver's so-called 'rigid mind' and Menzies's higher level of curiosity and perception, see John M. Naish, *The Interwoven Lives of George Vancouver, Archibald Menzies, Joseph Whidbey and Peter Puget: Exploring the Pacific Northwest Coast*, Edwin Mellen Press, Lewiston, 1996, especially p. 165.

23 Entry of 6 May 1792, Add. MS 32641, fo. 118, BL.

24 Entries of 6 and 23 June 1792, ibid., fos 137, 147.

25 Entry of 23 June 1792, ADM 55/27, fo. 113, PRO.

26 Cole Harris, 'Voices of Smallpox around the Strait of Georgia', in Cole Harris (ed.), *The Resettlement of British Columbia: Essays on Colonialism and Geographical Change*, University of British Columbia Press, Vancouver, 1997, pp. 3–30.

27 J. Sykes, 'View of Indian Village on Cape Mudge, Gulf of Georgia' (monochrome watercolour), View no. 44, HOA; J. Sykes (sketched), J. Landseer (eng.), 'Cheslakee's Village in Johnstone's Straits', in *Vancouver's Voyage*, vol. I, p. 346. For reproductions of these drawings and engravings see Robin Fisher, *Vancouver's Voyage: Charting the Northwest Coast, 1791–1795*, Douglas & McIntyre, Vancouver, 1992, pp. 41, 42.

28 Compare, for example, H. Humphrys, 'Port Dick' (monochrome watercolour), HOA, and H. Humphrys (sketched), B. T. Pouncy

(eng.) 'Port Dick, near Cook's Inlet', *Vancouver's Voyage*, vol. III, p. 151. For reproductions see Fisher, *Vancouver's Voyage: Charting the Northwest Coast*, pp. 86, 89.

29 *Vancouver's Voyage*, p. 627.

30 Michael E. Harkin, *The Heiltsuks: Dialogues of Culture and History on the Northwest Coast*, University of Nebraska Press, Lincoln, 1997, pp. 124–5.

31 *Vancouver's Voyage*, p. 1017.

32 Entry of 19 August 1792, ADM 55/27, fo. 134, PRO.

33 For this tendency in European attitudes see Robin Fisher, *Contact and Conflict: Indian–European Relations in British Columbia, 1774–1890*, University of British Columbia Press, Vancouver, 1977, pp. 81–2, 85.

34 *Vancouver's Voyage*, p. 1055.

35 Robin Fisher, 'Cook and the Nootka', in Robin Fisher and Hugh Johnson (eds), *Captain James Cook and His Times*, Douglas and McIntyre, Vancouver, 1979, pp. 81–98; and 'Muquinna', *Dictionary of Canadian Biography*, vol. 5, University of Toronto Press, Toronto, 1983, pp. 618–19.

36 See Yvonne Marshall, 'Dangerous Liaisons: Maquinna, Quadra, and Vancouver in Nootka Sound, 1790–95', in Fisher and Johnson (eds), *From Maps to Metaphors*, pp. 160–75.

37 See Entry of July 1792, Manby, fo. 96, UBC.

38 *Vancouver's Voyage*, p. 671–2.

39 Ibid., p. 1403.

40 *Cook's Journals*, vol. 3, p. 531.

41 *Vancouver's Voyage*, pp. 447–8, 464.

42 Entry of March 1792, Manby, fo. 64, UBC; *Vancouver's Voyage*, pp. 826–7.

43 For a detailed account of this incident see Greg Dening, *The Death of William Gooch*.

44 *Vancouver's Voyage*, p. 1145.

45 Ibid., p. 1156.

46 Ibid., p. 985.

47 Vancouver letter, left to be shown visitors to the Islands, 2 March 1794, Captain Cook collection number 116, Archives of Hawai'i.

48 For accounts of these developments see Ralph S. Kuykendal, *The Hawaiian Kingdom, I: Foundation and Transformation, 1778–1854*, University of Hawaii Press, Honolulu, 1938, pp. 29–51; and K. R. Howe, *Where the Waves Fall: A New South Sea Islands History from First Settlement to Colonial Rule*, Allen & Unwin, Sydney, 1984, pp. 154–8.

49 *Vancouver's Voyage*, p. 1160.

50 W. D. Westervelt, 'Kamehameha's Cession of the Island of Hawaii to Great Britain in 1794', *Twenty-Second Annual Report of the Hawaiian Historical Society for the Year 1913*, Paradise of the Pacific Press, Honolulu, 1914, p. 21. Westervelt quotes a Hawaiian account from 1862.

[51] Dening, *The Death of William Gooch*, pp. 3–9, 148–52.

[52] Bruce Trigger, *The Children of Aataentsic, vol. 1: A History of the Huron People to 1660*, McGill-Queen's University Press, Montreal, 1976, vol. 1, pp. 23–5; *Natives and Newcomers: Canada's Heroic Age Reconsidered*, McGill-Queen's University Press, 1985, pp. 169–71; and 'Early Native North American Responses to European Contact: Romantic Versus Rationalistic Interpretations', *Journal of American History*, vol. 77, March 1991, pp. 1214–15.

[53] Clayton, in Brown and Vibert (eds), *Reading Beyond Words*, p. 120.

[54] Bernard Smith, *European Vision and the South Pacific: A Study in the History of Art and Ideas*, Oxford University Press, London, 1960.

[55] I take this phrase from Bryan D. Palmer, *Descent into Discourse: The Reification of Language and the Writing of Social History*, Temple University Press, Philadelphia, 1990.

Archer: Whose Scourge?

I want to thank Peter Cruse of the Faculty of Medicine at the University of Calgary for his assistance in my study of the medical aspects of smallpox, and Alan Frost for his perceptive views about the transmission of *variola major* in the history of Australia and the Pacific basin. Thanks also to my commentators at the August 1995 Symposium at La Trobe University: Professors Iris Engstrand, University of San Diego; Francis Brooks, Flinders University; Greg Dening, University of Melbourne; Bryan Gandevia, University of New South Wales; Campbell Macknight, University of Tasmania; F. B. Smith, Australian National University; and Frank Fenner, John Curtin School of Medical Research, Australian National University, and former Director of the WHO Smallpox Eradication Campaign. Thanks also to CRA (Consolidated Riotinto Australia) Ltd for the Distinguished Visiting Fellowship that permitted this research and to my Mexicanist colleagues at La Trobe University, Steve Niblo and Barry Carr.

[1] Nathaniel Portlock, *A Voyage round the World*, London, 1789, p. 271.

[2] Donald R. Hopkins, *Princes and Peasants: Smallpox in History*, University of Chicago Press, Chicago, 1983, p. 2; and Joel N. Shurkin, *The Invisible Fire: The Story of Mankind's Victory over the Ancient Scourge of Smallpox*, Putnam's Sons, New York, 1979, p. 32.

[3] Alfred W. Crosby, *Ecological Imperialism: The Biological Expansion of Europe, 900–1900*, Cambridge University Press, Cambridge, 1986, p. 201.

[4] Alfred W. Crosby, *The Columbian Exchange: Biological and Cultural Consequences of 1492*, Greenwood Press, Westport, 1972, pp. 55–6; Crosby, 'Conquistador y Pestilencia: The First New World Pandemic and the Fall of the Great Indian Empires', *Hispanic American Historical*

Review, vol. 47, August 1967, p. 332; and John Hemming, *The Conquest of the Incas*, Penguin Books, London, 1983, p. 28. Hemming suggests that the disease could have been malaria rather than smallpox, which illustrates the paucity of solid information.

5 Ross Hassig, *Mexico and the Spanish Conquest*, Longman, London, 1994, pp. 152–4. Hassig points out that other diseases such as measles, influenza, mumps and malaria where the *Anopheles* mosquito lived were also important in the demographic catastrophe.

6 For the most recent and thorough assessment see Alan Frost, 'The Curse of Cain? The "smallpox" epidemic at Port Jackson', in *Botany Bay Mirages: Illusions of Australia's Convict Beginnings*, Melbourne University Press, Melbourne, 1994, pp. 190–210. Without any real evidence, some other historians attempted to link the British settlers with the 1789 epidemic. See especially Noel Butlin, *Our Original Aggression: Aboriginal Populations of Southeastern Australia, 1788–1850*, Allen & Unwin, Sydney, 1983, p. 175. Butlin suggested, but did not give evidence, that the infection of the Aboriginal population was a deliberate act of the British. See also Crosby, *Ecological Imperialism*, pp. 205–7; and Judy Campbell, 'Smallpox in Aboriginal Australia, 1829–31', *Australian Historical Studies*, vol. 20, October 1983, pp. 536–56.

7 For the most thorough study, see F. Fenner et al., *Smallpox and Its Eradication*, World Health Organization, Geneva, 1988, pp. 188–9; Shurkin, *The Invisible Fire*, p. 25.

8 For example, at the Cape of Good Hope in 1771 Marion Dufresne's surgeon attempted to confuse Dutch officials and to cover up the fact that there was smallpox aboard *Mascarin* and *Marquis de Castries* that killed (among others) Ahutoru, a Tahitian who was being returned from France to his island home. See Edward Duyker, *An Officer of the Blue: Marc-Joseph Marion Dufresne, South Sea Explorer, 1724–1772*, Melbourne University Press, Melbourne, 1994, p. 120.

9 Fenner, *Smallpox and Its Eradication*, p. 204. See also Francis Brooks, 'The First Impact of Smallpox: What was the Columbian Exchange Rate?', in Anthony Disney (ed.), *Columbus and the Consequences of 1492*, Columbus Quincentenary Conference and Institute of Latin American Studies, Melbourne, 1994, pp. 36–42. Brooks employs the term 'catastropher' to describe those historians who support the pandemic approach.

10 Francis Brooks, 'Revising the Conquest of Mexico: Smallpox, Sources, and Populations', *Journal of Interdisciplinary History*, vol. 24, Summer 1993, pp. 1–29. For a broad revisionist overview, see James Lockhart, 'Sightings: Initial Nahua Reactions to Spanish Culture', in Stuart B. Schwartz (ed.), *Implicit Understandings: Observing, Reporting, and Reflecting on the Encounters between Europeans and other Peoples in the Early Modern Era*, Cambridge University Press, New York, 1994, pp. 218–67.

11 Robert McCaa, 'Spanish and Nahuatl Views on Smallpox and Demographic Catastrophe in Mexico', *Journal of Interdisciplinary History*, vol. 25, Winter 1995, p. 398.

12 Ibid., pp. 420–31.

13 *Portlock's Voyage*, p. 271.

14 William Beresford (ed.), *A New, Complete, and Genuine History of a Voyage Round the World in the* King George *and* Queen Charlotte *under the command of Captains Portlock and Dixon. Undertaken and Performed in 1785, 1786, 1787 and 1788*, London, 1794, p. 103. Portlock's description of smallpox was corroborated a few years later by Etienne Marchand. See Charles P. Claret de Fleurieu, *A Voyage Round the World performed during the Years 1790, 1791, and 1792 by Etienne Marchand*, London, 1801, vol. 1, p. 328.

15 *Portlock's Voyage*, p. 271.

16 John Boit, 'Log of the Second Voyage of the *Columbia*', in Frederick W. Howay (ed.), *Voyages of the* Columbia: *to the Northwest Coast, 1787–1790 and 1790–1793*, Oregon Historical Society Press, Portland, 1990, p. 371. Also see 'John Hoskins' Narrative of the Second Voyage of the *Columbia*', in ibid., p. 196. Hoskins noted that the Nitinat chief Cassacan both bore the marks of smallpox and suffered venereal disease.

17 Warren L. Cook, *Flood Tide of Empire: Spain and the Pacific Northwest, 1543–1819*, Yale University Press, New Haven, 1973, pp. 80–1.

18 James R. Gibson, 'Smallpox on the Northwest Coast, 1835–1838', *BC Studies*, no. 56, Winter 1982–83, pp. 63–4.

19 Ibid., p. 64. Grigorh I. Shelikov wrote in 1786 about the Alaska possessions, '[The Natives] do not have nor ever have had smallpox'. See 'The Account of the Voyage of Grigorh I. Shelikov and his wife, Natalia Shelikova, from Okhotsk to the Coast of Northwest America and Return, Including a Description of the Islands and Native Peoples Encountered', in Basil Dmytryshyn, E. A. P. Crownheart-Vaughan and Thomas Vaughan (eds), *Russian Penetration of the North Pacific Ocean*, Oregon State Historical Society, Portland, 1988, vol. 2, p. 318. See also Robert Fortuine, *Chills and Fevers: Health and Disease in the Exploration of Alaska*, Alaska University Press, Fairbanks, 1989, pp. 227–8. Fortuine was less certain that the Spaniards should be blamed for smallpox.

20 See Robert Boyd, 'Smallpox in the Pacific Northwest: The First Epidemics', *BC Studies*, no. 101, Spring 1994, pp. 5–40; 'Commentary on Early Contact-Era Smallpox in the Pacific Northwest', *Ethnohistory*, vol. 43, Spring 1996, pp. 307–27; and 'Population Decline from Two Epidemics on the Northwest Coast', in John W. Verano and Douglas Ubelaker (eds), *Diseases and Demography in the Americas*, Smithsonian Institution Press, Washington, DC, 1992, pp. 249–55.

21 See Donald B. Cooper, *Epidemic Disease in Mexico City, 1761–1813:*

An Administrative, Social, and Medical Study, University of Texas Press, Austin, 1965; and Josefina Muriel, *Hospitales de la Nueva España*, 2 vols, Editorial Jus, México, 1960.

22 *Vancouver's Voyage*, p. 528.
23 Ibid., p. 559.
24 Ibid., p. 540.
25 Ibid., p. 540, note 1.
26 Robin Fisher, *Contact and Conflict: Indian-European Relations in British Columbia, 1774–1890*, University of British Columbia Press, Vancouver, 1977, p. 20. Although Fisher's work is almost twenty years old and there has been a great deal of new published research, he has not changed his views appreciably on population decline in the early era or contact. For a thorough discussion of abandoned villages, see Boyd, 'Smallpox in the Pacific Northwest', pp. 29–35, who supports the disease hypothesis commencing with pandemic smallpox.
27 Crosby, *Ecological Imperialism*, p. 203.
28 Cole Harris, 'Voices of Disaster: Smallpox around the Strait of Georgia in 1782', *Ethnohistory*, vol. 41, Fall, 1994, p. 592. See also Ann F. Ramenofsky, *Vectors of Death: The Archaeology of European Contact*, University of New Mexico Press, Albuquerque, 1987.
29 Harris, 'Voices of Disaster', p. 615.
30 *Instrucción*, Estado, legajo 20, ramo 5, AGI.
31 *Instrucción*, Articles 15–20, ibid. For a summary in English, see Herbert H. Beals, *Juan Pérez on the Northwest Coast: Six Documents of His Expedition in 1774*, Oregon Historical Society Press, Portland, 1989, pp. 24–8.
32 Dening, *Islands and Beaches*.
33 Fr Juan Crespi, Journal, Estado, legajo 43, ramo 10, AGI.
34 Translated from Martínez, Entry of 4 November, 1774, Journal, Guadalajara, legajo 516, AGI.
35 Peña, Journal, Estado legajo 43, ramo 9, AGI.
36 Crespi, Journal, Estado, legajo 43, ramo 10, AGI.
37 Martínez, Journal, Guadalajara, legajo 516, AGI.
38 Martínez, Journal, Guadalajara, legajo 516, AGI.
39 Crespi, Journal, Estado, legajo 43, ramo 10, AGI.
40 Pérez, Journal, Estado, legajo 20, ramo 11, AGI.
41 Martínez, Journal, Guadalajara, legajo 516, AGI.
42 Pérez, Journal, Estado, legajo 20, ramo 11, AGI; and Pérez to Antonio Bucareli, 3 November, Journal 1774, Estado, legajo 20, ramo 11, AGI.
43 Martínez, Journal, Guadalajara, legajo 516, AGI.
44 Campa, Journal, Guadalajara, legajo 515, AGI.
45 Bodega y Quadra, 'Navegación', in *Colección de Diarios y Relaciones para la Historia de los Viajes Descubrimientos*, Consejo Superior de Investigaciones Científicas, Instituto Histórico de Marina, Madrid, 1943, vol. 2, p. 103.

46 Hezeta, Journal, Estado, legajo 38-A, ramo 11, AGI.
47 Mourelle, Journal, Estado, legajo 38-A, ramo 4, AGI.
48 Ibid.
49 Campa, Journal, Guadalajara, legajo 515, AGI.
50 Campa, Journal, Guadalajara, legajo 515, AGI.
51 Hezeta, Journal, Estado, legajo 38-A, ramo 11, AGI.
52 Campa, Journal, Guadalajara, legajo 515, AGI.
53 Bodega to Bucareli, 13 October 1775, Estado, legajo 20, ramo 21, AGI.1
54 Mourelle, Journal, Estado, legajo, 38-A, ramo 4, AGI.
55 Ibid.; and Bodega 'Navegación', in *Colección de Diarios y Relaciones*, vol. 2, p. 124.
56 Arteaga, Journal, Estado, legajo 38-A, ramo 13, AGI; and Quirós y Miranda, Journal, Estado, legajo 38-A, ramo 14, AGI.
57 Juan Riobo, 'An Account of the Voyage Made by the Frigates *Princesa* and *Favorita* in the Year 1779 from San Blas to Alaska', *Catholic Historical Review*, vol. 4, July 1918, p. 222.
58 Ibid., p. 223; Aguirre, Journal, Estado, legajo 38-B, ramo 18, AGI; and Arriaga, Journal, Estado, legajo 38-B, ramo 19, AGI.
59 Although some Spanish observers believed that lust for iron and other metal items caused parents to sell their own children, most were prisoners taken in wars or individuals who lacked status and position in the Tlingit bands. See Archer, 'The Making of Spanish Indian Policy on the Northwest Coast', *New Mexico Historical Review*, vol. 52, January 1977, pp. 45–69; 'Cannibalism in the Early History of the Northwest Coast: Enduring Myths and Neglected Realities', *Canadian Historical Review*, vol. 61, December 1980, pp. 453–79; and 'Russians, Indians, and Passages: Spanish Voyages to Alaska in the Eighteenth Century', in Antoinette Shalkop (ed.), *Exploration in Alaska*, Cook Inlet Historical Society, Anchorage, 1980, pp. 129–43.
60 Camacho, Journal, Estado, legajo 38-B, ramo 16, AGI.
61 Bodega, 'Observaciones sobre el genio, caracter, armas y alimentos de aquellos naturales, terrenos y maderos de los montes circunvecinos a los puertos de la entrada Puerto de Bucareli', vol. 575 bis, MN.
62 Ibid.; and Arteaga, Journal, Estado, legajo 38-A, ramo 13, AGI.
63 Cañizares, Journal, Estado, legajo 38-B, AGI.
64 Arteaga, Journal, Estado, legajo 38-A, ramo 13, AGI.
65 Bodega, Journal, Estado, legajo 38-A, ramo 15, AGI.
66 Arriaga, Journal, Estado, legajo 38-B, ramo 19, AGI.
67 Bodega, Journal, Estado, legajo 38-A, ramo 15, AGI.
68 Mourelle, Journal, vol. 332, MN; and Bodega, Journal, Estado, legajo 38-A, ramo 15, AGI. It is interesting that Lapérouse, who visited nearby Lituya Bay ten years later, had an even more negative reaction to the labret, but also made no mention of pockmarks. See John

Dunmore (ed.), *The Journal of Jean-François de la Galaup de la Pérouse, 1785–1788*, Hakluyt Society, London, 1994, vol. 1, p. 125.

[69] Quirós, Journal, Estado, legajo 38-A, ramo 14, AGI.

[70] Bodega, Journal, Estado, legajo 38-A, ramo 15, AGI.

[71] Ibid.

[72] 'Lista de los ropares, armas, e instrumentos, que en un caxoncito se remiten a España', 27 December 1779, Estado, legajo 20, ramo 28, AGI. This document contains a catalogue of native items that were sent to the Spanish king.

[73] Arriaga, Journal, Estado, legajo 38-A, ramo 14, AGI.

[74] Diario de Ignacio de Arteaga, 1779, Estado, legajo 38-A, ramo 13, AGI.

[75] Martínez, Journal, Mexico, legajo 1529, AGI; and Serantes, Journal, Caja Fuerte, BNM.

[76] Ibid.; and Gonzalo López de Haro to Flórez, 22 September, 1788, Caja Fuerte, BNM.

[77] Martínez, Journal, Mexico, legajo 1529, AGI; and López de Haro to Flórez, 28 October 1788, Caja Fuerte, BNM.

[78] Ibid.; and Serantes, Journal, Caja Fuerte, BNM. Martínez kept the Russian papers and replaced them with ones written in Spanish indicating the date, his name, and the fact that the expedition was Spanish.

[79] Palacios, Journal, MS 1683, BNM; and Narvaez Journal, Clark.

[80] López de Haro to Flórez, 28 October 1788, Caja Fuerte, BNM.

[81] Martínez, Journal, Mexico, legajo 1529, AGI; and Palacios, Journal, Caja Fuerte, MS 1683, BNM.

[82] Ibid.

[83] Francisco de Eliza to Conde de Revillagigedo, 20 April 1791, Caja Fuerte, BNM; and Cosas, Journal, Historia, vol. 69, AGNM.

[84] Saavedra to Revillagigedo, 15 June 1794, Historia, vol. 71, AGNM.

[85] 'Aviso a los navigantes sobre la conservación de su salud', n.d., vol. 402, AGNM.

[86] See Ann M. Pallsovich, 'Historic Epidemics of the American Pueblos', in C. S. Larsen and G. R. Milner (eds), *In the Wake of Contact: Biological Responses to Conquest*, Wiley-Liss Publishers, New York, 1994, p. 93; Cole Harris, 'Voices of Disaster'; and Robert Boyd, 'Commentary on Early Contact-Era Smallpox in the Pacific Northwest', for good summaries of the impact of smallpox upon native populations of the continent.

[87] See F. O. MacCallum and J. R. McDonald, 'Survival of Variola Virus in Raw Cotton', *Bulletin of the WHO*, vol. 16, 1957, pp. 247–53. According to this study, under ideal conditions the smallpox virus could have survived for many months. More recently, some researchers have worried that the excavation of burial crypts might inadvertently release smallpox virus. See, for example, Arie J. Zuckerman, 'Infectious

Diseases: Palaeontology of Smallpox', *Lancet*, 22–29 December 1984, p. 1454; and P. D. Meers, 'Smallpox Still Entombed', *Lancet*, 11 May 1985, p. 1103. Meers noted that the smallpox virus remains viable for the longest periods in dried scab material—possibly up to 100 years in unusually cold, dry conditions.

88 Salamanca Apuntes, incordinados a cerca de las costumbres, usos y leves de los salvajes del Estrecho de Fuca, vol. 330, MN.

89 Lorenzo Sanfeliu Ortiz, *62 meses a bordo: La expedición Malaspina según el diario del Teniente de Navío Don Antonio de Tova Arredondo, 2 comandante de la 'Atrevida' 1789–1794*, Editorial Naval, Madrid, 1988, p. 167.

90 Saaveda, Entry of 15 June 1794, Journal, Estado, legajo 4290, AHN.

91 Cole Harris argues persuasively and passionately that the smallpox epidemic he dates to 1782 devastated the native population of Puget Sound and the Strait of Georgia. However, much of the evidence based upon oral traditions and the reminiscences of aged Native informants for this early period is very thin. See Harris, 'Voices of Disaster'.

Porter: The Career of William Ellis

1 C. A. Bayly, *Imperial Meridian, The British Empire and the World, 1780–1830*, Longman, London, 1989; Alan Frost, *Convicts and Empire: A Naval Question, 1776–1811*, Oxford University Press, Melbourne, 1980, and *Botany Bay Mirages: Illusions of Australia's Convict Beginnings*, Melbourne University Press, Melbourne, 1994; Philip D. Curtin, *The Image of Africa: British Ideas and Action, 1780–1850*, Macmillan, London, 1965.

2 For published accounts of Ellis's life, see John Eimeo Ellis, *Life of William Ellis, Missionary to the South Seas and to Madagascar*, London, 1873; William Ellis, *Memoir of Mary M. Ellis*, London, 1835; *Dictionary of National Biography*. The principal primary sources are Ellis's correspondence with Anderson, contained in the archives of the American Board of Commissioners for Foreign Missions (ABCFM) which are held at the Houghton Library, Harvard University; and his letters in the Council for World Mission Archive (CWM), held at the School of Oriental and African Studies, University of London. The publication here of material from the American Board papers is by permission of the Houghton Library, Harvard University; that from the CWM Archive is used by permission of the Archivist, School of Oriental and African Studies.

3 William Ellis to the Secretary, LMS, 3 November 1814, Candidates Papers 1796–1899, Box 5/16, CWM; R. Lovett, *The History of the London Missionary Society, 1795–1895*, 2 vols, London, 1899, vol. 1, p. 214.

4 Ellis to Rev. George Burder (LMS Secretary), 24 April 1816; and Ellis,

Affidavit before Hannibal McArthur JP, 9 September 1816, SS Box 2, File 3, CWM.

5 The phrase is used by Niel Gunson, *Messengers of Grace, Evangelical Missionaries in the South Seas, 1797–1860*, Oxford University Press, Melbourne, 1978, ch. 5, 'Innocents Abroad'.

6 Ellis to Burder, 10 December 1816, SS Box 2, File 3, CWM; Ellis was still explaining these expenses to the Directors three years later. See Ellis to Burder, 4 August 1819, SS Box 2, File 6, CWM. For Rowland Hassall, see *Australian Dictionary of Biography*, Melbourne University Press, Melbourne, 1966, vol. 1, pp. 521–2.

7 See the entry for John Williams, in *Australian Dictionary of Biography*, 1967, vol. 2, pp. 599–600.

8 Correspondence, *passim*, in SS Boxes 2 and 3, CWM.

9 Ellis to Burder, 24 November 1818, SS Box 2, File 6, CWM.

10 Ellis, John Davies and Charles Barff to Burder, 15 July 1820, SS Box 3, File 2, CWM.

11 For the Sandwich Islands Mission of the American Board of Commissioners for Foreign Missions, see Hiram Bingham, *A Residence of Twenty-One Years in the Sandwich Islands*, 3rd edn, New York, 1969 (Boston, 1849); Char Miller (ed.), *Selected Writings of Hiram Bingham 1814–1869: Missionary to the Hawaiian Islands*, Edwin Mellen Press, Lewiston, NY, 1988; Char Miller, *Fathers and Sons: The Bingham Family and the American Mission*, Temple University Press, Philadelphia, 1982; Patricia Grimshaw, *Paths of Duty: American Missionary Wives in Nineteenth-century Hawaii*, University of Hawaii Press, Honolulu, 1989; Sandra Wagner-Wright *The Structure of the Missionary Call to the Sandwich Islands 1790–1830: Sojourners Among Strangers*, San Francisco, 1990.

12 Bingham, *A Residence*, p. 161.

13 Ellis to W. A. Hankey (LMS Treasurer), undated, but late 1822, SS Box 3, File 8, CWM. There is a slight frostiness in Lovett's references to Ellis at this time in the centenary history of the LMS. See, for example, Lovett, *London Missionary Society*, vol. 1, pp. 218, 271. Still more strangely, there is no mention whatever of his later secretaryship of the Society.

14 Wagner-Wright, *Structure*, pp. 149–50; Miller, *Fathers and Sons*, pp. 37–8.

15 Ellis to Burder, 9 July and 18 November 1822, SS Box 3, Files 10 and 8, CWM. Bingham and Thurston, letter of welcome to Ellis, 23 February, with Ellis's reply, 25 February 1823, SS Box 4, File 3, CWM.

16 D. Tyerman to LMS Treasurer, 9 August 1822, SS Box 3, File 10, CWM.

17 Ibid.

18 Bingham, *A Residence*, pp. 165–7.

19 Bingham to Jeremiah Evarts (American Board of Commissioners for Foreign Missions Secretary), 27 October 1823, 12 November 1824, in Miller (ed.), *Selected Writings*, pp. 243, 261; Bingham to the LMS Directors, 8 June 1825, SS Box 5, File 4, CWM; Bingham, *A Residence*, p. 167.

20 Ellis to Burder, 30 October 1823, SS Box 4, File 3, CWM.

21 Ellis to [?], 26 October 1824, SS Box 4, File 6, CWM.

22 John Eimeo Ellis, *Life of William Ellis*, ch. 6; William Ellis, *Memoir*, pp. 151–3; correspondence in SS Box 5, File 4, CWM.

23 Ellis to Burder, 16 May 1825, from New York, SS Box 5, File 4, CWM.

24 Ellis to Burder, 8 July 1825, from Dorchester, SS Box 5, File 4, CWM.

25 Rufus Anderson, *History of the Sandwich Islands Mission*, Boston, 1870, pp. 59–60.

26 Ellis to [?], 26 October 1824, SS Box 4, File 6, CWM.

27 G. Burder to W. A. Hankey, 11 April 1826, and Dr T. H. Burder to Rev. J. Arundel, 27 May 1826, Home 4/8, CWM.

28 See his *Narrative of a Tour through Hawaii, or, Owhyee*, London, 1826; and *Polynesian Researches, during a residence of nearly six years in the South Sea Islands*, 2 vols, London, 1829.

29 Ellis, *Polynesian Researches*, vol. 1, p. ix.

30 Ellis, *Narrative*, Preface.

31 The visit was extensively reported in *The Times*, June–September 1824. The Hawaiian party left Oahu in November 1823, the king and queen died in July 1824, and the *Blonde* arrived in Oahu on 4 May 1825; Ellis left in September 1824 and arrived in London at the beginning of August 1825.

32 Maria Graham (comp.), *Voyage of HMS* Blonde *to the Sandwich Islands in the Years 1824–1825*, London, 1826. Graham was Captain Byron's cousin.

33 *Quarterly Review*, vol. 35, March 1827, pp. 419–45, quotation from p. 438; see also the Note with a letter from Na-Boki, p. 609, and ibid., vol. 36, June 1827, Note, p. 298. The Moravian missionaries were for the most part continental Europeans, especially German-speakers, noted for their 'civilizing' work in the West Indies, Cape Colony, Greenland, and Labrador.

34 William Orme, *A Defence of the Missions in the South Seas and Sandwich Islands against the misrepresentations contained in a late number of the* Quarterly Review *in a letter to the editor of the Journal*, London, 1827; Ellis to W. A. Hankey, 12 April 1827, SS Box 6, File 4, CWM; Gunson, *Messengers of Grace*, pp. 143, 170.

35 Elisha Loomis to Ellis, 21 July 1827, SS Box 6, File 4, CWM.

36 Ellis to Rev. J. Arundel, 21 June (from Dungannon) and 10 December 1827, Home 5/1, CWM; George A. Byron, *An Examination of Charges against the American Missionaries at the Sandwich Islands, as alleged in the Voyage of the Ship* Blonde, *and in the* Quarterly Review, Cambridge,

1828; J. Dyer (Admiralty) to Arundel, 13 April 1826, Home 4/8, CWM.

[37] Ellis to [Arundel?], 9 July 1829, from Edinburgh, Home 5/4, CWM.

[38] *Quarterly Review*, vol. 43, no. 1, 1830, pp. 1–54; quotations at pp. 1, 54.

[39] Ellis to Arundel, 21 June 1830, from Penrith, Home 5/5, CWM. Also Ellis to Arundel 8 June 1830, ibid.; and R. Southey to Rev. Neville White, 27 August 1830, in Charles Cuthbert Southey (ed.), *The Life and Correspondence of the late Robert Southey*, London, 1849–50, vol. 6, p. 114.

[40] Rufus Anderson to Ellis, 21 November 1827, 15 and 28 January 1828, 2.01/1, fos. 32–3, 40, 41, ABC. The series ABC/2.01 and 2.1 contain the Foreign Secretaries' 'Out' Letters of the ABCFM.

[41] Anderson to Ellis, 15 January 1828, 2.01/1, fo. 41, ABC.

[42] Charles Samuel Stewart, *Journal of a Residence in the Sandwich Islands, during the years 1823, 1824 and 1825; . . . With an Introduction and occasional notes by William Ellis*, London, 1828.

[43] Anderson to Ellis, 23 May 1828, 2.01/1, fos 54–6, ABC; Ellis to Jeremiah Evarts, 29 November 1828, 14/1, ABC. The series ABC 14, 'Miscellaneous Foreign Letters', consists of 7 volumes covering principally the years 1831–99 and 1910–19; it contains the extensive correspondence addressed to the Board and its officers in Boston by members of foreign missionary societies and other individuals overseas.

[44] Minutes of 17 December 1830, Minutes of the London Secretaries Association, vol. 1, British and Foreign Bible Society Archives, University Library, Cambridge; Ellis to Arundel, 23 February 1831, and Rev. Dr Paterson to Rev. John Clayton, 4 November 1831, Home 5/6, CWM; Ellis to Anderson, 31 March 1831, 14/1, ABC.

[45] Ellis to Anderson, 19 July 1832, 14/1, ABC; Anderson to Ellis, 2 January 1833, 2.01/2, fo. 23, ABC.

[46] Ellis to Anderson, 27 March 1830, 14/1, ABC.

[47] Ellis to Anderson, 20 April 1830; 14 November 1830; 31 March 1831; 28 February 1833, 14/1, ABC; 24 November 1838, 14/2, ABC; Anderson to Ellis, 2 January 1833, 2.01/2, fos 27–9, ABC.

[48] O. E. von Kotzebue, *A New Voyage round the World in the years 1823, 24, 25 and 26*, 2 vols, London, 1830, 'O Tahaiti', vol. 1, pp. 119–223 *passim*; for Bingham (referred to as 'Bengham'), see 'The Sandwich Islands', vol. 2, pp. 151–265. For the irritation it caused, see Gunson, *Messengers of Grace*, pp. 171–2.

[49] *Vindication of the South Sea Missions from the Misrepresentations of Otto Von Kotzebue, Captain in the Russian Navy, with an Appendix*, London, 1831, p. 11.

[50] Beechey's work was published in London, 1831; it was the subject of an article in the *Edinburgh Review*, vol. 53, March 1831, pp. 210–31; Anderson to Ellis, 2 January 1833, 2.01/2, fo. 29, ABC.

51 Ellis to Frederick Krohn (Berlin), 3 January 1833, and to Anderson, 28 February (enclosing Krohn's letters) and 2 June 1833, 14/1, ABC.
52 Anderson to Ellis, 30 January 1832, 2.1/1, fo. 400, ABC; 2 January 1833, 2.01/2, fos 24–7, ABC; Anderson to Ellis, 4 October 1837, 2.1/1 fos 470–1, ABC.
53 Ellis to Arthur Tidman (LMS Foreign Secretary), 20 September 1844, Home 8/8, CWM; letters of Ellis to Anderson in 14/4 (1860–71), ABC; William Ellis *The History of the London Missionary Society,* London, 1844; *The American Mission in the Sandwich Islands: A Vindication and an Appeal in relation to the proceedings of the Reformed Catholic Mission at Honolulu,* London, 1866.
54 Their correspondence during the 1830s contains many such examples.
55 For his confidence in the Aborigines' ultimate 'enjoyment of all the blessings of intelligence, civilization, and Christianity', see Ellis, *Polynesian Researches,* vol. I, pp. 21–2.
56 Ellis, *Narrative,* Preface.
57 Ellis to Anderson, 20 April 1830, 14/1, ABC.
58 Little direct correspondence seems to have survived either in the CWM Archives or the Buxton Papers; but see Ellis to Buxton, 15 December 1832, and Buxton to [Ellis?] 15 December 1835, Home 5/1, 6/9, CWM, and Buxton to Ellis, 27 January 1836, in Patricia Pugh, *Calendar of the Papers of Sir Thomas Fowell Buxton, 1786–1845,* London, 1980, p. 79.
59 For Philip's connection with Anderson and the ABCFM, see Andrew Porter, 'North American encounters with indigenous peoples and British missionary experience in Africa and the Pacific, c.1800–1850', in M. Daunton and R. Halpern (eds.), *Empire and Others: British Encounters with Indigenous Peoples, 1600–1850,* University College London Press, London, 1998, pp. 345–63. For brief references to Ellis and southern Africa, see W. M. Macmillan, *Bantu, Boer and Briton,* rev. edn, Clarendon Press, Oxford, 1963, pp. 161–6, 186; and Timothy Keegan, *Colonial South Africa and the Origins of the Racial Order,* Leicester University Press, London, 1996, pp. 140, 148. For a recent consideration of the contemporary South African debate, see Elizabeth Elbourne, 'Freedom at Issue: Vagrancy Legislation and the Meaning of Freedom in Britain and the Cape Colony, 1799 to 1842', *Slavery and Abolition,* vol. 15, 1994, pp. 114–50.
60 Ellis to Anderson, 12 April 1837, 14/1, ABC.
61 Ellis and Charles Barff, 17 June 1821, and Ellis, 10 March 1823, both to G. Burder, SS Box 3, File 5, Box 4, File 3, CWM.
62 Anderson to Philip, 5 July 1836, 2.1/1, fos 130–3, ABC.
63 Anderson to Ellis, 4 October 1837, 2.1/1, fos 469–70, ABC; Ellis to Anderson, 7 February 1838, 14/2, ABC. For the books in question, which indicate an informed overview from the mid-1830s of what was

seen as the relevant literature in the field of Indian–settler relations, see the Appendix.

64 *Report from the Select Committee on Aborigines (British Settlements), Parliamentary Papers,* 1837, vol. 7, 425, QQ. 4294–5, 4304–6, 4320, 4328 et seq., 4365, 4375, 4389, 4396–4402, 4416.

65 The description is from Ellis to Anderson, 25 April 1843, 14/2, ABC.

66 Ellis to Anderson, 22 June 1831, 14/1, ABC, and 25 April 1843, 14/2, ABC.

67 Ellis to Anderson, 2 June 1833, 16 December 1833, 18 April 1835, 14/1, ABC, and 7 February 1838, 14/2, ABC.

68 See, for example, George Pritchard's letters to Anderson, 1835–43, in 14/1–2, ABC.

69 Tidman to Chairman, LMS Board of Directors, 13 January 1840, and Freeman to Arundel, 24 February 1840, Home 7/7, CWM; Ellis to Arundel, 16 December 1840, Home 7/8, CWM, and 10, 17 May 1841, Home 7/9, CWM.

70 Andrew Porter, 'Cambridge, Keswick and late-nineteenth century attitudes to Africa', *Journal of Imperial and Commonwealth History,* vol. 5, 1976, pp. 5–34; John Mason Hitchen, Formation of the Nineteenth-century Missionary Worldview: the case of James Chalmers, PhD thesis, University of Aberdeen, 1984; David Hilliard, 'The Making of an Anglican Martyr: Bishop John Coleridge Patteson of Melanesia', in Diana Wood (ed.), *Martyrs and Martyrologies,* Studies in Church History, vol. 30, Blackwell, Oxford, 1993, pp. 333–45.

Van Kirk: Colonised Lives

I would like to thank Fran Gundry of the BCARS for inspiring this article by inviting me to give an anniversary lecture on the women of Fort Victoria in 1993. My research assistant Christopher Hanna was most helpful in unearthing subsequent chapters in these women's lives. Kathryn Bridge provided assistance with the photographs, all of which are published with the permission of the British Columbia Archives and Record Service. Thanks to University of British Columbia geographer Eric Leinberger for the maps.

1 See Sylvia Van Kirk, '*Many Tender Ties': Women in Fur Trade Society in Western Canada, 1670–1870,* Watson & Dwyer, Winnipeg, 1980, and Jennifer Brown, *Strangers in Blood: Fur Trade Company Families in Indian Country,* University of British Columbia Press, Vancouver, 1980.

2 For an excellent discussion of the ideology behind the colonisation scheme for Vancouver Island, see Richard Mackie, 'The Colonization of Vancouver Island, 1849–58', *BC Studies,* no. 96, Winter 1992–93, pp. 3–40.

3 For a further discussion of the differing experiences of the sons and daughters of these families in early Victoria, see Sylvia Van Kirk, 'Tracing the Fortunes of Five Founding Families of Victoria', *BC Studies*, nos 115 and 116, Autumn/Winter 1997–98, pp. 149–79.

4 The following synopsis of the origins of these five families is derived mainly from Van Kirk, *Many Tender Ties*.

5 John Work to Ermatinger, 15 February 1841, Edward Ermatinger Correspondence, BCARS.

6 Ibid., and 'Five Letters of Charles Ross, 1842–1844', *British Columbia Historical Quarterly*, vol. 1, April 1943, p. 107.

7 McNeill to Simpson, 5 March 1851, Simpson Correspondence Inward, D.5/30, HBCA.

8 For further discussion of the social controversy caused by the Beavers' arrival at Fort Vancouver, see Van Kirk, *Many Tender Ties*, pp. 154–7.

9 John Work to Ermatinger, 13 December 1834, Ermatinger Correspondence, BCARS.

10 Walter P. Ross & Mary Tait to Secretary, HBC, 13 June and 7 August 1845, A.10/19 and 20, HBCA.

11 John Miles to Robert Clouston, 21 December 1858, E/B/C62A, BCARS.

12 Annie Deans Correspondence, 29 February 1854, E/B/D343, BCARS; see also Jane Fawcett to sister Emma, 24 June 1860, Edgar Fawcett Papers, Add. MS 1963, BCARS.

13 Marion B. Smith, 'The Lady Nobody Knows', in R. E. Walters (ed.), *British Columbia: A Centennial Anthology*, McClelland and Stewart, Toronto, 1958, p. 479.

14 Dorothy B. Smith (ed.), *Lady Franklin Visits the Pacific Northwest*, Victoria, 1974, pp. 12, 22–23.

15 Dorothy B. Smith (ed.), *The Reminiscences of Doctor John Sebastian Helmcken*, UBC Press, Vancouver, 1975, p. 120.

16 George Stanley (ed.), *Mapping the Frontier: Charles Wilson's Diary of the Survey of the 49th Parallel, 1858–1862*, Macmillan, Toronto, 1970, p. 135.

17 H. H. Bancroft, *Literary Industries*, History Co., San Francisco, 1890, p. 534.

18 Martha Douglas Harris, Unpublished Reminiscences, BCARS.

19 Ibid.; Smith, *Reminiscences of . . . Helmcken*, p. 120.

20 Nellie de Bertrand Lugrin, *The Pioneer Women of Vancouver Island, 1843–1866*, Women's Canadian Club, Victoria, 1928, p. 64.

21 Augustus Pemberton Diary, 1856–1858, E/B/P37A, BCARS; *British Colonist*, 30 April 1859, p. 2; 20 and 21 May 1862, p. 3.

22 Victoria *Daily Chronicle*, 30 April 1864 and 4 May 1864. See also *British Colonist*, 26 August 1863, p. 3; 1 September 1863, p. 3; 27 September 1864, p. 3; and Victoria *Daily Chronicle*, 1 September 1863.

23 Bishop Edward Cridge Papers, vol. 7, 1868: pp. 68, 89, Add. MS. 320, BCARS.

24 Victoria *Daily Chronicle*, 24 April 1885; Carrie to Isabella, 17 August 1880, Wren Family Papers, BCARS.

25 John Tod Clipping File, BCARS.

26 Probate Records, Box 25, File 20 (1876), GR 1304, BCARS. The probate file of the McNeill Estate contains a complete inventory of the contents of this house which was auctioned off in 1876.

27 Captain McNeill's Letterbook, A/B/20 Si22, BCARS; Helen Meilleur, *A Pour of Rain: Stories from a West Coast Fort*, Sono Nis, Victoria, 1980, p. 203.

28 Will of Martha McNeill, 18 September 1883, BCARS. Shortly before her death in 1883, Martha McNeill dictated her will in Chinook jargon to a mixed-blood interpreter, Margaret Hankin, who then translated it into English.

29 Fort Victoria, School Register, 1850–52, Add. MS 2774, BCARS.

30 Smith, *Lady Franklin Visits*, pp. 11, 15–16.

31 Christ Church Cathedral, Register of Marriages at Fort Vancouver and Fort Victoria, BCARS; Smith, *Reminiscences of . . . Helmcken*, p. 297; Lucy Moffatt Clipping File, BCARS.

32 Stanley, *Mapping the Frontier*, pp. 8, 45.

33 Philip Hankin Reminiscences, p. 166, BCARS.

34 Christ Church Cathedral, Register of Marriages, BCARS.

35 W. Kaye Lamb, 'Letters to Martha', *British Columbia Historical Quarterly*, vol. 1, January 1937, p. 35.

36 Christ Church Cathedral, Register of Marriages, BCARS; Robert Belyk, *John Tod: Rebel in the Ranks*, Horsdal & Schubart, Victoria, 1995, pp. 187, 197.

37 Will of Charles Wren, 6 February 1864, Wren Family Papers, BCARS.

38 Christ Church Cathedral, Marriage Register, BCARS; Gordon Keith (ed.), *The James Francis Tullock Diary, 1875–1910*, Binford and Mort, Portland, 1978, p. 16; Cridge Papers, vol. 7, 1868, p. 32, BCARS.

39 John Tod to Ermatinger, 1 June 1864, Ermatinger Correspondence, BCARS.

40 Angus McDonald, 'A Few Items of the West', *Washington Historical Quarterly*, vol. 8, 1917, p. 225.

41 H. H. Bancroft, *History of the Northwest Coast*, History Co., San Francisco, 1886, vol. II, pp. 650–1. I have indicated by italic all the officers who settled in Victoria. My attention was first drawn to this quote by reading Janet Campbell Hale's fascinating autobiography, *Bloodlines: Odyssey of a Native Daughter*, Random House, New York, 1993.

42 Christine Welsh's film *Women in the Shadows* was released by the National Film Board of Canada in 1991. She was able to trace her

native female roots back to Jane, a Cree woman who married George Taylor, a Hudson's Bay Company sloopmaster. One of their daughters, Margaret, was the 'country wife' of Hudson's Bay Company Governor George Simpson in the 1820s.

43 See S. F. Tolmie, 'My Father: William Fraser Tolmie, 1812–1886', *British Columbia Historical Quarterly*, vol. 1, October 1937, pp. 227–40; Donald McNeill, Personal Record, 1924, BCARS.

44 Martha Douglas Harris, *History and Legends of the Cowichan Indians*, Victoria, 1901, p. 57.

Marshall: *The Great Map of Mankind*

1 *The Great Map of Mankind*, p. 72–3.

2 Nigel Leask, *British Romantic Writers and the East: Anxieties of Empire*, Cambridge University Press, Cambridge, 1992.

3 Kate Teltscher, *India Inscribed: European and British Writing on India 1600–1800*, Oxford University Press, Delhi, 1996, chs 4 and 6; Javed Majeed, *Ungoverned Imaginings: James Mill's* The History of British India *and Orientalism*, Clarendon Press, Oxford, 1992, pp. 21–40.

4 Teltscher, *India Inscribed*, pp. 5–6.

5 Sara Suleri, *The Rhetoric of English India*, Chicago University Press, Chicago, 1992, chs 2 and 3.

6 Mildred Archer, *India and British Portraiture, 1770–1825*, Sotheby, Park Bernet, London, 1979.

7 William Hodges, *Travels in India, During the Years 1780, 1781, 1782 and 1783*, London, 1793, p. 156.

8 Archer, *India and British Portraiture*, p. 255.

9 G. H. R. Tillotson, 'The Indian Picturesque: Images of India in British Landscape Painting 1780–1880', in C. A. Bayly (ed.), *The Raj: India and the British, 1600–1947*, National Portrait Gallery, London, 1990, p. 141.

10 Mildred Archer, *Company Paintings: Indian Painting of the British Period*, Victoria and Albert Museum, London, 1992.

11 Toby Falk, and Mildred Archer, *Indian Miniatures in the India Office Library*, Sotheby, London, 1981, pp. 26–7.

12 William Robertson, *An Historical Disquisition concerning the Knowledge which the Ancients had of India*, London, 1791, p. 282; see also Partha Mitter, *Much Maligned Monsters: History of European Reactions to Indian Art*, Clarendon Press, Oxford, pp. 143–4.

13 Raymond Head, 'Corelli in Calcutta: Colonial Music-making in India during the 17th and 18th Centuries', *Early Music*, vol. 13, 1985, pp. 548–53; Ian Woodfield, 'New Light on Mozart's London Visit: A Private Concert with Manzuoli', *Music and Letters*, vol. 76, 1995, pp. 187–208; '"The Hindostannie Air": English Attempts to Understand Indian Music in the late Eighteenth Century', *Journal of the Royal Musical Association*, vol. 119, 1994, pp. 189–211.

[14] Edward W. Said, *Orientalism*, Routledge & Kegan Paul, London, 1978, p. 22.

[15] Ibid., pp. 120–1.

[16] Ibid., p. 78.

[17] Ronald B. Inden, *Imagining India*, Basil Blackwell, Oxford, 1990.

[18] Bernard S. Cohn, 'The Command of Language and the Language of Command', in Ranajit Guha (ed.), *Subaltern Studies*, vol. 4, 1985, pp. 276–329.

[19] Bernard S. Cohn, 'The Peoples of India: From the Picturesque to the Museum of Mankind', unpublished paper, 1984.

[20] Teltscher, *India Inscribed*, pp. 204, 210.

[21] Thomas Metcalf, *Ideologies of the Raj: The New Cambridge History of India*, part III, vol. 4, Cambridge University Press, Cambridge, 1994, pp. 5–6, 14.

[22] David Kopf, *British Orientalism and the Bengal Renaissance: The Dynamics of Indian Modernization, 1773–1835*, Firma K. L. Mukhopadhyay, Calcutta, 1969, p. 2.

[23] David Kopf, 'European Enlightenment, Hindu Renaissance and the Enrichment of the Human Spirit: A History of Historical Writings and British Orientalism', in Nancy G. Cassels (ed.), *Orientalism, Evangelicalism and the Military Cantonment in Early-Nineteenth Century India*, Edwin Mellen Press, Lewiston, 1991, p. 23.

[24] Garland Cannon, 'Oriental Jones, Scholarship, Literature, Multiculturalism and Humankind', in Garland Cannon and Kevin R. Brine (eds), *Objects of Enquiry: The Life, Contributions, and Influences of Sir William Jones (1746–1794)*, New York University Press, New York, 1995, p. 47.

[25] O. P. Kejariwal, 'William Jones: The Copernicus of History', in Cannon and Brine (eds), *Objects of Enquiry*, p. 109.

[26] Suleri, *The Rhetoric of English India*, p. 4.

[27] Rosane Rocher, *Orientalism, Poetry, and the Millennium: The Checkered Life of Nathaniel Brassey Halhed, 1751–1830*, Motilal Banarsidass, Delhi, 1983.

[28] For a fuller statement, see P. J. Marshall, 'The Founding Fathers of the Asiatic Society', *Journal of the Asiatic Society*, vol. 27, 1985, pp. 63–77.

[29] Orme to Hastings, 14 January 1775, Add. MS 29136, fo. 17, BL.

[30] Cited in Graham Shaw, *Printing in Calcutta to 1800: A Description and Checklist of Printing in Late Eighteenth-century Calcutta*, Bibliographical Society, London, 1981, p. 4.

[31] C. A. Bayly, *Empire and Information: Intelligence Gathering and Social Communication in India, 1780–1870*, Cambridge University Press, Cambridge, 1996.

[32] David Ludden, 'Orientalist Empiricism: Transformation of Colonial Knowledge', in Carol A. Breckenridge and Peter van der Veer (eds), *Orientalism and the Postcolonial Predicament*, University of Pennsylvania Press, Philadelphia, 1993, p. 253.

33 Rosane Rocher, 'The Career of Radhakanta Tarkavagisa, an Eighteenth-Century Pandit in British Employ', *Journal of the American Oriental Society*, vol. 109, 1989, pp. 27–33; and 'Weaving Knowledge: Sir William Jones and Indian Pandits', in Cannon and Brine (eds), *Objects of Enquiry*, pp. 51–79; and 'British Orientalism in the Eighteenth Century: The Dialectic of Knowledge and Government', in Breckenridge and Van der Veer (eds), *Orientalism and Post Colonial Predicament*, pp. 215–49.

34 Rocher, 'British Orientalism in the Eighteenth Century: The Dialectic of Knowledge and Government', pp. 230–1.

35 Robertson, *Historical Disquisition*, p. 29.

36 Minute, 18 April 1781, in 'History of the Calcutta Madrassa: Establishment of the Madrassa and Objects of its Foundation', *Bengal Past and Present*, vol. 8, 1914, pp. 105–6.

37 Bayly, *Empire and Information*, pp. 78–88.

38 G. H. R. Tillotson, '"A Fair Picture": Hodges and the Daniells at Rajmahal', in Pauline Rohatgi and Pheroza Godrej (eds), *Under the Indian Sun: British Landscape Artists and India*, Marg, Bombay, 1995, pp. 65–6; and 'The Indian Picturesque', in Bayly (ed.) *The Raj*, p. 141. I have learned much about British artists and Indian landscape from Dr James Lancaster.

39 Woodfield, 'The Hindostannie Air', pp. 192–6.

40 *The Great Map of Mankind*, p. 77.

41 Ibid., p. 303.

Mackay: Exploring the Pacific, Exploring James Cook

1 *Captain James Cook and his Times*, 1979, pp. 59–80. Glyndwr Williams, *The British Search for the Northwest Passage in the Eighteenth Century*, Longman, London, 1962.

2 *Cook's Journals*, vol. 3, p. 309.

3 In 1994 Glyn Williams had a more successful visit to the other Ship Cove which Cook had used as a base. Ship Cove, Queen Charlotte Sound, New Zealand, is uninhabited and accessible only by sea or walking track. Glyn's visit was on the sloop *Cape Resolution*, sailed by Tim Beaglehole, son of J. C. Beaglehole.

4 J. C. Beaglehole, 'The Death of Captain Cook', *Australian Historical Studies*, vol. 11, no. 43, October 1964, p. 297.

5 E. Kolig, 'Captain Cook in the Western Kimberleys,' in Ronald M. and Catherine H. Berndt (eds), *Aborigines of the West: Their Past and Their Present*, University of Western Australia Press, Perth, 1980, p. 280.

6 Bernard Smith and Rüdiger Joppien, *The Art of Captain Cook's Voyages*, Yale University Press, New Haven, 1988, vol. 3, pp. 126, 200.

7 Arthur Kitson, *Captain James Cook*, John Murray, London, 1907; Alan Villiers, *Captain Cook*, Hodder & Stoughton, London, 1967; Richard

Hough, *James Cook: A Biography*, Hodder & Stoughton, London, 1994.

[8] J. C. Beaglehole, *The Exploration of the Pacific*, 3rd edn, Stanford University Press, Stanford, 1966, p. 314.

[9] Ibid., p. 315.

[10] J. C. Beaglehole, *The Life of Captain James Cook*, Hakluyt Society, London, 1974, pp. 713–14.

[11] This is the view of Tim Beaglehole, who sailed on the *Endeavour* across the Tasman Sea, around part of the New Zealand coast and from Cape Town to London. It is shared by John Longley of the *Endeavour* Foundation.

[12] See 'A Chart of New Zeland or the Islands of Aeheinomouwe and Tovypoenammu', in R. A. Skelton (ed.), *The Journals of Captain James Cook: Charts & Views*, Hakluyt Society, London, 1969, no. XII.

[13] *Forster's Journal*, vol. 2, p. 267.

[14] *Cook's Journals*, vol. 1, pp. 278–89.

[15] Ibid., vol. 2, p. 175.

[16] Gananath Obeyesekere, *The Apotheosis of Captain Cook: European Myth-Making in the Pacific*, Princeton University Press, Princeton, 1992.

[17] Ibid., p. 3.

[18] Ibid., p. 10.

[19] It is only fair to acknowledge that I was one of the writers attacked, on the basis of a paper on 'The New Zealand Legacy of Captain Cook', delivered at a conference at the Royal Society in 1990. The attack placed me in some very flattering company. As in the case of Hawaii, however, Obeyesekere manages to insult the culture he sets out to defend. In particular he disputes the force of Maori oral history and *Whakapapa*. See Obeyesekere, *Apotheosis*, pp. 135–6.

[20] Marshall Sahlins, *How 'Natives' Think: About Captain Cook, For Example*, University of Chicago Press, Chicago, 1995, p. 8.

[21] Obeyesekere's apparent dismissal of Pacific Islands oral tradition is ironic in this context.

[22] Philip Edwards, *The Story of the Voyage: Sea Narratives in Eighteenth Century England*, Cambridge University Press, Cambridge, 1994, pp. 1–4.

[23] *Campbell's Navigantium*, vol. 1, pp. xv–xvi.

[24] *Anson's Voyage*, p. 96. The reference makes the point that Glyn Williams's knowledge and analysis of the range of such eighteenth-century narratives is unsurpassed, a fact made clear both by the bibliography printed below and by the recently published *The Great South Sea: English Voyages and Encounters, 1570–1750*, Yale University Press, New Haven, 1997.

[25] *Forster's Observations*, p. 342.

[26] These ideas are explored in David Spadafora, *The Idea of Progress in Eighteenth Century Britain*, Yale University Press, New Haven, 1990;

and in R. L. Meek, *Social Science and the Ignoble Savage*, Cambridge University Press, Cambridge, 1976.

27 The troubles of Dr Hawkesworth are related in J. L. Abbott, *John Hawkesworth: Eighteenth century Man of Letters*, University of Wisconsin Press, Madison, 1982. His role is also described in Edwards, *Story of the Voyage*, ch. 5.

28 It was, for example, the work most borrowed from the Bristol Library in 1773–74. See Edwards, *Story of the Voyage*, pp. 91–2; and Paul Kaufmann, *Borrowings from the Bristol Library, 1773–1784: A Unique Record of Reading Vogues*, Bibliographic Society of the University of Virginia, Charlottesville, 1960, pp. 39, 201.

29 The role of Cook's voyages as a model is described in David Mackay, 'A Presiding Genius of Exploration: Banks, Cook and Empire, 1767–1805', in Robin Fisher and Hugh Johnston (eds), *Captain James Cook and His Times*, pp. 29–36; and 'The Great Century of Pacific Exploration', in John Hardy and Alan Frost (eds), *Studies from Terra Australis to Australia*, Australian Academy of the Humanities, Canberra, 1989, pp. 109–20.

30 Mary Louise Pratt, *Imperial Eyes: Travel Writing and Transculturation*, Routledge, London, 1992, pp. 30–1.

31 Strange to Banks, 3 December 1785, Banks, vol. 1, p. 215, Kew.

32 From *Voyage autour du monde*, cited in Urs Bitterli, *Cultures in Conflict*, Polity, Cambridge, 1989, p. 160.

33 *Forster's Observations*.

34 *Banks's Journal*, vol. 2, p. 130.

35 Glyndwr Williams, '"Far more happier than we Europeans": Reactions to the Australian Aborigines on Cook's Voyage', *Australian Historical Studies*, vol. 19, 1981, pp. 499–512.

36 *Cook's Journals*, vol. 1, pp. clxxii–cxcii.

37 Robin Fisher and Hugh Johnston (eds), *From Maps to Metaphors*. This volume also included a chapter by Glyn Williams.

38 Lynne Withey, *Voyages of Discovery: Captain Cook and the Exploration of the Pacific*, William Morrow, New York, 1987.

39 Greg Dening, *Islands and Beaches*; Cook makes a brief, inglorious appearance in *The Death of William Gooch*; and in *Mr Bligh's Bad Language: Passion, Power and Theatre on the Bounty*, Cambridge University Press, New York, 1992. Marshall Sahlins, *Islands of History*, University of Chicago Press, Chicago, 1985, is representative of his works in this context.

Index

DATE DUE

GAYLORD			PRINTED IN U.S.A.